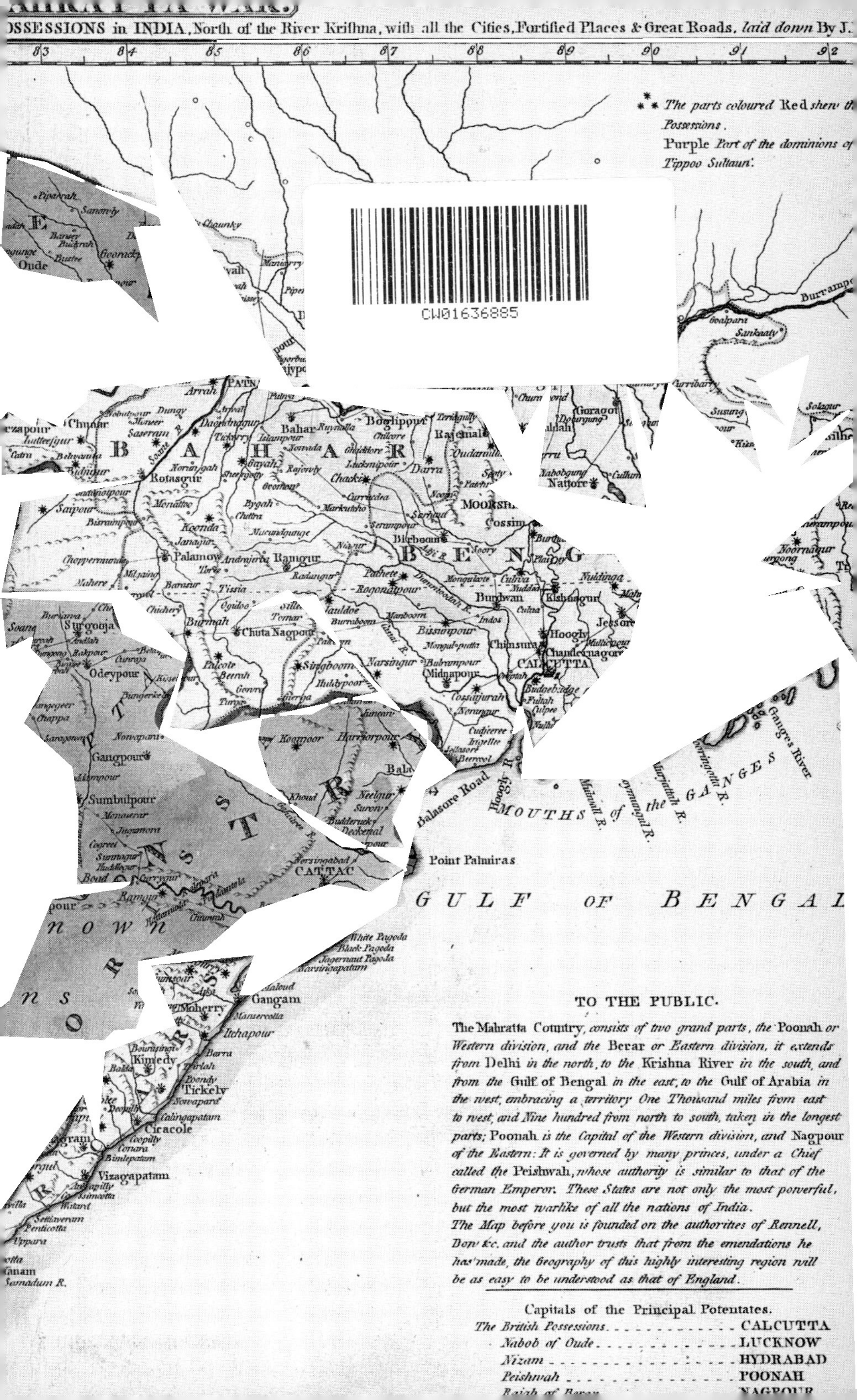

TO THE PUBLIC.

The Mahratta Country, *consists of two grand parts, the* Poonah *or Western division, and the* Berar *or Eastern division, it extends from* Delhi *in the north, to the* Krishna River *in the south, and from the* Gulf of Bengal *in the east, to the* Gulf of Arabia *in the west, embracing a territory One Thousand miles from east to west, and Nine hundred from north to south, taken in the longest parts;* Poonah *is the Capital of the Western division, and* Nagpour *of the Eastern: It is governed by many princes, under a Chief called the* Peishwah, *whose authority is similar to that of the German Emperor. These States are not only the most powerful, but the most warlike of all the nations of India.*

The Map before you is founded on the authorities of Rennell, Dow &c. and the author trusts that from the emendations he has made, the Geography of this highly interesting region will be as easy to be understood as that of England.

Capitals of the Principal Potentates.

The British Possessions	CALCUTTA
Nabob of Oude	LUCKNOW
Nizam	HYDRABAD
Peishwah	POONAH
Rajah of Berar	NAGPOUR

PUBLICATIONS
OF THE
ARMY RECORDS SOCIETY
VOL. 14

THE MARATHA WAR PAPERS OF ARTHUR WELLESLEY

The Army Records Society was founded in 1984 in order to publish original records describing the development, organisation, administration and activities of the British Army from early times.

Any person wishing to become a member of the Society is requested to apply to the Hon. Secretary, c/o the National Army Museum, Royal Hospital Road, London, SW3 4HT. The annual subscription entitles the member to receive a copy of each volume issued by the Society in that year, and to purchase back volumes at reduced prices. Current subscription details, whether for individuals living within the British Isles, for individuals living overseas, or for institutions, will be furnished on request.

Arthur Wellesley, Duke of Wellington, by Thomas Lawrence. Print from a lithograph drawing, reproduced by kind permission of Field Marshal the Lord Carver.

THE MARATHA WAR PAPERS OF ARTHUR WELLESLEY

January to December 1803

Edited by
ANTHONY S. BENNELL

Published by
SUTTON PUBLISHING LIMITED
for the
ARMY RECORDS SOCIETY
1998

First published in the United Kingdom in 1998
Sutton Publishing Limited · Phoenix Mill · Thrupp · Stroud · Gloucestershire

British Library Cataloguing in Publication Data

A catalogue record for this book is available from the British Library

ISBN 0 7509 2069 6

Endpaper map reproduced by kind permission of the British Library Map Room.

Typeset in Ehrhardt.
Typesetting and origination by
Sutton Publishing Limited.
Printed in Great Britain by
Bookcraft, Midsomer Norton, Somerset.

Contents

Maps

Preface

I have been honoured by the willingness of the Army Records Society to publish this selection of the Maratha War Papers of Arthur Wellesley. The aim has been to give a version of the events of 1803 which, while drawing heavily on the letters of Arthur Wellesley, has placed them in the context of some part of the correspondence he received during that year. Two letters here inserted he would probably never have seen; they give independent accounts of two of the military operations of the year.

I have been greatly assisted in the preparation of this volume by the ready cooperation of the Hartley Library of the University of Southampton, where the Wellington Papers are now housed. Material in copyright has been reproduced by permission. For the financing of a microfilm programme, which alone made possible the preparation of this volume in an acceptable time-frame, I am indebted to the Society for South Asian Studies and also to the Hartley Trustees. The West Sussex County Record Office, and the Chichester Public Library have been generous in the provision of microfilm reading facilities.

Readers are greatly in the debt of Elizabeth Lowry-Corry who has read both the final Mss and the typescript with detailed care. My friend and former colleague Brian Robson has again given me encouragement and support, and my wife has continued to sympathise with, if not to understand, my long-running obsession with the minutiae of Maratha history. Over the twin chronological and geographic voids, I salute the work of Colonel Gurwood, and the more recent editors of the *Poona Residency Correspondence* series. Finally, I commend the *period* to the next generation of scholars of Anglo-Indian history; there are many myths here yet to face critical scrutiny.

Anthony S. Bennell
March Square
Chichester
August 1998

Introduction

The second of the three contests of the British in India with the Maratha Confederacy can be seen as the classic period of British imperialism in India. It is certainly the stage in the process at which a self-conscious decision was taken that relations with the 'country powers' in India required a formidable advance of the political and therefore of the military frontier. At least until 1798, it was neither inevitable nor pre-ordained that the one European chartered Company in India with extensive territorial possessions should set itself to create what would afterwards be seen to be the foundations of paramountcy.

The scale of those territorial possessions needs to be briefly stated. The rich delta lands of Bengal, which the Company had ruled for less than forty years, gave the land-revenue base on which the bid for paramountcy was to be mounted. Enclaves of territory at Madras and Bombay were of limited extent. Linked to Bengal and to Madras were states in a condition of clientage, Oudh and the Carnatic. A disunited Maratha Confederacy controlled the greater part of western India, the Deccan, and 'Hindustan' as far north as Agra and Delhi. Tipu of Mysore was unreconciled to his earlier defeat by a coalition led by the Company in 1792. The Nizam of Hyderabad, one of the two surviving former Mughal rulers in India, retained a precarious independence, despite a united attack upon him by the Marathas in 1795.

The historic encounter of the Wellesley family with the policy and diplomacy of India came about by chance. It was in June 1796 that Cornwallis wrote a brief letter of introduction that Lieutenant-Colonel Arthur Wesley 'of my regiment' could present on arrival at Fort William Calcutta to Sir John Shore, then Governor-General. In the standard stilted langauge of letters of this type, which crowd the archive of senior figures in India, he is described as 'a sensible man and a good officer, and will I have no doubt, conduct himself in a manner to merit your approbation.'[1] It may be presumed that the acquaintance was a slight one, despite the position of Cornwallis as colonel of the 33rd. The elder brother of the young Colonel, Richard, second Earl of Mornington in the Irish peerage, later Marquis Wellesley, had made a number of attempts to secure for Arthur Wellesley a political appointment in Dublin. After a series of purchases and exchanges had advanced him to the rank of Colonel, at the age of twenty-seven, he determined to follow his regiment, then serving in India.

Early in 1797, as Arthur Wesley was approaching India, word reached London of the actions of Shore as Governor-General and Sir Robert Abercromby as Commander-in-Chief in giving way the previous year to the insubordination of the officers of the Company's army. This had led Henry Dundas, as President of the Board of Control, to appeal to Cornwallis to accept appointment to India a second time as Governor-General. Dundas believed that if he could persuade Cornwallis 'to forego the comforts of home for one year more of your life' it would be possible to introduce a measure of reform of the Company army, based in part on an earlier scheme of Cornwallis, which had been sent to India in January 1796 and had caused disquiet. His appeal followed the refusal of Pitt and Spencer to contemplate the appointment of Dundas himself as Governor-General. Cornwallis at first accepted the obligation of a further period as Governor-General, David Scott the Chairman of the Company commenting to Dundas on the advantages of Cornwallis being 'the announcer in Bengal river of his own appointment.'[2]

At this point the attempt of Dundas to impose on the Company his scheme of reform of its army collapsed. When the Court of Directors referred the matter to the Court of Proprietors, the arrangements were rejected, although redrafted by Cornwallis. Dundas at first hoped to resolve the dispute by legislation, but the naval mutinies of mid-1797, and other preoccupations prevented this. Cornwallis refused the appointment as Governor-General, to which he had been sworn in, and continued as Master-General of the Ordnance, being later appointed Lord-Lieutenant and Commander-in-Chief in Ireland.

Hobart, as Governor of Madras, had quarrelled intemperately with Shore, and thus forfeited his prospect of the 'reversion' to the Governor-Generalship, and Dundas determined to recall him. Mornington, who had accepted provisionally the appointment of Governor of Madras, with the prospect of reversion of the Governor-Generalship, had also gained from Pitt the undertaking that if Cornwallis was not appointed, the Governor-Generalship should be his. He had held no office other than that of a junior member of the Board of Control.[3]

The early years of Mornington as Governor-General saw the first steps on the road to paramountcy. Tipu of Mysore was attacked in February 1799, after the most nominal attempt at negotiation, following the publication by the Governor of Mauritius in January 1798 of a Proclamation stating that he awaited 'the moment when the French shall come to his assistance to declare war against the English who he ardently desires to expel from India.' Tipu was killed in his capital city Seringapatam in May 1799. Mornington had already secured an alliance with the Nizam of Hyderabad, displacing a French-officered force by a subsidiary Company force in October 1798. The ruler of Oudh was later compelled to accept a large subsidiary force and to surrender extensive territory to the Company. A successor to the Nawabship of the Carnatic was compelled, in the intervals of the ceremonies associated with the death of a relative, to accept a pension and his displacement from the direct rule of the territory. Mornington's reward for the achievements for his first year, seen as inadequate by its recipient who had asked for the Garter, was an Irish Marquisate in the title of Wellesley.

The opening for the East India Company to intervene in Maratha politics came in late 1802. What Richard Wellesley wished to secure was a pacified Maratha Confederacy that recognised British overlordship. This was to be the climax of his Governor-Generalship, the ultimate restructuring of the political system of the country powers in India, and the basis of his claim to high political office when he returned to England. His agents in the venture were to be the politicals on whom he had relied before, including Edmonstone, the head of the Fort William Secretariat, Barry Close the Resident with Peshwa Baji Rao, and John Malcolm, who had served both as a Private Secretary and as an Assistant Resident with the Nizam of Hyderabad and an envoy to Persia. But central to the evolution of the policy was to be the relationship of Richard Wellesley with his brother Arthur Wellesley, who had been gazetted a Major-General in April 1802.

The opportunity of intervention in the Maratha Confederacy arose from the conflict between the Sindes and the Holkars, the central fault line of the polity of the Maratha people. Late in October 1802, in the battle of Hadapshar outside Pune, Jaswant Rao Holkar had defeated the army of Peshwa Baji Rao, and some troops provided by

Daulat Rao Sinde. Baji Rao fled from Pune and after a period of hesitation, accepted the personal security of a small force of troops provided by the East India Company. Shortly before the battle of Hadapshar on 25 October 1802, Peshwa Baji Rao had sent to Barry Close, the British Resident at his court, an agreement accepting military support in return for the cession of territory. It was this agreement, once aware of the outcome of the battle and the events immediately following it, that Richard Wellesley wished to convert into a full subsidiary alliance. This Barry Close achieved in the Treaty of Bassein concluded on the last day of 1802.[4]

Note on Editorial Method

Arthur Wellesley wrote about 600 letters in 1803; they are almost all in print. To reprint all of these, together with the letters he received, would produce a volume of a bulk now unacceptable. The approach followed here in relation to Arthur Wellesley's own letters has been to select a proportion, and within this selection frequently to print parts of letters.

The letters written to Arthur Wellesley, preserved to an impressive degree of completeness in the Wellington Papers, present a different challenge. Selection is necessary here too, but in this case from among his correspondents. The central figures are the 'politicals', the Residents at the courts of the country powers, but also the members of the Fort William Secretariat. There are letters also from Arthur Wellesley's superior commander, Lieutenant-General Stuart, as well as from two subordinate commanders, Colonels Stevenson and Murray.

Many of the letters, both those written by Arthur Wellesley and those sent to him, deal extensively with political or diplomatic matters, including both relations with the 'country powers' and their internal administration. In these matters from late July 1803 Arthur Wellesley possessed extensive political authority, handled at the same time as a wide military command. The admixture of these two streams, the political and the military, gives the archive its unique character, and tells us much of the education of the thirty-four year old Major-General.

The 'authorised version' of the text of the letters of Arthur Wellesley is printed in the various editions edited by Gurwood and later by the Second Duke. The text there transcribed is from the copies that Arthur Wellesley retained, which he or a staff officer made at the time. These documents were probably literally 'sent to the printer' in the Eighteen Thirties; they can be regarded as 'holograph drafts' or 'holograph copies' although they have not here been so annotated. The printing of the despatches from them was accurate; there are few misprints. The proof sheets of these editions survive, and in the case of the first edition Wellington read the proofs and made amendments.

As printed last century the letters have few excisions, mostly turning on issues of officer discipline, but the censorship was not applied consistently, and it is not difficult to reconstruct the original text. There are a limited number of references to letters that do not appear to have survived. A small part of the archive is in cipher or with enciphered passages. The cipher is a relatively simple one and copies of the unciphered text are normally available. They have not been specifically annotated.

The papers in the Wellington archive are frequently not the only available source of a letter, and are often themselves copies. Letters were also widely copied for incorporation in the recorded Consultation processes. The carefully edited papers in the *Poona Residency Correspondence* series were prepared in part from the surviving archive of the Pune Residency, and in part from the Secret and Political Consultations of the various Presidencies. These can be found both in the Oriental and India Office Collections of the British Library and also in the National Archives of India.

A major Parliamentary Paper, the authority for which was given in June 1804, quoted extensively from the Governor-General's letters to the Secret Committee of the Court of Directors, and from the diplomatic correspondence in 1803 of the political officers of the Company. The *Notes on the Maratha War* published in India at the end of 1803, were reprinted in the Parliamentary Paper and also published separately in London. The texts of the conferences with the agents of the country powers in December 1803, which led to the two peace treaties, were published in India within a few months of these meetings. A copy of an important letter to the Secret Committee of April 1804, reporting on the diplomatic prelude to the Second Anglo-Maratha war and political events during the war, was captured by a French frigate and published in *Le Moniteur* in June 1805. It was printed in London in pamphlet form in August 1805.

It is from this material that James Mill was able within ten years to prepare those parts of his *History of British India* which dealt with the Governor-Generalship of Richard Wellesley, drawing heavily on primary material. The publication of the despatches of both Richard and Arthur Wellesley in the 1830s gave somewhat fuller documentation than that just cited, and created it in the form which has been normally used for scholarly work.

A standardised system of spelling of personal names has, in general, been chosen and carried through into the text of the letters. The Peshwa is given as Baji Rao, the other principal Maratha rulers as Daulat Rao Sinde, Raghuji Bhonsle and Jaswant Rao Holkar. The spellings used in

1803 were not consistent, and it seemed best to standardise, even if an arbitrary choice has been made.

Place names have been modernised, drawing on detailed maps mostly of the early twentieth century; spellings in these sources are not standardised, and it is possible to do no more than attempt internal consistency. Where a place cannot be identified, the form used in contemporary letters has been retained, in the hope that other researchers will be more successful. Place names prove frequently to be wrongly spelt but recognisable phonetically. Some are repeated. There are two rivers called Purna, one south of the battlefield of Assaye, flowing eastwards past Naulniah and emptying into the Godavari, the other south of the Satpura range and flowing westwards into the Tapti. The term 'ghat' is used both to refer to a ferry point on a river and also to a pass in a range of hills. Where the location at which a letter was written is defined only as 'Camp' without a place name, this is omitted.

Letters have been given in date order; for some the date of receipt by the addressee has been indicated; on other occasions the reader must assess this. Letters were sent to distant correspondents 'under flying seal' so that those responsible for onward transmission could be aware of content; this can sometimes be traced in the letters. Arthur Wellesley did not record on the text of letters he received the date of receipt. To the principle of placing the letters in date order there is an important exception: letters from the Fort William Secretariat, including those from Richard Wellesley, have been inserted in the text by date of their arrival with Arthur Wellesley in the Deccan, so that they are in the text directly followed by the actions to which they gave rise. This practice has not been followed for other correspondence, so that it is necessary for the reader to make his own assessment of the 'delays in the dak' of which the writers so constantly speak.

The location of the source of each letter is given, whether taken from printed material or from archives. Where available, the pagination in the Wellington Papers series 3/3 is given, although the letters are not now retained in the book form binding in which they were formerly held. The list of abbreviations given leads to the locations, printed or manuscript, of all letters.

Abbreviations

A Mss	Additional Manuscripts, British Library.
Grwd	*The Despatches of . . . the Duke of Wellington . . . from 1799 to 1818* compiled . . . by Lieutenant-Colonel Gurwood.
Home Misc	Home Miscellaneous Series, British Library Oriental and India Office Collections.
Martin	*The Despatches of the Marquis Wellesley* ed. Martin, M. (London 1837).
NLS	National Library of Scotland.
NLW	National Library of Wales.
NUL	Nottingham University Library, Bentinck Papers.
OIOC	British Library, Oriental and India Office Collections.
Parl Pps	Parliamentary Papers.
PRC	*Poona Residency Correspondence: English Records of Maratha History.*
SD	*Supplementary Despatches . . . of FM Arthur Duke of Wellington* 15 vols. (1858–72).
SNRR	Sinha, H.N., ed *Selections from the Nagpur Residency Records* 3 vols. (Nagpur 1950–53).
WP	Wellington Papers, University of Southampton.

Glossary

amil	a command of troops.
amildar	a chief.
Attavesi rivers	country between the Tapti and the Dumungunga.
banjara, brinjarri	a dealer in grain and salt following an army.
bheels, bhils	inhabitants of the hills of Malwa.
campoo	a disciplined brigade under European commanders in the Maratha service.
chauth, chaute	tribute or protection money claimed by the Marathas.
cossid	a courier or messenger.
cowle	a safe-conduct or amnesty, an agreement.
crore	a hundred lakhs.
dak, dawk	a relay of bearers or horses.
dewan	a minister, especially one concerned with the collection of revenue.
doab	the land between two rivers.
doolie, dooley	a conveyance for the sick and wounded.
durbar	the court of a ruler.
havildar	a sepoy non-commissioned officer.
Hindustan	lands to the north of the Narbada.
hircarrah	a messenger.
jagir	the territory ruled by a jagirdar.
Jats	a Hindu agricultural grouping in Rajastan.
jemadar	a junior sepoy non-commissioned officer.
karkun	an agent or messenger.
kharch	a gratuity or disbursement.
khas	land granted by a ruler.
killedar	the commander of a fortress.
kos	a measure of distance, about two miles.
lakh	a hundred thousand.
munshi	a representative or agent.
nullah	a watercourse, not necessarily a dry one.
pagah	the personal horsemen of a ruler.

pandit, pundit	a learned man.
parganah, pergannah	a district.
pindaries	irregular troops paid only by plunder.
Rajput	a Hindu warrior caste of northern India.
sanad	a treaty or agreement.
saranjami, seranjami	land assigned for the support of troops.
sebundy, sebundi	irregular sepoy soldiery, troops used for revenue duties.
silledar	state cavalry.
soucar	a banker.
subah	a large division of the Mughal empire, also an abbreviated form of subahdar.
subahdar	governor of a subah, a local commandant, the chief officer of a company of sepoys.
takur	a subordinate ruler in Gujerat.
taluk	the subdivision of a district.
talukdar	officer collecting the revenue of a taluk.
tannah	a schedule of revenue.
vakil	an authorised agent or messenger.
zemindar	a landholder.

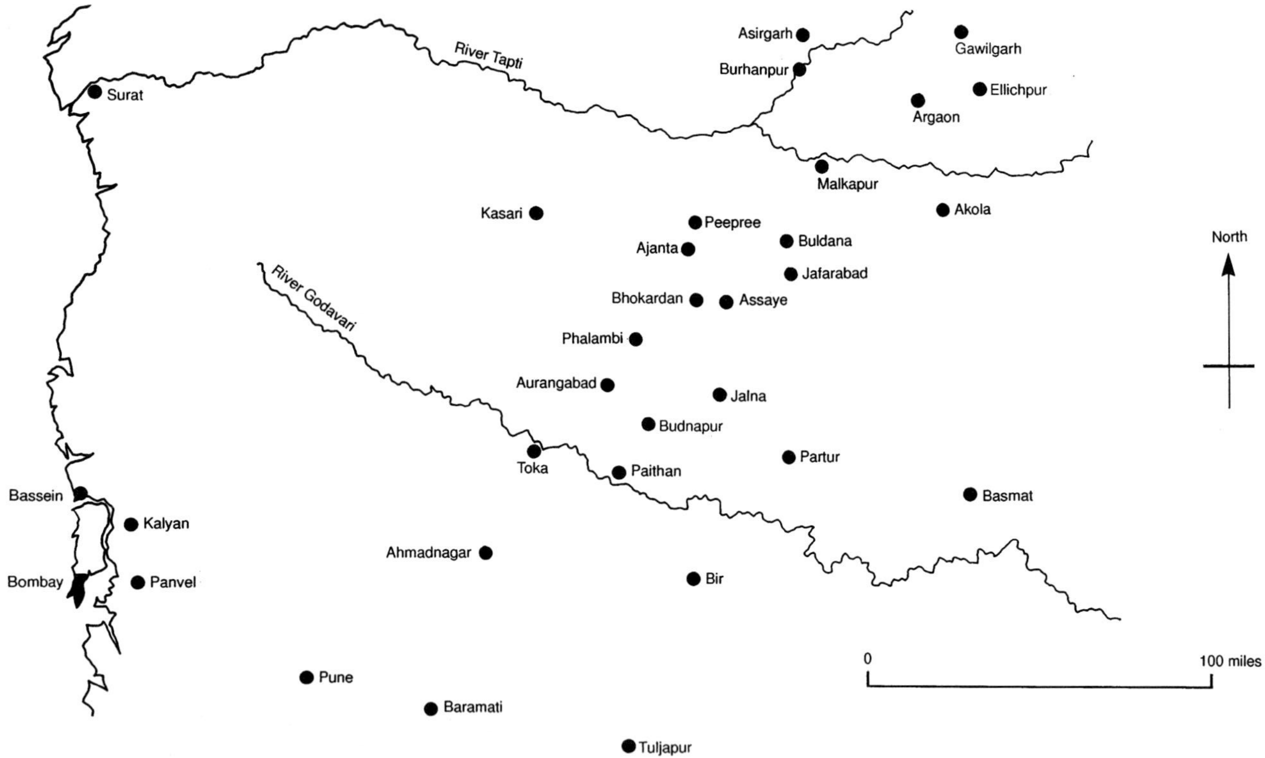

The setting of the Deccan campaign. (Aardvark Illustration)

I
Prelude – January to April 1803

Some while after the short campaign against Dhondiah Vagh, which ended with the battle at Conahgull on 10 September 1800, and in which he had commanded one detachment, while another was under the command of Colonel Stevenson, Arthur Wellesley had set out some thoughts on operations in Maratha territory 'as before long we may look to a war with the Marathas.' As is not unusual in such attempts, his projection was markedly accurate in some respects, and less so in others.

The analysis started from the premise that 'the season at which it is most convenient to commence a campaign with the Marathas is that at which the rivers, which take their rise in the Western Ghats, fill. This happens generally in the month of June.' Arthur Wellesley understood the timing of the south-west monsoon, not only from the Dhondiah Vagh campaign of 1800, but also from its relation to that of the attack on Seringapatam in May 1799. He would seem also to have been to some degree aware, in an age before regular meteorological records, of the variability of the monsoon, important in determining the extent to which rivers were a potential barrier. The rivers in the southern Deccan, the Bhima, the Kistna [Krishna], and the Toombuddra [Tungabhandra] flow from west to east. They are described by a modern geographer as flowing 'in broad shallow valleys maturely graded almost to their heads . . . entirely dependent on a rainfall concentrated in five or six months of the year, flowing over a thin soil-cover, and . . . almost dry in the hot weather.'[1]

The onset of the south-west monsoon was seen as the most suitable season for operations against the Marathas because Arthur Wellesley regarded their armies as 'principally composed of cavalry.' He believed that their scheme of operations against a British army would be 'to endeavour to cut off its communication with its rear, and impede the junction of its supplies from the Mysore country.' Having postulated operations during the south-west monsoon, he considered that a British army 'if good pontoons were provided' would be able to cross rivers without difficulty, but that the Marathas 'would never dare to detach a body across any river for the purpose of annoying our communications.' Further, the Deccan was 'in general . . . but ill supplied with water' and the advantage of certainty of supply offset the disadvantage of the destruction of cattle in heavy rain. The monsoon rain would 'fill many nullahs and an army has at this time some chance of being supplied with water.' Against these advantages, 'the inconvenience to be apprehended from the rains is trifling.' Arthur Wellesley went on to outline a scheme of operations in Maratha territory initiated from the northern boundary of Mysore. The events of late 1802 led to a conflict in a very different setting, and one in which the timing of operations depended on political realities rather than preferences related to climatic conditions. These operations were aggressive in intention, fought in the northern Deccan, and were not primarily against cavalry forces.[2]

On the evening of the 25 October 1802, after the decisive battle of Hadapshar outside the capital city, Barry Close as Resident with Peshwa Baji Rao wrote from Pune to the Governors of Madras and Bombay, and to James Kirkpatrick, the Resident with the Nizam of Hyderabad. He suggested to each of them that the prospective alliance with the Peshwa, and the probable requirement to restore him to his capital, made discreet military preparation urgent. The restoration of the Peshwa, if such should be ordered, would require the deployment of military force from the south, from the subsidiary force at Hyderabad, and from the area of Bombay.[3]

For Arthur Wellesley, serving as the Commanding Officer of Company troops in Mysore, the summons came on 12 November 1802, in a letter from Josiah Webbe, a former Secretary to the Governor of Fort St George Madras. This gave Arthur Wellesley warning that it was probable that the Company's political relations with the Marathas could well lead to an armed intervention, and there was 'a probability that an army would be assembled on the Toombuddra' [Tungabhandra] as a preliminary to a northward movement in the Deccan. Arthur Wellesley set himself to arrange the commissariat support of an army which might be involved in moving northwards into Maratha territory. In December 1802, when Barry Close the Resident with the Peshwa Baji Rao had left Pune and had begun the negotiations which were to lead to the Treaty of Bassein, Arthur Wellesley became involved in relations with some of the 'southern jagirdars', that is the lesser feudatories of Peshwa Baji Rao in southern Maharastra, with whom he had dealt during the campaign against Dhondiah Vagh. On these negotiations he reported both to his

Commander-in-Chief in Madras, Lieutenant-General James Stuart, and to Clive the Governor of Madras.[4]

In writing to John Malcolm, a key figure in the Secretariat at Fort William Calcutta, Arthur Wellesley stressed the importance of a move to Madras of Richard Wellesley, to enable him to supervise the evolving policy against the Marathas from a position of vantage with 'much earlier intelligence of every event.' It was also required because 'nothing but his presence can keep the government of Madras in a direct line.' The Governor of Madras was a nullity, and left to its own devices, in the absence of its Commander-in-Chief, the Madras Council might well so act as to endanger an army in the field. After an initial hesitation, this was advice that Richard Wellesley did not take. In the event, the robust handling of military advance in the Deccan by Stuart and Arthur Wellesley would have made this move otiose.[5]

Barry Close concluded the Treaty of Bassein with Peshwa Baji Rao on the last day of 1802. At almost the same time, Arthur Wellesley sent Close an assessment, which took a month to reach him, of the prospective movement north of a detachment from the Mysore territory tasked with the restoration of the authority of the Peshwa. He assumed assembly of the detachment at Harihar on 1 March and forecast an arrival at Pune at the end of April. He noted the political obstacles to the unopposed advance of a Company detachment [1,7].

For the detachment once arrived at Pune to rely on an extended logistic chain from Mysore when it faced the prospect of extended operations in the central Deccan would be to expose it to risk, and Arthur Wellesley, after consultation with his Commander-in-Chief, therefore stated to the Governor of Bombay, Jonathan Duncan, his requirements for a depot near to Bombay on which a detachment in the Deccan could call. It was to be a difficult association, and Arthur Wellesley was left with a confirmed scepticism of the effectiveness of the military authorities at Bombay which was to be important later [6]. The assemblage of force on the northern boundary of Mysore took most of January and February 1803. Arthur Wellesley questioned some parts of the logistic preparation, especially that of the provision of certain artillery pieces, to which Stuart responded cautiously [11]. In late February Stuart informed Arthur Wellesley that it seemed probable that 'a considerable detachment from this army will be directed to proceed beyond the frontier' [14]. Arthur Wellesley set out his recommended order of battle for the detachment, and suggestions for its supply.[6] Stuart's response, since he knew that Clive had selected Arthur Wellesley for the command of the detachment, was to ask him to join him and discuss these matters [15].

The logistic arrangements made, Stuart prepared the political directive for the detachment, and showed it to Arthur Wellesley in draft. Care was to be taken to conciliate the 'southern jagirdars' and to form a junction with the Peshwa, perhaps at Miraj, to form a junction with the subsidiary force advanced from Hyderabad and 'to proceed eventually to Pune, and establish an order of things in that capital favourable to the return of the Peshwa' [18]. Arthur Wellesley crossed into Maratha territory on 11 March. After two days he wrote to his brother the Governor-General; he was optimistic about the prospects of the movement of the detachment: 'all your plans will be carried into execution' [20]. But the central purpose of the letter was to seek from the Governor-General an assurance that Arthur Wellesley would retain the command in Mysore, while operating as commander of the detachment in the Deccan. This Arthur Wellesley stated as essential to ensure the continuity of supply from Mysore: this was an ostensible reason, the hidden point was that neither Richard nor Arthur Wellesley trusted the Government of Madras fully to support the Maratha venture.

To the north of the detachment as it advanced on the Deccan, forces loyal to Jaswant Rao Holkar, commanded by Mir Khan and Futteh Sigh Mania, fell back towards Pune. Good progress was made; by 14 March Arthur Wellesley felt able to forecast to Stevenson, the commander of the detachment moving westwards from Hyderabad, that he would reach Miraj by 5 April. He was anxious to arrange that his detachment would be joined by Peshwa Baji Rao. But on 30 March in Bassein, Barry Close had a five hour conference with Peshwa Baji Rao, on which he reported to both Richard and Arthur Wellesley that Baji Rao adamantly refused to join the Company detachment.[7]

By the first days of April, Arthur Wellesley knew that Jaswant Rao Holkar was withdrawing from Pune northwards towards Ahmednagar. He felt able to forecast that the detachment would arrive at Pune on 23 or 24 April.[8] The detachment reached Akluj on 15 April; it was now close to the forces which had moved from Hyderabad. In a letter to Richard Wellesley sent by Hyderabad, Arthur Wellesley reviewed the political and military situation which had been created by the junction of the two Company detachments. Looking beyond the occupation of Pune, he commented on the prospects of handling a possible northern combination of the Marathas determined to obstruct the restoration of the Peshwa under British control. He noted that Malcolm had explained to him why Richard Wellesley was 'anxious to bring these questions to a decision as soon as possible.' This was a reference to the realisation by Richard Wellesley that Ministers in London, the government of Addington, were not willing to give support to him against the Court of Directors and that the end of the Governor-Generalship was in sight. Arthur Wellesley spoke of this as a factor 'which must be conclusive to every friend of yours' [34].

As a means of frightening Peshwa Baji Rao, Jaswant Rao Holkar had threatened the firing of Pune on the approach of Company forces or those loyal to the Peshwa, and these messages had been passed by Close both to Fort William and also to Arthur Wellesley [32]. When he was within one extremely long forced march from Pune, believing that Amrit Rao was still in the city [38, 39], Arthur Wellesley pressed onwards over difficult ghat conditions and entered it, almost as Amrit Rao left. He had, by his own method, an accelerated cavalry movement covering sixty miles in thirty-two hours, met the central anxiety of Barry Close as Resident, that the Peshwa should not return to a fired city [40]. So it came about that on 20 April, Arthur Wellesley and John Malcolm were dating their letters from the capital city of Peshwa Baji Rao [41]. The moves of the two detachments, that commanded by Arthur Wellesley and that moved forward from Hyderabad, had achieved, as Richard Wellesley had intended, a political and military confrontation on the Deccan between the Company and the Maratha Confederacy.

I

Arthur Wellesley to Lieutenant-Colonel Close

Seringapatam
1 January 1803 [received 4 February]

Webbe[1] has desired me to write to you upon the subject of our operations to the northward, and although it is difficult to form an opinion on the subject of any military operations without knowing precisely their object, I comply with pleasure with his wishes . . .

I shall suppose our object to be to march the army to Pune, there to re-establish the Peshwa's authority. At this season of the year, I do not know of any natural obstacle to impede our progress, excepting the great distance. The principal object of art[ifice] is the fort of Dharwar, which I conclude that the Peshwa will have ordered the killedar to deliver up to us. If his Highness should not have given these orders, or if the killedar should not think it proper, we must make ourselves masters of that fortress. I am of opinion that it is to be taken by a coup de main and I should certainly attempt it. It may not however be thought proper to attack the place in this manner; but at all events, I do not conceive that it will stop the British army for more than a few days. It will also take three or four days to arrange our garrison in the place, and to remove thither our stores grain etc from Hullihall in Soondah.

After Dharwar shall be in our possession, I do not know of any place that will stop the British army for a moment. I will suppose that the army shall have arrived upon the Toombuddra, and that General Stuart will be prepared to advance from Harihar on the 1st of March. I do not think it possible that he could be there sooner; he has a very large and heavy equipment, which he brings from Madras; he has Carnatic cattle to move it; and he meets with the old disappointments in procuring them. He does not quit Madras till the 15th of this month; his troops and stores about the 12th; he has four hundred miles to march to Harihar, which will take him more than six weeks.

After quitting Harihar, he will have eight marches to Dharwar and from thence twenty two to Pune by Padshapur Chickoree [Chinchli?] Miraj and Tasgaum, and one more if he should go by Shahapur and Belgaum to Miraj. I should recommend the latter road, because I believe it will be convenient if not necessary to us to have possession of Belgaum, and by that road we shall be more certain of finding water than by the other. According to this account, I do not think you ought to look for us at Pune before the end of April . . .

Grwd (1837) i 391 (1844) i 321

2

Josiah Webbe to Arthur Wellesley

Madras
7 January 1803
[summary]

Webbe reported that an express from Close for the Governor-General had brought the text of the Treaty of Bassein, which he saw as containing 'all the material points.' He reported that 'the original object of Holkar was certainly to have established his paramount authority by making Baji Rao a pageant, by appointing Amrit Rao to be his dewan, and by retaining the sole command of the army. After the flight of the Peshwa, he seems to have intended the same thing by constituting Amrit Rao's son to be the new Peshwa.'

Webbe suggested that should the Company determine to settle disputes in the Maratha confederacy by force, the army could not reach the frontier before the end of February.

WP 1/135 fldr 1

3

Josiah Webbe to Arthur Wellesley

[Madras]
15 January 1803
[summary]

'Our preparations on the Toombuddra will probably dispose Holkar to an amicable negotiation.' If so, Webbe considered that Richard Wellesley should move to Bombay. Instructions of 30 December received from Fort William showed that the Governor-General planned to intervene in Maratha affairs as an ally of the Peshwa, to insist on an engagement, and if Peshwa Baji Rao declined, to take possession of territory as indemnity for the expense of military operations.

WP 1/135 fldr 2

4

Lieutenant-General Stuart to Arthur Wellesley

[Madras]
17 January 1803
[summary]

Stuart reported that he had received a letter from Richard Wellesley dated 8 January. This reported the intention of the Governor-General to embark for Madras at the end of January, possibly later visiting Mysore and Bombay, and his hopes that it would be possible 'to settle impending business by negotiation . . . in a few weeks.' Stuart noted the approval of the Governor-General of the military preparations so far made.

WP 1/135 fldr 2

5

Josiah Webbe to Arthur Wellesley

Madras
18 January 1803
[summary]

Webbe reported that he had received letters from both Malcolm and Richard Wellesley, from which he deduced that the Governor-General had decided to visit Madras and possibly travel to Bangalore. Richard Wellesley was reported to be 'sanguine in his expectation of accomplishing all his objects at Pune by negotiation and desires it to be understood that he has no intention of war.'

WP 1/135 fldr 2

6

Arthur Wellesley to Jonathan Duncan

Seringapatam
20 January 1803

General Stuart will have informed you that, adverting to the probability of the march of the army to Pune, and the possibility that our communication with Mysore and the seats of our resources of the army on this side of India might be precarious, and at all events would be difficult, on account of its length, I had proposed to him a plan for the formation of a depot at Panvel or Bassein, or some other place on the coast opposite to the islands of Bombay or Salsette, by means of the Government of Bombay . . .

The first point for consideration is the situation for the proposed depot. It should be somewhere on the coast, within reach of water carriage from Bombay, both that the depot may be formed without difficulty or great expense, and that it may be in the power of the Government of Bombay to provide for its defence with ease, supposing that the enemy should have a design to attack it. It should be at no great distance, and of easy access, from the ghat leading to Pune. It should have two gates at least if not more, all of easy access to cattle, and it should be of such strength as to render it probable that a small body of troops could keep it till reinforcements could be sent from Bombay . . .

The articles of which we shall be principally in want are food for Europeans, for our native troops and followers, and for our horses, military stores, medical stores, and money . . .

Grwd (1837) i 395 (1844) i 325

7

Arthur Wellesley to Lieutenant-Colonel Close

Seringapatam
21 January 1803

. . . I have the most positive assurances that our army will be joined by Goklah, and I believe them to be sincere, as his vakil who was here told me that his master has nothing to hope for from Holkar, as he had taken and given up to Balaji Kunjar, the brother of Holkar who has been put to death. His only reliance therefore was upon the English, and their endeavours to restore the power of the Peshwa.

I have not hitherto had any communication with any of the Patwurdans, excepting a civil letter from Chintomeni Rao and an answer from Bal Kishen Bhau to a letter which I wrote to him and sent by Govind Rao. I have at the same time desired Govind Rao to discover the intentions of the Patwurdans upon the present occasion. Bal Kishen Bhau declared that he considered himself as belonging to the English, and should join our army himself, and should do everything in his power to influence the others to adopt the same line of conduct. But he said that he could not answer for the others of the family . . .

Grwd (1837) i 399 (1844) i 329, WP 1/136

8

Lieutenant-General Stuart to Arthur Wellesley

Colar
1 February 1803

. . . If you have not already ordered the 7th Regt of cavalry to join the force under your immediate command that corps might join me in passing [Seror?] . . . Letters from Major Malcolm mention that the Governor General was to sail from Calcutta for Madras on the 25th January and as they have had northerly winds at Madras since the 25th he is soon expected at that Presidency.

Were it possible to procure at Seringapatam 100 bullock drivers to be sent to join us on the road as soon as possible to replace those who have deserted, it would be a great convenience to me. Major Symonds will pay them regularly the regulated pay of one and a half pagodas per mensem, and any trifling advance that may be made to them at Seringapatam Major Symonds being made acquainted with it, he will reimburse it.

WP 3/3/87 p. 3

9

Lieutenant-Colonel Close to Arthur Wellesley

Bassein
4 February 1803

I am extremely obliged by your communication of the lst [January]... You are perfectly right as to the object of our movements, and the route you have mentioned is the best and most direct from Mysore to Pune.

On the subject of Dharwar I have done all that was possible. Bapoji Sinde obtained his present place from Nana Fhadnavis and has never been obedient to the Peshwa and his Highness has therefore appointed Bal Kishen Gungur Dhur to the killedar of Dharwar. Sanads from the Peshwa on the subject I forwarded some days since to Lord Clive and copies are gone off to Bal Kishen Gunga Dhur by land . . .

The principal jagirdars on the Kistna seemed to be leagued against Goklah and Fateh Singh Mane and others of Holkar's sirdars. Mane has lately received a check at Karnada, a post belonging to the Pritti Niddi and has fallen back towards Pune, but Mir Khan is on his march from Pune towards Pandharpur and will probably endeavour to lay the Putwardan family and all their neighbours under contribution. He goes, most certainly to collect money, with a force of not less than 10 or 12,000 horse and 4000 infantry with guns, so that I hope his operations will have a favourable effect in making the different jagirdars feel it to be in their interest to unite with us to save them[selves] from the attacks of the common enemy.

Madu Rao Rastiah appears to be in some force near Pandharpur and the Peshwa considers this chieftain as firmly attached to his interests. I shall be happy to learn from you that the letters from the Peshwa which I have sent to Lord Clive respecting Dharwar have been put in a train for taking effect . . . I am afraid that Bapoji Sinde will refuse to deliver up Dharwar on the Peshwa's orders, but he may be induced to comply if threatened to be hanged in case of resistance . . .

You see that we ought to have a British force soon at Pune. As General Stuart's equipment is heavy, perhaps he may be induced to leave a part of it at Dharwar or some other post with a view to expedition.

WP 3/3/45 p. 3

10

Lieutenant-Colonel Close to Arthur Wellesley

Bassein
14 February 1803

I have been favoured with the intelligence you sent me through Sir William Clarke[2] and will be obliged to you for any further information you may be enabled to assist me with, respecting jagirdars and partisans on the Kistna. By the latest accounts from Pune, Holkar is much dissatisfied with Rastiah and the Bhau family, and has ordered the divisions under Mir Khan, Shalamunt Khan and Nagu Jevaji to proceed against them without delay. The force under these commanders is said to consist of not less than 16,000 cavalry, 4,000 infantry and 40 pieces of cannon. If this force really arrives on the Kistna it may induce the different jagirdars to unite, and make it their interest to accommodate with us, and cooperate with our troops for their safety.

I send you a statement of the whole of Holkar's force, taken from a letter which I received today from his camp. An abatement must of course be made in the numbers. Fateh Singh Mane's division I imagine has suffered much of late from loss in the field and desertion. I yesterday despatched a man by way of Miraj and Dharwar with instructions to discover if possible the situation of Baul Kishen Gunga Khan and make you acquainted with the subject with all expedition, but should this person [even] not be found, as I forwarded to Lord Clive an order from the Peshwa to Bapoji Sinde removing him from the charge of Dharwar and commanding him to deliver over the place to another officer, I trust we shall get hold of the fort without much delay or difficulty.

I have seen Mr Duncan on the subject of supplies and received assurances from him that every article mentioned in your letter of the 20th January will be ready in the requisite quantity at the proper time. To establish a depot on the coast in the Maratha territory would not be practicable at present, and that will not be necessary as cattle may be loaded from boats at Panvel with more facility perhaps than they could be from a magazine . . . The Konkan is now in the greater part in the hands of the ruling party at Pune, with whom we are not at peace yet, although we protect the Peshwa here. Amrit Rao's nearest party is at Kalyan.

I suppose Malcolm is by this time at Madras and that his Excellency is expected to arrive there soon. If we are to proceed by arms and negotiation, much work may occur in each of these departments . . .

WP 3/3/45 p. 9

10A

Statement of the force of Jaswant Rao Holkar

7 February 1803

Nagu Rao Jevaji 5000 cavalry
Shah Ahmed Khan 6000 cavalry 800 infantry
Mir Khan 5000 cavalry 4000 infantry 40 guns
Fateh Singh Mane 10,000 cavalry 2000 infantry
The whole of the above have assembled in the neighbourhood of Baramati, to be employed against the Bhau family and afterwards upon more distant objects.

Therefore [there are] with Holkar at Pune
Dukkuries 20,000 cavalry
Hindustani 10,000 cavalry
Holkar's own brigade 3000 infantry and 46 guns
Vicker's brigade 2500 infantry and 35 guns
Dodd's brigade 1500 infantry and 20 guns
heavy park of artillery 22 guns
two corps of aligoles guard the park, one of 700 and the other 1400.
Totals [for both groups taken together] 56,000 cavalry, 15,900 infantry and 157 guns of different calibres

WP 3/3/45

11

Lieutenant-General Stuart to Arthur Wellesley

17 February 1803

. . . My opinion respecting the importance of celerity of movement corresponds to yours.[3] The object is of unquestionable advantage but the means of accomplishing it will I am apprehensive be attended with many difficulties.

It is certain, as you have observed, with respect to hired cattle that the whole army cannot be capable of marching with expedition unless all its parts are so, and I fear that the movement of the mass of public and private carriages which will accompany our troops cannot be materially facilitated by any reduction there we may find it practicable to make of the number of public wheeled carriages.

The extreme length of our line of operations, in the event of our advancing to Pune, and the precarious nature of the communication with our magazines renders me anxious that we should possess means on our arrival there of prosecuting such operations as the course of circumstances might make it necessary to undertake. I therefore directed the park and magazine to be supplied to a greater extent than might be requisite in operations nearer our own frontier, and the same reasons made me desirous that the supplies of grain and provisions should be equally ample.

The greater part of the magazine and provisions, stores and all the private baggage are to be carried on the backs of bullocks, but I have found these during the present march to move as slowly and to fail as rapidly as the draft cattle. This it is true cannot be considered as a proof of the superiority of either plan, because the route and the nature of our movements have been favourable to the draft cattle and the carriage cattle were originally very bad. However the extent of our equipment will certainly delay the regular marches of the army, and it has appeared to be doubtful whether any plan can enable it to advance with all the departments with celerity equal to what you have in mind.

Expeditions may be made with all the celerity of which the march of infantry and guns is capable, but in these cases will probably find it requisite to disburden themselves of our encumbrances by throwing them into support. The number of carriages at present with the different divisions of the army does not much exceed your calculation, and I shall certainly abridge it in passing the frontier as much as may be practicable.

A variety of opinions is entertained by the artillery respecting brass twelve-pounders. They have been suggested to me by officers of experience in that corps as the most useful description of field guns that can be taken on service, as being equally movable with six-pounders and possessing much superior effect. Colonel Agnew and Captain Sir John Sinclair employed them with advantage to the southward, and the latter is of opinion with proper management of the charge they are a most efficient piece of ordnance. The failure of the carriages sent from the Residency must be owing to the bad quality of the wood of all the carriages furnished by the contractors.

As we have 24 tumbrils loaded with treasure, I fear that the elephants will not be equal to the carriage of the quantity contained in them . . . I certainly agree in your opinion of the advantage of all the draft cattle being the property of the public. I shall endeavour to effect that arrangement on our joining at the frontier. Indeed all the arrangements of the army and its departments must be adjusted there . . .

WP 3/3/87 p. 25

12

Arthur Wellesley to Lieutenant-General Stuart

Jingey Jalaub
17 February 1803

. . . The country through which I have marched has suffered much from a want of rain in the last season, a want which has been general in all the countries bordering on the Western Ghats and has been most severely felt to the northward. I understand that the crops have failed entirely in the neighbourhood of Harihar, that the country is quite burnt up, and forage for your army will be exceedingly scarce. Under these circumstances, I have again taken into consideration the proposition which I heretofore made to you to collect your army at that place.

If immediately upon your arrival in its neighbourhood it is your intention to enter the Maratha territory, and to advance upon your march as soon as your arrangements are made, the best thing to do would be to cross the Toombuddra at once, and encamp within the Maratha territory. You will then have both sides to forage in, whereas if you remain on this side you will procure nothing from the other . . . The country on the other side of the river is likely to afford you the greatest quantity of forage, as its produce is jowari of which the crop is earlier than ragi and the country is in general more fertile than that on this side. Besides, none of it will have been consumed, whereas there must have been a great consumption of the forage on this side by the cattle which have been in that neighbourhood for the purposes of formation of the depot, and belonging to the banjaras.

If you should be desirous not to advance into the Maratha territory till you should receive further advices, either from the Governor General or from the Resident at Pune, as a want of forage for any number of days must be fatal to the cattle and exceedingly detrimental to your ulterior operations, it is my opinion that it would be best not to approach Harihar, and not to collect the army in one body until you have determined to commence your march forward. In that case General Campbell might remain at Harponelly [Harpanshalli?] and forage as far as the Toombuddra to the northward, this division either opposite Hoonelly [Honnali] upon the Toombuddra or upon the Soolakairy Lake, and the main body of the army in the neighbourhood of Mayaconda. The whole would thus subsist with ease, and two days' easy march would join them at Harihar . . .

SD iv 8

13

Arthur Wellesley to Lieutenant-Colonel Close

Hooley Honore [Holehonnur]
22 February 1903 [received 15 March]

I enclose a letter from Govind Rao and another from Ball Kishen Bhau by which you will perceive that the dispositions of the chiefs of the Putwardan family are favourable to the Peshwa. They are all encamped on the Kistna. I shall send you Govind Rao's detail as soon as I receive it.

We are to halt in three divisions; General Stuart at Mayaconda, General Campbell at Harponelly [Harpanshalli?] and myself at Honnali, till further orders are received. General Stuart's cattle will recruit a little there, but not much, and I see no remedy but that which I have recommended to him, namely to diminish his monstrous equipment and leave behind everything not absolutely necessary. I shall see him at Mayaconda on the 26th and will try to persuade him to adopt this measure.

I might arrive at Harihar on the 25th and I am finely equipped for the service in every respect. I make long marches with the greatest facility and my cattle are all fresh . . . I have not heard where Gungur Dhur is, but Bapoji Sinde will certainly refuse to give up Dharwar till he sees our army approach it. The threat to use six baums of rope may then be useful. But at all events I think we can take it by a coup de main.

Grwd (1837) i 407 (1844) i 333

14

Lieutenant-General Stuart to Arthur Wellesley

Chittledroog
23 February 1803

I have been honoured by your letters of the 21st and 22nd, and return you many thanks for the details you have communicated to me relative to subsistence and forage. My apprehension of a want of either of these articles is in great measure removed by the tenor of a despatch from the Governor General which has been forwarded to me by Lord Clive.[4] This important communication . . . contains the principles and objects of his plans and describes the nature of the measures proposed for their execution.

I have received no orders from the Governor of Madras on the subject of this despatch. I expect however definite instructions in the course of a short period of time and I think it probable from the actual advance of the [Hyderabad] subsidiary force, from the movement of Holkar's chiefs stated in Colonel Close's last despatch, and from the necessity of supporting the southern jagirdars, that a considerable detachment from this army will be directed to proceed beyond the frontier without delay.

In order to be able to execute with promptitude the movement which I have thus anticipated, I have been desirous to assemble the army at Harihar, but I am prevented from adopting this step as yet by the consideration that, should there be be a delay in the transmission of his Lordship's sentiments, the subsistence of the cattle will be attended with considerable inconvenience. I shall therefore adhere to my former plan of halting at Myaconda where I shall expect to have the pleasure of seeing you.

You will perceive the importance attached by the Governor General to the favourable disposition and the cordial cooperation of the Maratha feudatories, indeed the prosecution of his Excellency's plans is made to depend in a great measure upon their support of our cause. It is therefore more than ever requisite to conciliate the attachment and encourage the assistance of all the jagirdars to the cause of the Peshwa with which our measures are connected. It has afforded me the greatest pleasure to learn by your last letter that the sentiments of the Patwurdans are so favourable to our views, and I would request you to continue your communications with them for the purpose of confirming the intentions which they have expressed. The progress of Holkar's chiefs to the southward will contribute to render their wavering, from the apprehension of the consequences of exposing themselves to his attacks. It may therefore be prudent to afford them expectation of the speedy advance of the British troops to their relief.

WP 3/3/87 p. 39

15

Lieutenant-General Stuart to Arthur Wellesley

four miles south of Myaconda
3 March 1803 [received that day]

I have received by express from Lord Clive . . . the measures to be adopted . . . a detachment of not less than 7,000 from this army should proceed into the Maratha territory, that it should advance as soon as the arrangements for its formation can be completed, and that it should be commanded by you. The objects of the advance have already been described in the Governor General's despatch.

In consequence of the above communication I have determined to assemble the army at Harihar and I have directed Major General Campbell and Lt Colonel Dallas to march from their present positions on the 5th and to arrive at Harihar on the 7th. I request you will put your division in movement at the same time, but as your able assistance must be useful to me in arranging the details of the plans which it will be necessary to form, and as the urgency of the service will not admit of the advance of your detachment being delayed after the army shall have assembled at Harihar, I am desirous that you should join me as soon as may be practicable, leaving your division to be conducted to the rendezvous by the next senior officer.

I shall march from here the day after tomorrow, be at Kundewarra on the 6th and arrive at Harihar on the 7th. Major Malcolm is coming to us post and I trust may reach us before you cross the Tungabhandra . . . I am anxious that you should receive this letter with the least practicable delay that you may inform Goklah by his vakil, if he is still with you, of your coming to his assistance . . .

WP 3/3/87 p. 49

16

Arthur Wellesley to Lieutenant-General Stuart

Honnali
4 March 1803

I had the honour of receiving yesterday your first letter of the 3rd, and I have stopped here this day in order to see the vakils, to write letters to the sirdars on the frontier, and to make various arrangements preparatory to the march of the troops. I shall go to Harihar tomorrow morning, and shall join you at Kundewarra on the 6th. This division will march from hence on the 6th and will be at Harihar on the 7th. I have given orders that the banjaras may be collected. They will be in good time . . .

Grwd (1837) i 417 (1844) i 341

17

Arthur Wellesley to Lieutenant-Colonel Close

Honnali
4 March 1803

You will have learned from Lord Clive's instructions to General Stuart of the 27th February that everything ends at last in my going forward with a detachment, and that the main body of the army is to remain on the frontier with a view to its defence, or to giving support to the advanced division if it should be necessary. The army joins, consequently, at Harihar on the 7th and I shall move forward as soon afterwards as circumstances will permit. But as I sent to General Stuart yesterday detailed arrangements for detaching a body of about the strength stated in Lord Clive's instructions,[5] I imagine that all preparations for my march will be in readiness in a very few hours after the army shall join. I shall leave this tomorrow for General Stuart's camp to forward them, and you may depend upon my not losing one moment of time.

I enclose my last letters from Govind Rao, from which you will perceive the state of opinions and intentions of the jagirdars upon the frontier. Besides this, Goklah's vakil in my camp still assures me of the determination of his master to adhere to the cause of the Peshwa, and to join me. I have desired Govind Rao to urge Bal Kishen Gunga Dhur to come and meet me, and if Dharwar is not to be got by force, I shall at least try what I can do by fair means and threats . . .

Grwd (1837) i 418 (1844) i 311

18

Lieutenant-General Stuart to Arthur Wellesley

Harihar
9 March 1803

. . . Although I have considered it expedient to avoid prescribing the particular plan of the operations of your detachment, yet I judge it necessary to state certain principal objects which, in my judgement, ought to regulate the course of your proceedings.[6]

1. To encourage the southern jagirdars to declare in favour of the Peshwa's cause, to employ every means to reconcile their mutual animosities, and to induce them to unite their forces with the advancing detachment, for the purpose of reestablishing his Highness' government.

2. To proceed to Miraj and form a junction with the Peshwa, or should that measure be deemed unadvisable on the part of his Highness, with such of his chieftains and troops as may be able to meet you there.

3. To open a communication and form a junction with the subsidiary force under Colonel Stevenson, and the contingent of his Highness the Nizam.

4. To proceed eventually to Pune, and establish an order of things in that capital, favourable to the return of the Peshwa, and the attainment of the ends of the late treaty . . .

I have not noticed in the foregoing orders the conduct to be observed on your part in case of opposition of any chieftain, and in particular Jaswant Rao Holkar, from whom we are led to expect most opposition to your proceedings. The instructions of the Governor General and Lord Clive contain no orders and afford no positive rule to guide my determination on this important head.

I infer however from the spirit of those instructions, that if the majority of the southern jagirdars, and the sentiments of the body of the people, are found to declare in favour of the restoration of Baji Rao, the British detachment ought to persevere in the endeavour to reestablish his authority, and should the detachment, during the prosecution of that endeavour encounter the hostility of any individual jagirdar, that they are to employ, in concert with the well-affected jagirdars, every practicable means to overcome his opposition. In the event therefore of any single feudatory opposing resistance to the restoration of the Peshwa, after you have ascertained that the sentiments of the majority of the chieftains are favourable to that measure, I am of opinion that the instructions which I have received justify me in authorising you to compel his submission . . .

Grwd (1837) i 423 (1844) i 345, Parl Pps [5, 22 June 1804] p. 103, PRC x 81

19

Lieutenant-General Stuart to Arthur Wellesley

near Harihar
10 March 1803

Finding more forage here than I had at first expected will enable me to continue on my present ground until the 12th in hopes of seeing Major Malcolm . . . General Baird applied to me this morning for permission to avail himself of General Lake's leave to return to England, which I have granted him. Accordingly he leaves camp for Madras in a day or two . . .

I hope the letter I forwarded to you from Goklah last night contained information of a pleasant nature. I had no person in my camp that could read Marathi . . . I acquainted Colonel Close yesterday by express of your march and sent him a state of the force under your command. I wish to have a copy of your proposed route to enable me to calculate the probable time of your being able to form a junction with the subsidiary force. This, once accomplished, will set my mind at ease.

WP 3/3/87 p. 55

20

Arthur Wellesley to Richard Wellesley

Karisgy on the Werdah
13 March 1803

You will be anxious to hear from me as soon as possible after I have entered the Maratha territory. . . . I crossed the Toombuddra at Havanoor yesterday, and marched to this river, and made another march towards Savanore this day. We have been well received by the inhabitants of the country, the villages are all full, and the camp is well supplied with forage and provisions. I have no doubt whatever but that I shall be able to bring forward, for the service of the Peshwa, all the jagirdars in the southern part of the empire, and I think all your plans will be carried into execution . . .

Grwd (1837) i 432 (1844) i 351

21

Lieutenant-General Stuart to Arthur Wellesley

Harihar
15 March 1803 [received 16th March]

I have been honoured with your letter of the 13th and the paper of intelligence forwarded with it. I entirely concur in the justness of your reasoning and conclusion regarding the conduct ascribed to Bapoji Sinde. I cannot at present believe the account of his having admitted to the charge of this fort [Dharwar] any individual from Holkar, but even if a confirmation of that account is received . . . it should not induce us to change the mode of proceeding with respect to Dharwar which was described in my instructions to you. Everything at present requires the early advance of your detachment, your junction with Colonel Stevenson, and the final accomplishment of the objects of your proceedings . . .

Should our plans succeed, Dharwar will of course submit to whatever arrangement may be adopted with regard to it. That fortress might have been considered necessary as a post and a depot had the whole army advanced, but this necessity is considerably diminished by the continuance of the main body of the army on the frontier . . . I trust that you will succeed in conciliating the cooperation of Bapoji Sinde . . . Major Malcolm arrived this morning and proposes setting out with a light party to join you, as there are many points he wishes to explain more fully to you . . .

WP 3/3/87 p. 72

22

Lieutenant-Colonel Close to Arthur Wellesley

Bassein
15 March 1803 [received 23 March]

I have been favoured with your letter of the 22nd [February] and am happy to find that you have received such acceptable accounts from the Patwurdan family, whom Holkar and Amrit Rao are doing all that is possible to conciliate. Baul Kishen Gunga Dhur I would hope has long ere this opened a correspondence with you and advanced towards Dharwar with the aim of obtaining possession of that fort agreeably to his late appointment.

Without being too sanguine however, one can scarcely expect that Bapoji Sinde will be persuaded to surrender his authority unless urged by threats and impressed by fear. Very few of the Peshwa's posts have surrendered to the ruling party at Pune. Sevanghur close to that capital continues firm to his Highness' interest, and he has lately received possession of Saverndrug in the Konkan. I conceive you were perfectly right therefore in recommending to General Stuart to lighten his equipment. After we get possession of Dharwar the troops I imagine will have little to do in besieging . . . Stevenson[7] . . . on the 7th inst was a little this side of Bidar [Bedur] on his way to Parenda . . .

As usual all the parties concerned in the present difficulties negotiate or correspond with each other. The Berar man it is said is displeased with the Peshwa for having united his interests with us, and Sinde we hear regards that event with almost equal ill humour. By the last advices Collins had joined him but not seen him in business.

His Excellency has recommended that the Peshwa should offer a fort, a jagir, or money to Holkar to induce him to leave Pune and allow his Highness to return in peace to his capital. But his Highness thinks that Holkar should sue for pardon and not expect reward and thus the matter stands. The truth is indeed that Holkar is not to be satisfied with any such offer and in the state of things I think that the army ought to advance to Pune with the least possible delay.

WP 3/3/45 p. 20

23

Lieutenant-General Stuart to Arthur Wellesley

17 March 1803 [received 19 March]

. . . The sirdars coming with you and their assurances of a hearty and cordial cooperation is very satisfactory . . . Major Malcolm will probably inform you of a very extraordinary proposal I had made to me by the Madras Government to detach a part of my army to support the civil authority in Malabar, the rebellion in that province having become serious.[8] Fortunately it was not a positive order, only the necessity of the measure strongly urged, which I cannot agreeable to my own judgement of the present state of affairs comply with . . .

WP 3/3/87 p. 77

24

Lieutenant-General Stuart to Arthur Wellesley

Gubghurry
18 March 1803 [received 20 March]

. . . I am much disappointed in the number of banjaras I expected from the Ceded Districts. I estimated them at 15,000 at least, in place of which they do not amount to 8,600. I have 4,000 with me on the road to join about 2,000 and Major Munro writes to me on the 15th that there are not 2,000 more in the Ceded Districts and these are loading at different places at so great distance that it is impossible to ascertain when they may be able to join me. We have no information as yet of the Baramahal banjaras having entered the Mysore country. I am afraid that we can have no dependence upon them . . .

WP 3/3/87 p. 79

25

Lieutenant-General Stuart to Arthur Wellesley

[undated, but about 24 March 1803]

I am honoured with your letter dated the 21st from Dharwar, which is very satisfactory.

As it is not impossible your views may point to the chief command on the Coromandel coast, I think it proper to inform you that I have this day written officially to the Chairman of the Court of Directors to inform him that it is my intention after the present service is over, and I shall have completed the necessary military arrangements that may become requisite in consequence, to resign the situation I at present hold under the Government of Fort St George.

This I judge it necessary to do, to prevent the Court of Directors from alleging that I took it by surprise by a hasty and unlooked for resignation, and I shall be particularly happy if this intimation to you may in any shape tend to assist in forwarding your views.[9]

WP 3/3/87 p. 70

26

Arthur Wellesley to Lieutenant-General Stuart

Erroor on the Kistna
1 April 1803

. . . I arrived here on the 31st March and have halted for two days in order to establish at this place a field hospital . . . I have taken the opportunity of this halt to have a general muster of the cattle attached to the different corps and departments . . . and although they have made a long march from Seringapatam in a short space of time, and in a season very unfavourable, they are still capable with very little assistance of moving the grain provision and ordnance stores for which they were hired. The Company's draught cattle are in high condition. I have now in this camp 10,000 banjara bullocks with full bags. The daily consumption of the bazaars is 200 [bullock loads] so that I have a supply which will last fifty days . . .

It is needless to enter into a detail respecting the animosities between the chiefs[10] in whose hands is placed the power over the countries through which this detachment has passed . . . Since the year 1800 when I was in this country before, it has been one continual contest for power and plunder between the different chiefs who have armies under their command . . .

I have prevailed on all these chiefs to cease their contests for the present and to join this detachment with the troops which would otherwise be employed in the plunder of the country or in the prosecution of their private quarrels, and to cooperate with me in the service of the Peshwa. They have allowed me the use of the supplies of the countries under their management or protection, on payment, and have protected the people belonging to my camp in their passage through their countries . . .

My next object must be to join Colonel Stevenson . . . It is now reported that Holkar with the main body of his army is gone towards Hindustan by the Ninderrah ghat. If that should be the case, the junction will not be difficult . . .

Grwd (1837) 457 (1844) i 372

27

Lieutenant-General Stuart to Arthur Wellesley

Humpsagor
1 April 1803

I have been honoured with your despatch dated the 29th and I am happy to find that you have been joined by Goklah.

With respect to the 3,000 pindaris it is unquestionably highly advantageous to the general interest in the present state of affairs to remove any cause that is calculated to occasion a continuance of the warfare that has prevailed amongst the southern jagirdars, or that is likely to increase the means of opposition and annoyance within Holkar's control, or to produce any disturbance in the countries in your rear . . .

The dismissal of the pindaris might occasion all these consequences, and as there was no means of providing for their support without allowing them to plunder or taking them into pay, I am of opinion that in adopting the latter alternative you have acted in the manner most conformable to the advantage of our cause in general . . .

Should the report of the movement by Jaswant Rao Holkar towards the northward be confirmed, you will be able to advance on a more direct line and with more expedition to Pune, concerting with Colonel Stevenson a plan for the junction of the detachments nearer to that capital than might have been expedient under other circumstances . . .[11]

WP 3/3/87 p. 113

28

Lieutenant-Colonel Close to Arthur Wellesley

Bassein
2 April 1803 [received by 11 April]

Appearances at Pune become more favourable daily. I send you a copy . . . of a letter of the 29th March from a brahmin in my employ at Pune[12] . . . Holkar you will perceive is certainly destined for Chandore beyond the Godavari and Amrit Rao as certainly prepared to follow him. The party of Holkar's infantry under Hurnaut Singh and Makin Singh that remained within eight or ten kos of Pune you will find have proceeded to the northward in circumstances of great distress, having suffered greatly by desertion and been obliged to leave three pieces of cannon behind them.

As Mir Khan, Shahamut Khan, Nagu Jewaji and Futteh Singh Mania now act for themselves and can subsist only by plundering the southern jagirdars, I trust you will not find it difficult to keep the latter strictly neutral at least, and as to the former I presume that they will not offer much obstruction to your march.

The Peshwa's lady, and the lady of his brother Chimnaji reside in his Highness' dwelling at Pune, and there is every reason to believe that when Amrit Rao marches, Govind Rao Pranspy who has charge of Sevanghur will proceed to occupy the city on the part of the Peshwa. Indeed I think it not impossible that Pranspy may endeavour to beat up Amrit Rao's quarters in the course of his march. It is not improbable I think that Mir Khan etc may retire before you towards Gardoon as you advance. Should they wish however to avoid your line and remain behind you on the Kistna, it may be a question whether you ought to disturb them at the expense of time, or come briskly on to Pune. In such a state of things General Stuart's army must keep them in check. Cut off from Holkar they must soon decay and sink, and under every circumstance your first object must be to bring the Peshwa up the ghats.

If Holkar does not return from the northward, and at present there is no prospect whatever of his coming back, you may possibly find it unnecessary to bring Colonel Stevenson to the west of the Bhima. From any point on that river near Parenda he could keep Holkar in check, should he attempt to return to Pune or disturb the Nizam's frontier. There is certainly nothing at present to prevent Colonel Stevenson from coming on to Pune except that in doing so he might leave the Nizam's country rather exposed, and except also that as yet you are rather too distant from him. You see that in all my statements I conclude that you will be joined and assisted by the Peshwa's sirdars, who separated from him at Mhar, although some of the jagirdars on the Kistna may decline being active and be neutral.

The Peshwa has sent directions to his killedars between the Kistna and Pune to give you constant information of what passes in the neighbourhood and to assist you to the utmost of their power.

WP 3/3/45 p. 49

29

Lieutenant-Colonel Close to Arthur Wellesley

Bassein
9 April 1803 [received by 16th April]

This morning I was made happy by your letter of the 2nd inst. It came by way of Pune which is evidently the most expeditious route . . . I enclose a copy of my last letter to his Excellency.[13] Sinde is certainly angry but I think neither wise nor bold. The Berar man is probably not to be duped and as for Holkar and Sinde they have heated passions to extinguish and much to discuss before they can possibly come to an arrangement. I am still of opinion that after we assemble at or near Pune we shall have little to fear from Maratha combinations.

Holkar has again repeated his orders to Mir Khan Shahamut Khan etc to join him by way of Gardoon and has recommended to Amrit Rao to watch the approach of the English troops and as they draw nigh to Pune to set fire to the city and retire with his people to the northward. But how Amrit Rao will act God knows. He seems at present to be much engaged in preparation for the marriage of his son . . . I conclude that Mir Khan will retire before you by the route of Gardoon as directed.

The 78th Regiment joined us yesterday. I shall see Colonel Murray tomorrow morning and arrange with him about his moving. I think he will march for Kalyan in the course of three or four days; from thence we can move to the vicinity of Panvel. I shall hope to hear from you or Malcolm every day by one channel or another. Goklah's letter for the Peshwa I have sent to the durbar. His Highness urges me so constantly for assistance of cash to enable him to move from hence and mount his dismounted mankaries and followers that I am absolutely afraid to propose to him that you should afford any aid to Goklah. Were I to start the subject I should have endless application from him, which could not be complied with.

If you think however that by assisting Goklah you would not draw other demands of a similar nature, you may act in the case as you judge proper, and I doubt not but I should be able by some mode to obtain payment from the Peshwa of the sum you may be induced to disburse on this occasion.

WP 3/3/45 fldr 3 p. 77

30

Lieutenant-General Stuart to Arthur Wellesley

[Bellasousy?]
10 April 1803 [received 16 April]

I have had the honour to receive your letters dated the 4th and 5th and I am happy to observe that everything goes on so well with you. I trust that your expectations regarding the movement of Holkar and his chiefs will be confirmed. It will be a great point effected if we can establish the Peshwa at Pune without opposition, for the influence of his regular authority supported by our army may do a great deal to prevent troubles . . .

I am glad that your endeavours to satisfy the banjaras succeeded so well. I shall make a proper use of the result of your investigations with respect to those with me . . . The cavalry are ordered by Government to be completed to their war establishment, the infantry corps not in the field to recruit their supernumeries and three extra battalions to be raised.

WP 3/3/87 p. 129

31

Lieutenant-Colonel Close to Arthur Wellesley

Bassein
11 April 1803 [received 18 April]

Yesterday evening only I was favoured with your important despatch of the 20th March.

As Jaswant Rao Holkar is on the Godavari and Mir Khan Shahamut Khan etc are about to proceed to the northward to join him, I conclude that you will pursue your plan of coming on by the route of Jejuri which seems admirably well calculated for the attainment of the objects you have in view. Our aim will be in due course to join you as soon as possible after you have taken up your proposed ground in the vicinity of Pune.

The detachment here will march the moment its bullocks arrive from Bombay. A few of them are come already and Colonel Murray tells me that he will be able to move on the 15th inst. In this case, he will be at Kalyan on the 18th where the Peshwa will proceed to join him with all haste. Kalyan is not more than two marches from the Bhoor ghat which is at present rather rough and difficult. As your convoys will have to frequent it much, I suggest that on your arrival near Pune you should send off a party of your pioneers to clear it and make it easily passable for loaded cattle.

I have attended to what you have written to General Stuart about Appah Sahib's pindaris. When we meet I hope there will be no difficulty in settling matters respecting them agreeably to your wishes. Amrit Rao is still at Pune apparently preparing for the wedding of his son. However there cannot be a doubt but he will soon proceed to join Holkar along with Mir Khan, Shahamut Khan etc.

Your letters to me should be delivered to Narrainji who has charge of the dak at the Sungam, unless something should occur to disturb him in the conduct of his office.

Sinde with his own mouth has given the most formal assurances to Colonel Collins that he has no intention to obstruct our alliance with the Peshwa, or to take any steps to interrupt the friendship which he pursues with the Company.[14] I have the pleasure to enclose copies of my last address to his Excellency and of an important despatch just received from Colonel Collins . . .

WP 3/3/45 p. 65

32

Lieutenant-Colonel Close to Arthur Wellesley

Bassein
11 April 1803 [two letters of the same date]

I have still to mention that your latest despatch is dated 3rd inst from Miraj.

However I conclude that you are coming on well, as Colonel Stevenson in a letter of the 7th inst says that Mir Khan and Shahamut Khan were returning to the northward with an appearance of agitation, occasioned I am sure by your appearance. Colonel Murray is doing all that is possible to arrange and complete his equipment and he will certainly march on the 17th inst for Kalyan.

I formerly mentioned that the ladies of the Peshwa's family resided in his dwelling at Pune. They are in the care of Balaji Patwardan who, in case of the departure of Amrit Rao, will assume charge of the city. By all account however Amrit Rao had not made up his mind to moving. He is still engaged about the marriage of his son, and he tells the Peshwa that if he be forced to quit Pune he will not move until he has set fire to the city and reduced it to ashes.

The Peshwa therefore has requested me to mention these circumstances to you, and suggests that Amrit Rao's design may be frustrated if on your arrival within eight or ten kos of Pune you should detach a detail to Kishen Gunga Dhur and the other Maratha sirdars who separated from his Highness at Mhar, to make a forced march to Pune, and use all possible means for the protection of the ladies of the Peshwa's family and the saving of the city from being ruined by fire.

The propriety of such a movement, his Highness is sensible, must depend upon circumstances, and should be made only in the event of your thinking that it might be attended by the desired effect.

WP 3/3/45 p. 85

33

Lieutenant-Colonel Close to Arthur Wellesley

Bassein
12 April 1803

. . . Colonel Murray will march for Kalyan on the 15th or 16th inst from whence we shall proceed to occupy Panvel. Your letter of the 3rd inst is the latest I have received from you . . . Your approach begins to make some noise at Pune. Amrit Rao however still keeps his ground there.

WP 3/3/45 p. 89

34

Arthur Wellesley to Richard Wellesley

Camp at Akluj
15 April 1803

You will be anxious to hear from me, and to receive my opinion of the state of our military affairs in this country, and I take the earliest opportunity of writing to you afforded by the junction of the Nizam's army. My march to this place has been unopposed, and I have received from the country all the assistance that it could afford. . . .

The question whether the supposed confederacy will be formed and whether we shall have to contend with it ought to be brought to a decision as soon as possible.

First because if we are to have a war we shall carry it on with great advantage during the rainy season.

Secondly because we are ready and the supposed enemy are not, and every day's delay after this time is an unnecessary increase of expense to us, and an advantage to them.

Thirdly because we shall immediately ascertain the views and intentions of the Peshwa regarding the alliance in general, and we shall leave no time for intrigues among the jagirdars in his and our interest.

Fourthly because nothing but our determined and early opposition to the confederacy can save us from it, supposing it to exist. To withdraw from our arrangements with the Peshwa will rather accelerate its attack, with the addition of the Peshwa's force.

In order to bring this question to a decision the Peshwa should be urged immediately, if possible before he should arrive at Pune, to desire Sinde to recross the Narbada. This chief ought at the same time to be pressed upon this point by our minister at his camp, and all the screws, menaces etc might be brought to bear upon him, upon his Frenchmen, and upon the Raja of Berar . . .

I think it probable that a system of menace towards Sinde, his Frenchmen, and the Raja of Berar, will put a stop to the negotiations for the formation of the confederacy, to which there are already many natural obstacles, particularly as we and the Nizam are prepared, and already in the field. But if Sinde should refuse to give an unequivocal symptom of his good intentions by retiring across the Narbada I can have no doubt of the confederacy and for the reasons I have above stated we ought to attack it without loss of time. The operations in this event will be of a nature so general that it is difficult to give an opinion concerning them. The battle must be fought either on the Nizam's frontier or near Pune by these troops, but the impression which will put an end to the contest, like that which will prevent the confederacy, must be made from the northern frontier of Bengal and from Midnapur.

This letter is already of a greater length than I intended to make it and contains a consideration of points which require a more detailed discussion than I can give them at present, but still I think it is best to send it to you. Malcolm has apprised me of the reason for which you are anxious to bring these questions to a decision as soon as possible, of the validity of which I am fully sensible. But exclusive of these reasons, which must be conclusive to every friend of yours, those of a military nature, to which I have above alluded, are decisive.

Gwrd (1837) i 494 (1844) i 396, WP 1/143

35

Arthur Wellesley to Colonel Collins

Somergaum at the junction of the rivers Nira and Kurrah
17 April 1803 [received 25 April]

After so much time has elapsed since I have had any communication with you, it gives me the most sincere pleasure to commence one by the expression of the great gratification I received in the perusal of your despatch to the Governor General of the 25th [March] a copy of which reached me yesterday from Colonel Close . . . you drew from the prince with whom you were sent to negotiate a declaration which must be regarded as formal, and to which must be attributed the future peace of India, if he should act in conformity to his declaration.

You will have heard from Colonel Close that I am advancing towards Pune with a detachment of the army, which is so well equipped and composed that I should not be apprehensive of the consequences if it were opposed by all the forces in Hindustan. I am now within a few marches of Pune where I expect to arrive on the 22nd or 23rd. Colonel Stevenson with the subsidiary force in the service of the Nizam reinforced by one European regiment together with his Highness's contingent is one march up the Bhima towards Gardoon. He will leave there, within the Nizam's frontier, all his Highness's troops and will take a position with those of the Company upon the Bhima between Pune and Gardoon . . .

My first object after I shall reach Pune will be to bring up the Peshwa from Bassein, for which I have arranged a plan and have communicated it to Colonel Close. According to this plan he ought to arrive at Pune at the end of this month. But I cannot answer for the movements of His Highness's person and therefore cannot say when he will reach that city. I shall afterwards take up such a position as will appear most likely to enable the troops to subsist with facility in an exhausted country and to form a junction, if that measure should be necessary, in which I shall wait the results of the pending negotiations.

SD iv 58

36

Lieutenant-Colonel Close to Arthur Wellesley

Bassein
17 April 1803

Our hircarrahs I am afraid are timid, lazy or negligent. Our latest favour from you is dated 7th [April]. I enclose copy of a letter of the 9th from Colonel Collins.[15]

To the northward there seems to be a great deal of talk about effecting a reconciliation between Sinde and Holkar and forming a general combination against us, but I consider it all to be merely talk. No progress whatever seems to be made towards the accomplishment of such objects.

Yesterday evening Colonel Murray showed his line to the Peshwa who was delighted with its appearance and performance. The Colonel was to have moved this morning towards Kalyan but unfortunately a few of the bullocks are still to arrive, so that he cannot march before tomorrow evening. The party that was at Kalyan has retired and the place is now in possession of the Peshwa's troops. Mir Khan etc have fallen back, I hear to Gardoon. Amrit Rao has at last moved from Pune and appearances indicate that he is destined to join Mir Khan.

Pune I hope will now escape injury. The inhabitants however have a notion amongst them that Mir Khan will send a party to set fire to the principal streets and buildings, but this can be suggested only by their fears. If we find that you approach so as to afford the prospect of your being in the vicinity of Pune by the time you have mentioned, we shall manage I think to reach the bottom of the ghat by the end of the month at furthest . . .

WP 3/3/45 p. 94

37

Arthur Wellesley to Lieutenant-General Stuart

Somergaum
17 April 1803

. . . You will observe the communication to Lord Wellesley of the intention of burning Pune. With a view to prevent the execution of this plan, I have written a very civil letter to Amrit Rao to announce my approach in which I stated that I shall take measures to ensure the safety and tranquillity of the city on my arrival there. I think it possible that this letter may draw from him an answer and that he will send me a vakil. If he does and remains at Pune I shall keep up the correspondence till I get within reach of Pune with the cavalry, when I shall move forward briskly to prevent the execution of this horrible plan.

Grwd (1837) i 499 (1844) i 399

38

Arthur Wellesley to Lieutenant-Colonel Close

Camp four miles west of Baramati
18 April 1803

I have just received your letter of the 11th. The cossids who brought it, and who left Pune on the 16th in the morning report that Amrit Rao marched five days ago. I think this report is probable, but if I should find that it is not true and that Amrit Rao is still at Pune, I shall do something of the kind that you recommend but in a more effectual manner. I shall march tomorrow night with the cavalry . . . The Patwurdan and Goklah, in my opinion, are not to be trusted in a business of this nature.

Grwd (1837) i 503 (1844) i 402

39

Lieutenant-General Stuart to Arthur Wellesley

Hoospet
19 April 1803

I have been honoured with your letters dated 11th and 12th [April] and I am happy to find that your junction with the subsidiary force was so nearly effected, and that you expected to reach Pune at so early a date as the 20th of this month. I highly approve of your instructions to Colonel Stevenson . . . to leave the Nizam's contingent upon His Highness' frontier . . .

I have not heard from Colonel Close for a considerable length of time, and I am not aware of the arrangement that has been made regarding the Peshwa's movement to Pune. The force with him at Bassein I should suppose to be sufficient under present circumstances to escort him thither and his speedy return appears to be necessary to enable us to decide upon the conduct to be observed towards the northern states, of whose confederacy there seems to be little doubt . . .

I do not propose going any lower down the river. I shall probably be detained here for a few days by a General Court Martial . . . after which I propose returning up the river keeping in the Ceded Districts until I shall ascertain the steps necessary to be taken by this army . . .

WP 3/3/87 p. 133

40

Lieutenant-Colonel Close to Arthur Wellesley

Bassein
21 April 1803

I wrote to you yesterday and now have the pleasure to acknowledge your favour of the 13th [April] from Akluj.

Accompanying [this] are letters from the Peshwa to his sirdars, numbered to correspond to the enclosed list. I am extremely happy to find that you have not lost Appah Sahib . . .

Amrit Rao has sent off his guns on the 18th inst from Pune and was about to follow them. He seems disinclined to join Mir Khan. He has plundered the city to the last rag. We shall be at Kalyan by the 26th and shall then be only two marches from the bottom of the Bhore ghat. When it is ascertained that you have approached near to Pune, Colonel Murray will forward a party to take possession of Panvel in order that your supplies may come on to that place. I hope the Peshwa's cavalry will come on in your front in order to save Pune from fire or further depradation. The inhabitants are going off, but would return immediately if encouraged by the approach of protection.

I am infinitely happy to find that you do not complain yet of want of forage.

WP 3/3/45 p. 107

II
Confrontation – May to July 1803

The occupation of Pune on 20 April 1803 by the detachment under the command of Arthur Wellesley opened a new phase in the relations of the Company with the Marathas.

Arthur Wellesley wrote to his brother the Governor-General from Pune in a suitably triumphalist style. 'In all great actions there is risk, which the little minds of those who will form their judgement of yours will readily perceive' [42]. Anxious to outline the defence against criticism of the movement forward into Maratha territory, he contended that Jaswant Rao Holkar would have been forced by the inadequacy of plunder in the Deccan to move into the lands of the Nizam, which the Company were bound by treaty to defend. It followed that 'we should have had to deal with this confederacy at all events.' But because of the speedy advance to Pune, 'the scene of action must be at a distance from the Company's territories.'

Arthur Wellesley added that the detachment he commanded 'was in such a state of preparation as to insure its speedy success.' Overstatement to the Governor-General in Fort William may have had later an influence on policy; 'matters in general have a good appearance. I think all will end as you wish' [42]. There was also a deliberate side-blow at James Kirkpatrick, the Resident at Hyderabad, who had written both to Fort William and to the commander of the subsidiary force presaging a confederacy of the Maratha powers against the Company [43].

Restoration of Peshwa Baji Rao to his capital was protracted, Barry Close commenting to Arthur Wellesley on 28 April that 'you can conquer a kingdom under the most menacing circumstances in less time than I can move the Peshwa to re-accept his crown' [50]. The delay rankled with Close, who three months later mentioned it again to Arthur Wellesley. 'I did expect that when you arrived at Pune he [Peshwa Baji Rao] would have jumped from the depth of his depression at Bassein and decidedly hastened back to his capital. You have witnessed his mortifying behaviour at that glorious but critical moment.'[1]

Baji Rao was also totally unwilling to tackle issues on which the Resident was concerned to make urgent progress. For the detachment commanded by Arthur Wellesley to be able to face the potential confederacy against it to the northward, it was essential that there should be assistance from the Maratha horse of the lesser feudatories of Peshwa Baji Rao. The 'southern jagirdars' who had joined and moved with the detachment northwards from the Kistna had to be conciliated. There had been no negotiations or commitments during the march northwards to Pune, but clearly hopes of improved feudal status were harboured. Barry Close, Arthur Wellesley and John Malcolm pressed Peshwa Baji Rao on these matters during a discussion held on 14 May [78,79,80]. Promises were certainly received, and taken at first at their face value, but it soon became evident that Baji Rao dealt with requests of this type by procrastination. Close and Malcolm met with prolonged frustration in their attempts to achieve resolution of issues of status or requests for financial aid.

The Company 'politicals' needed to establish whether the restoration of the Peshwa was likely to lead to the formation against the Company of a hostile confederacy of the major Maratha rulers. This was the danger to which Arthur Wellesley had directed the attention of the Governor-General in the letter he had sent to Fort William through Hyderabad from Akluj on 15 April [34]. Various intelligence sources gave some indication of the probability of this combination, but to a marked extent Arthur Wellesley, John Malcolm and Barry Close were dependent upon the correspondence from Colonel Collins, the Company Resident with Daulat Rao Sinde. In his first letter to Arthur Wellesley, Collins commented that 'the good disposition of the Maharajah cannot be relied on' [46]. Within a few days, the action of Jaswant Rao Holkar, after his move away from Pune, in levying a heavy contribution from Aurungabad, a city within the territories of the Nizam of Hyderabad, led Collins to add that he was certain 'that Holkar, as well from Sinde as from the Berar Rajah, has received the most positive assurances of support and cooperation' [57].

Raghuji Bhonsle, the Raja of Berar, moved westwards with his army along the Purna valley towards the camp of Daulat Rao Sinde. At the least, the intention of combining to oppose the two British detachments could be assumed. When word of this movement reached Pune, Barry Close believed that there was a possibility of an advance by Sinde on the capital city 'in fourteen or fifteen marches' and initiated the first of a series of suggestions made to Arthur Wellesley urging redeployment, not only of his own detachment and of the subsidiary force commanded by Colonel Stevenson, but also of the army of reserve far to the south commanded by Lieutenant-General Stuart [59]. Arthur Wellesley was less alarmed. 'The report of his intended march has been circulated for the purpose of intimidating the Nizam' [62]. But he urged on Lieutenant-General Stuart a position north of the Kistna which would so place him as to make possible a rapid movement to Hyderabad, should that be necessary following the expected death of the Nizam, and place him close also to the homelands of the southern jagirdars. This recommendation was adopted.[2]

Conciliation with Amrit Rao, with whom Arthur Wellesley had been in correspondence shortly before the final dash to Pune, also faltered. This was seen as the second issue on which pressure on Peshwa Baji Rao was needed, but there seemed to be little hope of an agreement between the half-brothers. This failure was ultimately decisive in determining the attitude of Barry Close and John Malcolm to the Peshwa. They could now see no prospect of working with Baji Rao in a manner that at all met their view of his best interests [151].

In a lengthy political note, John Malcolm had earlier emphasised the need to 'act independent of any expectation of efficient aid from the Peshwa' [128.] After the 'very strong remonstrance' of 23 June, he recommended the creation of an independent feudal status for Amrit Rao, and argued that even if this led Peshwa Baji Rao to leave Pune and seek asylum with either Daulat Rao Sinde or Raghuji Bhonsle, this was a hazard that must be accepted [151]. Later, in mid-July, Arthur Wellesley gave Amrit Rao a contingent undertaking that, despite the hesitations of Baji Rao, the Company accepted an obligation to ensure his safety [170]. Negotiations with Amrit Rao, through agents, led to a treaty with him in mid-August [232,233].

As well as taking emergency measures to alleviate the supply crisis with which Arthur Wellesley was faced in mid June 1803, Close again urged a variation to the military deployment. Arthur Wellesley had ordered forward the subsidiary force which Stevenson had brought from Hyderabad [117]. In a letter to Close in which he stated that the whole venture would be 'a useful lesson to Governments and to us all,' Arthur Wellesley surveyed deployment alternatives. He doubted whether if he moved his own detachment forward into the Nizam's territories, while still remaining south of the Godavari, the supplies held by the subsidiary force would be sufficient for both detachments. On the other hand withdrawal across the Bhima, quite apart from its political effects, could expose Stevenson's detachment, certainly if the confederacy included Jaswant Rao Holkar [137].

Barry Close suggested rather that Arthur Wellesley should detach to the river Godavari a King's unit, two sepoy battalions and two regiments of native cavalry, and at the same time arrange that Lieutenant-General Stuart should send forward from the Kistna two sepoy units to Hyderabad. A further supply train should be prepared at Hyderabad and sent to the Godavari with the two sepoy battalions there [140]. This advice was not taken. As Arthur Wellesley saw it, if hostilities with the Marathas were to follow after an interval, the deployment that Close envisaged would make necessary either a recall of Stevenson or the movement northwards of a significant reinforcement from Stuart to the area of Pune. The dilemma was the multiple potential calls on the army on the Kistna. It was not only the reserve for the detachments north of Pune, there were also the contingencies of a French attempt to recapture Pondicherry, of the need for a reinforcement to Hyderabad in the event of disturbances following the death of the Nizam, and the continuing rebellion in Malabar. As the supply crisis seemed to have slightly eased, Arthur Wellesley deferred taking a decision [142].

The alliance between the major Maratha rulers remained in prospect. The critical discussion at the durbar of Daulat Rao Sinde was that of 28 May. In this the Company Resident Colonel Collins followed detailed instructions from Fort William [87]. These instructions required the Resident to seek to secure the withdrawal of Daulat Rao Sinde north of the Narbada river. Failure to do so would hazard the potential advantages to Sinde of the alliance that Richard Wellesley wished to offer to him. The Resident attempted to bring Sinde to a declaration of his intentions, and cautioned him that some of his actions appeared to indicate hostility. Collins failed to secure a clear indication of intention, Sinde confining himself to saying, in full durbar, that he could not answer the points raised by the Resident until he had held discussions with Raghuji Bhonsle and that only after these had taken place could the Resident be informed 'whether it was peace or war' [95,96].

Arthur Wellesley saw this procrastinating reply as justifying immediate hostilities, but these he was scarcely in a position to attempt. Shortly after the onset of the monsoon in the first days of June, his detachment was struck by acute supply difficulties. There was heavy mortality among the bullocks belonging both to the 'public departments' and also to the banjaras who had come with him from the territory to the north of Mysore. There were clear limitations in the effectiveness of the supply line from Bombay, to which Arthur Wellesley had devoted much care in earlier planning.

The detachment was forced to leave supplies at its camp site at least twice, on the mornings of 5 and 19 June. Arthur Wellesley now attempted to secure additional banjaras from the Pune region, and to enhance the capacity of his own detachment to move supplies by the purchase of additional bullocks. He was foiled in both ventures. The banjaras of the region, perhaps influenced by those that he had brought forward from the south, refused to join him, and it proved impossible to purchase additional bullocks. Arthur Wellesley suspected that the reluctance to assist him followed from the attitude of the durbar of Peshwa Baji Rao [136].

The informal triumvirate of Arthur Wellesley, Close and Malcolm could take some comfort from the realisation that Jaswant Rao Holkar was holding back from joining the supposed confederacy. He was soon moving northwards away from the probable area of operations, evidently attaching greater importance to an attempt to regain traditional Holkar territory, reportedly granted to him by an agreement with Sinde, than to any joint venture against the Company. On 19 June, Arthur Wellesley felt sufficiently confident of the withdrawal of Holkar to forecast to Stuart, the Commander-in-Chief Madras, that there would be no confederacy including Holkar.[3]

But the need to bring Daulat Rao Sinde and Raghuji Bhonsle to the point of decision remained. News from Europe now suggested that the war between Britain and France was about to be resumed. On the assumption that the instructions to which the Resident with Sinde was working had been outdated by events, Arthur Wellesley now urged Collins that he should give a time-limit to the durbar within which a clear declaration of intention should be made. Such a declaration by the two Maratha rulers would need to be supported by a withdrawal of forces from the immediate frontier of the territories of the Nizam of Hyderabad [149]. Writing to the Governor-General in early July, he drew from this correspondence the conclusion that the Resident had 'gone on a false notion from the beginning; he has supposed that peace was concluded between Holkar and Sinde, because Sinde's ministers have told him so.'[4]

Earlier, on 10 May and 4 June, Arthur Wellesley had twice directly hinted to his brother the Governor-General that delegated and overriding political authority needed to be granted to a single political or military figure in the Deccan. There was no suggestion that he should be the mandated authority. On 10 May he had noted that 'we are playing a little at cross purposes here . . . We ought to have some authority here to settle matters with all these chiefs, under some general authority from you. The state of affairs varies daily' [75]. He repeated the plea almost a month later, on 4 June. 'I wish there were powers here to act at once, and to direct the negotiations with the different Maratha chiefs to certain points as they arise. These questions occur daily, and nearly six weeks elapse before your orders can be received upon every fresh occurrence.' [101]

There were hints in private letters reaching the politicals in the Deccan from Fort William that either revised instructions or delegated authority would be sent, but it was not until 18 July that Arthur Wellesley received, to use his own description, 'extraordinary powers, for the purpose of concluding whatever arrangements may become necessary, either for the final settlement of peace, or for the active prosecution of war' [175,176]. Before these instructions arrived, clear in his own mind what the situation required, and having received a forcible statement from Barry Close [162] Arthur Wellesley had sent the sharpest of instructions to the Resident with Sinde that the two Maratha rulers must either withdraw from the Nizam's frontier or face military operations [167].

The last days of peace saw the continuation of a pattern by now established. The two Maratha rulers refused to discuss with the Company Resident 'the issue of peace or war' despite persistence by Collins in attempts to do so [185,187]. At a final major durbar session on 31 July, there was discussion of a series of schemes of withdrawal and disengagement. These were perhaps designed to continue the negotiation rather than to resolve it [200,203]. When Collins had agreed that he would send one of these schemes in writing to Arthur Wellesley for consideration, acting in so doing directly against his orders, the Marathas submitted it in a different form, and the Resident, finally unwilling to negotiate further,left their camp. [203]

In a letter evidently designed as a public declaration of the Company position on the whole aborted negotiation process, if such indeed it can be called, Arthur Wellesley wrote to Daulat Rao Sinde [211]

> 'You must stand the consequences of the measures which I find myself obliged to adopt, in order to repel your aggressions. I offered you peace on terms of equality, and honourable to all parties. You have chosen war, and are responsible for all consequences.'

Negotiation, for which Richard Wellesley and the Fort William Secretariat had sent detailed instructions, had never taken place. It had been evaded at least partly because both Sinde and Bhonsle wished it not to take place. Both believed that they could still bring Jaswant Rao Holkar into their confederacy against the Company. They had also placed themselves, with their armies, on the frontiers of the territory of the Nizam, the traditional Maratha plunder ground, and from that position they refused to withdraw. Had negotiation been attempted, the statement of Richard Wellesley of the territorial concession which he hoped to secure [175] suggests that these were terms which the Marathas would never have accepted.

In the timing of the outbreak of hostilities, which the Marathas left to themselves would almost certainly have postponed until after the monsoon season and possibly longer, the personal decision of Arthur Wellesley was paramount. The influence of Barry Close and John Malcolm was real, but the final interpretation of the instructions of Richard Wellesley, in relation to a changing situation and the political needs of the Governor-Generalship, was that of his brother. He did not see the outcome of the contest as doubtful, although there was a proviso. It would be necessary to 'strike such a blow during the rains as will give us the superiority, and keep our rear in tranquillity'.

41

Arthur Wellesley to Lieutenent-Colonel Close

Pune
20 April 1803

After I wrote on the 18th, I heard that Amrit Rao still remained in the neighbourhood of Pune, that he had removed the Peshwa's family to Sevaghur, that many people were flying, and all believed the town would be burnt. In consequence of this information, I marched last night with the cavalry, and arrived here this day about two and the town is safe . . .

I was detained about six hours in getting the cavalry guns through the Bhoor ghat, in consequence of which I imagine that Amrit Rao received intelligence of my march at such time as to enable him to depart this morning before I arrived. The infantry will be here the day after tomorrow and on the next day I shall move towards the ghats. We have marched sixty miles since yesterday morning.

I am in your house, and have some of the troops quartered in your stables. I eat your forage and grain also.

Grwd (1837) i 505 (1844) i 403

42

Arthur Wellesley to Richard Wellesley

Pune
21 April 1803

. . . Matters in general have a good appearance. I think they all will end as you wish. The combined chiefs, of whom we have heard so much, have allowed us to come quietly, and take our station at this place, and notwithstanding their threats have taken no one step to impede our march or to divert our attention to other objects. Here we are now in force in a position from which nothing can drive us and in which we shall gain strength daily . . .

I conclude that we should have had to contend with this confederacy at all events, or at least that we should have had a war with the Maratha powers in some shape even if this Treaty with the Peshwa had not been concluded. Upon this point I have only to observe that the establishment of Holkar's power at Pune, founded as it was upon repeated victories over Sinde's troops, would probably have occasioned demands upon the Nizam. But supposing that I may be mistaken I declare that from what I have seen of the state of this country, it would have been impossible for Holkar to maintain an army in the Deccan without invading the Nizam's territory . . .

Supposing therefore that you should be blamed for adopting a course of measures in which there is a distant risk that you may have a contest with the Maratha powers, you have the satisfaction of reflecting that in consequence of those measures, the scene of action must be at a distance from the Company's territories, and that you are in such a state of preparation as to insure its speedy success. At all events it is probable that, if you had not adopted those measures, either the Company or their ally must have suffered all the evils of war, without having the same means of averting them or limiting their duration.

In all great actions there is risk, which the little minds of those who will form their judgement of yours will readily perceive in that which I am now considering. But their remarks ought not to give you a moment's uneasiness, and I have in this letter made you acquainted with a fact which must silence every objection to your measures, and which I shall take care to send in an official form through the channel which I believe to be the source of the croaking which I hear.

Grwd (1837) i 506 (1844) i 406. Partly printed PRC x 95

43

Colonel Murray to Arthur Wellesley

Kalyan
22 April 1803 [received by 26 April]

I had the honour of sending you a return of the troops under my command at the beginning of the month since which time I have been reinforced by HM 78th regiment and two howitzers. On the 17th inst I marched from Soopara leaving the 78th regiment to follow the next day. I arrived at Kalyan this morning and expect the 78th, which is now at Bundy [Bhiwandi?] early tomorrow.[1]

My present intention is to halt here till his Highness the Peshwa shall arrive, which cannot be before the 27th as Colonel Close writes me that he cannot prevail upon him to quit Bassein before the 25th inst. As I have not yet had the honour of receiving any orders from you, I have endeavoured that my movements should correspond with what I conceived might meet your wishes. With regard to my future movements I am anxious to receive your orders, as I do not know whether you would wish that the corps which I command should escort the provisions for your army and take up a position which might cover the convoy, or attend the Peshwa to the ghats. I shall hold myself in readiness to execute whatever you may be pleased to order on the subject. At this season of the year there is unfortunately a great deficiency of water. Between this and Panvel, which is twenty miles, there is none.

I have not yet been able to procure sufficient information on the other route to give you the necessary information; I trust however that I shall be well acquainted with them before we meet. The sirdar who commanded here for Amrit Rao evacuated the place about ten days ago and returned to the Bhoor ghat.

WP 3/3/79 p. 9

44

Colonel Murray to Arthur Wellesley

Kalyan
23 April 1803 [received by 26 April]

. . . HM 78th regiment passed me this morning and I am now in readiness to proceed wherever you may be pleased to direct. My principal object in despatching this hircarrah is to ascertain if this communication is open and in that case to bring back your orders. I am informed by the Peshwa's people that detachments of Amrit Rao's army occupy Abtah and Karnala. Both these places are near Panvel. In case you should wish that we should escort what is expected from Bombay one or two troops of cavalry would be of great assistance. I am informed that there is no want of forage below the ghats. Hitherto we have found it in the greatest profusion.

WP 3/3/79 p. 4

45

Arthur Wellesley to Colonel Stevenson

Pune
23 April 1803

I have received your letters of the 19th . . . With regard to that letter in which you have copied an extract from one which you have received from the Resident, I have to observe that whatever may be the Resident's private opinion, it would be as well that he should refrain from a communication of it.[2]

The fact is, here I am at Pune unopposed and in strength, and the Resident knows or ought to know that those chiefs who are supposed to intend to combine against us, have not yet made peace, and cannot have settled any plan of operations.

It is true that as we have taken into our hands the bone for which they have been contending for some years, not one of them is well pleased, and each gives out that the whole will combine against us. But there are many considerations which must be maturely weighed by at least two of the parties, Sinde and the Raja of Berar, before they will venture upon a war with the English, particularly when we are prepared and they are not . . .

Grwd (1837) i 511 (1844) i 407

46

Colonel Collins to Arthur Wellesley

25 April 1803 [received by 1 May]

. . . The strong approbation you give of the manner in which I conducted myself in the important conference of the 24th [March] affords me infinite satisfaction . . .

[I wish I were confident?] that the declaration of Sinde on the foregoing occasion was formal, and that the peace of India will be preserved should the Maharajah act in conformity to the assurances which he then made. But as the ministers of this prince are eternally urging him to oppose the completion of the arrangements lately concluded at Bassein, the good disposition of the Maharajah cannot be relied on, on account of his inability to pay his army without pecuniary aid which his ministers alone can supply. Therefore as Sinde is by no means master of his own conduct, I rejoice that your force is fully equal to all events which may possibly occur . . .

I had written this far when I received certain advices of Holkar within four kos of the city of Aurungabad. This chieftain publicly declares his intention of laying waste the country of our ally the Nizam. As this intelligence is of importance I must convey word of it immediately to the Governor General. Depend on my writing to you every material occurrence that passes at this durbar . . .

I had almost forgot to mention to you that this court objected to the advance of the British army, not of the Nizam's troops, to Pune. In fact the ministers of the Maharajah had been informed that the English forces were approaching the Maratha frontier by the route of Hyderabad.

WP 3/3/53 p. 1

47

Statement of Sinde's forces at Burhanpur

[summary]
25 April 1803

Cavalry: 13,200 Hindustani and 2000 Deccani cavalry commanded in the main by 'different native sirdars'

Infantry: 26 sepoy battalions;
commanded by Pohlman 7 battalions
by Colonel Doddernique [Dudrenec] 7 battalions
in the pay of Begum Sumroo commanded by Colonel Saleur 4
in the pay of Ambaji Inglia commanded by Major P Shepherd 4
commanded by Major Brownrigg 4 and 1000 matchlock men
Each sepoy battalion consisted of nearly 700 rank and file.

Ordnance: a range of heavy and field pieces were listed under each commander totalling 30 heavy guns and 161 field pieces, and an additional park of artillery listed as 25 heavy guns and 100 field pieces.[3]

WP 3/3/53 p. 4

48

Arthur Wellesley to Lieutenant-General Stuart

Pune
26 April 1803

I did not march this morning as I had intended as I heard last night that Holkar had made three marches towards this place, and I thought it proper to halt a day to ascertain the truth of this report.

The result of my enquiries is that he has marched towards the Nizam's frontier, and that he was on the 21st at a station about 8 kos from the Godavari, and at a small distance from the frontier of Holkar's, of the Nizam's and of Sinde's territories. He had not on that day had the interview with Ambaji Inglia which it was supposed would produce a peace between Holkar and Sinde, and it is reported that Ambaji Inglia had sent to the Raja of Berar the boy Khande Rao Holkar, who is a great bone of contention between Sinde and Holkar, and that this circumstance may delay the negotiation for peace. If they are only delayed till the Peshwa's arrival here, and we shall be enabled to take up a better position for the defence of the Nizam's frontier, I think all will end well.

I intend tomorrow to march towards the hills. I believe the Peshwa was to leave Bassein yesterday.

Grwd (1837) i 517 (1844) i 411

49

Arthur Wellesley to Colonel Murray

Pune
26 April 1803 [received 30 April]

I have had the honour of receiving your letters of the 22nd and 23rd inst.

I learn from Lt Colonel Close that he has communicated to you the wishes of his Highness the Peshwa respecting the movements of your detachment, according to which you are of course to conduct yourself. The Colonel however has informed me that he has requested you to send off five or six companies to Panvel with two guns, for the purpose of occupying that place and of affording security to the supplies which will have been forwarded thither from Bombay. I conclude that you will have complied with this request and that the troops on their march to Panvel will have driven off the troops belonging to Amrit Rao occupying Abtah and Karnala. If that should not have been done it appears to me a very necessary measure, and I request you to turn your attention to it. The ghat I am informed is exceedingly bad, and some time will elapse before you will be able to bring up all your carriages. A part of your troops therefore might be employed in clearing the road to Panvel of enemies, while the remainder should move your advanced carriages up the ghat, and no time would be lost.

I have written to the government of Bombay for certain articles of supply, which must be forwarded by means to be furnished within that settlement. I request you to afford protection to such of them as you may hear are prepared to leave Panvel, when your troops shall move from that quarter towards the Bhoor ghat. I send from here banjara bullocks to load with rice, but it will be some time before they will arrive at Panvel, and they may be too late for your troops, and at all events an escort from this camp will go with them, which will be sufficient for their protection, particularly if the road should be cleared by you.

Gurwd (1837) i 519 (1844) i 413

50

Lieutenant-Colonel Close to Arthur Wellesley

Kalyan
27 April 1803

. . . You see that you can conquer a kingdom under the most menacing circumstances in less time than I can move the Peshwa to re-accept his crown. I shall be happy when I get him hither, but fear I shall still have difficulty in getting him to ascend the ghats, and until he shows himself at Pune, it will not be possible for me to direct his attention to the different important points you have stated for adjustment . . .

WP 1/148

51

Lieutenant-Colonel Close to Arthur Wellesley

Kalyan
28 April 1803 [received 1 May]

. . . From hence the Peshwa will be accompanied by Khande Rao Rastiah with his quota, consisting of about 1000 infantry and a few horse . . . and by the Dubari jagirdar with his party of cavalry consisting of two or three hundred. I conceive myself that it may be best that none of the horsemen should descend the ghat to meet his Highness, as in ascending the pass with the people that go from hence, his Highness will be sufficiently squeezed and dusted.

Should you be encamped near the pass when his Highness ascends, any compliment you may think proper to pay him as he passes will be highly acceptable . . . We have abundance of forage here, that is dry grass which answers well for bullocks, so that the cattle you send to Panvel may benefit by the duty. Colonel Murray is now in high marching order.

WP 3/3/45 fldr 5 p. 120

52

Lieutenant-General Stuart to Arthur Wellesley

Hoospet
29 April 1803 [received 8 May]

I have had the honour to receive your despatch of the 21st [April] from Pune and I congratulate you on your arrival at that capital and on the favourable consequences which must ensue from that event . . . I am happy to observe by your letter to me that the people are returning to Pune and furnishing you with supplies.

Your cattle from the circumstances of your march must be in a very reduced state, and you may find it difficult to supply your hopes from the side of Bombay. There are more carriage bullocks with me than I am likely to require and I could send you 2,000 and perhaps a greater number without inconvenience. I would therefore be glad to know whether you require a supply of cattle from this frontier, and if you do, the number which you will want, the route by which they should be sent and the escort proper to accompany them. Supplies of military and provision stores could be forwarded to you by these cattle if you should stand in need of them.

I have continued to receive treasure from the Collectors in the proportion required for the army: the amount in my treasury is equal to the disbursement of the force assembled for nearly four months and I could furnish you with a supply, if it were expedient to send it. I wish to know your sentiments upon this point . . . The state of the country will render a considerable escort necessary and it will be more convenient for you to draw money from Bombay, but circumstances may disable that Presidency from complying with your demands to the necessary extent.

WP 3/3/87 p. 151

53

Lieutenant-Colonel Close to Arthur Wellesley

Kalyan
29 April 1803

. . . I am labouring like a galley slave to move the Peshwa but cannot say when he will leave this place. I have some little hope that he will march the day after tomorrow. I hope your expectation of finding forage at Tallyguam [Talagaon] has not been disappointed. Our bullocks here have abundance.

Major Scott with the detachment from hence is arrived at Panvel, where I hope that the supplies that you want immediately will soon be landed. A good storehouse has been discovered in the town which has many excellent buildings. On this subject you will learn more from Colonel Murray who has [secured] 400 carriage bullocks for you and will send them off immediately to Panvel.

Ram Dyale has not given me much satisfaction since I left Pune. I do not allow him to open the akbars from Sinde's camp or from Hyderabad, and I would have you treat him with caution . . . Nanamji and Kundi Rao the newswriter are excellent men . . .

WP 3/3/45 fldr 5 p. 122

54

Colonel Murray to Arthur Wellesley

Kalyan
30 April 1803

. . . This corps marches for Panvel tomorrow morning and early the following day I shall arrive there. . . . From Panvel to the foot of the ghats is two marches, so that unless detained by the Peshwa I should be at Cassowli on the 4th of May.

The only inconvenience under which I at present labour is the want of money. I hope however that on our reaching the ghats this will be remedied. The government of Bombay sent with the Paymaster 50,000 rupees only and that in gold mohurs which are not current. I have got from the shroffs attached to the Pune Residency a small supply, barely sufficient for the payment of a few banjaras which were hired at the suggestion of Colonel Close and are sent to Panvel. I shall be happy to receive your instructions relative to the gold mohurs. I cannot dispose of them at present without a loss of six and a half per cent.

I am sorry to find from your description of the ghats that we are likely to meet with so much difficulty in getting up the cannon. This will be to us the more distressing [in] that I have only twenty pioneers who are not very fit for the service in which they are employed. However I hope as our pieces are light that in the course of one day with the assistance of the troops we shall be able to get all the wheel carriages above the ghats . . .

WP 3/3/79 p. 6

55

Lieutenant-Colonel Close to Arthur Wellesley

Kalyan
30 April 1803 [received 3 May]

. . . It must doubtless be difficult to ascertain the real designs of Amrit Rao in sending the karkun to you. He is certainly dissatisfied with Holkar and he knows probably that Sinde's resentment towards him has not much abated, and as you have astonished him by suddenly seizing Pune and adopting a secure position, he may now possibly think that under present appearances nothing better can occur for him than repossession of his jagir.

A long while since I prevailed on the Peshwa to write to him in terms entreating that he would separate from his colleagues and come into Bassein, but his views were then large and he treated the invitation (which at my instance was repeated) with contempt. The Peshwa's enmities, God knows, are but too lasting and too easily excited. He is certainly exasperated against Amrit Rao. At the same time I think we need not despair of seeing them reconciled. The misfortune is that all the chieftains that are hostile to the Peshwa sting him constantly with reproaches for his having united himself with us, by which they say he has shown himself a traitor to his nation, has abdicated his government, degraded himself from the rank of a brahmin and a Maratha, and become literally an outcast. This you see may help to make peacemaking a difficult task. To conciliate Amrit Rao and settle him suitably is assuredly a great object. I am infinitely glad therefore that you are in friendly correspondence with him. If he separates himself from his companions, there will be an opening for urging his case.

Hitherto I have thought that I have done much in keeping the Peshwa staunch to the alliance. His mind is so timid and unsteady and his temper so capricious that I could not be certain of him, and Sinde's hopes turned for a long time on the probability that he could be easily drawn off from us. I am now convinced that the more he sees of us, the more he likes us, and when his remaining doubts are replaced by full confidence, we may be able to give his mind a proper direction. The worst of it is that with a variety of exceptionable qualities, he is slow and indolent and averse to business, unless it is conducted in his own crooked and sinister way . . .

At political lying the Marathas are a match for the world. The utmost pains have been taken to establish the belief that Ambaji Inglia had a meeting with Holkar but the lie was always palpable from the correspondence of Colonel Collins. A form of theatrical humbug is now conducting with young Khande Rao Holkar, and Bapu Phurkia is exerting all his ingenuity to give it full effect.

I hope that you have favourable accounts of your supplies. I am afraid that much time will elapse before Mr Duncan can collect the number of bullocks that you have called for. Other banjaras and dealers I hope will now assemble at Pune and frequent your camp, and when they come in numbers you will be able to hire or purchase bullocks as occasion may require. The man from whom Colonel Murray hired the 400 could furnish more, but appears to be doubtful whether his hire will be duly paid.

WP 3/3/45 p. 124, WP 1/148

56

Arthur Wellesley to Colonel Stevenson

Panowullah
30 April 1803

There are reports here that Holkar intends moving upon Hyderabad with a light army, and they appear to come from something like authority. However I do not believe these reports, although we ought to be prepared for everything from a disposition so wild and unmanageable as Holkar's is represented to be.

I therefore recommended you to have an eye to your right, and if you find that Holkar really makes this dash at Hyderabad, you must move upon that place as quickly as you can. You will of course prevent the pindaris from cutting off your communications. Indeed they will not venture to attempt it, when there is such a body of horse in your camp, and they ought to be cut up most unmercifully whenever they are caught . . .

Grwd (1837) i 529 (1844) i 420

57

Colonel Collins to Arthur Wellesley

near Burhanpur
1 May 1803 [received by 9 May]

. . . I am satisfied in my own mind that Holkar, as well from Sinde as from the Berar Raja, has received the most positive assurances of support and cooperation, since otherwise he would scarcely have ventured to draw on himself the resentment of the English government in the manner which he has done. And hence I am led to conjecture that Sinde, Raghuji, and Holkar have confederated for the purpose of obstructing the completion of the arrangements lately concluded at Bassein.

The Berar Raja has made three marches towards Amrauti accompanied by Jadu Rao Bhaskar, Sinde's most confidential minister. Two days since the Maharajah intimated to me that he should shortly move from hence in order to follow the Bhonsle with whom he is to have an interview at Badauli [Buldana]. The European officers in the service of Sinde have been prohibited from visiting me by the minister, and war with the English is publicly talked of in the camp. The British subjects in the Maratha service are ridiculously alarmed on this occasion . . .

WP 3/3/53 p. 16

58

Colonel Collins to Richard Wellesley

near Burhanpur
2 May 1803 [seen by Arthur Wellesley by 9 May]
[summary]

Collins forwarded a response by Sinde to the Governor-General following complaint on a demand for chaute. As he regarded the reply as 'highly improper' Collins informed Sinde that if he intended travelling to Pune, he would as Resident accompany him, but if Sinde planned to travel into the territory of the Nizam to meet the Raja of Berar, the Resident must ask for an escort and leave his camp.

Collins reported that in northern India Perron was actively levying new troops, despite having obtained Lake's consent, should he leave Sinde's service, to enter Company territory and move to Lucknow. He noted also that a body of cavalry of about 10,000 was about to leave Sinde's camp for Hindustan.

PRC ix 191

59

Lieutenant-Colonel Close to Arthur Wellesley

Panvel
2 May 1803

I . . . am this moment favoured with your letter of the 1st, the same conveyance having brought me the enclosed important despatch from Collins . . .[4]

If Sinde moves on 6th May as he threatens, he may reach Pune in fourteen or fifteen marches, and be in time to cross the Godavari before the river swells, and as his intentions cannot be friendly and Holkar's are already hostile, I conceive that it occurs forcibly for consideration at this crisis whether General Stuart should not move on with all expedition to Hyderabad, allowing Colonel Stevenson's force to join yours or act in concert with you, should Sinde really cross the Godavari with a view to obstruct our alliance with the Peshwa . . .

Last night I informed the Peshwa of your having sent the Mysore cavalry with some infantry to the Bhoor ghat to cover his approach to Pune and he appeared to be much satisfied with the arrangement. I think it is proper therefore that the troops should continue at Panowullah, although his Highness may be gratified by your coming forward yourself to receive him at the head of the pass or thereabouts.

Words cannot express what I feel on account of his Highness's tardiness, although there cannot be a doubt that his remaining behind me today is to be attributed to indisposition.

WP 3/3/45 fldr 5 p. 138. Partly printed PRC ix 194

60

Colonel Murray to Arthur Wellesley

near Panvel
2 May 1803

. . . I am sorry to inform you that there will be more delay in loading the stores at Panvel than was supposed. Captain Young informs me that the small boats were two days in coming up the river and that the large ones cannot come up at all. Perhaps at the springs [spring tides?] which are nearly setting in they may be more expeditious.

The Peshwa is not yet arrived and Colonel Close seems to think that he will not be here today. He complained last night of a slight fever. This however will make no difference to my movements. I shall march tomorrow morning to Barva or Chauk as will be most convenient for water. I find that the country is perfectly quiet . . . I shall therefore leave only one European officer with 60 men as a guard at Panvel and one company of sepoys to proceed with a convoy of supplies for this detachment . . .

WP 3/3/79 p. 8

61

Lieutenant-General Stuart to Arthur Wellesley

8 miles south west of Hoospet
3 May 1803

I have had the pleasure of receiving your letter of the 24th [April]. Your measures with respect to the banjaras and the repair of the carriages are in my opinion highly proper. I trust that the Peshwa's return will before you receive this have given efficiency to our footing at Pune, and enabled you to see clearly the line of measures which it will be most advisable to pursue.

In a despatch from Major Kirkpatrick dated the 28th [April] I have received accounts of depradations having been committed by

Holkar's parties to the Nizam's country, and it is affirmed that Holkar has himself advanced near Aurungabad. In the situation of that chieftain, circumscribed by the advance of British troops, and the position of Sinde's army, and pressed for the means of subsisting his people, I think it probable that he will attempt to overrun the Nizam's country, as it is likely to be the only one open to his incursions that has not already been plundered. It appears likely that both Sinde and the Bhonsle would encourage that design, although they might profess friendship to us. Should these conjectures be just, you will have to concert your measures with a view to the triple objective of maintaining our footing at Pune, showing a formidable force to Sinde, and driving back Holkar. I trust however that every conjecture on this point will not be verified, as it will be more desirable in my judgement to conciliate than to reduce Holkar.

From the tenor of the last despatches received overland . . . it would be fortunate could we get all our Maratha affairs arranged and settled, before the French armies arrive in this country, as that event may not improbably occasion our having more upon our hands than we shall know well how to manage.

WP 3/3/87 p. 153

62

Arthur Wellesley to Lieutenant-General Stuart

Pune
3 May 1803 [received 14 May]

. . . It is my opinion that it is by no means certain that Sinde will advance to Pune and that it is most probable that the report of his intended march has been circulated for the purpose of intimidating the Nizam.

However it is as well to be prepared with a consideration of the measures to be adopted in case Sinde should advance to Pune. I have no doubt whatever that the force which will be here when the Peshwa shall arrive will be more than equal to contend with his, of which I enclose you an account.[5]

I also am of opinion that Colonel Stevenson's force with the Nizam's army is fully equal to the defence of the Nizam's country against either Holkar or Sinde. If both should unite in an attack on the Nizam's country, Colonel Stevenson and I must cooperate or join in the defence of it, leaving at Pune a sufficient force for the protection of the Peshwa's person against straggling parties, on the other hand if both should approach Pune Colonel Stevenson must come nearer to me.

You will probably be desirous that I should give my opinion regarding Lieutenant-Colonel Close's proposal . . . In the event of Sinde's advance our military position ought to be such as to give confidence to those connected with us and to show the wavering and our enemies that we are really in strength. It will not answer to move at once to Hyderabad as you would thereby leave open the Raja of Mysore's country and the Company's, and would remove the check upon the southern jagirdars. But if you were to cross the Tungabhandra and move to Mudghal you would be nearer the scene of action at Pune, within twelve or fourteen marches of Hyderabad, and close upon the southern jagirdars. You would also be in a better situation to defend the Company's frontier.

In six weeks from this time the rivers which rise in the Western Ghats will fill. I know that native armies are then very incapable of carrying on their operations, and you will be so near the Kistna that you can decide whether you will cross it and at once carry your decision into execution . . .

Grwd (1837) i 534 (1844) i 423, PRC ix 193

63

Lieutenant-Colonel Close to Arthur Wellesley

Panvel
3 May [1803] 1 pm

Uneasy at the tardiness of the Peshwa, I yesterday despatched a sharp note to Raghunath Rao from whom I have just received an answer promising me in the most positive manner that his Highness will be here in the course of the day. The hircarrah who brought his answer reports that at eight o'clock this morning his Highness' flag was hoisted at a spot two kos this side of Kalyan and that his horses were saddled and his attendants in every respect ready to move . . . Colonel Murray marched this morning for Chauk.

WP 3/3/45 fldr 5 p. 134

64

Lieutenant-Colonel Close to Arthur Wellesley

Panvel
3 May [1803] 6½ pm

. . . The Peshwa is this moment coming in and in order that the pass may be clear for his ascent, I have recommended to Colonel Murray to pursue his march to Khandala and there await your further orders. I hope therefore that he will ascend the pass on the day after tomorrow. Taking up the guns and carriages may be a little troublesome but he will have the assistance of the pioneers. I am anxious that the Colonel may experience no delay in clearing the pass, in order that the Peshwa may have no excuse for further tardiness. . . .

Captain Young tells me that the whole of the 10,000 bullock loads (the first demand) will be collected here in the course of a very few days. The rice already landed is in the most part exposed to the weather, but the Captain means to place it under cover soon, that is to lodge it in houses in the town, to which there is access only by narrow back streets, from which I apprehend that when the bullocks arrive they cannot be loaded without much delay. He could construct proper cover here, had he orders for the purpose, but he is uninformed yet whether it be your intention to have a permanent depot here, or only to draw off such supplies as you may require for immediate use. Indeed I think you ought to have an officer here who is in possession of your ideas touching the supplies you need to draw off from here at this or any other period . . .

WP 3/3/45 fldr 5 p. 140

65

Colonel Collins to Governor-General

near Burhanpur
4 May 1803 [seen by Arthur Wellesley by 10 May]

I have the honour to forward a translate and copy of Daulat Rao Sinde's reply to my letter under date the 2nd inst.[6] I know not whether the road from Badauli to Pune be short and easy as the Maharajah asserts, but it is certainly not the usual route from hence. However should Sinde really intend to proceed to Pune, according to his positive assurance, I shall not fail to accompany him thither . . .

PRC ix 195

66

Colonel Collins to Arthur Wellesley

near Shapora
7 May 1803 [received by 12 May]

I am this instant favoured with your letter of the 2nd inst for which accept my thanks. I wish from my heart and soul that Holkar and Sinde may not have accommodated their differences but I have strong reason to believe that this accommodation has actually taken place through the mediation of the Berar Raja. My agent at this durbar assures me that Sinde's ministers acknowledge that the Maharajah has made peace with Holkar and my newswriter at Aurungabad apprises me that Jaswant Rao talks publicly of this event. The name of this vakil is Jaswant Rao Ramchand.

Balaji Kunjar is expected here today or tomorrow so that I shall soon know whether Sinde is disposed to accept the friendly proposals of the Governor General but I have not the most distant hope of attaining the objects of my mission. In truth the ministers of this court do not require the aid of a subsidiary force from the English government.

When Sinde has received the communications with which Balaji Kunjar is charged on the part of the Peshwa, he intends I understand to proceed by forced marches to Badauli in order to have an interview with the Berar Raja . . .

WP 3/3/53 p. 23

67

Arthur Wellesley to Colonel Murray

Panowullah
7 May 1803 [received that day]

I delayed to answer your different letters upon the subject of the refusal of the killedar to deliver up the fort of Karnala to the Peshwa's officers, till I should have an opportunity of conversing with Lt Colonel Close upon that subject . . . I have determined that I will not suffer the Peshwa's authority to be trampled upon in the manner which it has been by the killedar of Karnala, and that the detachment under your command shall be immediately employed in getting possession of that fort for his Highness . . .

Grwd (1837) i 551 (1844) i 434

68

Colonel Murray to Arthur Wellesley

Cassowli
7 May 1803

An hircarrah whom I sent to Apta and Karnala returned last night. In the fort there are 400 men only under the command of Walaji Rao Deo Gura. Abba Lamba a sister's son of [Naru Punt] Churkedi ran away from Apta and is supposed to be in the fort. At Goolscond which is at the foot of the fort there are 50 men of the Peshwa's troops and at Apta 100 belonging to Churkedi. These last parties have no communication with the troops in Karnala.

WP 3/3/79 p. 16

69

Colonel Murray to Arthur Wellesley

Cassowli
7 May 1803 half past 9 pm

I have this moment received your orders of this day. I shall march at twelve and expect to reach Chauk about seven or eight o'clock. From the report I had the honour of sending you this morning, I should hope that there will not be much difficulty in the attack of Karnala and your orders both with regard to the breaching and example shall be strictly attended to. As there appears to be a few of the Peshwa's troops there, perhaps instructions that they should obey my orders might prevent some difficulty. I think a few cavalry may possibly be of some use.

WP 3/3/79 p. 17

70

Arthur Wellesley to James Kirkpatrick

8 May 1803[7] [received by 15 May]

. . . It is unfortunate that his Highness the Nizam's territories should be so situated as to be liable to the predatory invasions of the Marathas, and it must be obvious to his Highness that no army can give them complete protection. Those places in which there are the greatest riches and which may happen to be unprotected must suffer, and it is for this reason that it is advisable that his Highness should at an early period adopt measures for the defence of the rich cities placed like Aurungabad upon his extreme frontier. In case there should be a contest with the Maratha powers the operations which may be necessary for the general defence of his Highness' territories must oblige the army to leave some of these places at a distance . . .

Grwd (1837) i 540 (1844) i 427 and ii 1459

71

Colonel Murray to Arthur Wellesley

Chauk
9 May 1803

I arrived at this encampment yesterday morning at eight o'clock. At three I went to examine Karnala which is about nine or ten miles from hence. I found it in appearance much stronger than I expected. The fort is at the top of a very high hill of considerable extent covered with jungle. There are several paths which lead to it, the principal one from Apta which is situated exactly at the foot of the hill. I was prevented from going into Apta by finding that Abba Lamba had come down from the fort with a considerable number of his people, they said 700 but that must have been an exaggerated account.

As from the inspection of the fort last night it appeared to me that we could not bring cannon to bear upon it, till we had established ourselves on the hill, and that it would be absolutely necessary to make roads, I have determined to march close to it that I may be ready to make use either of the scaling ladders or guns as may be judged proper. It appears to me of much consequence to prevent the troops at Apta from rejoining those in the fort and particularly to get possession of Abba Lamba who is reported as the cause of the fort's resistance. With this view I propose marching this evening with the 78th Regiment to Apta to surprise that point and secure the people that are in it. If I succeed I shall push over one or two companies over the hill to find out where the defences commence and it is possible they may secure some important point. I propose leaving orders with the next senior officer to strike the camp two hours after I have marched, to proceed to Karnala and to appear at the pass that leads to the fort on a different side from Apta about daylight; from that side likewise I shall push up a few men. From this movement it is very possible that the killedar may surrender but I shall not summon him till I am prepared for a vigorous attack in the case of refusal.

It appears extraordinary that at Apta there should be a small party of the Peshwa's troops, and I believe likewise some in service of Churkedi. I have sent to bring the karkun here and I intend to keep him with me till we reach the place, so that he may point out the Peshwa's troops and prevent any mistake that might otherwise occur. I had the honour of receiving your letter of the 8th this morning enclosing the letters for Angriah and the killedar of Karnala. The killedar I understand expects an attack; he has been threatened with it by some of the Peshwa's ministers.

I am now in the greatest distress for money; neither sepoys nor followers have the means of procuring subsistence. I have written to the Bombay government on the subject, who I conclude will refer me to Colonel Close's shroffs. I hear from Panvel that some treasure is to pass through this camp for your army. I hope that you will excuse my stopping a small part of it, which may be replaced from the cash which the shroffs of the Residency engaged to furnish to us. The followers are particularly distressed and will inevitably desert, and what is of much consequence, a considerable sum is due to the banjaras who threaten to desert unless they are paid. As some difficulty appears to have arisen at Panvel with regard to escort I have appointed Captain Young to the command of the troops there. I propose sending immediately to the top of the ghats one month's complete supply for this corps. The bullocks may be employed in carrying forward the stores for your army.

WP 3/3/79 p. 19

72

Arthur Wellesley to Colonel Collins

9 May 1803 [received by ?17 May]

. . . It appears that matters are taking a serious turn in your quarter and although I should be happy to see you at Pune, I should be much more pleased if I should hear that Daulat Rao Sinde had prevailed upon you to remain at his court.

The confederacy against which according to appearances we may have to contend is composed of persons and powers among whom there can be no common interest excepting that of plunder and there are many sources of jealousy and enmity. They will soon find that they have everything to lose by hostilities with the English government and such is the state of our military preparations that they have but little to gain. Some of them please God may come in for harder blows than they expect and upon the whole we may reasonably look for the speedy dissolution of this confederacy . . .

The prince at whose court you have resided is one of the principal members of the confederacy; he has most to lose and least to gain in the contest because whatever may be the success of this plundering expedition, his troops are not of that description to partake in its benefits in proportion to their numbers and importance, and his territories are most exposed to our invasions.

His mind also appears to be adverse to the course of measures which his ministers have adopted, he is of a disposition to take sudden measures in consequence of the failure of the military operations, against those who have advised him, and it appears that he has a great respect and regard for you.

Under all these circumstances I anxiously hope that he may have endeavoured to prevail upon you to remain with him, and that you may have stayed . . .

SD iv 73

73

Lieutenant-General Stuart to Arthur Wellesley

Hospet
10 May 1803

. . . The Peshwa's tardiness in returning to his capital at a time like the present is most unaccountable and provoking.

I am sorry to tell you a letter received last night by express from the Resident at Hyderabad informs me that Holkar has encamped in the vicinity of Aurungabad, made a demand on that city of a crore of rupees, and that they have agreed to give him eleven lakhs and sent him soucars as hostages and security for the payment. Whether that sum would content him or not, the paper of intelligence sent to Hyderabad does not say, but mentions that he threatens to lay some other cities under contribution, and even to march to Hyderabad itself.

We have expended all the forage on both sides of the river at this place. I am now on my march to a lake within fifteen miles of Bellary where I shall try to stay while the forage lasts and I must then proceed further down the river.

WP 3/3/87 p. 165

74

Richard Wellesley to Arthur Wellesley

Fort William
22 April 1803 [received 10 May]
[summary]

Arthur Wellesley was instructed to report to Hobart (Secretary of State for War) and Castlereagh (President of the Board of Control) on the progress of the detachment. He was also to send to Fort William his estimate of the time at which it would be possible for a subsidiary force to be established at Pune, and the balance of forces in the Deccan to be returned to Mysore or to Company territory.

Home Misc. 616 p. 931

75

Arthur Wellesley to Richard Wellesley

Chinchore near Pune
10 May 1803

I have received this day your letter of the 22nd April . . . I cannot fix the time at which the troops can return to their stations, but I still think we shall not have a war. We are playing a little at cross purposes here. Colonel Collins encourages Sinde to march to Pune, or rather does not object to that march, which ought to be done at present.

Colonel Close and I think that the Peshwa ought to write to Sinde to inform him that he has regained his power and that he must not come here, and that I ought to write a letter to Sinde in similar terms. The consequence of his coming will be a contest preceded by a long Maratha negotiation in the course of which he will intrigue with all the Peshwa's chiefs, shake their allegiance, and throw the country which is getting into order into a new scene of confusion. It is better by far that the contest should be at a distance, but there is a better chance of avoiding it entirely if we keep him away.

We ought to have some authority here to settle matters with all these chiefs under some general instructions from you. The state of affairs varies daily, and before orders can come from Bengal upon any question the circumstances that ought to guide the decision have entirely changed . . .

Grwd (1837) i 557 (1844) i 438

76

Colonel Murray to Arthur Wellesley

near Karnala
10 May 1803

I carried into execution the movement which I had the honour of communicating to you yesterday and I am now encamped before Karnala.

I am sorry however to inform you that I was not successful in taking Abba Lamba, as he had escaped from Apta in the early part of the night. I had certain information that he was there about twelve or one o'clock in the forenoon with three or four hundred Scindians and Arabs. But alarmed at the return of the corps under my command and acquainted with its determination, he did not think it prudent to wait our attack.

After passing one or two small guards of the Peshwa's we reached Apta about half past one; at the last I was informed that we should meet at the entry of the town with 200 Arabs and Scindians in the service of Abba Lamba. Two or three companies however passed without opposition, and I had concluded that the place was evacuated when I perceived something like a column of two or three companies coming out of the village to our left. I concluded them to be the Scindians and sent an officer with a company to stop them. This they would not submit to, and on their retreating towards the river an unfortunate foray commenced. It did not do much mischief and was instantly checked. One man was shot when stealing on a sentinel with several others and another I fear belonging to the Peshwa was stabbed by a sergeant after he had fired his piece at him. In the struggle of securing, the guards being ignorant of what they were, few people were hurt.

It appears that since our return to Chauk the alarm in the fort has been great. I believe now that the killedar will surrender but he has been informed indirectly that I will not be satisfied till he has evacuated the place. I have not judged it right to send your summons or indeed any other as I am not prepared for an immediate attack in case of refusal. But some people from the fort and one of the Peshwa's officers have been with me to know my intentions and I have told them that he has no chance left. I have some expectation that he will come down this evening or early tomorrow morning. Should however contrary to my expectation the place hold out, I have little doubt of taking it by escalade in a few days after the arrival of the ladders. In obedience to your orders I shall march without loss of time to join your army when this service is over.

WP 3/3/79 p. 21

77

Colonel Murray to Arthur Wellesley

near Karnala
11 May 1803

I have to acquaint you that the pickets which I had pushed close to the fort of Karnala took possession of the gate without resistance at eight o'clock this morning. His Highness' troops are now on their march to occupy the place and I have ordered mine to return to camp as soon as they shall arrive.

I have not had, till a few hours ago, any direct communication with the killedar. Between him and the Peshwa's officer however several messages have passed, and he understood through that channel the fate that awaited him. The summons I have had no occasion to use; I reserved it till the arrival of the scaling ladders and cannon.

The killedar sent his son to me this morning to receive my orders. I informed him that his father must quit the place without delay and was at liberty to take his private baggage with him. It appears to me very evident that there was no intention on the part of Abba Lamba or the killedar to give up the fort. I have ordered a salute to be fired from the fort on his Highness' colours being hoisted.

I shall march from hence to Chauk tomorrow morning and the day following to Cassowli, and as I presume the road is now finished I hope to ascend the ghat on the 14th. The scaling ladders were brought to camp this morning and the guns are arrived at Panvel. As I do not know whether you might want them for any other purpose I shall direct Captain Young to keep them till he receives your orders. I am happy to find that there were only two people killed at Apta, one of whom certainly was an Arab, and the other was killed when attempting to cut down a sergeant of the 78th. Three or four only are slightly wounded and doing well.

WP 3/3/79 p. 23

78

Lieutenant-Colonel Close

Memorandum to Peshwa's Ministers

11 May 1803
[summary]

Close sent a request that Baji Rao should write to Sinde not to come to Pune, suggested that the Peshwa should furnish cavalry only in support of the Company's troops and that these should be provided by the 'sirdars and jagirdars . . . present and assembling in Pune' by giving them financial aid.

PRC vii 75

79

Arthur Wellesley – Subjects on which the Peshwa is to be pressed

Pune
14 May 1803
[summary]

In a briefing note, Arthur Wellesley listed in all eleven of the southern jagirdars, with statements of various claims for funding or requests for confirmation of office or landed title. Of the eleven, only two (Goklah and Appah Dessaye) were destined in the event to join his detachment later in the year.[8]

SD iv 82

80

Arthur Wellesley to Lieutenant-General Stuart

Pune
15 May 1803

I saw the Peshwa last night according to his appointment. The object of my visit was to press his Highness to relieve the distresses and to attend to the requests of those chiefs who had come forward in his cause with me, and thus to excite them to fresh exertions in his service and to bring forward others who still remained behind.

It was agreed between me and Colonel Close that he should begin by pressing [the Peshwa] to prepare the army which he is bound by treaty to produce, and that then he should be informed of the distresses and claims of the chiefs, whose troops it was certain that his Highness would enumerate among those to be appointed to join the British detachment. In the course of the conversation his Highness showed much quickness and ability, and I observed that he appeared particularly anxious to perform all the stipulations of the treaty, of course at the smallest possible expense to himself.[9] But he gave satisfactory assurances that he would immediately commence to settle with the different chiefs who had come here with me, and that in proportion as his Highness should satisfy them, he would signify the same to the Resident and they were thenceforward to be considered as part of his Highness' contingent . . .

Upon the whole we were all satisfied with the meeting . . .

Grwd (1837) i 574 (1844) i 449

81

James Kirkpatrick to Arthur Wellesley

Hyderabad
15 May 1803 [received by 25 May]
[summary]

The Resident had received the letter from Arthur Wellesley of 8 May. The Nizam's principal minister, Azim ul Umara, had hesitated to use the delegated powers given to him. The action taken by Arthur Wellesley following the moves of Holkar into Hyderabad territory had been welcomed by the court of the Nizam.

WP 3/3/60

82

Colonel Collins to Arthur Wellesley

Camp near Ghorasgaon
[17 May 1803 ?][10] [received by ?24 May]

. . . Rest assured that I shall not leave this court while my presence can in any way tend to promote the good of the public service.

I am sorry my dear General I cannot agree with you in thinking the present confederacy of the two principal Maratha jagirdars was formed for the attainment of plunder in the Nizam's country. On the contrary I am of opinion that the confederacy originated at least on the part of Sinde and of the Berar Raja from apprehension that their interest and influence in the Maratha state would eventually be injured in a material degree by means of the engagement which the Peshwa has lately contracted with the British government, and therefore that should those chieftains ultimately resort to the plundering of the territory of our ally the Nizam this measure would be adopted solely with a view of inducing our government to relinquish these engagements.

Believe me it would be needless to point out to this court how vulnerable Sinde's possessions are in Hindustan, since his ministers are but too well aware of the danger to which the Maharajah is exposed in that quarter. Yet they flatter themselves that General Perron is in sufficient force to prevent the English troops from making any permanent conquest there. They are indeed sensible that the country is open to invasion and consequently liable to devastation, and are prepared to retaliate on the Company's districts in the Doab . . .

I understand that Jaswant Rao Holkar has moved from the vicinity of Aurungabad in consequence of your late military arrangements.

WP 3/3/53 p. 26

83

Merrick Shawe to Arthur Wellesley

Fort William
27 April 1803 [received by 14 May]
[summary]

Arthur Wellesley was instructed to send to Henry Wellesley in England an account of events in the Maratha empire. Orders for his own conduct after the restoration of Baji Rao had been drafted for the consideration of Richard Wellesley and were expected to be sent as soon as the present despatches for Europe had been completed.

A Mss 13,778 f. 7

84

Colonel Collins to Arthur Wellesley

near Ghorasgaon
19 May 1803 [received by 23 May 1803]

. . . Since I proposed leaving Daulat Rao Sinde his ministers have been more than usually civil in their behaviour towards me. With respect to the Maharajah, his conduct has been invariably attentive and even kind. I do not think that Sinde's army will march to Pune until the conclusions of the approaching rains and that it will never advance thither so long as the troops under your command retain their present position.

WP 3/3/53 p. 29

85

James Kirkpatrick to Arthur Wellesley

Hyderabad
19 May 1803
[summary]

Kirkpatrick explained that the sirdar at Aurungabad, which had just been plundered by Holkar, had a brother who had quarrelled with the Nizam. The Resident also noted that he had urged the employment of Mir Khan by the Nizam, and that it seemed possible that this might be agreed.[11]

WP 3/3/60

86

Lieutenant-General Stuart to Arthur Wellesley

near Comply, bank of the Tungabhandra
19 May 1803

I have had the honour to receive your letter dated the 11th [May].

I am sorry to find that the Government of Bombay have been unable to fulfil the expectation which they raised with respect to a supply of money. I send you tomorrow one lakh of pagodas in gold coins which I understand are current in the Maratha country. We have few or none of the rupees you mention and only 34,000 Bahadry and Sultany pagodas which are sent. The money is to be carried on an elephant and two camels, which are all the camels with me at present. The escort consists of two companies commanded by a captain and a subaltern from the corps escorting the boats to the Malpurba. It will not however wait the movements of that corps but proceed with all due expedition to Sangoly and then to Pune by the western route.

I came here this morning, and tomorrow the ordnance and departments cross to the other side of the river, it requiring boats, working parties and elephants to transport the perishable stores, rice and sheep. There is already so much water in the river, the troops will follow the day after . . .

Everything by the accounts of some hircarrahs of mine who came in last night, is perfectly quiet from Miraj to the banks of this river.

WP 3/3/87 p. 173

87

Neil Edmonstone to Colonel Collins

Fort William
5 May 1803 [received by Collins by 26 May and seen by Arthur Wellesley by 24 May]
[summary]

In a note intended to form the basis of detailed instructions and sent to Collins to be implemented at once, the Governor-General directed that Sinde should be informed of the necessity of his immediately crossing the Narbada and returning to Hindustan. The purpose of his position could be seen only as the subversion of the arrangements between the Peshwa and the British government, and the re-establishment of his own ascendancy over the Peshwa.

Sinde was to be informed of the contents of the Treaty of Bassein, reminded that the Peshwa was fully entitled to use British assistance to restore him to his throne, and that Sinde had invited the cooperation of the British power in this.

The Resident was to inform Sinde that he must retire or hazard the advantages of protection of his own government which the Treaty of Bassein offered to him. Collins was to offer both a subsidiary force, a defensive guarantee, and British mediation in any demands Sinde had either on the Peshwa or on Jaswant Rao Holkar. Military operations against British remonstrances would lead to measures of precaution, and accession to a confederacy against British power would lead to hostilities and 'justify the destruction of his power.'

Parl Pps [5, 22 June 1804] p. 128, Martin iii 93, PRC ix 198

88

Neil Edmonstone to Lieutenant-Colonel Close

7 May 1803 [received by Close 22 May and seen by Arthur Wellesley by 23 May] [summary]

The Resident was instructed to satisfy the Peshwa of the British intention to avoid interference in his government, but also to mediate between the Peshwa and his jagirdars. An attempt should be made to conciliate the Peshwa towards both Jaswant Rao Holkar and Amrit Rao. The subsidiary force of six battalions and infantry and an artillery detachment should be established at Pune as soon as possible.

'The proceedings of Major General Wellesley must be regulated in a great measure by the information which he may receive from the Resident with Daulat Rao Sinde with respect to the effect produced on Sinde by the representations which Colonel Collins was instructed to make to that chieftain by the orders of the 5th [May].'

The troops employed for the restoration of the Peshwa were to return to British territory. The army under Lieutenant-General Stuart was to separate, once Arthur Wellesley had indicated that this could safely be done, unless there was reason to fear a return to Pune of Jaswant Rao Holkar. Once done, this would 'satisfy the principal Maratha jagirdars that the British government had no views beyond the express stipulations of the Treaty of Bassein.'

'If Major General Wellesley and Colonel Close should be convinced of the hostile intentions of Sinde or Holkar, the army must be properly employed to disperse Holkar's forces, and to drive Sinde beyond the Narbada. In such an event, the earliest notification should be sent to General Lake at Fatehghar, who will be ordered to seize Agra Mathura Koil and Delhi and other places (probably Kalpi) and to take or disperse Sinde's troops in those quarters. These suggestions are stated, but no reason exists to countenance an apprehension that Sinde, Holkar, the Raja of Berar, or any other power, will now attempt to frustrate the Treaty by hostilities.'[12]

Parl Pps [5, 22 June 1804] p. 136, PRC x 97

89

Arthur Wellesley to Lieutenant-General Stuart

Pune
23 May 1803

I have the honour to enclose the copy of a dispatch received yesterday by Lt Colonel Close. The orders contained therein will bring matters to a speedy issue. The dispatch from me to which the Governor General refers in his letter to Colonel Close was a private letter which I wrote to him on the day that I was joined by Colonel Stevenson, to inform him of that event and the general situation of our affairs at that moment. I sent it by Hyderabad . . .[13]

Grwd (1837) i 586 (1844) i 459

90

Arthur Wellesley to Colonel Collins

Pune
24 May 1803

. . . You will have received the Governor General's instructions of the 5th [May]. The consequences will be either that Sinde will not come to Pune or that if he should move this way we shall know what line we are to follow. You have a fine field open for you, and if you should succeed firstly in drawing from Sinde a declaration of his peaceable intentions and secondly in prevailing upon him to recross the Narbada as a proof of the reality of those intentions, you will deserve the thanks of your country . . .

Colonel Stevenson is now up at Paithan. I march in that direction in the course of a few days. I have been detained here for material to repair some of my carriages, but these are now arrived from Bombay and I shall march in three or four days.

SD iv 93

91

Arthur Wellesley to Colonel Stevenson

Pune
25 May 1803

I enclose the copy of a paper which I have received from Major Kirkpatrick from which it appears that Mohipat Ram imagines that you have assured him that the British government will pay half the expense to be incurred by taking Mir Khan into the Nizam's service. I conclude that this is a misconception of Mohipat Ram, but the sooner he is undeceived the better . . .

Grwd (1837) 588 (1844) i 461

92

Arthur Wellesley to Richard Wellesley

Pune
27 May 1803

. . . It is evident that the Peshwa's confidence in us increases daily. He calls for our assistance frequently to support and enforce, by our influence over the jagirdars and other chiefs, his authority and orders, and he pays attention to our recommendation of their claims upon his government . . . I have had a correspondence with Amrit Rao the result of which is that he has written a letter which he calls an engagement . . . in which he promises that from that moment he will separate himself from the Peshwa's enemies, and he requests that the British government will intervene to reconcile him to his brother and to obtain for him a provision in the state.

If we succeed in reconciling the Peshwa with Amrit Rao, the interior of this state will be settled as far as it can be at present, and this defection will shake the nerves of the members of the congress to the northward . . .

Your instruction to Colonel Collins of the 5th [May] will have arrived just in the proper time. The Treaty of Bassein is in fact a better security to Holkar and to Sinde for the possessions they have extorted from the Peshwa, and those lying to the southward of the Narbada, than either of those chiefs could have under any other arrangement which could secure the Peshwa's power. They will see that clearly, and their sense of their own interest will combine with their fears to prevent a war . . .

I propose to march from hence in a few days. I am detained here only by the want of iron to repair the wheels of my ordnance carriages. If I should find that the congress to the northward determine upon war, my first operation will be to seize upon Ahmednagar, by which Sinde will lose a territory worth nine lakhs of rupees and which he extorted some years ago from the Peshwa. Malcolm is still very unwell; he was talking of going back to Mysore but I have prevailed upon him to stay with me some time longer.

The letter from the Court of Directors to the Governor of Fort St George is shocking. I hope that you do not propose to stay in India longer than the end of this year. Such masters do not deserve your services.[14]

Grwd (1837) i 593 (1844) i 464. Partly printed in Parl Pps [5, 22 June 1804] p. 146

93

Arthur Wellesley to Lieutenant-General Stuart

Pune
27 May 1803

The banjaras with this division have sustained great losses in cattle and they appear to apprehend much greater and are very unwilling to continue with the troops . . .

Since the 20th April my banjaras have sold nothing as the troops have been subsisted entirely upon the produce of the country purchased in the bazaar. I have therefore thought it necessary, to secure their services and their goodwill in the present situation of our affairs, to make them a present of two rupees for each bullock they may have . . .

I find the banjaras and indeed all the people of the Mysore country and the Carnatic very averse to staying in this country. It is true that forage and all kinds of provisions are uncommonly dear. I therefore take the liberty of recommending to you to bring forward as many hired bullocks as possible, and to depend less upon the banjaras for supplying your troops than I have.

The more I see of them the more I am convinced that we have entirely mistaken the character of these people. Unless they are permitted to plunder the country through which they pass or to have profits such as the native armies are able to give them from plunder, they will not follow the troops to any distance from the place at which they usually reside. I have had the greatest difficulties with them, and they have deceived me and broken their engagements upon every occasion. Colonel Stevenson who has another set has been obliged to punish and even put some to death for plunder in the Peshwa's country . . .

Grwd (1837) i 597 (1844) i 466

94

Colonel Stevenson to Arthur Wellesley

28 May 1803
[summary]

Stevenson had received Arthur Wellesley's letter of 25 May. It seemed most unlikely that Mohipat Ram had so misunderstood matters as to believe that Stevenson had given an assurance that the Company would bear half of the costs of engaging Mir Khan in the service of the Nizam. The agreement which he had been pressed to sign had in any event been dependent upon Arthur Wellesley's consent.

WP 3/3/60

95

Colonel Collins to Richard Wellesley

near Chikhli
29 May 1803 [seen by Arthur Wellesley by 4 June]
[summary]

Following the arrival of the instructions of the Governor General of 5 May, Collins reported on an interview in Sinde's durbar of 28 May. In this he gave to the durbar for the first time a copy of the Treaty of Bassein, and received confirmation that it was seen as containing no stipulations prejudicial to the interests of Sinde.

Collins then noted in durbar discussion 'that negotiations had of late been carried on between Daulat Rao Sinde and the Berar Raja, that these chiefs were . . . to have an interview shortly . . . that the Maharajah had concluded a peace with Jaswant Rao Holkar, in whose camp a vakil now resided on the part also of Raghuji Bhonsle, that Sinde had likewise avowed an intention of proceeding with his army to Pune accompainied by the Berar Raja' and that putting these points together, he suspected 'designs adverse to the interests of the British government.' Collins therefore sought an explanation of the nature of the engagement entered into by the three Maratha rulers.

Sinde's ministers refused to give any reassurance, saying that this could be done only after an interview with the Raja of Berar. Collins explained that measures of precaution at the frontiers of Maratha territory would be taken, and that a march on Pune or attack on the territories of the Nizam would be considered an act of aggression. Sinde finally stated that after the interview with Raghuji Bhonsle, the Resident would 'be informed whether it would be peace or war.'

Martin iii 159, PRC ix 234, Parl Pps [5, 22 Jun 1804] p. 153

96

Colonel Collins to Arthur Wellesley

30 May 1803 [received by 4 June]

. . . Anxiety of mind and the extreme heat of the weather have affected my health. This letter therefore will be short . . . Colonel Close will apprise you of the unsuccessful issue of my conference with Sinde consequent on the notes of instructions which I lately received from the Governor General. But although the Maharajah made so stout a reply, I cannot believe that his ministers will venture to involve him in a war with the English, since should the event be unfavourable to this state, of which there can be little doubt, the whole responsibility would rest with the ministers who have all along acted in opposition . . . It is absolutely necessary that the Peshwa should instantly prohibit the advance of Sinde to Pune, for the Maharajah has positively assured me that he has been invited to proceed thither by Baji Rao and that since the return of his Highness to his capital.

I really am too much indisposed to write more at present. Pray let me know of your movements after marching from Pune.

WP 3/3/53 p. 32

97

Arthur Wellesley to Lieutenant-Colonel Close

Pune
31 May 1803

. . . I proposed to march on the 3rd June being fully prepared for that purpose. From the communications however which I have had with the different chiefs in the service of the Peshwa, who accompanied my march to his city, I find that notwithstanding his Highness' positive promise to me in your presence, no steps have been taken to satisfy the claims of any of them. These chiefs therefore appear to entertain great anxiety upon the subject of my approaching march. Some of them have determined to ask for permission to return to their homes, and none are prepared to march with the British troops under my command.

Under these circumstances I think there is strong reason to apprehend that the whole of the troops of the Peshwa will disband when I shall commence my march from Pune. You will be aware how strongly I am urged by the situation of affairs of the government of the Peshwa to the northward and by the advanced state of the season to commence my march at the earliest possible period. But in hope that some arrangement will be made, I have no objection to halt until the 4th, on which day I must march.

Grwd (1837) i 608 (1844) i 476

98

James Kirkpatrick to Arthur Wellesley

Hyderabad
3 June 1803
[summary]

The Resident reported that he had received the letters sent to him by Arthur Wellesley on 25 and 29 May. The ministers of the Nizam were not prepared to engage with Mir Khan for a force of more than 3000. He had been concerned to learn of the commitment allegedly entered into by Colonel Stevenson. After a further attempt to secure acceptance by the Nizam's ministers of the obligation to engage some part of Mir Khan's force, he would at worst inform the ministers that Colonel Stevenson had acted without authority. He noted that the health of the Nizam was failing rapidly.[15]

WP 3/3/60

99

Colonel Collins to Richard Wellesley [copied to Lieutenant-Colonel Close]

near Chikhli
3 June 1803 [seen by Arthur Wellesley on 8 June]
[summary]

Collins reported that Daulat Rao Sinde and Raghuji Bhonsle were to meet between their two camps on 4 June. The principal minister of Sinde had reported on his meetings with Raghuji Bhonsle. Collins added that he had learnt from several sources that the force of the Berar Raja consisted of 'ten battalions of infantry and 20,000 cavalry'.

PRC ix 258

100

Arthur Wellesley to Colonel Collins

Charowli
4 June 1803 [received 9 June 1803]

I marched from Pune this morning and I shall continue my marches towards the river Godavari. Colonel Stevenson has crossed that river at Paithan. I have just received your letter of the 30th May and Colonel Close has sent me that which you have transmitted to him of the same date.[16] I am concerned that Sinde should not have given you at once the answer which I think he will give you in the end.

I observe that in the 16th paragraph of the note of instructions to you the Governor General requires that Sinde should instantly explain himself without reserve. But instead of making this explanation, he tells you that when he will meet the Raja of Berar he will let you know whether it is to be peace or war. That very answer might justify an immediate attack upon Sinde's possessions. But when it is connected with the probable delay of the arrival of the Raja of Berar and of the proposed meeting, which after all I believe will never take place, it appears to be absolutely necessary that there should be some further explanation.

You will observe that I am directed to regulate my conduct in conformity to the instructions to you and to Colonel Close. But it is obvious that unless I am to consider Daulat Rao Sinde's delay to explain himself as a refusal, I cannot act, and unless he is called upon to fix a time when he will give his explanation, we shall be obliged to remain in the situation which we ought particularly to avoid, namely with the armies in the field incurring all the expense and inconvenience of war without any of its honours or advantages.

You will observe that the object of all the Governor General's instructions is to bring the question to a speedy decision, and to break up the army in this quarter. The necessity of this becomes the more evident when we reflect upon the intelligence of the 11th March received from Europe last night, from which it appears that there is a probability of the renewal of the war with France.

SD iv 105

101

Arthur Wellesley to Richard Wellesley

Charowli
4 June 1803

I marched from Pune this morning and shall proceed towards the Godavari. I am sorry to tell you that, notwithstanding our strong recommendation of the southern jagirdars and the Peshwa's officers to his Highness, his solemn promise to me that he would satisfy their claims in order to secure their future services, and the assurances of his servants from time to time to Colonel Close that his Highess was taking measures to satisfy them and to send out an army with me, I have not got with me one Maratha horseman . . . The Peshwa trusts none of his ministers and pretends to do his own business, although his time is much taken up by religious ceremonies and his pleasures and he is very undecided. These faults in his character, added to a slowness natural to every Maratha negotiator, render hopeless the conclusion of any important transaction.

In the meantime the season is advancing, the rivers which rise in the Western Ghats will soon fill, and then if I am not on the spot to urge the chiefs [the southern jagirdars] to take all the trouble and to make all the arrangements which are necessary to cross the rivers with the troops, months will elapse before they will overtake me, even if the Peshwa should settle their claims as far as to induce them to march from Pune at all.

This conduct of the Peshwa would appear as treachery, but I declare that I do not suspect him of treachery. I really believe that he thinks his only safety is in the alliance with the Company, and that he wishes to carry into execution all the stipulations of the treaty. But he is incapable himself of doing business, he will not trust his ministers, and he is jealous of and detests his sirdars. The news which came from England yesterday makes it very desirable that we should break up in this quarter . . .

I wish that there were powers here to act at once and to direct the negotiations with the different Maratha chiefs to certain points as they arise. These questions occur daily, and nearly six weeks elapse before your orders can be received upon every fresh occurrence. At this moment Colonel Collins ought to be ordered to press Sinde to give an answer, particularly as he is wavering between peace and war, and time, which is all that Sinde requires and which is fatal to us, will be gained by the necessity of waiting for your orders unless Colonel Collins should attend to my suggestion. A communication ought also to be opened with Holkar and the Raja of Berar upon the subject of the Treaty of Bassein, and endeavours made to separate them from Sinde, and the Peshwa ought to be made to show his correspondence with Sinde. I conclude however that Colonel Close will ascertain whether his Highness has written to that chief as he asserts that he has.

Grwd (1837) i 614 (1844) i 481, WP 3/3/2 fldr 1 p. 23

102

Lieutenant-Colonel Close to Arthur Wellesley

Pune
5 June 1803

. . . I am extremely happy to find that you have pressed [Colonel Collins] on the necessity of his still urging Sinde for a decided reply. The aim of his durbar is to trifle away the period of the monsoon during which his army shut in between the rivers must be entirely helpless, and deprives us, in the event of a rupture, of the advantage of attacking immediately his northern provinces and laying siege to Ahmednagar on the rising of the river . . . I conclude that the Colonel will immediately comply with your wish that he should deprive Sinde of the benefits of evasion by insisting on his fixing a time within which he will give his definitive answer.

The bad state of your banjara bullocks is certainly a matter of great urgency. I am endeavouring to draw some of the banjara maistries to a private conversation with me, in the hope that by giving them a cowle from the Company, and a party of sepoys for their protection, I may be able to prevail upon them to engage to serve for supplying your army. The progress I may make in this business shall be reported to you. Colonel Murray has taken possession of his barracks and moved his line so as to connect with them. The sick of the 84th are comfortable indeed, and the rest of the troops with the assistance of huts and bungalows will soon be substantially covered. I have had a visit from the Chinchore soucar who says that he will punctually adhere to his agreement . . .

WP 3/3/45, p. 146

103

Arthur Wellesley to Major Malcolm

6 June 1803

I return your letters and I am much obliged to you for the perusal of them.[17] I am glad to see that our conduct in this quarter is approved of. It is very desirable that you should bring on the chiefs and I hope that you will succeed in your negotiations, but prevail upon them to hasten a little as otherwise the Bhima will fill and they will find it difficult and tedious to cross that river . . .

Grwd (1844) i 486, SD iv 107

104

Lieutenant-Colonel Close to Arthur Wellesley

Pune
6 June 1803

Your despatch of the 5th I received this morning. Colonel Murray immediately sent off a party to take charge of the rice left at Charowli. He had only sixty carriage bullocks at command which he despatched, but tomorrow I hope we shall be able to collect a sufficient number to bring in the whole of the rice in two or three trips. I shall attend to your directions about the depot. I am in negotiation with some banjaras and I hope to make some progress with them . . .

I have written to Mr Duncan telling him that we are pressed now for the two lakhs . . .

WP 3/3/45 p. 156

105

Lieutenant-Colonel Close to Arthur Wellesley

Pune
7 June 1803

I send you the brahmin's news of yesterday and a copy of a letter from Bombay containing intelligence about Holkar.

Bistnapah is moving off and Goklah only talks of moving, not having procured the necessary cash yet from the durbar. Appah Dessaye is to pay us a visit this evening. Nothing has yet been finally settled for him, but he will probably march soon. Appah Saheb is constantly offended . . .

We have not succeeded yet in procuring bullocks for bringing on the rice from Charowli but I may get some off today. The weather still holds up, but the supplies from Panvel come faster than Major Spens can erect cover for them.

I have this morning received a letter from Collins dated Chikhli 3rd inst. Raghuji Bhonsle had arrived at Mulkapur and it had been settled that he and Sinde were to meet midway, each attended by 200 horse. Jadu Rao Bhaskar had rejoined Sinde and appeared to be greatly disgusted at the state of things at court. Balaji Kunjar had been frank enough to say that he thought it would not be possible for Sinde to march to Pune before the rains . . . I shall furnish you with a copy of the Treaty of Bassein as soon as possible.

WP 3/3/45 p. 183

106

Colonel Collins to Richard Wellesley

near Chikhli
7 June 1803
[summary]

Collins reported that he had sent his munshi to Raghuji Bhonsle, to whom Richard Wellesley had sent a letter and the text of the Treaty of Bassein. Sinde had refused Ambaji Inglia permission to move to Hindustan.

Collins explained that 'should Daulat Rao Sinde intimate to me after a conference with Raghuji Bhonsle that he is desirous of maintaining the relations of friendship that formerly subsisted between his sarkar and the British government or should he even express a wish to become a member of the general defensive alliance, I shall in either event explicitly state to the Maharajah that your Excellency required in proof of the sincerity of his friendly disposition towards the English and their allies that he should immediately recross the Narbada and repair to his possessions in Hindustan.'

Collins noted that the monsoon was not yet sufficiently severe to make the roads impassable.

PRC ix 261

107

Lieutenant-Colonel Close to Arthur Wellesley

Pune
8 June 1803

I am favoured with your letter of the 7th and return the packet that accompanied it. This new demand for troops is considerable but I hope distant. I hope in God your forage improves. Part of the rice you left at Charowli is come in and a large proportion of the remainder will come in this evening. I have elephants camels and carriage bullocks at work and Colonel Murray has 200 of his best carriage bullocks now out grazing.

The bullocks that brought the supplies from Panvel are hired I believe for the trip. The owners obstinately refuse to move a yard beyond this place on any terms. I am still in communication with some banjaras but cannot get on with them as I wish; they say they have sent off all their bullocks and could not collect them in less than a month. I will persevere however and may succeed.

The Peshwa has passed an order on me to Goklah for 75,000 rupees to be paid out of the the two lakhs to be received from Mr Duncan, and I have ventured to give 10,000 rupees to Goklah to enable him to move, the remainder to be discharged when I receive the bill of exchange from Mr Duncan. Should I not receive this bill soon, you are to assist Goklah in the interim, taking his receipt for what you advance. Lingum Pundit has just been here and Goklah marches to join you tomorrow . . .

We make the basket boats here in great style. We have covered three large ones and our progress in working will increase. The brahmin had no news of any sort yesterday. The principal sirdars will soon be off to join you I hope, and then we shall press the Peshwa for an answer on Amrit Rao . . .

WP 3/3/45 p. 195

108

Colonel Collins to Arthur Wellesley

near Chickhli
9 June 1803 [received by 18 June]

I received your favour of the 4th inst this morning.

It is indeed greatly to be regretted that Sinde should not at once have told me whether he intended to obstruct the completion of the Treaty of Bassein, nor can your concern exceed that which I have felt from his refusing an instant explanation.

I perfectly recall the 16th paragraph of the Governor General's instructions to me and am very sensible of the necessity of bringing the Maharajah to a speedy decision on this important point. But I am not aware that any other means could have been used for effecting that purpose, than those which I have already adopted, since every argument with which the Governor General had furnished me was brought forward in order to induce Sinde to give the required explanation. I likewise exerted all my powers of persuasion towards the attainment of the same end, and when I perceived that both arguments and persuasion were alike ineffectual, I then explicitly stated in the Governor General's own words what the Maharajah had to expect should this explanation be withheld . . .

I conceive that you will agree with me that it would have been inconsistent with the dignity of the British character had I pushed my importunities further after Sinde had declared that he could not then afford the satisfaction that I demanded without a violation of the faith which he had pledged to the Raja of Berar, and that immediately after his interview with that chief I should be informed whether there would be peace or war, since in fact this declaration left it to the discretion of our government to commence immediate hostilities.

You will ere this reaches you have been apprised that the meeting between Sinde and the Berar Raja has, contrary to your conjecture, actually taken place. You will likewise learn from my correspondence with Colonel Close that the Berar Raja has received a letter from the Governor General which is likely to produce the happiest effects . . .

I am however by no means so confident . . . as to neglect any necessary measures for bringing this court to a speedy decision. Be assured therefore that the day after Sinde and Raghuji Bhonsle have held a private conference together I shall demand of the Maharajah an immediate explanation of his intentions, and should he decline giving me an explicit answer I shall in this case declare that his refusal will be considered as an avowal of hostile designs against the British power.

We had only light showers until the night of the 7th, but since then it has rained violently and incessantly. My dining tent has three feet of water in it this morning and the ground all around is impassable for carriage and draught cattle. My health is very indifferent as I have a fever attended by gouty symptoms. This will account for my employing an amanuensis on the present occasion.

WP 3/3/53 p. 36

109

Lieutenant-Colonel Close to Arthur Wellesley

Pune
10 June 1803

. . . Your accounts of your cattle are most unhappy. From the enclosed minutes of a conversation which Malcolm and I had yesterday with the Peshwa you will perceive that I am anxious to hire some banjaras for you.[18] Raghunath Rao writes to me today that he is busy on the subject and will see me on it tomorrow.

If you purpose the plan you mentioned to me of establishing a little depot on the Goor river, or anywhere in that neighbourhood, it is probable that with the assistance of the recovered cattle belonging to the corps here, a considerable quantity of grain would be advanced from here with little delay. If you adopt the plan in question then give me as early intimation on the subject as you possibly can. I could probably procure coolies to convey supplies to an advanced depot during the rains on terms as cheap as bullocks could possibly be hired for the purpose. Colonel Murray has 18,000 rupees in readiness for you which will be forwarded tomorrow or next day . . .

Supplies come in from Panvel and cover is rising fast for them. I hope in God your forage improves. I expect to get some banjaras but if the place of the advanced depot will answer, our means of carriage for that purpose will I doubt not be adequate. Four large boats are finished and others are in hand. We shall be able to convoy them to the proposed stations, but the people of this country do not know how to work basket boats on the water. Perhaps a few of your pioneers may be spared for the purpose.

The brahmin's news of yesterday was a meeting had taken place between Sinde and the Berar Raja and that their plan was to invite Holkar and secure his person. Today a report prevails in the city that Holkar had ascended the Cassabari ghat and he has designs against Gujerat.

WP 3/3/45 p. 199

110

Colonel Murray to Arthur Wellesley

Pune
10 June 1803

. . . I expect the first division of the pontoons in two or three days. Shall I forward them immediately or wait the arrival of the whole. I have the honour to enclose a state of the treasure . . .[19] Captain Mathison reports to me weekly and at all times when it is increased or considerably diminished. I will send regular reports to you. Colonel Close informs me that he will have some treasure to send you tomorrow or the next day. Mine shall accompany it.

WP 3/3/79 p. 27

111

Arthur Wellesley to Lieutenant-Colonel Close

11 June 1803

. . . Certainly your conference with the Peshwa was as satisfactory as words could be. However I hope that he will write to Sinde and the Raja of Berar, and that he will now enter heartily into the cause in which we are embarked for his government. The settlement with the chiefs [the southern jagirdars] will then advance rapidly and they will soon join me . . .

I move a short distance daily, and get a little forage, and just keep alive; I dread a fall of rain however. I am now able to carry all my loads, and if I can get the bullocks required from Bombay and promised by Mr Duncan, and those on the subject of which I wrote yesterday to you and Colonel Murray, I shall still weather these little difficulties and mishaps . . .

Grwd (1837) i 636 (1844) i 497, WP 3/3/46 fldr 2 p. 54

112

Colonel Murray to Arthur Wellesley

[Pune]
11 June 1803

I received last night a most melancholy account of the roads below the ghats. Captain Young seems to despair of the pontoons getting on without the assistance of elephants. These I have not to send him. All I could do was to send 150 gun lascars to join the two companies and I have ordered the officer in command to go down the ghat to meet the pontoons. I have likewise directed a party I sent for the 12 pounder carriages to join this detachment . . . I have heard nothing of Mr Duncan's 2000 bullocks. I fancy that they have not yet arrived at Panvel . . .

WP 3/3/79 p. 30

113

Lieutenant-Colonel Close to Arthur Wellesley

Pune
11 June 1803

. . . We are now employed on the fifth boat, so that we shall soon have the number you require. I shall let you know when the whole are finished and you must tell me when they ought to be forwarded and what people you have allotted for working them in the water. I shall attend to your wishes about the purchases of bullocks etc and the care of those we have and may have in charge of the Bombay servants . . .

WP 3/3/45 p. 209

114

Colonel Collins to Richard Wellesley

near Chikhli
12 June 1803
[summary]

Collins having established that there had been a substantive meeting between Sinde and Bhonsle, and found that his agent failed to obtain any satisfaction when the durbar was 'urged to declare whether this court intended peace or war' addressed a memorial to Daulat Rao Sinde saying that refusal or further delay would be taken as 'an avowal of hostile designs.' Should Sinde decline giving the satisfaction now demanded, Collins requested a party of horse to escort him to Aurungabad.

Parl Pps [5, 22 June 1804] p. 474, Martin iii 170, PRC ix 262

115

Colonel Collins to Arthur Wellesley

near Chikhli
12 June 1803

. . . It is my intention to leave this court the instant I can receive grain sufficient for the subsistence of my sepoys etc from hence to Aurungabad. I am told that no provisions of any kind are procurable on the road thither. I have written to the Commander in Chief[20] forwarding a copy of my memorial and apprising him of the reply which Sinde gave to it. When I addressed you on the 9th [June] I did not know that the Berar Raja and Sinde had held a private conference, this circumstance not having been communicated to me until the afternoon of the same day.

WP 3/3/53 p. 40

116

Lieutenant-Colonel Close to Arthur Wellesley

Pune
12 June 1803

. . . Early tomorrow morning I shall send off supplies of cash to you. . . A draft of a letter from the Peshwa to Sinde has been prepared and given to Raghunath Rao who approves of it highly. I think it will be adopted and forwarded by the Peshwa and if so a similar one will be sent by his Highness to the Raja of Berar. Balaji Kunjar has been obliged to acknowledge to Collins that the Peshwa did write to Sinde discouraging him from coming to Pune. On this subject I shall send you some papers tomorrow.

WP 3/3/45 p. 228

117

Arthur Wellesley to Colonel Stevenson

Angah
14 June 1803

. . . I am at present encamped about twenty miles to the southward of Ahmednagar and I intend to seize that place immediately if there should be a war. I shall afterwards cross the Godavari and act in cooperation with the troops under your command. I wish you to move towards Aurungabad with a view to be prepared to make the arrangements which I informed you the Nizam's government had in contemplation as soon as you shall receive a communication of their wishes upon the subject . . .

I would not wish you to move your main body from Aurungabad till that post shall have been secured . . . If the question of peace or war shall remain undecided for any length of time I must still remain to the southward of the Godavari till I can seize Ahmednagar. In that case I shall be either on the road to Paithan or on that from Pune to Aurungabad and your hircarrahs will find me on one or the other. I shall let you know which as soon as I have found out on which there is most forage.

If by the slowness and indecision of all transactions in which the Marathas are concerned I should be detained on this side of the Godavari till that river shall have filled, which I think probable, I must get you to speak to Mohipat Ram and Sukhruder to collect boats for me at Toka at which place I propose to cross if possible. Toka is, I believe, within the Nizam's territories and is the place where the last of the rivers that fill the Godavari falls into it. It is on the road from Pune to Aurungabad. . . .

Grwd (1837) ii 5 (1844) i 501

118

Lieutenant-Colonel Close to Arthur Wellesley

[Pune]
14 June [1803] [received 16 June]

. . . Six boats are finished in a capital style and they shall be sent off to the Bhima and the Goor without loss of time. Two for the Inderowny shall go off in about three days which I conclude will be time enough as we have had but little rain and there is no alteration in the rain yet. I have the prospect of procuring a few people who can work boats in the water. My progress on the point I will write to you tomorrow.

The banjara man who agreed to supply 4000 bullocks begins to act in a manner which does not please me. However I shall hope to succeed though perhaps not within the stipulated period which wears away fast . . . I sent you a supply of cash yesterday and today I received 14,000 rupees from the Chinchore soucar.

Not a word more about Gujerat from Mr Duncan or any other quarter. Colonel Murray I believe writes to you about the progress of the bridge from Panvel. We have not been able to open a channel yet for the purchase of bullocks . . .

WP 3/3/45 p. 232

119

Colonel Murray to Arthur Wellesley

Pune
14 June 1803

The accounts of the pontoons do not improve. The two first were five days from Panvel to Chauk distant only 12 miles. One cause of the delay may be the want of officers to enforce exertion which will be remedied when the sepoys and lascars join them. Provisions continue to arrive from Panvel. Six hundred bags arrived this morning, and I am sorry to acquaint you that the greater part of this is spoiled by the incessant rain they have had since leaving Panvel. I fear more will arrive in the same state . . .

I am very sorry that I can give you no flattering prospect of purchasing cattle here. Major Spens is still making every enquiry but hitherto without success. Colonel Close is not more likely to succeed at present, from what I could learn this morning . . .

WP 3/3/79 p. 32

120

Lieutenant-Colonel Close to Arthur Wellesley

Pune
15 June [1803]

. . . I have strong promises from the durbar about the banjara bullocks and I live in hope. The six boats for the Bhima and the Goor are finished and I hope to get them off tomorrow accompanied by two sepoys of the Bombay battalion who can work basket boats properly, and will be able to teach any people that may be procurable for such business. I have sent off materials for the repair of the boats now at the Bhima but I am sorry to learn that the boat on the Goor is not repairable. There is another however lower down the river which may be brought to the ford when the water rises a little and any repairs it may require may be completed hereafter. The boat people at the Bhima and the Goor . . . it may be proper perhaps to put . . . on pay as they will probably be much employed by the public. The Peshwa has revised the draft of the letter for Sinde and I expect to receive the amended draft from the durbar any moment . . . The weather is very wet and I am afraid that the roads in the Konkan must be very deep.

WP 3/3/45 p. 236

121

Colonel Collins to Arthur Wellesley

15 June 1803 [received by 27 June]

. . . I think that the Berar Raja is averse to war but at the same time that he is inclined to adhere to the present confederacy. I fancy that he expects to derive some advantage by acting the part of mediator on this occasion. I have apprised this chief of the content of my memorial to Sinde under date the 12th [June] by which he will clearly perceive that this court has declared that peace or war depends entirely on himself.

Sinde has informed me that if the weather should continue fair until the day after tomorrow he will then grant me an audience in the presence of the Berar Raja . . . The Maharajah also promises that this conference shall be decisive, but you well know what kind of people these Marathas are, and how little reliance can be placed in their assurances . . .

WP 3/3/53 p. 50

122

Arthur Wellesley to Lieutenant-Colonel Close

Angah
16 June 1803

I have received your letter of the 14th. I sincerely hope that you may succeed in getting us some bullocks and in bringing forward the banjaras. I have got a few bullocks from the Nizam's country, but so few that they do not replace the casualties even amongst the Bombay carriage bullocks. We have had rain which has done much mischief to our weak cattle. In short nothing but the required assistance from Pune can keep us in the field.

I hear good accounts of Ahmednagar; it is full of everything we want. The property of this country is lodged there. The capture of that place will relieve our immediate distresses and will give everybody spirits. But the resources of Pune must keep us in the field during the rainy season. My people got 3000 bullocks in one month, besides the cattle purchased by individuals and bazaar people.

Have you got any description of Ahmednagar? . . .

Grwd (1837) ii 10 (1844) i 506, WP 3/3/46 fldr 2 p. 59

123

Lieutenant-Colonel Close to Arthur Wellesley

[Pune]
16 June 1803

. . . By different letters from European officers in Holkar's army dated 2nd [June] almost the whole of his infantry was on that day near the Tapti, to the westward of Burhanpur. Money was plentiful amongst them and the general idea was that they would soon move to the eastward so as to be near the meeting between Sinde and Raghuji Bhonsle.

I cannot give you any satisfactory answer about the banjara bullocks yet. Six fine boats were despatched this morning, four for the Bhima and two for the Goor. They are accompanied by two sepoys who are good boatmen and two more sepoys of the same description shall follow tomorrow. Two boats for the Inderowny will be ready in two or three days and shall be despatched with one good boatman whom I have secured. Now that he has procured a few boatmen some of the country people may be induced to act with them . . .

The rains continue here and the rivers have swelled considerably.

WP 3/3/45 p. 240

124

Lieutenant-Colonel Close to Arthur Wellesley

[Pune]
17 June 1803

. . . My endeavours shall be applied to procure from the Peshwa an answer to Amrit Rao's despatch the moment that our progress in respect to other pressing objects will permit. The letter which his Highness has drafted for Sinde and the Raja of Berar is not despatched yet, and till it goes off I cannot venture to press the durbar on any subject to which it is openly averse . . .

WP 3/3/45 p. 242

125

Arthur Wellesley to Colonel Collins

near Angah
18 June 1803 [received 29 June]

I have just received your letter of the 9th and I am much concerned that my letter of the 4th should have given you any uneasiness.

It appeared to be probable at the moment I wrote it that Sinde and the Raja of Berar would never meet, and under that notion which I see was erroneous I suggested to you the propriety of urging Sinde to name a day on which he should give his answer to your inquiries. I am of opinion that you pressed him as hard as was possible, and that a Maratha durbar only could have withheld an answer at that time. I hope that before now the wished for private meeting will have taken place and that you will have had an opportunity of pressing Sinde for an explanation.

It is very desirable that we should know at an early period how we stand . . .

SD iv 118, WP 3/3/46 fldr 1 p. 15

126

Lieutenant-Colonel Close to Arthur Wellesley

Pune
18 June 1803

. . . Raghunath Rao is confined to his house by the ceremonies attendant on the celebration of his marriage. I therefore paid him a visit this forenoon. I was happy to learn from him that the Peshwa had despatched the proposed letter to Sinde desiring him to refrain from coming to Pune . . . It is not sent exactly as Malcolm and I wished it to be, but it is right in all essential points. But perhaps the whole subject may be of little importance considering the stage to which, by Collins' last letter, matters have arrived at Sinde's court . . .

Your comments on Ahmednagar are flattering.[21] Raghunath Rao has promised to send me an head hircarrah who was employed there for 17 years. When he comes I shall send him to you. If you lay siege to the place, I suppose you will send for the two twelve pounders and two 5½ inch howitzers at present with Colonel Murray.

Edmonstone's letter of the 30th May . . . hints that the Peshwa might be induced to cede lands in Bundelkhand in lieu of Savanore and the ceded part of Buncapur. Would it be [in] our interest if such an exchange took place?

The weather will probably clear up soon and if so would you wish that more rice be brought hither from Panvel? It would certainly be at hazard of being wet and spoiled. We have now I believe about 8000 bullock loads.

We send off two boats today to Inderowny. I have not heard from the ford at the Bhima yet but I hope our boats there work well. Four sepoys are gone there with them who are capable of leading the management of basket boats to the country people. I have sent only two boats to the Goor. Would you have me send two more? If you attack Ahmednagar your communication at these rivers ought to be easy and secure . . .

WP 3/3/45 p. 244

127

John Malcolm to Arthur Wellesley

[Pune]
18 June 1803
[summary]

Malcolm reported that by a letter from Shawe[22] he understood that steps were to be taken to give adequate delegated powers. He sent a memorandum. 'I have lost all faith, God knows I never had much, in this court . . . If we place any dependence whatever in the aid of this court we shall be liable to constant disappointment, and we ought not to engage in hostilities unless we are prepared to take their weight on our own shoulders.'

WP 3/3/70

128

John Malcolm – Memorandum

Pune
18 June 1803
[summary]

In an extended political appreciation, Malcolm noted that all that would be obtained from Peshwa Baji Rao in the event of hostilities would be 'a neutral inaction' and that there would be no 'zealous cooperation' from the southern jagirdars. British interests required that the contest should be undertaken despite the conduct of the Peshwa. To retreat would expose both the territory of the Nizam and possibly that of the Company to danger. Assuming the preservation of the position at Pune, no Maratha force would be able to invade Company territory to the south.

'In the early and complete settlement of affairs in this empire, our best political security both against native and European enemies is to be found, and unless a very positive danger threatens, this object should engage for a period the undivided efforts of the British government.

'If the English government engages in a contest with the confederacy on the grand scale, and under the circumstances I have supposed, they should act independent of any expectation of efficient aid from the Peshwa, nor do I think it necessary to wait for the assent or cooperation of that prince in any measure or negotiation which policy might dictate, with the whole or separate chiefs of the confederacy, though it would no doubt be desirable to conciliate the Peshwa to the proceeding to be adopted if that could be done without the sacrifice of any object connected with the interests of the British nation.

'His Highness' adherence to friendship would be secured by the superiority of our force at Pune and his non performance of some of the most essential articles of the Treaty might be urged by the British Resident as a sufficient excuse for the British government departing from forms and pursuing a line of action which his conduct renders indispensable for the safety of the interest of the alliance.'

A Mss 13, 746 f. 182, WP 3/3/70

129

Arthur Wellesley to Lieutenant-Colonel Close

18 June 1803

. . . I apprised you yesterday of the intelligence I had received of Holkar's movements which I believe to be authentic. A man came in from his camp this morning who says that he left him on the 11th on his march northward, that he appeared to be in a hurry, that he was making long marches leaving behind everybody that could not keep up with him, and that it was reported in his camp not only that he intended to cross the Tapti but likewise the Narbada and to go into the Holkar territory to the northward of that river.

I think his crossing the Tapti at all, if he should afterwards cross the Narbada, looks very like a breakup of the confederacy. I do not think it probable that Holkar would trust the defence of Chandore to Sinde, if he is to be involved in hostilities with us . . .

Grwd (1837) ii 12 (1844) i 507

130

Colonel Murray to Arthur Wellesley

near Pune
19 June 1803

. . . By the returns of the magazine here and at Panvel which I had the honour of forwarding to you some days ago you will see the state of our supplies. It is not the intention to send up any more perishable articles at present, so I learn from a letter to Major Spens from Captain Moor. In this case should we be successful in procuring cattle it will be necessary to purchase rice here to keep up our depot to the quantity you have ordered, which at present and probably for some time will be very expensive, as there is a rise in the price of this article since your departure.

I am much afraid that there is not much prospect of a supply of cattle. . . From the slowness with which you have been supplied with bullocks I have thought it unnecessary to apply to Bombay for others to replace those which marched with you. I know they could not get them. I am very desirous to complete our complement for the guns, and from Lieutenant Goodfellow's report I think it improbable that you will be able to spare any again from the pontoon establishment. I shall therefore write pressingly upon this subject requesting that a sufficient number may be collected ready to join me when the season will permit.

Lt McArthur of the Scotch Brigade arrived here last night from Erroor with a few recovered sepoys. Captain Buchan had not reached Erroor when he left it. I have written to Mr Duncan on the subject of our money affairs but as yet have received no answer. Either our paymaster manages very ill or Colonel Close gets all the money, for we can get none here. Our cash yesterday amounted to two rupees exclusive of the dollars which are coming.

WP 3/3/79 p. 41

131

Lieutenant-Colonel Close to Arthur Wellesley

Pune
19 June 1803

. . . There has been a dreadful fall of rain below the ghats and we have had our share here, but the sky is now clearing and we are again blessed with a little sunshine. No part of the last monsoon was so severe as the beginning of this, so that I trust that we shall now have a fair interval. The rivers here rose high but have greatly subsided again . . . Collins in his last despatch, you will observe, mentions that by his information Holkar was moving to the eastward to be near Sinde and the Bhonsle.

I feel all that you have said to me about bullocks and shall exert myself to procure them with proportionate solicitude. True it is, however, that the banjaras are cursedly averse to employ their cattle during the rains, but the durbar shall have no peace till I succeed . . .

The boats for Inderowny are off. I shall have two more for the Goor tomorrow or next day, and when ready they shall be despatched, especially as I am afraid that there is no serviceable boat on the Goor except those that were sent thither three or four days since . . . I have hopes of being able to send you in the course of tomorrow or the next day an hircarrah or two who have long resided at Ahmednagar and possess minute information of the place.

WP 3/3/45 p. 251A

132

Arthur Wellesley to John Malcolm

20 June 1803

I have received your letter of the 18th with the memorandum enclosed, and I agree almost entirely in the opinions which you have given. Till the question with the confederacy is decided we must stick to our ground in this country, otherwise the Nizam and we eventually must suffer. Even supposing that by withdrawing we could stop the hostilities, which I doubt, we should only defer them to a period at which probably we should be less prepared than we are at the present moment. But as soon as there shall be no threat of the confederacy either by the withdrawing of Sinde or from the success of the war, it is my opinion that we ought either entirely to new model the alliance or to withdraw from it . . .

The greater experience I gain of Maratha affairs, the more convinced I am that we have been mistaken entirely regarding the constitution of the Maratha empire. In fact, the Peshwa never had exclusive power in the state. It is true that all treaties have been negotiated under his authority and have been concluded in his name, but the chiefs of the empire have consented to them. The want of this consent on the part of any one of them . . . or of power in the head of the empire independent of these chiefs is the difficulty of this case at the present moment . . .

In what manner then ought the alliance to be modelled? In my opinion we ought to withdraw from Pune and leave some chance that the principal chiefs may have the power of the state in their hands. We ought to keep up our connection with the Peshwa so that he might not be trampled upon. At the same time, we ought to increase our influence over the chiefs of the empire, in order that it may preponderate in all possible cases in which the state shall be called upon to decide. In short I would preserve the existence of the state and guide its actions by the weight of British influence, rather than annihilate it and establish new powers in India by the subsidiary treaty . . .

Collins is just in the right state. The fellow [Daulat Rao Sinde] will explain himself, and will ask him to stay, and will pretend that he cannot move off on account of the rain, the swelling of the rivers, or because my troops are in this country, and thus the matter may hang on for some time longer. I think that if the war had not been still doubtful, Collins would have got an answer inimical to his memorial. The truth is they are all shaking, and if the allies [the southern jagirdars] had come out of Pune with me, there would be no war . . .

Grwd (1837) ii 20 (1844) i 513

133

Lieutenant-Colonel Close to Arthur Wellesley

Pune
20 June 1803

. . . I am doing all that is possible to procure bullocks but cannot I am sorry to say give you any favourable accounts of my progress. I am to see Raghunath Rao tomorrow and then Malcolm and I will press him most strenuously on the answer to be given to Amrit Rao . . .

Enclosed is a despatch just come in from Collins.[23] I am afraid the vagabonds to the northward will wheedle us out of the monsoon. I send you also a paper of news from Mir Khan's camp received last night. Colonel Murray sends off some arrack to you tomorrow and I shall accompany it by supplies of cash from the two soucars. I conclude that the rains in your quarter have begun to abate . . .

WP 3/3/45 p. 253

134

Arthur Wellesley to Colonel Stevenson

21 June 1803
[summary]

It was not now necessary for Stevenson to occupy Aurungabad, since Mohipat Ram had moved there. Arthur Wellesley doubted if there would be a war, since Sinde had promised satisfaction to Collins and Holkar had crossed the Tapti. It followed that Stevenson could not be attacked by the confederacy. It remained important to avoid offensive action.

Grwd (1837) ii 28 (1844) i 517

135

Colonel Murray to Arthur Wellesley

Pune
22 June 1803

By my latest accounts, several of the pontoons have got to the top of the ghat. There are by this time probably six there, but they cannot be forwarded as all the bullocks are required to bring the remainder from Panvel to the ghat . . .

A Maratha who has been in our service as a guide etc since we left Bassein has undertaken to provide some hundred cattle. I have confidence in this man, and have allowed him an advance of cash. There is another man from Pune who has come forward and promises to procure some hundreds. He requires likewise an advance which I have agreed to, provided he gets a security on whom we can depend.

I hope the convoy of arrack which left us yesterday morning will reach you in safety.

WP 3/3/79 p. 43

136

Arthur Wellesley to John Malcolm

22 June 1803

. . . The alleged want of bullocks at Pune is too ridiculous. I make no doubt but that in the town of Pune alone there are not a smaller number than 50,000 bullocks at this moment.

I have not written to the Governor General for a length of time. I do not like to communicate to him my sentiments of the Peshwa nor do I wish to deceive him. I agree with you that strong measures are necessary but how are they to be carried into execution?

Holkar has made one march from the Tapti. It is reported in his camp that the expedition to Gujerat is deferred for two months. He is now supposed to be going to Chooli Myhissur on the Narbada. This place appears to be not far from Ujjein and Indore. It is very clear that the confederacy is not firm yet . . .

Grwd (1844) i 520, SD iv 120

137

Arthur Wellesley to Lieutenant-Colonel Close

23 June 1803

I return Colonel Collins' dispatch of the 16th.[24] It is rather less pacific than the last but I think it probable that the confederates have not yet arranged their matters, that Holkar has not yet come into their views, and that for that reason they wish to delay the decision for some time longer. Holkar's object would appear to be to get hold of the Holkar territory and his game to effect it by a war between Sinde and us. If there should be no war between Sinde and us, he will get hold of that territory, but not so certainly, either by a peace mediated by the Raghuji Bhonsle and guaranteed by him, or by the continuation of the contest with Sinde . . .

If the answer of Sinde to Collins should be at all peaceable and friendly, in my opinion we ought to accept it, and I ought to inform him that I intend to recross the Bhima and to break up the army as soon as I find that he commences to recross the Narbada. What has happened already and the situation of this body of troops are sufficient proofs that we cannot carry on a war in this country after having been four months from Seringapatam and having marched nearly 700 miles, without having the assistance of the resources of Bombay and Pune. The government of Bombay is unable, and will always be so with its present instruments, to afford us any assistance, and the Peshwa is both unable and unwilling . . .

The difficulties however in which this corps is likely to be involved, will be a useful lesson to governments and to us all, first to avoid entering into a treaty with a prince, the only principle of whose character is insincerity, and next to avoid if possible to enter upon a campaign at the distance of 700 miles from our own resources, not only <u>not</u> having the government of the country on our side, but in the shape of a friend, our worst enemy . . .

Grwd (1837) ii 33 (1844) i 521

138

Lieutenant-Colonel Close to Arthur Wellesley

Pune
23 June 1803

. . . Malcolm will have told you that yesterday we made a desperate struggle at the durbar to obtain a proper answer for Amrit Rao, and prevail on the Peshwa to take some effective measures for supplying us with the 4000 bullocks promised us some time since through Govind Naig. The first point is still in suspense, but it grieves me to the soul to acquaint you that I have just received a note from Raghunath Rao telling me that there are no bullocks and that the sarkar cannot assist us with any at this time, but that in the course of twenty days the government may be able to collect some from those at pasture, that Govind Naig will be able to assist us with coolies, that we shall also have some asses to carry grain to camp at the rate of six rupees per cooly per trip and 6½ per ass per trip, a hire so shockingly exorbitant as to put me out of all temper.

Yesterday evening we spoke . . . to the Peshwa's ministers warning them in the most solemn manner that if the Peshwa failed to furnish the bullocks you would be obliged to return hither, and the Governor General to pursue such separate courses as he might judge necessary for the security of British interests. Beyond this we can say nothing and hopes of aid are now at an end.

Malcolm sends you two letters from Collins, in one of which he says that if he does not receive a decided answer soon, he will leave Sinde's camp. That ere this the question of peace or war could have been decided was within your expectation when you marched from here, and that in order to determine your course, the question should be immediately decided, was evident. The question decided whether of peace or war by Collins coming off, and you would either return hither with credit or lay siege to Nuggur, which as you observe would serve to relieve your immediate wants. I conceive therefore that you should write to Collins ordering him to quit Sinde, if the question of peace or war be not decided within a fixed number of days from the date of your despatch.

If events require you to lay siege to Ahmednagar we should be able to send rice etc by trips from here till the siege should terminate, or to the Goor should you establish a post there . . .

I have examined one man respecting the works at Nuggur but his information is by no means satisfactory. The people of the durbar assure me that they have sent for a man near Lhoghur who served seventeen years as killedar of Nuggur and that he may be expected to arrive every hour . . .

WP 3/3/45 p. 257

139

Lieutenant-Colonel Close to Arthur Wellesley

Pune
24 June 1803

. . . I shall soon make you acquainted with our late proceedings at the durbar. They are calculated to put it in the Governor General's option to do what he pleases in respect to this wretched government, which is not to be roused by either events or menaces.

This morning I sent off the supply of treasure to you, and during this day we have despatched some rice to you on asses bullocks and men's heads. We shall continue to send off this article to you daily in the largest quantity possible till we receive further directions from you. Colonel Murray, who writes to you I believe, expects 300 bullocks in from pasture grounds tomorrow, which he understands are serviceable. It is impossible to procure any species of conveyance here to serve on any terms except by the trip.

Malcolm, apparently quite recovered, proceeded to join you this forenoon. The Maratha sirdars are still here, but they still talk of joining you. Malcolm will tell you that every possible screw has been resorted to to put them in motion. I hope you have a dak direct to Collins.

WP 3/3/45 p. 261

140

Lieutenant-Colonel Close to Arthur Wellesley

Pune
25 June 1803 [received 26 June]

Last night I was favoured with your letter of the 23rd and have since given it a mature consideration. When I last wrote to you on the subject of your present difficulties, it did not occur to me to embrace the situation of Colonel Stevenson's army, which should it continue on this side of the Godavari should certainly be strong enough to meet the confederates, although I must agree with you in what you have said about Holkar, and shall accordingly give the hint to Collins that you have suggested.

If Collins' next despatch brings accounts of a rupture, your first object must certainly be to lay siege to Ahmednagar, should you find that measure feasible, but if his next despatch should leave the question of peace or war in a state of uncertainty, I would pursue the following plan.

I would detach to the ferry on the Godavari near Colonel Stevenson the 74th, two native battalions and two regiments of cavalry. With the party I would send if possible a park of four six pounders. From General Stuart's army I would send if possible two native infantry corps, without guns, to Hyderabad. These two corps should be ordered to march with all possible speed, and should they leave a few men behind to come up in the rear, it would be attended with little inconvenience.

Early intimation of these moves should be given to Major Kirkpatrick, who should be directed to collect and prepare for movement all the provisions he can for the supply of the troops under Colonel Stevenson. As the two native corps approach to Hyderabad, Major Kirkpatrick should send off the supply of provisions for Colonel Stevenson, escorted by the two native battalions now at Hyderabad, without their guns. The junction of the two corps on the Godavari would make Colonel Stevenson completely formidable and enable him I think to act beyond the Godavari on the Nizam's frontier, even [during?] the rains . . . and in the face of the confederacy. But without the aid of the two battalions from Hyderabad I conceive that the force under Colonel Stevenson, though strengthened by the proposed detachment from your army, would not be sufficiently numerous to make us wholly confident . . .

I shall say no more on the foregoing sketch but have brought it to your consideration, subject to any modification you may think capable of improving it. I am aware that the plan would require some time to bring it fully into effect, but it is recommended only under the supposition that the equipment of the different branches of the confederacy is not so efficient at present as to allow of their making any movements profitably for the purpose of bringing British troops to action . . .

WP 3/3/45 p. 243

141

Lieutenant-Colonel Close to Governor-General

Pune
25 June 1803 [received at Fort William 14 July]
[summary]

Close reported on two meetings with ministers of the Peshwa. He hoped to secure the support of the Peshwa's government in securing 4,000 bullocks needed to keep the detachment commanded by Arthur Wellesley capable of movement, the appointment of an agent of the Peshwa to be based in the camp, and an answer from the Peshwa on the terms of conciliation to be put to Amrit Rao. Save on the second of these objectives, he had made little progress.

Close and Malcolm in a 'review of the state of things to the northward' spoke of the attempt being made by Daulat Rao Sinde and Raghuji Bhonsle to conciliate Jaswant Rao Holkar and urged 'the necessity of some rational policy being adopted for the purpose of defeating their schemes and preventing the menaced combination from reaching any point of maturity or acquiring any accession of strength.' The two political officers were careful to mention the report of a conversation on the 14th June with the munshi employed by Colonel Collins in which the Raja of Berar had stated that he possessed hereditary claims to the Peshwaship.

NLW Clive 283 PRC x 104, A Mss 13,598 f. 152, Grwd (1837) ii 8, Parl Pps [5, 22 June 1804] p. 487, WP 3/3/45

142

Arthur Wellesley to Lieutenant-Colonel Close

26 June 1803

. . . I am fully aware of the necessity of strengthening Colonel Stevenson, if I should be obliged to draw off. Indeed that measure is so obviously necessary that I considered the propriety of joining Colonel Stevenson myself with my whole corps. But the objection to that measure was the danger of increasing his consumption so far as to distress him for provisions at the moment when we might be called upon to act . . .

Another objection to reinforcing Colonel Stevenson at all, and that applies still more strongly to sending the large detachment from this corps which you have proposed, is the risk that in consequence thereof, this corps may never be of sufficient strength or so composed as to be able to march forward from Pune supposing that there should be a war . . .

We must certainly keep Colonel Stevenson in such strength as to ensure his safety in his advanced position, but in deciding upon the degree of strength I must give him . . . I must consider . . . the strength of the enemy, their present state, their probable future state and their immediate designs. However as I told you before my prospects have so much improved within these last two days that I have strong hopes that I shall be able to retain my position, and if any of my modes of procuring bullocks succeed, I shall entirely recover.

Grwd (1837) ii 45 (1844) i 530

143

Lieutenant-Colonel Close to Arthur Wellesley

Pune
26 June 1803

We send off 600 to 700 bags of rice to you every day and shall continue to do so until we hear from you . . .

Malcolm will have told you that the Peshwa refuses to do anything about Amrit Rao's business. The paper we drew out in consequence has been delivered to the durbar . . .

WP 3/3/45 p. 267

144

Lieutenant-Colonel Close to Arthur Wellesley

Pune
27 June 1803

I am favoured with both your letters of the 25th and shall immediately consult with Colonel Murray what is best to be done in the present state of things. Our alarms from your want of rice were so great that we have been sending off this article to your camp on mens' heads for these three days past – a small supply is just now going off, but we shall send no more until we receive your further instructions . . .

WP 3/3/45 p. 269

145

Lieutenant-Colonel Close to Arthur Wellesley

Pune
28 June 1803

. . . Colonel Murray will have told you that we have just despatched from hence to camp by coolies 2,800 Bombay loads of rice, which makes upwards of 1400 light bullock loads. The Colonel is now sending off forage for your 500 bullocks on their way to Coraygaon, and the loads of rice for there will leave this as expeditiously as possible, that is I hope in the course of the day. It will now be necessary that you should inform us of the quantity of rice that you wish to be sent to camp from hence in addition to the quantity already despatched by coolies and the 500 bullock loads about to be despatched.

Your depot here is diminishing fast. Colonel Murray tells me that he has taken means to have more rice brought hither from Panvel. The quantity there I believe is not less than 10,000 light loads but as there will be drafts on it soon, perhaps you ought to have more sent to Panvel from Bombay . . .

I am happy indeed to find that you have the prospect of being able to keep your position. But if you remain near Nuggur and Colonel Stevenson continues beyond the Godavari he must be liable to an attack in case of a rupture without your being able to sustain him without great delay, especially if scantily supplied with conveyance. Besides, you would be obliged to move so immediately as to be under the necessity of leaving Ahmednagar in your rear. At present I have not a distinct view of your prospects supposing you may be able to keep your present position and in consequence my objections as above stated may be weakly founded.

As I view things at this conjuncture, I think to give us a prospect of success in the event of a rupture and to provide against possible cases, Colonel Stevenson should be competently reinforced, so as to allow him to operate with confidence beyond the Godavari while the river continues full, and that you should have the means at the same time of laying siege to Nuggur with a fair prospect of carrying the place. My plan I conceive provided for these two great objects. If Colonel Stevenson cannot subsist a larger force than is now with him, it may be a question whether he ought to continue beyond the Godavari as the river must now soon fill.

In respect to taking two battalions from General Stuart's force, he may certainly not be disposed to part with them, but independently of these two corps, the detachment from your army that I mentioned would probably secure Stevenson beyond the Godavari. Stevenson's corps thus reinforced, you would still I think have force enough to meet any portion of the confederate troops that could be opposed to you, with Stevenson in advance. But I have to repeat that the whole of this observation might have appeared to me to be unnecessary had I a distinct view of your present projects. If it be in your view to march from your present position to support Stevenson when seriously menaced, I am afraid that your movements could be not quick enough to be effectual, and in my conception it is an invariable principle that to give us speedy success against the confederates, Ahmednagar should not be an enemy's post in our rear but be so circumstanced as to serve as a depot for our support . . .

WP 3/3/45 p. 275

146

Lieutenant-General Stuart to Arthur Wellesley

Mudghal
28 June 1803

. . . yesterday I forwarded to you a copy of a despatch from Lord Clive on the subject of the proceedings of this army, and apprised you of my intention to recross the Tungabhadra.

In the present state of the Carnatic, this measure seems to be absolutely necessary in order to provide the means of acting with proper effect against the French force that is expected, and I trust that it will not be productive of any material disadvantages to our interests in the Maratha empire. The great distance to which you have proceeded appears to render the active cooperation of this army with your force entirely inconsistent with the safety of the Carnatic.

Even should hostilities occur with the Maratha chiefs I therefore consider it as a principle that . . . this army cannot be spared from the protection of the Company's possessions. It does not either appear to me that the return of this army will occasion any unfavourable effect to the negotiations with the principal Maratha chiefs, for according to Colonel Collins' last despatch the question of peace or war was on the point of being decided, and nearly thirty days must elapse between the date of that despatch and the receipt of intelligence of the return of this army, in which time the above question, I should conceive, must be finally determined.

The Resident at Hyderabad has repeatedly expressed the greatest confidence in being able to secure the succession to the Nizam in case of His Highness' death without the assistance of this army, and the settlement which has been made at Pune with some of the southern jagirdars, the peaceable disposition manifested by others, and the internal jealousies among them all, induce me to think that they will not attempt to molest the general tranquillity after the return of this army within our boundary . . .

WP 3/3/87 p. 210

147

Colonel Collins to Arthur Wellesley

near Selore
29 June 1803 [received 4 July 1803]

I return you many thanks for your obliging letter of the 18th inst.

As it is equally my duty and inclination to act conformably to your sentiments and opinions in the present critical situation of affairs in this quarter I must confess that I felt much uneasiness at the idea of your disapproving of any part of my conduct. However your last kind letter has removed any apprehension of that sort, and I am now as light as a feather . . .

You will perceive that Sinde intends to proceed to the ghat of Ajanta after having disclosed to me his final determination. I understand this ghat is only 35 kos distant from Aurungabad and although Sinde says he shall not ascend it yet I dare say you will not altogether rely on his veracity on this occasion.

My own opinion is that the ministers of the Maharajah would gladly avoid war with the English provided they could obtain a modification of some parts of the Treaty of Bassein. But I shall be able to write with more certainty on this subject the day after tomorrow. In the meantime I can assure you that Jadu Rao Bhau, Sinde's most confidential servant, appears to have great influence in the counsels of the Berar Raja.

I wish you would consider some mode of reconciling the Peshwa to Jaswant Rao Holkar; could this be effected, the chiefs here would soon become mighty complaisant.

Forage is scarcely procurable in these parts; grain of any description bears a most extravagant price. In short the distress in Sinde's camp is very great.

Pray let me hear from you sometimes.

WP 3/3/53 p. 66

148

Lieutenant-Colonel Close to Arthur Wellesley

Pune
29 June 1803 11 am

I am this moment favoured with your letter by express of yesterday's date, and trust that my despatch of yesterday will before this time have satisfied you on the subject of it. When I wrote to you on the 27th I was apprehensive that we had despatched more rice to your camp by coolies than you would immediately require.

A proportion of forage for your bullocks at Coraygaon was despatched from here yesterday, and more sent off this morning, so that they will be well supplied: the 500 large loads for them went off this morning in part, and the remainder is now under despatch and will be off in a few hours. You will of course let Colonel Murray know what quantity of rice you require from hence at this juncture. Coolies are to be had in abundance to work by the trip, and some even on monthly pay but at a high rate.

The tappal naik at Bajapur writes that Luksmur Naik the banjara will set off from that place in ten or fifteen days with 3000 laden bullocks. He only waits till forage shall be procurable on the road . . . I sent off 30,000 rupees to you yesterday morning.

WP 3/3/45 p. 275, 3/3/54 fldr 1 p. 16

149

Arthur Wellesley to Colonel Collins

29 June 1803 [received 3 July]

. . . I proceed to give you my opinion on the present state of our affairs. I think it is much altered in many respects since the Governor General wrote the instructions under which you have been acting lately. You will perceive by late letters from Colonel Close that it is probable that the Treaty of Bassein will not work as was expected, even in the Peshwa's durbar: and on the other hand the intelligence received from England in the beginning of June gives great reason to believe that the war with the French may have been renewed. Every circumstance therefore points out the necessity that if possible the war with the northern Maratha chiefs should be avoided . . .

The motive for war . . . with these chiefs at the present moment cannot be the fear of the immediate or even remote consequences of the establishment of our power in the government of Pune, but it must be a desire to regain that object of ambition for themselves . . . the question whether there will be peace or war does not in my opinion depend on the fact whether the confederacy is formed or not, or on any political question excepting upon the hope of advantage or the fear of loss entertained by the chiefs in the camp with you. To withdraw from the alliance with the Peshwa if it were practicable after what has passed, would affect this question only in this manner; it would give reason to our enemies to suppose that we wanted confidence in ourselves and that their menaces had had their effect and their hope of advantage from the war would be increased.

. . . Our course of action at this moment ought to be calculated in such manner as to increase their sense of danger and decrease their hope of gain from the war as the best means of preserving the peace. There is no doubt but that at this moment Sinde's territories on this side of the Godavari and at Broach are exposed to certain loss, and that those of the Raja of Berar bordering upon the seacoast are in the same situation . . . This therefore appears to me to be the time best calculated for bringing these chiefs to a decision on the question of peace or war.

On this ground I would immediately send a memorial to Sinde stating the earnest desire of the British government to remain at peace. I would explain the defensive and innocent nature of the treaty of Bassein, the security it affords to the territories of each of the chiefs and the provision it makes for the peace of India. I would point out the right which the Peshwa had to conclude that treaty independently of Sinde. I would repeat his declared approbation of the measure in his letters to Colonel Close. I would advert to the fact that neither he nor his ministers have ever made any detailed objection to any part of the treaty, I would recall to his recollection his friendly declaration to yourself, and I would contrast that declaration with his recent declared doubt whether there should be peace or war.

I would call upon him to perform his engagement to explain that doubt in three days from the delivery of that paper, and would announce my intention of departing on that day if I should not then receive his explanation. At the same time I should call upon him to act in conformity with his declarations and if he were inclined for peace he should withdraw his army from the Nizam's frontier into its usual stations, and allow us to withdraw our troops to our own territories. If Sinde should not give the explanation which you require and should not act in conformity to his declaration, you cannot stay in his camp one moment after the time fixed by yourself for your departure.

. . . If I saw the smallest prospect of avoiding the war by any political negotiation I should recommend you to enter upon it, but under present circumstances nothing can be done till the Raja of Berar and Sinde will have withdrawn from the Nizam's frontier.

SD iv 123

150

Lieutenant-General Stuart to Arthur Wellesley

near Moosky
30 June 1803

I have been honoured by the receipt of your letter of the 19th inst. I regret exceedingly the difficulties which you have experienced in consequence of the casualties among your bullocks and the want of grain.

Anxious to furnish you from this quarter with such assistance as it may be in our power to afford, I have resolved on sending you 5,000 carriage bullocks, 2,000 of which will be loaded with rice and 50 with kegs of arrack, and on forwarding at the same time the three lakhs of pagodas which I formerly mentioned to you, one of which you know is intended for the subsidiary force. The treasure will be carefully packed in gunnies and carried on bullocks, a spare bullock for each load will accompany it, besides a proportion of bullocks loaded with grain for the use of those conveying the treasure. The above convoy will leave this camp tomorrow evening under an escort of the 1st battalion of the 10th regiment commanded by Major Peter Dallas. A brigade of three pounder gallopers with their limbers drawn by bullocks has been attached to this corps on this duty.

Major Dallas has been instructed to cross the Kistna at the Kalachabootra ghat, to advance by the route which borders upon the left banks of the Bhima and the Seena and passes near Eedgerr, Colburga, Akul Cottah, Salapoor and Parenda. This route appears to be the most eligible in every view, for if you have marched upon the Godavari, no river will occur to obstruct the convoy in following you, and if you have returned to the Bhima it can divert the route to you there without great difficulty. Major Dallas has been instructed to continue his route until he effects a junction with you, should he find the country safe and receive intelligence of your situation, but if otherwise to wait at Parenda for your orders, and in all cases to obey your instructions.

Everything requires that your force should be as efficient as possible. The above supply will reach you at a time when you may have sustained further losses and it may be of service. My vicinity to the Company's country, and the probable destination of a considerable part of this army, enable me to spare that supply with little inconvenience. Should you have any apprehension of the safety of the convoy, or judge it necessary, you will of course reinforce it on the march from your army, or should you be able to relieve it at Parenda or any other place on the march without inconvenience, it would be desirable that you should detach a party for that purpose, as Government may wish for the speedy return of that battalion into the Company's districts.

I have directed the sutlers in this camp to forward by the present escort as much wine spirits and other supplies to yours as they can find carriage bullocks for, or coolies, but not wheel carriages.

WP 3/3/87 p. 212

151

John Malcolm – Memorandum

30 June 1803
[summary]

In a further extended memorandum, Malcolm reviewed the courses of action that were open to the Company in the Deccan.

'If Sinde and Raghuji Bhonsle persist in their refusal to give a direct and explicit answer to the just and moderate demands of the Governor General their ultimate design must be to attack the English government and its allies and their professions to the contrary can only be intended to gain time.'

Malcolm then noted the 'very strong remonstrance'[25] which had been delivered to the durbar of Peshwa Baji Rao on 23 June, and added that the principles which the durbar was following were 'incompatible with the obligations of friendship which the Peshwa has contracted . . . are at variance with all political wisdom, and . . . render all plans of cooperation in a war between that prince and the British government wholly impracticable.' On the conciliation of Amrit Rao, Malcolm outlined a scheme of gift of territory, title of which had been transferred to the Company by the Treaty of Bassein. This 'would secure his attachment to the English government and he would be thrown back to a station where he could give the Peshwa no just cause of alarm as he would be completely removed from the scene of intrigue with either Holkar Sinde or the Bhonsle.'

Malcolm recognised that such a transfer of territory would excite the jealousy of the Peshwa 'to a pitch that might make him secretly disaffected to the alliance, perhaps lead him to intrigue with Sinde or the Bhonsle, or possibly impel him to the still greater extreme of flying from Pune. I have contemplated all these events and I am satisfied none of them could be attended with any effects which could counter-balance for a moment the solid advantages to the British interest which must accrue from the adoption of the plan which I have suggested.'

Malcolm concluded by pointing out that should the Peshwa flee from Pune this would free the Company 'to substitute a more efficient local authority at that city.' Even if Baji Rao's subsequent actions were hostile, 'there cannot exist a doubt but that he would be found to the full as impotent as an enemy as he has hitherto proved himself as an ally.'

WP 3/3/70, A Mss 13,746 ff. 196–204 where dated 4 July

152

Colonel Collins to Richard Wellesley

near Salore
2 July 1803
[summary]

After insistence, Collins secured his first interview for a month with Daulat Rao Sinde, and remonstrated 'against the evasions which the servants of the Maharajah had practiced in order to render the written promise of their master of no avail.' He sought the 'final determination' of Sinde both as to whether it should be peace or war, and also on his intentions in respect of the Treaty of Bassein. On the first the Resident received assurances on the continuance of the 'relations of friendship' but on the second was informed that the reply he sought could be given only in the presence of the Raja of Berar. Collins warned that he could not be held responsible if hostilities followed. The evasion of the questions he had put 'could only be practised with a view to afford time for the junction of the forces of some other sirdar.' He agreed to stay a few days longer, and was told that he would receive a proposition for the withdrawal of both British and Maratha forces.

PRC ix 303, WP 3/3/53 p. 68

153

Arthur Wellesley to Lieutenant-Colonel Close

4 July 1803

Malcolm has communicated to me your letter to him.[26]

I acknowledge that in the event of a war I have no fears for Colonel Stevenson's safety, considering that the enemy's force is certainly divided, that they cannot bring it to bear upon the Colonel till I shall be within reach of him, and that therefore that they can bring upon him is not very well equipped. If I am mistaken upon this point, I must make up my mind to forego one of two objects, either the capture of Ahmednagar or the security of the Nizam's frontier. I do not think it would be proper to try the siege of Ahmednagar excepting in full force, and if Colonel Stevenson is not in sufficient force I must either reinforce him at the expense of leaving Ahmednagar in the hands of the enemy, or I must draw him back to the Godavari possibly across that river and leave the Nizam's territories beyond that river defenceless.

The only part of my force that it has ever been supposed I could send him consistently with the plan of attacking Ahmednagar is the cavalry. But considering the state of my supplies and the total deficiency of country cavalry with this division from the failure of the sirdars that is the part of my corps which I may most want. From the last letter from Colonel Collins of the 29th June I think it probable that we may expect from him something which will give us a tolerably clear idea of the views and intentions of the chiefs . . .

Grwd (1837) ii 64 (1844) i 539

154

Colonel Collins to Governor-General

near Jamner
6 July 1803 [seen by Arthur Wellesley by 11 July]
[summary]

In a durbar discussion on 4 July Collins sought from both Sinde and Bhonsle confirmation that there was no intention to obstruct the engagements made at Bassein. This he failed to secure, and was challenged on the advance of British troops towards the Ajanta ghat. He argued that 'to evince the sincerity of their present professions, it was indispensably requisite that Daulat Rao Sinde should recross the Narbada and the Bhonsle repair to

Nagpur.' As he failed to secure this, he was 'inclined to infer that their friendly professions are insincere.'

Martin iii 236, PRC ix 305, Grwd (1837) ii 67, Parl Pps [5, 22 June 1804] p. 166

155

Lieutenant-Colonel Close to Arthur Wellesley

Pune
6 July 1803

. . . The Madras battalion I think we can spare from hence under certain limitations. If you take Nuggur I think it should be thrown into that place, but if from any cause you should be induced to cross the Godavari without taking Nuggur, you must send it back to us on your marching from Nuggur. This I think is all that should be hazarded under the internal state of things here . . . The Peshwa is about to make a run to Wahen to bathe in the Kistna. It is impossible to withhold him from this foolish trip.

WP 3/3/45 p. 331

156

Arthur Wellesley to Richard Wellesley

Peepulgaum
8 July 1803

I have not written to you since the day I marched from Pune [4 June] because in fact matters have remained exactly in the same state . . . Holkar has crossed the river Tapti with his whole army and appears disinclined and I hear has positively refused to trust his person in the same camp with Sinde.

Notwithstanding Colonel Collins' assertion, Indore has not been given over to Holkar, and I believe that the peace which the

Colonel supposed to have been concluded is only a cessation of hostilities, which Sinde has been prevailed upon to grant by Raghuji Bhonsle in order to gain time for the negotiation of a peace, and of which Holkar has taken advantage in order to place the Tapti between his army and that of Sinde.

In the meantime we who were ready on the 4th June have lost that month and part of this for our operations and unless Colonel Collins has attended to a second representation which I made to him at the end of June we are as far from our point as we were in the month of May. The Colonel has gone on a false notion from the beginning. He has supposed that peace was concluded between Holkar and Sinde because Sinde's ministers had told him so, and he has had no other information and has never produced any one proof of the fact, the truth of which he believed and invariably asserted. Under this notion he has been timid and has afforded them time to conclude the peace and to intrigue which is all that they desired . . .

Grwd (1837) ii 74 (1844) i 544

157

Colonel Collins to Arthur Wellesley

near Jamner about 12 kos from the Ajanta ghat
8 July 1803 [received by 14 July]

I have to acknowledge and thank you for your very able and friendly letter of the 29th [June] which I should have replied to ere now had I not been kept in suspense for several days past respecting the real intentions of this court. Even to this hour I have not received the letters which Sinde and the Bhonsle have written to the Governor General. However these chiefs are to have a meeting this day at which my munshi is requested to attend for the purpose of receiving the kharitars.

In the meantime a copy of the address of Raghuji Bhonsle has been sent to me with an assurance that Sinde's will be exactly to the same purport. That you may be enabled to form a judgement of its tendency I enclose an extract from it, and I shall also forward a transcript of the whole letter to Major Malcolm by this dak. I do this in order to give you time, because it is my intention to call on you and Colonel Close officially to say whether, once Sinde has declined crossing the Narbada immediately, there appears to you any other required proof that he can give you of his intention not to oppose the completion of the Treaty of Bassein.

I have directed my munshi to demand the copy of any treaty which the Bhonsle or Sinde may have formerly concluded with the Peshwa, and should this not be attainable, I have directed Mirza Bauker to demand whether the engagement referred to by these chieftains militate in any respect [against] those lately contracted by his Highness with the British government.

Since my interview with Sinde and Raghuji on the 4th inst my munshi has had a conference with the latter in which he gave the most solemn assurance of his intention to pursue peace with the English and at the same time declared that he has not the most distant idea of opposing the arrangements lately concluded at Bassein. Mirza Bauker says that he thinks the Raja was sincere in this occasion and that he only keeps the field from an apprehension that the Peshwa may wrest from him certain possessions which he formerly obtained . . . and to which he consequently has not legal claim . . .

WP 3/3/53 p. 74

158

Colonel Collins to Richard Wellesley

near Jamner
9 July 1803 [seen by Arthur Wellesley by 14 July 1803]

I do myself the honour to forward two letters to your Excellency's address from Maharajah Daulat Rao Sinde and Raghuji Bhonsle the Raja of Berar . . .[27] Both declare 'they will never manifest any intention of disturbing the stipulations of the treaty of nineteen articles concluded at Bassein between the British Government and Rao Pandit Pradhan [Peshwa Baji Rao] provided that the British Government and Rao Pandit Pradhan will never disturb the conditions of the treaty subsisting from remote times between Rao Pandit Pradhan's Government and Raghuji Bhonsle Daulat Rao Sinde and the other sirdars of the Maratha empire.' . . .

PRC ix 310, Parl Pps [5, 22 June 1804] p. 501

159

Colonel Collins to Arthur Wellesley

Jamner
9 July 1803

Conformable to what I wrote you yesterday Mirza Bauker Khan asked Raghuji Bhonsle for a copy of the treaty referred to by him in his letter to the Governor General. The Bhonsle said that he had left it with his other papers at Nagpur. My munshi then asked whether that treaty contained any stipulation adverse to the engagement concluded at Bassein between the Peshwa and the British government. Raghuji declared that this treaty contained no stipulation opposite or prejudicial to those engagements.

WP 3/3/53 p. 84

160

Colonel Collins to Lieutenant-Colonel Close [copied to Arthur Wellesley]

Camp near Jamner
9 July 1803 [received by Arthur Wellesley by 14 July]

. . . Last night I was assured by an intelligent person that the Berar

Raja had obtained the consent of the Maharajah to send off the boy Khande Rao to [Jaswant Rao] Holkar, either this day or tomorrow, and should that measure actually be adopted I have not the least doubt that Jaswant Rao Holkar will shortly form a junction with Raghuji Bhonsle and Daulat Rao Sinde. . . . These chieftains may have determined upon this interview for the purpose of effecting a solid and permanent accommodation between Sinde and Holkar previously to the return of Raghuji Bhonsle to his capital . . .

As to Sinde and the Bhonsle Raja, it might be unreasonable to suspect that they meditate hostilities against the British government or its allies, from the recent assurances which they have given in writing to the Governor General. Nevertheless I must confess I do not wish to rely implicitly on their faith but would infinitely rather obtain some proof of their friendly disposition more unequivocal than professions and promises . . . I beg leave to request your opinion whether the friendly assurances which Sinde has lately pledged to his Excellency should be regarded as satisfactory, or whether you can suggest any other proof of their insincerity that would in your judgement be less equivocal . . .

PRC ix 313, Parl Pps [5, 22 June 1804] p. 500

161

Arthur Wellesley to Lieutenant-Colonel Close

Baungaum
10 July 1803

I return your letters. In my opinion Colonel Collins has not accounted in a satisfactory manner either for his own assertion that peace has been made between Sinde and Holkar or for that of his munshi that we should attack the latter. In this extraordinary despatch one of the most extraordinary parts is that he has given as proof of a peace between these chiefs that Sinde has made sacrifices of territory to Holkar, whereas that fact requires proof, as well as every other part of the letter . . .[28]

Grwd (1837) ii 77 (1844) i 546

162

Lieutenant-Colonel Close to Arthur Wellesley

Pune
10 July 1803

. . . When I reflect on the systematic course of deceit and treachery pursued by Daulat Rao Sinde from the period when he put his troops in motion in consequence of the defeat which his army sustained in this neighbourhood from Jaswant Rao Holkar, I cannot flatter myself that the pacific liberal and candid mode of proceeding, adopted and still persevered in by the Governor General, to impress Sinde with a just sense of his interest and dissuade him from his present adverse and arbitrary course, will be attended with the desired effect . . .

As you are now prepared and conveniently situated for eventually laying siege to Ahmednagar, you ought to dispatch a letter to Colonel Collins informing him of this circumstance and entreating him to apprise Sinde that if he advanced a single kos nearer to the Nizam's territory Colonel Stevenson will act on the offensive and his fort of Ahmednagar be immediately besieged, and that besides he must expect to be exposed to such other operations from the British government as circumstances may permit . . .

You ought further to fix a period at the lapse of which Sinde and Raghuji Bhonsle should be required to commence retiring towards their respective dominions. The length of this period should be regulated in reference to the present state of your preparations and projects . . .

PRC ix 314, Parl Pps [5, 22 June 1804] p. 502

163

Arthur Wellesley to Colonel Collins

11 July 1803 [received 15 July]

. . . I have seen your letter to the Governor General of the 6th. It occurs to me that Sinde and the Raja of Berar may be inclined to withdraw to their own capitals if they should be assured that we would withdraw likewise. I certainly propose to repass the Bhima myself and to order Colonel Stevenson to repass the Godavari as soon as I find those chiefs commence their march towards their own territories, and I shall break up the army in this quarter as soon as I shall be convinced that they no longer threaten the territories of the Peshwa or the Nizam, and are settled the one to the northward of the Narbada the other at Nagpur. I communicate to you these intentions in order that you may make such use of them as you may think proper.

SD iv 136

164

Arthur Wellesley to Colonel Stevenson

Sangwi
13 July 1803

. . . In respect to Mohipat Ram's[29] proposal that you should move nearer to the Ajanta ghat, I object to it on this ground that when you have once advanced you cannot retire again, and the negotiations to induce Sinde to withdraw may take much time and you may be distressed for forage in your advanced position. It is also my intention, if we should commence hostilities, to desire you to approach the ghat as near as you can with convenience in order to check Sinde in his endeavours to ascend it with his guns, and it will be necessary that you should have as much fresh forage in your power as possible at this time. I therefore think that on the whole it is best that you should not approach the ghat or move from your present position till you shall hear further from me . . .

Grwd (1837) ii 78 (1844) i 547

165

Arthur Wellesley to Daulat Rao Sinde

14 July 1803 [received on 21 July]

. . . Whatever respect I may have for your word, so solemnly pledged as it is in your letter to the Governor General . . . common prudence requires that I should not trust to that alone for the security of the Company and its allies, which has been given to my charge. Accordingly I call upon you if your professions are sincere to withdraw with your troops to their usual stations across the river Narbada. You were the first by your hostile measures and declarations and the expression of doubts of the duration of the peace between the Honourable Company and your government, and by the movements of your troops, to render necessary corresponding measures of precaution by the Company's government, and you ought to be the first to withdraw your troops, if your intentions are really as pacific as you profess them to be . . .

Grwd (1837) ii 88 (1844) i 554, Parl Pps [5, 22 June 1804] p. 194

166

Arthur Wellesley to Colonel Murray

14 July 1803

I have received a letter from Colonel Close from which I learn that a banjara has engaged to attend this body of troops with 5000 bullocks at monthly hire, that these bullocks are in the first instance to receive their loads at Panvel, and to proceed thence to join me. The loads which I should wish to receive are rice . . .

Grwd (1837) ii 85 (1844) i 551

167

Arthur Wellesley to Colonel Collins

14 July 1803 [received 20 July]

I have had the honour of receiving your letter of the 9th inst and I have taken into consideration the subject upon which you have desired that I should communicate to you my opinion.

Daulat Rao Sinde and the Raja of Berar have declared in their letters to the Governor General that they have no intention to obstruct the arrangement concluded at Bassein between the British Government and the Peshwa, and that they are desirous of maintaining the relations of amity which so long subsisted between the British Government and them, and that they will not ascend the Ajanta ghat or march towards Pune. I am sorry to observe however that they still intend to advance with their armies to the Ajanta ghat upon the Nizam's frontier notwithstanding their peaceable declarations . . .

If there had been no hostile declarations from Sinde and the Raja of Berar, common prudence would have prevented us from viewing with indifference the assembly of their armies upon the Nizam's frontier, and the British Government must have insisted upon their withdrawing. Pacific declarations would not in that case have been deemed sufficient security for the Nizam, nor can they in that at present under consideration particularly as I have pointed out the great advantages which those chiefs will derive from the delay to commence hostilities.

I am therefore decidedly of opinion that if the Raja of Berar does not withdraw to Nagpur, and if Sinde does not remove his armies to stations usually occupied by his troops north of the river

Narbada, their intentions must be considered hostile, and we ought to take advantage of our position to attack them without loss of time. Accordingly I have written a letter to Daulat Rao Sinde . . . If you should find that Daulat Rao Sinde and the Raja of Berar remain encamped in the neighbourhood of the Nizam's frontier, I request you to deliver that letter . . .

Grwd (1837) ii 82 (1844) i 549

168

Colonel Collins to Arthur Wellesley

16 July 1803

Last night I was favoured with your despatch of the 11th of this month. In the conference which I held with Sinde and the Berar Raja on the 4th inst they promised to give the Governor General assurances in writing of their intention never to oppose the completion of the engagements concluded at Bassein between the British government and His Highness the Peshwa. But as those chiefs were four days in consulting on the terms of their letters, I did not obtain a copy of the Bhonsle's letter until the 8th nor did I receive a transcript of Sinde's until the day following. These circumstances will account for any delay in replying to your favour of the 29th [June] which reached me on the night of the 3rd [July].

On the next day my interview with Sinde and the Berar Raja took place, when such concessions were made on their part as I conceived might justify a suspension of the measures which you have recommended me to pursue . . . I am ordered by the Governor General to consult with Colonel Close as well as with yourself . . . and it was in consequence of this order that I advanced those questions to Colonel Close in the conclusion of the fourth paragraph of my official despatch to the Colonel under date the 9th inst. I have been thus particular that you may not suppose me guilty of any unnecessary delay in replying to your friendly letter of the the 29th June as likewise to account for not having instantly adopted the measures therein advised.

By the direction of the Governor General[30] I have lately demanded an explanation from Sinde respecting certain orders which have been transmitted to the Bundelkhand chiefs from this durbar of a nature highly hostile towards the British government. I have also called on the Maharajah to state the objects of the detachment now serving under Dharran Rao Pundit on the northwestern frontier of the Company's territories. Should Sinde refuse to countermand the orders above referred to or decline to explain himself regarding the objects of Dharran Rao's detachment, I am in this event instructed to apprise the Maharajah 'that his refusal to comply with these just requisitions will place him in the condition of a public enemy to the British government and will compel the British government to commence immediate hostilities against him.' You will soon be informed of the result of my remonstrance on the foregoing points. At present Sinde seems disposed to evade giving any reply thereto, so that it is extremely probable that I may soon be obliged to leave this court.

I still continue very unwell.

WP 3/3/53 p. 88

169

Lieutenant-Colonel Close to Arthur Wellesley

16 July 1803
[summary]

Close sends 'with great pleasure a copy of a despatch to your address from the Governor General conveying to you the powers which in your present situation you require.' He has copied them to Stuart 'hinting that should he not have crossed the Tungabhandra when the packet comes to hand, it might be a matter of consideration with him whether he should not remain on this side of that river until he should hear from you . . .' Close adds 'I conclude that you will now make a vigorous effort to bring these chieftains to the field.'

WP 3/3/1

170

Arthur Wellesley to Amrit Rao

16 July 1803

I was in hopes that before this time I should have been enabled to communicate to you the final result of the repeated recommendation of your situation which I have made to the Peshwa, but hitherto His Highness has come to no decision in respect to your case.

I feel most sensibly the difficulties under which you labour and you must be convinced that I have done everything in my power to remove them. However although I cannot at present tell you that anything is absolutely settled for you with the Peshwa, you may depend upon it that the British Government will take care that you shall have such a provision as will be gratifying to you, provided you continue in the manner in which you have conducted yourself since you last wrote to me.

Gwrd (1837) ii 94 (1844) i 557

171

Arthur Wellesley to Lieutenant-Colonel Close

Sangwi
17 July 1803

. . . I have apprised Daulat Rao Sinde of my intention to take advantage of the position of the Company's troops to attack his possessions if he should advance one step towards the Nizam's frontier after the receipt of my letter, or if I found that he did not withdraw his troops to their usual stations north of the river Narbada. I have not fixed when he should withdraw, firstly because I wish to keep in my own breast the period at which hostilities will be commenced, by which advantage it becomes more probable that I shall strike the first blow, if I should find hostile operations to be necessary, [and] secondly [because] there is every prospect to expect instructions from the Governor General applicable to the present situation of affairs in India as well as in Europe . . .

Gwrd (1837) ii 96 (1844) i 559

172

Arthur Wellesley to Colonel Collins

17 July 1803 [received by 26 July]

. . . The only difference between the letter which I wrote to Sinde and that which Colonel Close proposed that I should write is, that I have not fixed a day on which Daulat Rao Sinde should depart. My reasons for preferring the mode which I have adopted are that it leaves me the choice of the day on which to commence my operations, supposing them to be necessary, it renders greater the probability that I shall strike the first blow, and it leaves matters open so far as that, if the Governor General should alter his plan I can alter my proceedings. On the other hand to fix a day for his [Daulat Rao Sinde's] departure has an appearance of harshness and hostility which is entirely inconsistent with the spirit of the Governor General's instructions. I mention these circumstance to you lest you should suppose that there is any difference of opinion between Colonel Close and me upon the main point.

SD iv 139

173

Colonel Collins to the Governor-General

Camp near Jalgaon
17 July 1803 [seen by Arthur Wellesley on 21 July]
[summary]

Reporting on a discussion with Sinde held on the 16th July, Collins first reported the denial by the durbar of any responsibility for the orders to the Bundelkhand chiefs to prepare to attack Company territory, about which he had been instructed to protest. Finding Sinde 'particularly complaisant' he renewed pressure urging the return of the Maharajah to Hindustan. He was assured that as soon as Sinde and the Berar Raja received 'favourable answers' to the letters which they had sent to the Governor General, they would 'repair to their respective countries.'

Collins felt that 'the disposition of this court had of late undergone a change so material as to afford reasonable grounds to hope that the intention of opposing the arrangement concluded at Bassein was altogether abandoned.'

PRC ix 337, Parl Pps [5, 22 June 1804] p. 508, WP 3/3/53 p. 92

174

Richard Wellesley to Arthur Wellesley

Fort William Calcutta
26 June 1803 [received 18 July]

The present state of affairs in the Maratha empire and the security of the alliance lately concluded between His Highness the Peshwa and the British Government require that a temporary authority should be constituted at the least possible distance from the scene of eventual negotiation or hostilities with full powers to conclude upon the spot whatever arrangements may be necessary either for the final settlement of peace or for the active prosecution of war. It is therefore necessary during the present crisis to unite the general direction and control of political and military affairs in Hindustan and the Deccan under a distinct local authority . . .

I hereby appoint you to the chief command of all the British troops and of the forces of our allies serving in the territories of the Peshwa of the Nizam and of any of the Maratha chiefs, subject only to the orders of His Excellency Lt General Stuart or of His Excellency General Lake. I further empower and direct you to assume and exercise the general direction and control of all the political and military affairs of the British Government in the territories of the Nizam the Peshwa and of the Maratha states and chiefs . . .

I authorise and empower you to commence and conclude negotiations with any of the Maratha chiefs and jagirdars on the part of the British Government for the purpose of promoting the general objects of the alliance lately concluded with His Highness the Peshwa or of that subsisting with His Highness the Nizam. This general authority especially empowers you either directly or through the representatives of the British Government to negotiate and conclude any engagements with Daulat Rao Sinde with the Raja of Berar or with Jaswant Rao Holkar which may induce those chieftains to retire with their forces within the limits of the respective dominions or to afford any other satisfactory pledge of their respective pacific intentions towards the British Government and its allies . . . It is my particular intention by these instructions to enable you to conclude such arrangements with any of those chieftains either separately or combined as may preclude or frustrate any confederacy or other measures directed to the subversion of the Treaty of Bassein or to the injury of our rights and interests or those of our allies . . .

Grwd (1837) ii 49, Martin iii 149, PRC ix 287, Parl Pps [5, 22 June 1804] p. 162

175

Richard Wellesley to Arthur Wellesley

Fort William Calcutta
27 June 1803 [received 18 July]

The conduct of Sinde and the Raja of Berar requires a special notification to you of my views and intentions with regard to the operations of your army and to such political proceedings as may be connected with a state of war between the British Government and those chiefs.

On receipt of this dispatch you will desire Colonel Collins to demand an explicit declaration of the views of Sinde and of the Raja of Berar within such a number of days as shall appear to you to be reasonable consistently with the due attention to the period of the season and to the facility of moving your army and of prosecuting hostilities with the advantages which you now possess. If that explanation should not be satisfactory on such grounds as in your discretion you may state to Colonel Collins you will desire Colonel Collins to repair to your camp under a proper escort.

In that event or in any other state of circumstances which may appear to you to require hostilities consistently with the general tenor of my instructions you will employ the forces under your command in the most active operations against Sinde or the Raja of Berar or against both according to your discretion . . .

The entire reduction of Sinde's power would certainly afford considerable security to our interest; in the event however of a peace with Sinde which should leave his power in existence among the states of India the most desirable arrangement would be [the following].

Firstly, Sinde should cede to the Company all his possessions rights and pretensions within the countries to the northward of a line drawn from the north frontier of Gohad to the frontier of Jainagar, together with all his possessions etc to the northward of Jainagar.

This cession would include Agra Delhi and the remainder of the Doab of the Jumna and the Ganges. The Mughal [Emperor's] person would necessarily fall under our protection. This article must be a special stipulation of the treaty.

Our frontier towards the ceded provinces of Oudh would then be formed by the small state of Gohad and by the Rajput states of Jainagar and Jodhpur. The Rana of Gohad to become tributary to the Company: Gwalior to be occupied by the Company. Defensive alliances to be formed with Jainagar and Jodhpur.

By this arrangement the Marathas would be excluded from the north of Hindustan and from communication with the Sikhs.

Secondly, Sinde to cede Broach and all his maritime possessions.

Thirdly, Sinde to cede all his possessions rights etc in Gujerat.

Fourthly, Sinde to cede all his possessions etc southwards of the Narbada . . .

From the Raja of Berar I would wish to acquire the whole province of Cuttack so as to unite the Northern Circars by a continued line of sea coast with Bengal . . . The district of Gurry Mundelah has been an object to the Nizam. This object to be pursued according to circumstances in the event of war with the Raja of Berar . . .

The precise time of action from Oudh and in Cuttack cannot now be stated, but I will seize Agra Delhi, take the person of the Mughal [Emperor] under British protection, and occupy the Doab together with Cuttack at the earliest practicable moment after I shall have learnt that you deem hostilities inevitable, or as soon as such measures of precaution may appear to me to be requisite . . .[31]

Grwd (1837) ii 53, Martin iii 153, PRC ix 291, Parl Pps [5, 22 June 1804] p. 164

176

Arthur Wellesley to Colonel Collins

near Sangwi
18 July 1803 [received 24 July]

. . . His Excellency has been pleased to entrust to me extraordinary powers for the purpose of concluding whatever arrangements may become necessary either for the final settlement of peace or for the active prosecution of war. I request you to be so kind as to communicate this circumstance to Daulat Rao Sinde and the Raja of Berar. You will be so kind at the same time to inform those chiefs that consistently with the principles and uniform practice of the British government, I am perfectly ready to attend to their interests and to enter into negotiations with them . . . But they must first withdraw from the position which they have taken up upon the Nizam's frontier and return to their usual stations in Hindustan and Berar respectively . . .

. . . If you should find those chiefs obstinately determined to remain in their positions upon the Nizam's frontier you will be so good as to inform them that I have requested you to withdraw from the camp of Daulat Rao Sinde and accordingly you will leave it on the following day . . .

I have reports from hircarrahs that two brigades of Sinde's with guns are at the Ajanta ghat at this moment, and that Gopal Bhau's detachment of cavalry are above the ghat, but the latter have received orders to retire which they appear disinclined to obey. Before you quit Sinde's camp it would be very desirable that you should endeavour to ascertain the general position of his troops and the numbers and description in each station, and by whom commanded . . . I request you also to endeavour to ascertain the same circumstances respecting the troops of the Raja of Berar . . .

Grwd (1837) ii 99 (1844) i 561, PRC ix 340

177

Arthur Wellesley to Lieutenant-Colonel Close

18 July 1803

. . . This day I have written to Collins to desire him to withdraw if he cannot prevail upon Sinde and the Raja of Berar to move away. I have also desired Colonel Stevenson to move forward if he finds that Colonel Collins comes away, and to watch the ghats so as to attack Sinde with advantage if he should attempt to pass through them. I have written most fully to General Stuart upon the subject of his crossing the Toombuddra [Tungabhandra].[32] He is of opinion that he ought to adopt that measure, but whether he will adopt it or not depends upon the orders he will receive from Madras . . .

Grwd (1837) ii 101 (1844) i 563

178

Arthur Wellesley to Colonel Stevenson

18 July 1803

. . . If you should receive notice from Colonel Collins that he has withdrawn from Sinde's camp, you will be so kind as immediately to take up a position as near to the Ajanta ghat which leads into the Nizam's territories as the conveniences of water and forage will permit. From this position you will watch with vigilance the designs and movements of Daulat Rao Sinde and the Raja of Berar. If you should find that those chiefs attempt to ascend that or any other ghat you will fall upon them immediately before they shall have time to deploy their forces above the ghat.

I do not however propose that your troops should descend the ghat but only that they should attack that part of the enemy which shall ascend. It is possible that they may leave the Ajanta ghat and endeavour to penetrate by the Cassabari ghat towards Aurungabad. You will in that case move towards the latter and place yourself in such manner as to attack them with advantage if they attempt to pass there . . .

Grwd (1837) ii 102 (1844) i 563

179

Arthur Wellesley to Jonathan Duncan

18 July 1803 [received 23 July]

. . . The troops serving in the territories of the Gaikwar are included among those placed under my command, and I shall be obliged to you if . . . I may receive from Bombay returns of the strength and state of the equipment of those forces, their present distribution and the names of the officers who command them. I am also desirous of having a sketch of the territories of the Gaikwar which it is intended that the troops should defend, and any topographical account of the country from which I may be able to form a judgement respecting its great communications, as well with the seacoast as with the territories of the Holkar family, of Sinde etc and with those lately ceded to the Company by the Peshwa . . .

Grwd (1837) ii 104 (1844) i 564, Parl Pps [5, 22 June 1804] p. 505

180

Colonel Murray to Arthur Wellesley

Pune
18 July 1803

The arrack which you have ordered in your letter of the 16th shall be sent off tomorrow. I understand you have left Peepulgaum and I do not know exactly where to direct the bullock drivers to go. The coolies which were sent with the gunny bags made a demand of an increase as the distance was greater, of which I could not judge. Those bullocks will be directed to go to the ferry at Serroor. The officer there will direct them how to proceed . . .

WP 3/3/79 p. 91

181

Colonel Murray to Arthur Wellesley

Pune
20 July 1803

. . . This morning we put together three of the pontoons. Everything seems to answer very well except the carriages. There are now thirty above the ghats including the four here. These thirty will make a bridge 200 yards long. One great defect of the carriages is the slightness of the pole and another is the weakness of the bolt which fastens the two parts of the carriage together. Would you wish us to prepare some spare poles and bolts which at the same time might be made stronger . . .

WP 3/3/79 p. 94

182

Colonel Collins to Arthur Wellesley

near Jalgaon
20 July 1803
[summary]

Collins had just received the letter to him from Arthur Wellesley of 14 July and that to Daulat Rao Sinde. Jadu Rao Bhau had just appointed the afternoon of 21 July for a meeting with Collins' munshi. He decided not to await this, but report to Arthur Wellesley at once the arrival of his letters.

Grwd (1837) ii 107 (1844) i 581, PRC ix 343, Parl Pps [5, 22 June 1804] p. 509

183

Lieutenant-General Stuart to Arthur Wellesley

South bank of the Tungabhandra
20 July 1803 [received by 30 July]

Lord Clive in a despatch of the 15th inst has suggested to me the necessity of reinforcing the troops in advance, in order to enable you to secure more effectually the objects of your general measures, and the necessity of removing the remaining part of this army into the Carnatic . . . Lt Col Close in a letter to Mr Webbe of the 3rd [July] mentions a reinforcement of two native battalions as necessary to the full accomplishment of your plans . . .

I have therefore determined to add two native battalions to the amount of your force and with this view I request you will detain the 1st battalion of the 10th under Major Dallas and I shall detach to you the day after tomorrow the 1st battalion of the 4th regiment commanded by Major Hill. I shall forward to you under escort of that corps 2½ lahks of pagodas in gold and as many banjara and hired cattle as can be sent.

Should the whole of the remaining part of this army return to the Carnatic, the Ceded Districts from the weakness of the force left in them would be exposed to internal commotions, our frontier would be deprived of all protection, no check would remain upon the conduct of the southern jagirdars and the Nizam's subjects and the communication with your force would be liable to interruption.

To prevent these consequences I have recommended to Lord Clive that a detachment composed of 1 regiment of native cavalry 5 companies of European infantry 2 battalions of sepoys and a proportion of artillery should be left by this army on the frontier. I have proposed that the above detachment should occupy a position in the neighbourhood of Mudghal where its position will be equally favourable to the protection of Mysore and the Ceded Districts and to the preservation of order amongst the southern jagirdars and the Nizam's subjects. The detachment can eventually proceed to join you, or to the Carnatic, as the emergency of public affairs may require . . .

PRC ix 344 WP 3/3/87 p. 329

184

Arthur Wellesley to Colonel Collins

21 July 1803 [received 26 July]

I have just perused the copy of your despatch to the Governor General[33] enclosed in your letter of the 18th to Colonel Close the contents of which have given me the greatest satisfaction. If there be any truth in a Maratha durbar we shall now have peace.

I consider my letter to Daulat Rao Sinde a complete answer to that which he wrote to the Governor General, and when he will have been informed that the Governor General has trusted to me extraordinary powers to settle all these questions, he will probably be of the same opinion and will be satisfied with it.

I now enclose one to the Raja of Berar to a similar purport which I request you to deliver to that chief, and I beg you to apprise him at the same time of the powers given to me by the Governor General, and that I cannot wait to commence my operations for any further letters or orders from his Excellency.

SD iv 143

185

Colonel Collins to Arthur Wellesley

near Jalgaon
21 July 1803
[summary]

Collins reports that he received, late on 20th July, his copies of the letters from the Governor-General giving Arthur Wellesley extensive delegated authority. He reports on a discussion with Jadu Rao Bhau on the letter from Arthur Wellesley to Daulat Rao Sinde. Jadu Rao Bhau was warned that 'in the event either of evasion or of procrastination in the present instance the British troops would enter upon action without further delay.' Jadu Rao explained the letter to Sinde and proposed to visit the Raja of Berar. Collins' munshi was sent to give a similar message to the Raja of Berar. Collins reported that 'the late change in the language of the ministers of the Maharajah induces me to hope that your requisition will be shortly complied with.'

Grwd (1837) ii 110 (1844) i 581, PRC ix 346, Parl Pps [5, 22 June 1804] p. 512

186

Lieutenant-General Stuart to Arthur Wellesley

22 July 1803

Major Hill's battalion crossed the river and marched this morning to join you, giving escort to 3,200 hired bullocks carrying 1,000 loads of rice and two and a half lakhs of pagodas and to nearly 1,000 banjara bullocks also loaded with rice. The Major will proceed to the Kalachabootra ghat and Parenda from whence he will direct his movement according to your orders. The hired cattle are placed under the care of a European officer of the 4th who is to be allowed a pagoda a day while so employed, and I have promised the owners a gratuity of a pagoda a day for each bullock that they shall produce in your camp at muster in good order and fit for immediate service, the same as was promised to the owners of the other bullocks previously sent to you, which I request you will order to be paid accordingly. The banjaras are likewise sent on the same terms with the former, namely to sell their rice at five seers a rupee without reference to the price of rice in your camp at the time that they may deliver it to you . . .

I have received no despatches from Lord Clive since I wrote to you on the 20th [July] and I am now making preparations to carry into effect the arrangement communicated in my letter of that date . . .

WP 3/3/87 p. 241

187

Colonel Collins to Arthur Wellesley

near Jalgaon
22 July 1803
[summary]

Collins' munshi had returned and reported that the Raja of Berar was not well disposed towards the request made by Arthur Wellesley. Raghuji Bhonsle sought assurances from Peshwa Baji Rao similar to those given by Arthur Wellesley. There had been a conference between Sinde and Berar lasting several hours on 21 July. Since Collins did not feel free to leave Sinde's court without specific authority from Arthur Wellesley, he asked for guidance on his course of action if Sinde or Berar refused to separate and retire.

Grwd (1837) ii 113 (1844) i 582, PRC ix 348, Parl Pps [5, 22 June 1804] p. 512

188

Jonathan Duncan to Arthur Wellesley

Bombay
23 July 1803
[summary]

Duncan responded to Arthur Wellesley's letter of 18th July, by forwarding returns of the troops at Bombay, Surat, and in Gaikwar territory. He noted that the fortress of Baroda was capable of successfully sustaining a siege, that the Attavesi territory near Surat was safeguarded by troops commanded by a Commission, including a military officer, and that a force under Lieutenant-Colonel Woodington was ready to attempt the reduction of Broach. He forwarded a sketch of the Gaikwar's territories, and reported that the Commission at Surat and Major Walker, the Resident at Baroda, had been instructed to correspond with Arthur Wellesley.

Parl Pps [5, 22 June 1804] p. 506

189

Lieutenant-General Stuart to Arthur Wellesley

on the banks of the Noogorcy
23 July 1803

. . . I enclose an invoice of the treasure sent under the escort of the 1st of the 4th. That corps, with its convoy, were all across the river yesterday evening, and proceeds on its march towards the Kalachabootra ghat this day, if not prevented by the weather; it has rained hard all day. Amongst our banjaras present with this army, 3,000 [in number] we have been able to select bullocks to carry 900 loads of rice that are in a condition to perform the journey to your camp. Lt Griffiths with his convoy are now crossing the Kistna and as he was plentifully supplied with forage on his march and as I have directed him to employ expert [drivers?] to assist in getting the bullocks across the river, I am hopeful that he will not have many casualties on reaching the northern bank.

Major Dallas is proceeding on his march towards you.

WP 3/3/87 p. 243

190

Arthur Wellesley to Richard Wellesley

Sangwi
24 July 1803
[summary]

Arthur Wellesley reviewed the relations with Sinde and Berar, believing (on the basis of the letter from Collins to Richard Wellesley of 18 July) that there had been 'a change of counsel' in the durbar. He then detailed 'the weak and confused state of the Peshwa's government' and the 'wavering disposition of the southern chiefs.' Other difficulties which his detachment faced included the rebellion in the Gaikwar's territories, and the probability of disturbance in the Hyderabad territories following the anticipated death of the Nizam. Arthur Wellesley explained the action which he had taken, despite the opposition of Peshwa Baji Rao, to preserve his relationship with Amrit Rao. He reported that he had attempted to open a negotiation with Jaswant Rao Holkar (destined not to reach him) sending Holkar a copy of the Treaty of Bassein and assuring him of the peaceful intentions of the Company towards him.

Grwd (1837) ii 120 (1844) i 572, Parl Pps [5, 22 June 1804] p. 510

191

Colonel Collins to Arthur Wellesley

Jalgaon
24 July 1803 [received by 29 July]
[summary]

Collins recorded that he had sent a memorandum to Sinde and Raghuji Bhonsle almost exactly in the words of Arthur Wellesley, and awaited a reply. He intended to leave camp if the Maratha chiefs appeared determined to retain their present positions. The troops seen by hircarrahs sent by Arthur Wellesley in the Ajanta ghat were those of Berar Raja; they had since been withdrawn. The brigade sent north to Hindustan consisted of seven battalions of infantry and 500 cavalry; Sinde had eleven battalions of infantry with him.

Grwd (1837) ii 132 (1844) i 584, PRC ix 350, Parl Pps [5, 22 June 1804] p. 514

192

Colonel Collins to Arthur Wellesley

Jalgaon
25 July 1803 [received by 29 July]
[summary]

Collins' munshi had held a long conference with Jadu Rao Bhau and had formed the impression that Jadu Rao felt it would be advisable for Sinde to withdraw. Collins sent Arthur Wellesley a listing of Sinde and Berar forces.

Grwd (1837) ii 135 (1844) i 585, PRC ix 353, Parl Pps [5, 22 June 1804] p. 515

193

Statement of the force now at Jalgaon

Sinde
25 July 1803

Under the command of Colonel Pohlman; 500 Hindustani horse, 7 sepoy battalions, 500 matchlock men, 8 heavy guns and 4 field pieces.

Under the command of Colonel Saleur and in the pay of the Begum Sumru; 4 sepoy battalions, 2 heavy guns and 30 field pieces

Under different native sirdars; 12,000 Hindustani horse and 2,000 Deccani horse

Under the command of Bapoji Sindhia 4,000 Hindustani horse

Park of artillery; 25 heavy guns and 100 field pieces

Each sepoy battalion is nearly 700 rank and file.

Raja of Berar

Under the command of different native sirdars 20,000 Hindustani horse

Under the command of Beni Singh 6,000 infantry and 35 field pieces

500 camels carrying rockets and 500 carrying shutarnals

Disposition of the above forces: the Maharajah with the whole of his cavalry is encamped to the north of the range of hills called the Ajanta ghat, ten kos from the pass of Phardapur and from that of Ajanta, which is impassable for guns. On the right of the Maharajah at a distance of two kos Colonel Pohlman is posted with his brigade; about a kos to the rear of Colonel Pohlman, Colonel Saleur is posted with the corps of Begum Sumru. Gopal Bhau having been left in the Deccan by the Maharajah on his return to Hindustan in the year 1801, and the strength of his detachment having at different times varied according to circumstances, the exact number of his troops cannot be ascertained. It is however certain that he has been repeatedly and positively ordered to join the Maharajah.

The Raja of Berar is encamped two kos to the left of the Maharajah with the whole of his artillery cavalry and infantry. Colonel Shepherd with the whole of the regular infantry of Ambaji Rao has already crossed the Narbada [to the north].

Colonel Dudrenec and Major Brownrigg with battalions of sepoys and a large part of artillery marched from Jalgaon towards the Narbada on the 18th instant.

Grwd (1837) ii 135 (1844) i 586, PRC ix 354, Parl Pps [5, 22 June 1804] p. 516, WP 3/3/53 p. 125

194

Lieutenant-General Stuart to Arthur Wellesley

18 miles from Adoni
25 July 1803

I have had the honour to receive your despatch dated the 15th inst. I entirely concur in your opinion and Colonel Close's, regarding the designs of Sinde and I consider your letter to that chieftain to be highly seasonable and proper. If Sinde permits hostilities to occur, it will be plain that his intentions all along have been hostile, and by commencing the war at this period, we will possess the advantages of acting against him before his plans have been matured, and while his operations are confined by the rivers. If hostilities occur, it will however be unfortunate that they have taken place at a crisis when the probable arrival of a large French armament may be expected to require a considerable disposable force to oppose their designs.

I have written to Piele [at Seringapatam] to send you the lakh of pagodas which you have mentioned. It appears to me that the safest mode of forwarding it will be to send it by a party of Mysore horse and on the road by which Major Hill's corps is advancing. The Mysore horse can overtake that corps before it is able to leave the north bank of the Kistna and can accompany it to your camp . . .

I separated this morning from Major General Campbell's division and marched eight miles towards Adoni. He marches from his present ground in the morning and encamps on the south bank of the river close to the ferry, so as to be in readiness to cross and resume the station I lately occupied in the neighbourhood of

Mudghal. One of his battalions, the 12th, is now on the north bank of the river; it never crossed to this side.

I have sent with Major Hill's corps a brigade of six pounders mounted on galloper carriages, as you may probably wish to have them to employ as disposable guns.

WP 3/3/87 p. 246

195

Arthur Wellesley to Major Walker[34]

26 July 1803

From the tenor of letters which I have this day received from Colonel Collins, it is probable that that officer will have departed from the camp of Daulat Rao Sinde by this time, and if that be the case, I propose to commence hostilities against that chief and the Raja of Berar immediately.

From papers received from the Government of Bombay I understand that you have directed that preparations should be made in Gujerat for the attack of Broach. I request you to urge forward these preparations as much as possible, and to desire the officer in command of the troops to be in such a state and position as to be able to make the attack upon Broach as soon as I shall send him notice that I have commenced hostilities in this quarter.

Grwd (1837) ii 135 (1844) i 580, Parl Pps [5, 22 June 1804] p. 513

196

Colonel Collins to Arthur Wellesley

26 July 1803 [received 31 July]
[summary]

In an interview on 25th July with Daulat Rao Sinde, in which Collins had advised Sinde to give the satisfaction that Arthur Wellesley was seeking, Jadu Rao Bhau had replied that the Maratha chiefs were within their own territory, had promised not to march to Pune, that they needed reassurance from Peshwa Baji Rao, and that their negotiations with Jaswant Rao Holkar were not completed. Collins had replied that their position was one threatening to the Company, that they could send vakils to Pune after they had withdrawn, and that it would be easier for them to negotiate with Holkar from further north. Jadu Rao Bhau had asked for time to reply, and Collins had finally agreed to await a reply on 28th July.

Grwd (1837) ii 137 (1844) i 587, PRC ix 356, Parl Pps [5, 22 June 1804] p. 517

197

Colonel Collins to Arthur Wellesley

near Jalgaon
26 July 1803

I have to acknowledge and thank you for your private letters of the 17th 19th and 21st inst.

I concur entirely with you that if there be truth in a Maratha court we shall now have peace. To confess my real sentiment I have not a doubt but that Sinde and his confidential minister Jadu Rao would willingly retire from the Nizam's frontier although I do not believe that the Maharajah could at present be prevailed upon to recross the Narbada.

However, as the greater part of his infantry has been detailed to Hindustan and as Suddasheo if not Ambaji Inglia also will shortly repair thither with a detachment of cavalry, I do not conceive any danger could be apprehended from Sinde's continuance in the Deccan, provided the Bhonsle will return to Nagpur. But on this last head I am rather doubtful having some notion that Raghuji had entertained a latent hope of being elevated to the masnad. However he must now see the folly of attempting to dethrone Baji Rao if he ever indulged such an idea, of which I have no proof . . .

WP 3/3/53 p. 130

198

Arthur Wellesley to Colonel Collins

Sangwi
29 July 1803 [received 3 August]
[summary]

In response to the letters from Collins of the 24th and 25th July, Arthur Wellesley noted that he was relieved that Jadu Rao appreciated the potential consequences of the dispute. Since Daulat Rao Sinde was probably concerned at the disgrace of withdrawal, Arthur Wellesley feared that he might promise to withdraw and not do so. In that event Collins was to write that he could trust the Maratha chiefs no longer and that if Sinde and Berar did not separate the following day he would start operations. Arthur Wellesley outlined the prospective operations against Broach and Ganjam, and firmly instructed Collins to withdraw from Sinde's camp.

Grwd (1837) ii 137 (1844) i 582, PRC ix 371, Parl Pps [5, 22 June 1804] p. 516

199

Arthur Wellesley to Colonel Murray

30 July 1803

Upon the whole I think that it will be as well to send down coolies from Pune and bring up a supply of rice from Panvel, if Captain Young has it not in his power to send you one. The Mysore banjaras will I dare say take 1200 bullock bags, and 600 lately ordered to camp will reduce your stock very much.

I have no fear of the forts between Pune and Panvel, and Angria will I think be as quiet as the others, if we are tolerably successful at first. Much depends on the first blow. I have no intention to keep the howitzers or the 12 pounders.

General Campbell has taken up a position with a corps in the doab of the Kistna and the Tungabhandra which relieves me from all anxiety respecting my rear and your position at Pune. I should now wish therefore to secure the boats upon the Godavari rather better than they are secured at present, by sending forward a battalion to that river. But I cannot venture to do that till I am joined by a battalion from Pune.

I wish therefore that you would order forward the 2nd battalion of the 3rd. They shall return to you with the ordnance and artillery as soon as the siege of Ahmednagar is concluded. Captain Campbell shall return after tomorrow's march with the Bombay company.

Grwd (1837) ii 149 (1844) i 599

200

Colonel Collins to Arthur Wellesley

Jalgaon
30 July 1803 [received 3 August]
[summary]

Collins reported an interview with Sinde held on 29th July. Familiar arguments were repeated and he again received the reply that further consultation with the Raja of Berar was necessary. Collins finally said it was evident that the sole objective of Sinde was to gain time, and that he was under orders to leave as soon as it was clear that the Maratha chiefs did not mean to withdraw.

Gwrd (1837) ii 151 (1844) i 588, PRC ix 373, Parl Pps [5, 22 June 1804] p. 520

201

Arthur Wellesley to Lieutenant-General Stuart

30 July 1803

I have to acknowledge the receipt of your letters of the 16th 18th and 20th.

. . . I have certainly recovered much in point of means of moving, and I have not received any very great injury from the late rains. When the cattle which you have sent shall reach me I shall be well supplied. I have besides some hopes founded however upon promises that I shall be able to bring forward the services of a large number of the Pune banjaras . . . I am infinitely obliged to you for the further reinforcement and supply which you state in your letter of the 20th you intended to send me. This makes me quite easy respecting the enemy in our front, and the position of General Campbell's division secures my communication with and the tranquillity of the countries in my rear . . .

Grwd (1837) ii 146 (1844) i 597

202

Arthur Wellesley to Colonel Collins

Rooie on the Seenah
31 July 1803

I have had the honour of receiving your letter of the 26th inst. I am concerned that there should have been any fresh delay on the part of Daulat Rao Sinde to engage to depart with his troops to their usual stations beyond the Narbada and particularly that the ministers of that chief should have given such futile reasons for refusing to comply with my requisition that Daulat Rao Sinde should retire . . .

In respect to the treaty between Sinde and Holkar notwithstanding the boasted union it now appears that the peace is not yet concluded. But that can be no reason why Sinde and the Raja of Berar should be allowed to remain encamped in a position in the neighbourhood of the Nizam's frontier. On the contrary it ought to be a reason for which Sinde at least should be induced to move with his troops into those territories which he ought to guard against Holkar's depredations. These futile reasons for remaining with their troops in their position on the Nizam's frontier are the strongest proofs of the insincerity of the declarations which the chiefs have made, and I hope that if they should not have satisfied you in your interview you would have withdrawn from their camp, according to the request conveyed in my letter of the 18th inst.

But in case you should still be in their camp when this letter shall arrive, I repeat the request made in my letter of the 29th that you should withdraw forthwith, if they should not commence their march with all their troops towards their usual stations. The fact that Sinde has not concluded his peace with Jaswant Rao Holkar, which is now acknowledged, is the strongest reason for pressing forward at the present moment the decision whether there should be peace with security, or war. Besides it is in conformity with the instructions from the Governor General.

Gwrd (1837) ii 149 (1844) i 600, Parl Pps [5, 22 June 1804] p. 518

203

Colonel Collins to Arthur Wellesley

Camp near Jalgaon
1 August 1803 [received 5 August]
[summary]

Collins having been detained by heavy rain throughout 31 July, the Maratha chiefs pressed for a further interview, and to this Collins agreed. In a full durbar discussion with both Sinde and Berar, three propositions of timed withdrawals on both sides were put to Collins, who agreed to transmit the third of these to Arthur Wellesley provided he was promptly given it in writing. He was again delayed by monsoon rains and when the letter from Bhonsle was received, it proved to be in different terms from those agreed. Collins' response was to determine to leave as soon as the roads were passable.

Grwd (1837) ii 155n (1844) ii 591n, PRC ix 379, Parl Pps [5, 22 June 1804] p. 522

204

Arthur Wellesley to Lieutenant-Colonel Close

Walki
1 August 1803 [received 3 August]

I enclose a paper which I received yesterday from Colonel Stevenson. It is the copy of a letter written to Salabat Khan by an agent of his in the Bhonsle's camp . . . The enclosed paper . . . contains intelligence that the Peshwa is treating with the enemy. I should pass unnnoticed this intelligence, if I had not observed that Salabat Khan's correspondent in Raghuji Bhonsle's camp is far more intelligent than the general run of these news writers, and I know that he writes accounts of almost everything that passes in the durbar of that chief.

But whether the intelligence is true or false, it is very certain that we have not the smallest knowledge of the nature or the objects of the communications passing between the Peshwa and Sinde, or the Raja of Berar, notwithstanding the obvious necessity that we should have that knowledge, as well as the stipulations of the treaty which provide for it . . .

I most earnestly request you to adopt all means in your power to find out what passes in the Peshwa's durbar, and particularly the nature and objects of his communications with Sinde and the Raja of Berar. If representations founded on the treaty will not produce the effect of disclosing what we must know, let other means be adopted. Let expense be incurred to gain the necessary intelligence . . .

I am aware that although you may make a friend of Raghunath Rao and even of Suddasheo Munkaiseer, you will not be able to guide the Peshwa's councils, because in fact he is guided by nothing excepting his own caprice and resentment. But you will have intelligence of what is passing in the durbar on which we can rely, instead of groping in the dark as we do at present. If the Peshwa should be really carrying on a correspondence with Sinde in breach of the treaty, we may in this manner have it in our power to lay hold of it, and thus have a ground for making a solid arrangement of the Pune government . . .

Grwd (1837) ii 159 (1844) i 602

205

Arthur Wellesley to Jonathan Duncan

Walki
2 August 1803
[summary]

Arthur Wellesley set out his recommendations on the defence of Gujerat and of the districts depending upon Surat. He listed the total forces available, 2,900 Europeans and 4,400 sepoys and gun lascars. He noted that 'the districts depending upon Surat can be entered by an army from the eastward only by the road which leads by Songarh,' that 'there is no passage for an army . . . through the Satpura hills between the rivers Tapti and Narbada, except by skirting the province of Malwa' and that 'the country is open north of the river Narbada.'

Since 'the armies which may invade Gujerat and the districts depending upon Surat can penetrate either from the northward of the Narbada or the southward of the Tapti by Songarh only' Arthur Wellesley suggested that given a single commander and the scale of the forces available to Daulat Rao Sinde 'the Chief most likely to invade those territories' it should be possible so to move the Company force as to protect both approaches.

He then listed recommended garrisons for a series of posts, including Surat and Baroda, and recommended that a series of small detachments should be called in, and replaced by sebundi forces. This left for 'service in the field' a body of artillery, the 65th and 86th Regiments and four sepoy battalions. These he suggested should be deployed in two detachments, one north of the Narbada and in front of Baroda, and the other south of the Tapti between Surat and Songarh.

Locations were recommended for a series of formed magazines. It was also proposed that commanding officers should have sufficient carriage for one month's provisions. Colonel Murray, who was recommended for command in the Gujerat and Attavesi, should be 'desired to attend to the requisition of the Resident at Baroda and of the civil authority of Surat.' An attempt should be made to conciliate the Bheels while avoiding both involvement in their affairs and attempts to collect 'tribute'.

Grwd (1837) ii 166 (1844) i 607, PRC ix 385, Parl Pps [5, 22 June 1804] p. 525

206

Arthur Wellesley to Colonel Murray

Walki
2 August 1803

I have received your letter of the 31st. The rice is not yet come in, but if we should find it damaged we must call for an additional quantity. In the meantime however I requested you in my letter of the 24th of July to take measures to keep the depot at Pune full . . .

Grwd (1837) ii 164 (1837) i 606

207

Lieutenant-Colonel Close to Arthur Wellesley

Pune
3 August 1803

. . . I have long felt great uneasiness at the failure of my endeavours to procure from this durbar satisfactory information or documents relative to the intercourse which is carried on between the Peshwa on our side and Daulat Rao Sinde and Raghuji Bhonsle on the other.

On one occasion when Major Malcolm was present I pressed Raghunath Rao on this point with great earnestness and the only answer I could obtain from him was that the Peshwa for a considerable time past had not heard from Sinde's camp. On more recent occasions when I urged Raghunath Rao on the same subject and on the propriety of the Peshwa's renouncing Balaji Kunjar, he has told me that the Peshwa holds no communication with Balaji Kunjar who has long since ceased to correspond with the durbar but that to restrict the operations of this person was the sole object of the late mission of Kistnaji Bowanni.

On pressing Raghunath Rao to inform me of the opinion of the Peshwa and the principal persons of the durbar relative to the designs of the northern chiefs in adopting the evasive conduct which they have so long pursued, I have always been told by him that the Peshwa and his servants had but one opinion on the subject which was that Sinde and Raghuji Bhonsle had it in view only to spin out the present season and to intimidate the British government into a compliance with their demands relative to the Treaty of Bassein, but that these chieftains however menacing their conduct would in the end refrain from war.

The obstinate indisposition of this durbar to declare the particulars of its intercourse with the northern chiefs is of itself but too strong a ground of suspicion against its good faith and the purity of its intentions. But to this may be added the extraordinary circumstance of the Peshwa or any of his servants having never manifested the least indignation at Raghuji Bhonsle's having laid claim to the Peshwa's masnad, or at this chieftain and Sinde having set Kashi Rao Holkar aside in order to make room for Jaswant Rao Holkar against whom his Highness has ever declared the most rooted enmity . . .

WP 3/3/45, A Mss 13,599 f. 21

208

Colonel Collins to Arthur Wellesley

near Tondapur
3 August 1803 [received 6 August]

I have the honour to acknowledge the receipt of your letter under date the 29th ult and to apprise you of my having left the camp of Daulat Rao Sinde . . .

Although the weather began to clear up yesterday at noon and no rain fell during the night yet I found the road to this place exceedingly deep. It is now one o'clock in the afternoon and my escort is not yet arrived although it marched at half past four this morning.

I purpose ascending the Phardapur ghat tomorrow and proceeding as far as the town of Ajanta provided the gun bullocks are in a condition to perform the journey. I have apprised Colonel Stevenson that I should this day leave the camp of Daulat Rao Sinde on consequence of his refusal to retire from his present position and of my intention to prosecute my march to Aurungabad with all practicable expedition . . .

Grwd (1837) ii 184 (1844) i 620, PRC ix 400

209

Colonel Collins to Arthur Wellesley

Camp near Nizamabad
4 August 1803

I have the honour to acknowledge the receipt of your letter of the 31st [July] and to apprise you of my arrival at Nizamabad, a walled town appertaining to his highness the Nizam and situated three miles south of the Ajanta ghat.

It will not be possible for me to proceed on my journey towards Aurungabad until the 6th instant, as the escort and all my baggage are still in the pass, and cannot reach this ground before one or two o'clock tomorrow morning. It has rained incessantly and most violently from sunrise till sunset today, which unlucky event has tended greatly to retard the march of my detachment. It was half past four o'clock when the escort marched from Tondapur this morning.

PRC x 117

210

Colonel Stevenson to Arthur Wellesley

4 August 1803

I find the banjara tribe very difficult to manage either by argument or interest; they are defiant to force. The only prevailing argument is a favourable nuzzar and I find that I must submit to their terms or continue stationary. My treasury is now very low and I am under the necessity of borrowing a lakh of rupees from Rajah Sukhruder and Mohipat Ram in order to settle the accounts of the banjaras and take off their remaining stock, which is principally chinna, at the rate of five seers to the rupee. I shall receive sufficient for two month's supply for the 3rd and 6th regiments native cavalry and deposit what cannot be carried in Aurungabad from which it can most likely be easily withdrawn for some time to come.

I delayed the payment of my troops this last month until the 20th as I had no other expectation of a supply of money except the lakh of rupees coming forward with your treasure and the three lakhs of rupees that the Resident at Hyderabad promised to despatch about the 28th July. I cannot reasonably expect arrival of this supply till after the 20th of the present month. I have no doubt however that your treasure will arrive in time enough to assuage the wants of the troops and do not foresee any material circumstance that is likely to impede my forward movements. The only difficult part is to bring the banjaras to a point about carrying, but that for the present is settled and they have signed agreements to carry a month's grain . . . As they will receive advances for further supplies of the common grains, they may be expected to return with them before my present supply is consumed.

The rains are incessant but not very heavy and will not prevent me from moving ground on the 6th so as to take a direction on the Ajanta road. On the 7th I may march three or four miles further. Perhaps I may halt on the 8th, by which time I hope to receive further instructions from you. But in the event of not receiving any particular orders, I shall march forwards on the 9th as far as the weather and other circumstances will allow. The 2nd of the 9th has been advanced with their guns some days past about fifteen miles on the Ajanta road, for the protection of the public bullocks that were sent there as the best place for forage, and the pioneers have repaired the only bad [portion of] road betwixt Aurungabad and Ajanta, which is at a point where the battalion is stationed. The public bullocks and pioneers return to camp tomorrow, but the battalion and guns will remain there until joined by the horse.

WP 3/3/84 p. 364

211

Arthur Wellesley to Daulat Rao Sinde

[Walki]
6 August 1803

I have received your letter . . . You will recollect that the British government did not threaten to commence hostilities against you, but you threatened to commence hostilities against the British government and its allies. When called upon to explain your intentions, you declared that it was doubtful whether there would be peace or war, and in conformity to your threats and your declared doubts, you assembled a large army in a station contiguous to the Nizam's frontier.

On this ground, I called upon you to withdraw that army to its usual stations, if your subsequent pacific declarations were sincere. But instead of complying with this reasonable requisition, you have proposed that I should withdraw the troops which are intended to defend the territories of the allies against your designs, and that you and the Raja of Berar should be suffered to remain, with your troops assembled, in readiness to take advantage of their absence.

This proposition is unreasonable and inadmissible, and you must stand the consequences of the measures which I find myself obliged to adopt, in order to repel your aggressions. I offered you peace on terms of equality, and honourable to all parties: you have chosen war, and are responsible for all consequences.

Grwd (1837) ii 178 (1844) i 616

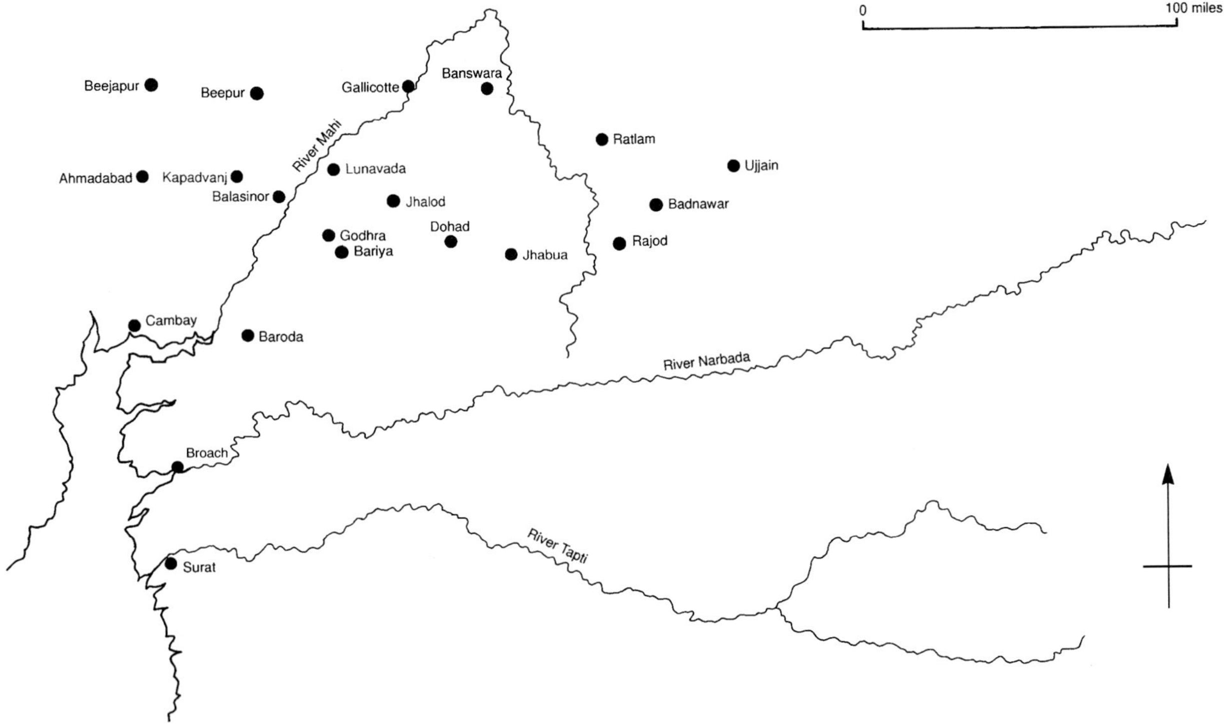

The setting of the Gujerat campaign. (Aardvark Illustration)

III
The Road to Assaye – August, September 1803

While waiting for the outcome of the negotiations with Sinde and Berar, Arthur Wellesley was in correspondence with the Governor of Bombay, Duncan, on the security of Surat, which he considered 'certainly must tempt strongly the cupidity of every Maratha chief.' A few days later, he noted that the committee at Surat which brought together the civil and military authorities, had failed to put ammunition or provisions into Songhur, a position important for the defence of both the Attavesi and of Surat. He was evidently concerned that a recent retreat in the area appeared culpable, and might call for court martial action.[1]

In a major paper written just before the outbreak of hostilities [205] Arthur Wellesley had reviewed the objectives of the group of forces answerable to the Bombay Presidency, the command of which had now devolved upon him. He had recommended unified command; 'one officer of rank should be appointed to command in the Attavesi and Gujerat.' Surat should be placed in a state of defence, and certain lesser forts garrisoned by sebundi troops. Other forces available, two King's regiments and four battalions of sepoys, should be grouped in two detachments, one north of the Narbada in front of Baroda, and the other south of the Tapti between Surat and Songhur. Colonel Murray was recommended for this command. Arthur Wellesley had noted that he would require 'the full confidence of government'.

British ascendancy in Gujerat had been established only in the previous year, and as Governor of Bombay Duncan was anxious to safeguard the position of Walker, the Resident at Baroda, by leaving with him the right to effect control of military resources. This he saw as endangered by the wide military and political delegated authority given to Arthur Wellesley by the orders of 26 June [174] 'the Governor-General not being minutely aware how the Gaikwar territory straggles though the Attavesi.' Any change in the political and military control in

Gujerat might 'produce a change perceptible to the natives with inconvenient consequences at this crisis.' Duncan appeared to agree to cooperate with the detailed proposals on deployment and on command set out by Arthur Wellesley despite 'the very dangerous experiment of separating the military local control from the Resident at Baroda.'[2]

As Resident with the Gaikwar's government, Walker doubted whether it would be appropriate to seek the support of the Gaikwar's troops against Daulat Rao Sinde. He spoke of these forces as being 'in a state of alliance with [Sinde's] government.' Since he also believed that their assistance would be ineffectual, he suggested that it might be better not to seek it. Duncan, Close, and Arthur Wellesley all reacted vigorously to this. Duncan commented that if he had appreciated that the forces of the Gaikwar could be said to be in close alliance with Sinde, he would have attempted to send all the force against Broach from Surat. Close contended that Daulat Rao Sinde could have 'no claim to the neutrality of the Gaikwar state' and Arthur Wellesley that 'it can never have been intended that the Company should protect the Gaikwar state unless the Gaikwar should also assist the Company with its forces against the enemies of the British government.'[3] At the same time, Arthur Wellesley expressed the strongest doubt on a series of operations suggested by Walker [252]. He reiterated that the central objective of the Company forces on the coast remained the seizure of Broach, which had been ordered by the Governor-General. If these suggestions were not followed, he hoped that he would 'not be considered responsible for the consequences.'

Duncan now set out his objections to both the deployment and the command structure proposed for the forces on the coast, while stating that the decision was one for Arthur Wellesley. 'I will most readily and cordially coincide with you in the whole proposed system if you can . . . preserve the necessary consequence of the Resident at Baroda.' He considered that serious harm would result from the withdrawal of military authority from the Resident [256]. Colonel Murray, recommended by Arthur Wellesley for the command of the forces in Gujerat [205] was evidently surprised at the position taken up by the Governor of Bombay [257,258]. Arthur Wellesley's reaction was forthright; he now resolved to leave the command of Gujerat and the Attavesi to the local military authorities: 'at this distance from the scene of action and under the difficulties of communication, I could not pretend to conduct so disjointed a piece of machinery.'[4]

Malcolm, who had moved away from the army via Pune to Bombay for his health, discussed these matters with Duncan. He was shown the letters from Arthur Wellesley. Malcolm attempted to calm the Governor, assuring him that the outbreak of hostilities and the 'ambiguous conduct of Holkar' required the scheme of defence which Arthur Wellesley had indicated, but that there had been no intention to degrade the consequence of the Resident at Baroda.[5]

Together Duncan and Malcolm created new instructions to the commanding officer of the detachment in Gujerat; these safeguarded the capability of the Resident with the Gaikwar to call on troops if this was necessary. Malcolm reported this action to Arthur Wellesley [288].

At Pune, Barry Close remained anxious about the attitude of Peshwa Baji Rao to his alliance with the Company. It was seen to be contingent and even disingenuous. Barry Close reported to Arthur Wellesley that the advocacy of an arrangement with Amrit Rao, to which they had both attached the greatest importance, had harmed relations with the Peshwa. Discussion was possible on a major issue of exchange of territory [224] but the desperate shortage of money of the durbar was evident. Close did not 'expect to see the Peshwa disburse any money for any purpose except to feed brahmins and to forward his pleasures' [269]. At the end of August, when joined by Appah Dessaye as well as Goklah, Arthur Wellesley had to determine to pay these two feudatories of the Peshwa from Company funds; this decision Close welcomed.[283] As Resident at Pune, Close was concerned with the logistic chain, which stretched back to the army on the Tungabhandra and also to Mysore, and which brought forward supplies as well as money. He reported just before the battle of Assaye that 2½ lakhs of rupees had been sent forward to the army [305].

The correspondence of Collins with Arthur Wellesley suggests that Sinde at least, perhaps in distinction from Raghuji Bhonsle, believed that the withdrawal from his camp of the Company Resident did not necessarily involve hostilities. The guidance from Arthur Wellesley which Collins sought was very clear. Having taken his decision for hostilities, Arthur Wellesley was not of a mind to be diverted by questionable attempts to reopen negotiation. 'Mere pacific professions unaccompanied by facts will not persuade me that their intentions are sincere' [235,242]. Having arrived at Aurungabad, Collins reported to Arthur Wellesley on the suggestions of Mohipat Ram, a major ruler within the territory of the Nizam of Hyderabad, of ways to improve the supplies required by the two detachments, comments which demonstrated the limitations on the power of the subordinate rulers in Hyderabad [267]. After discussions with Arthur Wellesley at

Aurungabad on 29 August, Collins wrote to the Governor-General clearly appreciating that his services were unlikely to be required in the Deccan.[6] In early September, Arthur Wellesley sought his help in the retention of a source of intelligence in the camp of Daulat Rao Sinde, but this Collins had to explain was no longer possible [295,298].

Arthur Wellesley had been given in late June a detailed formulation of the political objectives of the prospective campaign [175]. Once it had been appreciated in the Fort William Secretariat that the outbreak of hostilities was probable, this was refined [261]. In response, Arthur Wellesley reported evidence that Jaswant Rao Holkar was holding aloof from the other Maratha rulers, and noted that this was no time to attempt the restructure of the government of Peshwa Baji Rao. Further points he set aside until the time for negotiation came [262].

It had always been understood that the first objective of the detachment commanded by Arthur Wellesley was to be the capture of Ahmednagar. The capture of the pettah, or outer fortress, was followed, after an artillery bombardment, by the acceptance by the killedar of terms of surrender of the fortress [218,219,223]. After arrangements had been made for the settlement of the territory dependent on the fort, Arthur Wellesley moved his detachment to the Godavari, which was crossed at Toka. Meanwhile, the commander of the subsidiary force at Hyderabad, Colonel Stevenson, reported to Arthur Wellesley his supply difficulties [212,215] and his movement in the first instance northwards to approach the Ajanta ghat [217,220]. On 13 August came the first reports, subsequently proved not to be correct, of Maratha movement through the Ajanta. Stevenson appeared to be planning withdrawal or dispersal of his force to secure supplies [227,228] and to this Arthur Wellesley objected strongly. 'Dash at the first party that comes into your neighbourhood . . . a long defensive war will ruin us' [237].

Intelligence now arrived of a threat to the territories of the Nizam of Hyderabad from the 'eastern ghats', that is passes through the Ajanta range of hills south and east of the modern town of Buldana. Daulat Rao Sinde and Raghuji Bhonsle had moved their forces eastwards on the northern side of the Ajanta range [238]. In response, Stevenson moved his detachment northeastwards [245,248] and ultimately sent a small party through the 'Badowli ghat' [259]. But this Maratha movement had been a diversionary tactic, and was promptly reversed. By 25 August Stevenson knew that a Maratha entry into the lands of the Nizam through the Ajanta pass was in progress [264].

As Arthur Wellesley was moving from the Godavari towards Aurungabad, where he met Colonel Collins, Stevenson was withdrawing southwards, capturing Jalna on 2 September. The Marathas had meanwhile moved towards the Godavari, and appeared to be threatening a cavalry dash on Hyderabad. There was word also of the southward movement of their infantry; two deserters from one of the brigades of Daulat Rao Sinde came into Aurungabad on 2 September [278]. Arthur Wellesley moved south and east, while staying on the northern bank of the Godavari [284,287]. He resolved to instruct Stevenson to undertake a military movement towards Berar, and reinforced him for this purpose, but Stevenson evidently considered his force insufficiently strong to attempt this [293,294].

A reinforcing convoy, including an additional sepoy battalion, finally joined Arthur Wellesley on 18 and 20 September. He was now confident that he could move both detachments northwards towards the Marathas, who had withdrawn from the Godavari to a position protective of the Ajanta pass. In a series of letters, Stevenson reported his position to Arthur Wellesley, surmising that the two Maratha rulers were withdrawing, possibly towards the Ajanta pass [303,304]. In a final letter before the two commanders met at Budnapur on 21 September, and planned their approaches to Bhokrdan, Stevenson suggested a coordinated attack. He also reported an alleged suggestion of negotiation by Daulat Rao Sinde, but one which was tentative and could have been disowned [304].

The events that formed the crisis of the career of Arthur Wellesley in India on 23 September 1803, the day of Assaye, are here recorded in his own words [306]. One example of a letter by a participant, an unknown cavalry officer, is also given [306A]. The archival record appears to provide no fresh evidence on the most intriguing issue of all, namely the explanation for the prolonged delay in the junction of the Hyderabad subsidiary force and the main detachment. Is it fanciful to imagine that Stevenson wrote a long explanation of what happened that day, as he did for the capture of Burhanpur and Asirgarh [345,353] and for the far less controversial issue of the contribution forced on Burhanpur [407] and that Arthur Wellesley decided that its proper destination was the campfire? Loyalty to subordinates was important to the young Major-General.

Of the reality of the victory that had been secured there was little doubt. It is here stated in the measured periods of the Fort William Secretariat.

'During this severe and brilliant action, the conduct of Major General Wellesley united a degree of prudence, and of dauntless spirit, seldom equalled and never surpassed. It is impossible to bestow any commendation superior to the skill, magnanimity, promptitude and judgement displayed by Major General Wellesley on this memorable occasion; nor can any instance be adduced from the annals of our military glory of more exemplary order, firmness, discipline and alacrity, than was manifested by the British troops in every stage of the arduous contest which preceded the splendid victory of Assaye.

The whole line, led by General Wellesley in person, advanced to the charge with the greatest bravery and steadiness, without its guns, against a most severe and destructive fire of round and grape, until within a very short distance of the enemy, whom the British troops compelled, notwithstanding their superior numbers, at the point of the bayonet to abandon their guns and relinquish the field of battle, which Sinde's infantry had maintained with much obstinacy for more than three hours.'[7]

212

Colonel Stevenson to Arthur Wellesley

[near Aurungabad]
6 August 1803

The rains and winds for some days have caused many casualties amongst the public cattle and on their arrival in camp yesterday I found many of them in so bad a state that it became necessary to send some of military stores into Aurungabad, for which purpose I countermanded my orders for marching, but propose moving about five miles tomorrow to take up a position in the Ajanta road, and my movement must afterwards be guided by the weather and the condition of the bullocks . . .

A packet has this instant arrived from Colonel Collins to Major Kirkpatrick and the hircarrahs report that yesterday evening at six o'clock Colonel Collins was at Ajanta and Sinde had moved nearer to the ghat, and it is generally reported that they have moved their camp for the benefit of ground as they [had] been a long time in very damp ground and the late rains had made a movement necessary . . .

WP 3/3/84 p. 352

213

Lieutenant-Colonel Close to Arthur Wellesley

Pune
8 August 1803

I sent you yesterday a translation of a letter from our newswriter in Holkar's camp mentioning that a plan was laid by the confederates to inveigle the Peshwa off from hence to join them . . .[1]

After the Peshwa fled from Pune, Holkar and Amrit Rao did all that was possible to prevail upon him to return. Sinde at the same time urged him to come off to Broach, and you know at that period it was my object to detain him on the coast, whither he had gone at my instance. Sinde and the Bhonsle seem to have had it [at] first in mind to march in form to Pune and there arrange matters with the Peshwa in the manner they might judge most advisable.

Since they have found that plan however to be attended with too much hazard, they seem to have determined to lie on the frontier and to use all the means of intrigue for effecting their purpose by drawing off the Peshwa to their camp and conciliating the Peshwa's jagirdars so as eventually to have their aid. That is, Sinde defeated in his plan of forcibly effecting his purpose, seems to have renewed these efforts of negotiation, which failed while the Peshwa was on the coast.

There cannot be a doubt but that the Peshwa is anxious to pursue friendship with Sinde, although all my information states that he has no intention whatever to separate from the English. At all events, in the present state of things, great delicacy seems to be requisite in the management of the Peshwa, who you know is free and loose and may fly whither he pleases. This circumstance alone suggests the expediency of considering at an early time what should be done under the occurrence of some possible events. It is notorious that the Peshwa when big with a scheme, and there is not a more fickle man alive, is not confidential with his ministers whom, as he can manage, he keeps in a state of insignificance. Supposing things to be a worse state than from my information I have reason to apprehend, it should be our aim to remove Sinde and the Bhonsle as quickly as possible from the frontier.

WP 3/3/47 p. 428

213A

Message from a newswriter in Holkar's camp

30 July 1803 [received by Close by 7 August]

Holkar has moved from hence [no place given] for Mhaisur by the Sendwar route. Yesterday a warm altercation took place between

Holkar and Mir Khan, the latter representing loudly the want of subsistence for his troops. He was appeased at length by Holkar, who assisted him with some money, told him that as Khande Rao Holkar had been delivered up and the Holkar territories restored to him, all difficulties would soon be removed, that the only matter which required attention was the discussion on foot with the English, that this however would soon be adjusted, and that then Mir Khan should be rewarded with a suitable jagir. These assurances with the money apparently satisfied Mir Khan and the different commanders. Holkar distributed also a little money to the other troops of his army.

A corps of 10,000 horse is left in this neighbourhood, Holkar having proceeded light to Mhaisur. The purpose of his march thither is to seat Khande Rao Holkar on the masnad with all solemnity, and make some arrangements for settling the Mhaisur district and regulating the town, both of which are to be placed under the authority of Mulkar Shamji formerly dewan to the late Mulka Rao Holkar. These points adjusted, he and Khande Rao, according to reports prevalent here, are to return to Chopra and afterwards he is to consult with Raghuji Bhonsle and then proceed to attack Baroda in Gujerat. In this plan he has sent Raghuji Bhonsle's vakils back to him with assurances that he will soon return from Mhaisur . . .

Holkar has promised to give Sinde 25 lakhs of rupees to assist in bearing his expenses. Raghuji Bhonsle it is said has already paid the sum to Sinde for Holkar, who is to make it good to the former on his return from Mhaisur . . . The sirdars and others of his troops observe now to each other that Holkar formerly was no more than a vagrant freebooter but of late he is become an established sirdar with acknowledged authority.

Grain in camp is still at the high price of two seers for the rupee.

A Mss 13,599 f. 56

214

Lieutenant-Colonel Close to Arthur Wellesley

Pune
8 August 1803

I had just written the accompanying letter to you when I was favoured with your despatches of the 6th inst . . . I am in dread about the weather and am very sorry that you have had so much cause to complain of it. Allow me to wish you all success in the glorious attainment of your immediate object.

I am just returned from Raghunath Rao. I believe that we understand each other better than heretofore. He has assured me in the most solemn manner that neither Sinde nor the Bhonsle have desired the Peshwa to come off to their camp. He says however that formerly Sinde wrote to the Peshwa complaining of his having come off with me from Bassein but that since the Peshwa concluded the Treaty of Bassein, he has been firm in his resolution to adhere to us. I expect that the durbar will propose some scheme for adding to the number of the Maratha horse now serving with you.

I have told Mr Duncan that the Peshwa has allotted the remainder of the third year's rent of Ahmedabad for the subsistence of the Maratha cavalry serving under your orders and requested his aid to procure a speedy payment of the sum due. When necessary you must make advances on the strength of this fund . . . I shall draw upon Mr Duncan immediately for the remainder of the two Gaikwar lakhs, including the difference of exchange. The whole amounts to about 16,000 rupees. This sum I shall remit to you for the use of Appah Dessaye . . .

WP 3/3/47 p. 420

215

Colonel Stevenson to Arthur Wellesley

Camp four miles north of Aurungabad
9 August 1803

I marched almost six miles this morning towards Ajanta and must confine myself to the same sort of distance tomorrow as well on account of the reduced state of the public cattle as to bring forward the banjaras on which I entirely depend, having only 450 serviceable bullocks in the grain department. As I have sent some ordnance and provision stores into Aurungabad I shall be able to get forward as fast as I can to bring on my banjaras and if the present fair weather continues the cattle in general that have survived will recover strength.

I had a pair of hircarrahs arrive from Sinde's camp yesterday – the third day after leaving it – who report that Sinde and Bhonsle have sent all their heavy baggage to their respective capitals and that it was the discussion in their camps that Bhonsle was to enter the Nizam's country to the eastward and Sinde by Ajanta, that Bhonsle's troops were collected and ready to move but that Sinde's were still dispersed for forage.

Another set of hircarrahs, arrived this day, left Sinde's camp on the 7th, say that Sinde had assembled his principal officers and desired all that had good horses and were ready to die with him to be ready to march, that those that [were reluctant?] to follow his fortunes or had poor horses to go to Burhanpur, that four month's pay should be issued before they marched. They confirm the report of sending away the baggage and his horses still at forage. They report also that Bhonsle had promised four month's pay before his troops marched and confirm his having sent his baggage to Nagpur. His horses are considered to be generally in good order.

I have sent 1000 horse 500 foot and two guns from the Nizam's troops to cover the banjaras with 6000 bullocks at Basmat and have sent 500 horse to Paithan, to which place I have ordered the treasure and rice coming from Hyderabad. As Paithan is only thirty miles from Aurungabad the present escort of two companies with the 500 horse will choose a favourable opportunity of bringing it forward from that place.

As I think that Aurungabad may prove a useful place for the troops to assemble at if the campaign should be of any length, I have left all Mohipat Ram's troops for the protection of that place except three or four companies that come on as a covering party for two eighteen pounders which are all the guns that I [can muster?] in addition to four twelves, ten sixes, besides two galloper sixes and four galloper three pounders. Many of the Nizam's commanders brought guns with them, but the late rains killed their bullocks or rendered them unserviceable, and the guns are sent to Aurungabad.

I expect to meet Colonel Collins tomorrow and from the information received from him may form some opinion of my further movements.

WP 3/3/84 p. 364

216

Lieutenant-Colonel Close to Arthur Wellesley

Pune
9 August 1803

I am favoured with your letter of the 7th. As this memorandum is a very judicious paper that cannot fail of having a good effect,[2] I shall give it in to the durbar with a few lines from myself. I shall now have Raghunath Rao in a good humour, and I trust the conduct of the durbar will improve, although the Peshwa's mind is a melancholy mixture. Be assured that I shall labour incessantly to bring him into the line you desire.

I shall collect all the money I possibly can for you here. I learn from the durbar that Goklah is much distressed again for want of cash. Perhaps you may be able to assist him with an advance on the strength of the fund which I formerly mentioned to you.

I think I have the prospect of being able to purchase some cattle for you; should I disburse any of your money for such purpose? The head Chitty of Pune used always to attend the Peshwa's army in the field, and he now agrees to attend your camp in order to furnish supplies if I assist him in the [interim?] with 10,000 rupees to be paid back by him in the course of four months. I am to see him tomorrow at the desire of the durbar and I shall probably agree to his terms. He is a responsible person . . . I am much concerned that you have not heard from Major Dallas, who must be retarded by the rains. Malcolm's convoy is come in safe. We have fine weather now, and I hope you are released from the burden of the heavy rains.

WP 3/3/47 p. 436

217

Colonel Stevenson to Arthur Wellesley

Camp at Chavak
10 August 1803

My march led through a pass this morning to Chavak where I am now encamped. The distance does not exceed three miles and nearly nine miles from Aurungabad. The pass is narrow but had been made easy by the pioneers.

I met Colonel Collins this morning, who is of the opinion that the Ajanta pass is not practicable for guns and will prove difficult to loaded cattle . . . It is not likely that the enemy will attempt to enter by this ghat but as Sinde has not yet collected his cavalry there is no doubt I shall be in good time to prevent it. As Sinde has detached almost all his infantry, it is most likely he will attempt a predatory war, in which case he will prefer entering the Nizam's country in a more easterly direction where he will enter immediately into a more cultivated and populous country. He can have very little inducement to go round to the westward as that country has already been plundered and is totally desolated. I shall however use my best endeavours to get good information of his movements and be ready at all points.

I propose marching to Phulambri about six miles tomorrow and if I find Sinde disposed to attempt the Ajanta pass shall send a detachment to prevent him as, from the report I have of that pass, a battalion will defend it against any troops and the fort of Nizamabad is about two or three miles on this side to the southward of it. I have not yet got a good account of the advance of my banjaras on which I entirely depend for supplies but from the reports I received this morning I have reason to expect they will join me tomorrow.

Since writing the above I have been informed by Colonel Collins that you took the pettah of Ahmednagar by storm and expect the fort in a few days.

WP 3/3/84 p. 368

218

Arthur Wellesley to Lieutenant-Colonel Close

10 August 1803

I have the pleasure to inform you that I last night established a battery of four iron twelve pounders to take off defenders at the distance of about 400 yards of the fort which appears to succeed capitally. We suffer some little inconvenience for want of good platforms but nothing else. There is no doubt that this fine stone wall will be breached.

Have you ever hinted to Raghunath Rao that I propose to keep possession of this fort for the benefit of the allies.[?]

Our party at the battery have capital cover and a very tolerable communication from camp. We had only one pioneer killed and two wounded in establishing the battery and I believe two artillerymen wounded when it opened.

A Mss 13,599 f. 72

219

Arthur Wellesley to Lieutenant-Colonel Close

11 August 1803 7 pm [received 13 August]

The capitulation is settled nearly in the words I dictated this morning, and the terms are the same, excepting that the garrison march out at twelve instead of six. The hostages are in our hands and know what is to happen to them in case the treaty should be broke. I have stopped all our works and hope to write to you from the fort tomorrow. Malcolm is so ill as to be obliged to quit camp and I shall be obliged to you if you will ask Elphinstone to come up and assist me. If he assents beg of him to come here as soon as he can.

A Mss 13,599 f. 76

220

Colonel Stevenson to Arthur Wellesley

Camp north of Phulambri
11 August 1803

I marched this day about five miles to Phulambri and must halt tomorrow to bring in my banjaras. I detach a battalion with its guns about ten miles in advance tomorrow to put as good a mask as possible to our necessities. On the 13th I hope to march to Nygaum which is eleven miles and shall allow the battalion to move in advance about seven or eight miles.

The Marathas continue quiet below the ghat except about three or four hundred infantry and six guns that have advanced to Phardapur about three kos from Ajanta. It is reported, but does not gain belief, that Holkar has attacked and cut up 4000 irregular infantry that were coming from Ujjein to join Sinde. Bapoji Sinde is in the Basmat country with 15,000 horse. As I have not heard anything of him lately I know not whether he is there as a friend to the Peshwa or to Sinde. Gopal Bhau is still moving about betwixt Elora and the Cassabarri ghat.[3]

WP 3/3/84 p. 374

221

Lieutenant-Colonel Close to Governor-General [copied to Arthur Wellesley]

Pune
11 August 1803
[summary]

The Resident reported the discussion with two ministers of Baji Rao on 10th August which followed his presentation of the memorandum of Arthur Wellesley. He had protested when it had been suggested that the Peshwa should urge Sinde and Berar to return to Burhanpur to prepare to attack Jaswant Rao Holkar and to send vakils to Pune to discuss peace with the Company. The ministers also suggested that the forces of Appah Dessaye and Goklah should be employed against Amrit Rao.

Close reminded the ministers of the scheme of transfer of Peshwa territory in Bundelkhand. On this he was assured of the Peshwa's interest, provided that the Company subsidised a regiment of native horse and restored certain territory near Surat. Close saw nothing 'to encourage the hope that the Peshwa will be led to make these direct declarations, or preserve that decisive conduct so urgently demanded of him.' He noted that Baji Rao had been anxious to avoid a personal interview with the Resident since the time when 'he was urged to agree to some rational arrangements for an accommodation with Amrit Rao.'

WP 3/3/47 p. 440

222

Jonathan Duncan to Arthur Wellesley

Bombay Castle
12 August 1803

I have had the honour of receiving your letter [of 2 August 1803] in answer to mine of the 23rd [July] . . . I have only to assure you of the entire acquiescence and sincere and ready cooperation of this government in the[se] alterations . . .

The appointment of Colonel Murray will be put in orders . . . and the discontinuance of the local military authority hitherto exercised by the civil authority at Surat and by the Resident at Baroda may . . . be announced at the same period. General Jones being at the Presidency will of course remain here under the present arrangement.

PRC x 122, Parl Pps [5, 22 June 1804] p. 541

223

Arthur Wellesley to Richard Wellesley

Ahmednagar
12 August 1803

The weather cleared up so much on the 7th inst as to allow me to march to this place on the 8th. I had in the morning dispatched a messenger to the killedar of Ahmednagar to require him to surrender his fort, and on my arrival in the neighbourhood of the pettah, I offered cowle to the inhabitants. This was refused, as the pettah was held by a body of Arabs, who were supported by a battalion of Sinde's regular infantry and a body of horse, encamped in an open space between the pettah and the fort.

I immediately attacked the pettah with the pickets of the infantry, reinforced by the flank companies of the 78th regt., under the command of Lt Colonel Harness, in another place with the 74th regt. and 1st batt. of the 8th, under the command of Lt Colonel Wallace, and in a third with the flank companies of the 74th and the 1st batt. 3rd regt., under the command of Captain Vesey. The pettah wall was very lofty, and defended by towers, and had no rampart, so that when the troops had ascended to the attack, they had no ground on which they could stand, and the Arabs who occupied the towers, defended their post with the utmost obstinacy.

At length they were obliged to quit the wall, and fled to the houses, from which they continued a destructive fire upon the troops. Sinde's regular infantry also attacked our troops after they had entered the pettah. In a short time however after a brisk and gallant contest, we were completely masters of it, but with the loss of some brave officers and soldiers . . . The enemy's loss was from the nature of the contest necessarily much greater than ours, and on the night of the 8th all that part of their force which was not required for the defence of the fort went off to the northward, including all the Arabs who survived the contest in the pettah, excepting a small number who attended one of their wounded chiefs, who could not be removed farther than the fort.

On the 9th I reconnoitred the ground in the neighbourhood of the fort, and on that evening Lt Colonel Wallace with 5 companies of the 74th regt, and the 2nd batt. 12th regt, seized a position within 400 yards of it, on which in the course of that night a battery was constructed for 4 guns, to take off the defences on the side on which I proposed to make my attack. This opened at daylight on the 10th, and it was so advantageously placed and fired with such effect as to induce the killedar to desire that I should cease firing, in order that he might send a person to treat for his surrender.

In my answer I told him that I should not cease firing till I should have taken the fort, or he should have surrendered it, but that I would listen to whatever he was desirous to communicate. Yesterday morning he sent out two vakils to propose to surrender the fort, on condition that he should be allowed to depart with his garrison and that he should have his private property.

Although I consented to this proposal, it was five in the evening before the hostages arrived in camp, without whose presence

I refused to stop the fire from the British batteries. According to his engagement however the killedar marched out of the fort this morning, with a garrison consisting of 1400 men, and the troops under my command took possession of it. In this manner has this fort fallen into our hands, our loss since the 8th has been trifling, which I attribute much to the spirit with which our attacks on that day were carried on . . .

Grwd (1837) ii 193 (1844) i 625

224

Lieutenant-Colonel Close to Richard Wellesley

Pune
13 August 1803 [seen by Arthur Wellesley by 15 August]
[summary]

Close reported a discussion with Raghunath Rao held earlier on 13th August. The Peshwa was now prepared to agree to vary the Treaty of Bassein by substituting territory in Bundelkhand for cessions on the Deccan and in Gujerat.

The Peshwa was anxious to retain in his own possession the district of Olpad near Surat, estimated to yield a revenue of Rs 3.16 lakhs. The territory to be ceded in Bundelkhand 'from those parts of the province most contiguous to the British possessions' was calculated to yield an annual revenue of Rs 36,16,000 although shown 'in the Pune registers' as yielding Rs 62 lakhs.

These cessions were to be 'understood as clearing the Peshwa of the imputation of all failure . . . in regard to his engagements.' Raghunath Rao sought a disbursement or 'durbar-kharch' of Rs 1.5 lakhs. The Peshwa also sought Company payment of a force of 5,000 Maratha horse, expected to cost Rs 15 lakhs annually. The proposed agreement would include an undertaking by the Peshwa to provide at his cost a force of 6,000 horse and 4,000 infantry in time of war.

PRC x 111 [where wrongly dated 3 August], WP 3/3/47 p. 458, A Mss 13,749 f. 57

225

Lieutenant-Colonel Close to Arthur Wellesley

Pune
13 August 1803 [received 15 August]

We are overjoyed at having the news of the capitulation, which happily completes all your purposes without the hazard of any casualties amongst your brave fellows . . .

Poor Malcolm's sufferings on account of his fatigues are most distressing. I shall endeavour to get him down to Bombay to try the effect of the sea air, which will no doubt restore him. Mr Elphinstone has started to join you, full of joy. He is escorted by some of my troopers. I shall try to procure a few good bullocks for you. Enclosed is a copy of my last letter to his Excellency. I hope that you will approve of the Peshwa's proposition. I think it shows that he is decidedly with us, however languid his government.

WP 3/3/47 p. 456

226

Arthur Wellesley to Jonathan Duncan

Ahmednagar
13 August 1803 [received 15 August]
[summary]

In responding to a letter from Duncan of 8 August, Arthur Wellesley noted that nothing had been done, at least until the 21 July, to relieve the troops at Songhur, and that supplies had been moved to them at irregular intervals. 'The service cannot be carried on in this manner.'

'In consequence of the success of the troops under my command, and as it is my intention to pass the Godavari immediately, by which means I shall check the operations of any enemy by Songhur towards Surat, and as Jaswant Rao Holkar has passed the Narbada and it being reported that he intends to attack Gujerat, I would wish, if you approve of the plan which I proposed for the organisation of the troops . . . that you would allow them all, excepting those allotted for the defence of Surat, Songhur and Parneira, to move towards the river Narbada as soon as possible.'

Parl Pps [5, 22 June 1804] p. 539, Grwd (1837) ii 187 (1844) i 628

227

Colonel Stevenson to Arthur Wellesley

Camp at Phulambri
14 August 1803 6 am [received by 16 August]

The delays occasioned by the banjaras on whom I depend entirely for supplies prevented my advancing so quickly as I wished, in obedience to your orders, to the Ajanta ghat, and by the report of the officer about ten miles in advance the enemy are said to have entered the Nizam's country by the Ajanta ghat.

Lt Colonel Kenny sent his adjutant with his first report and I sent orders by Lt Wingfield for the battalion to join the line this morning. But finding by letters that Salabat Khan received last evening that they have not ascended the ghat when his hircarrah passed it yesterday evening, I countermanded my orders for the battalion's return to the line in so abrupt a manner and have ordered Salabat Khan and Nur ul Umrah with their troops to join the battalion in advance this morning and I propose going out with the pickets in the course of the day to get further information and confirmation.

Salabat Khan's letters report that Sinde and Bhonsle have sent back their infantry and guns to Hindustan and at the head of their respective horse entered the Ajanta ghat yesterday morning and were to be joined by Gopal Bhau as he with his troops were to form the advance. The pindari horse are to move in their divisions to endeavour to cut off our supplies.

The above is the important information contained in Salabat Khan's letter. My supplies and banjaras require my immediate attention and will render it expedient that I return to Aurungabad to give security to that place, and as far as my resources allow, I intend to move in an easterly direction to offer such protection to that rich country as is possible against predatory horse and particularly to endeavour to secure 6000 bullock loads of rice which I expect from Basmat.

I shall also find it expedient to incline towards Mungy Puttan [Paithan] where I expect some grain and where I have directed my treasure from Hyderabad, with 2000 bullocks load of rice, to come to. I have sent three sets of hircarrahs to look out for this convoy, which is escorted by one company of native infantry, to bring them to Paithan where I think they will be safe. If you find it convenient to send some support to the company with the treasure it may be serviceable. They are ordered to come by the direct route from Hyderabad to Aurungabad till they meet my hircarrahs who will direct them to Paithan.

I have detailed the duties which will require my immediate attention and shall otherwise keep the troops employed according to contingencies. The advance battalion under Colonel Kenny is ten miles north of my camp and thirty miles south of the Ajanta ghat. I enclose a note from Colonel Kenny dated half past six yesterday evening.

WP 3/3/84 p. 376

227A

Lieutenant-Colonel Kenny to Colonel Stevenson

13 August 1803 5 o'clock pm

An hircarrah of Salabat Khan is just come in and he says that Sinde and Bhonsle are crossing the ghats with horse only. 7000 already over. I send Mr Wingfield on horseback to give you timely notice.

WP 3/3/84 p. 380

227B

Lieutenant-Colonel Kenny to Colonel Stevenson

13 [August 1803] half past six pm

I have just received your message from Mr Wingfield and will be ready to move off at four o'clock at the latest, though I do not think that I have anything to apprehend from them and they have only horse and probably will not move at night. I have been to the top of a very high hill near my ground and though I could not perceive their tents I could clearly see the smoke of their encampment and what I thought a village burning. It seemed about the distance of five or six miles from the foot of the pass. I have received your note by the hircarrah. The enemy I think about twenty miles from here.

WP 3/3/84 p. 382

228

Colonel Stevenson to Arthur Wellesley

[Camp at Phulambri]
14 August 1803 [pm]

I am glad I can contradict the reports I forwarded yesterday. I rode out to the advance post this morning and find that the enemy have not entered the Nizam's country but have disappeared from the vicinity of the Ajanta ghat and have marched in an easterly direction. I think I shall be able to prevail on my banjaras to follow me up to Jafarabad which is situated for defending all the eastern ghats.

WP 3/3/84 p. 384

229

Arthur Wellesley to Lieutenant-Colonel Close

Ahmednagar
15 August 1803

I have received your letter of the 13th in which you have enclosed the dispatch to the Governor General of that date.

I approve entirely of the proposed change. There is every reason to believe that the people and chiefs of Bundelkhand wish to pass under the British government, and the transfer can be made immediately without the smallest difficulty. The transfer of the other districts to the southward is very remote and will be attended with difficulties.

I also approve of the proposed mode of raising 5,000 Maratha horse, and I am almost inclined to request you to take measures for raising them immediately. They would be very useful to us . . .

Grwd (1837) ii 203 (1844) i 635

230

Lieutenant-Colonel Close to Arthur Wellesley

15 August 1803
[summary]

Close explained that the Peshwa's minister, Raghunath Rao, had anticipated the possible capture of Ahmednagar and had asked what arrangements were to be made for the control of captured territory. Close had given a generalised reassurance that the fort would be garrisoned by the Company, and that after the end of the war the Peshwa could rely on the judgement of the Governor-General. Noting Arthur Wellesley's anxiety not to offend the Peshwa on this, Close added 'you may proceed to finish your proposed arrangements without further reference to me. I shall however keep you informed of all that passes on the subject. If in the end it should appear to be necessary I shall of course tell Raghunath Rao that a minute and accurate account will be kept of revenue resulting from the Ahmednagar districts for his Highness' satisfaction, and that the amount received will be applied to assist in defraying the expenses of the war.'

WP 3/3/47 p. 490

231

Arthur Wellesley to Colonel Collins

Camp at Ahmednagar
15 August 1803

I have had the honour to receive your letter of the 13th.[4]

Colonel Stevenson has my directions to watch closely the movements of Sinde and the Raja of Berar and attack immediately the troops of either of those chiefs which may move towards him. He will of course move towards the Badauli ghat if he should find that they intend to penetrate by that road.

It is impossible for me to say that Holkar is not on his march to join those chiefs. But if Raja Mohipat Ram is the subahdar of Aurungabad, and you have received that intelligence from him, I think it is to be doubted. But even if it should be true, as my cavalry commenced their march from hence yesterday and the infantry will arrive upon the river before the cavalry will have passed it, I expect I shall join Colonel Stevenson at least as soon as Holkar will have joined the other chiefs.

The Marathas have long boasted that they would carry on a predatory war against us; they will find that mode of warfare not very practicable at the present moment. At all events, supposing that they can carry their design into execution, unless they find the British officers and soldiers in the same corrupted enervated state in which their predecessors found the mussulman in the last century, they cannot expect much success from it.

A system of predatory war must have some foundation in strength of some kind or other. But when the chiefs avow that they cannot meet us in the field, when they are obliged to send the principal strength of their armies upon which the remainder depend to a distance lest it should fall into our hands, they must have little knowledge of human nature if they suppose that their lighter bodies will act, and still less of British officers if they imagine that with impunity they can do the smallest injury, provided only that the allies who are to be first exposed to their attacks are true to their own interests.

Grwd (1837) ii 202 (1844) i 634

232

Arthur Wellesley to Lieutenant-Colonel Close

16 August 1803 [received 19 August]

I enclose the copy of the translation of the engagement made with Amrit Rao, which I received this morning from Malcolm. In my opinion, it will not be proper to communicate this instrument to the Peshwa's government. The best thing to do will be to inform Raghunath Rao that I had reason to expect that Amrit Rao would join the British army, and that in that case I was very desirous that the Peshwa should cease all hostility against him, and that I would engage for Amrit Rao's conduct. If you approve of this plan, I request you to adopt it . . .

Grwd (1837) ii 205 (1844) i 637

233

Treaty with Amrit Rao

[summary]

By this engagement, Amrit Rao and after his death his son were guaranteed a revenue of seven lakhs of rupees, taking into account as part of that sum the revenues of the territories that he already occupied. He was to move to meet Arthur Wellesley, with his available cavalry and infantry, within nineteen days.[5]

Grwd (1837) ii 206 (1844) i 637

234

Colonel Stevenson to Arthur Wellesley

[Phulambri?]
16 August 1803

. . . I have sent parties of native cavalry to the distance of twenty miles in various directions but no pindari horse have been seen, nor any reports prevailed of depradations in any of the villages that they passed except some foraging horse having committed some acts of plunder and as I cannot discover that any horse of any description have ascended the ghats I am of opinion the mischief was committed by the foraging horse from our own Mogul troops. Sinde is at Peepree and Raghuji two or three kos to the northward of him yesterday evening. Tomorrow being a festival they were to remain quiet but it is reported in their camp that they were to advance to the eastern ghats the following day. I propose marching towards Jafarabad tomorrow.

WP 3/3/84 p. 386

235

Colonel Collins to Arthur Wellesley

Camp at Aurungabad
16 August 1804 [received 18 August]

. . . I have no doubt that Sinde heartily repents ere this not having complied with your requisition. As yet he has not dismissed my agent who resides in his camp and this man apprises me that the Maharajah advanced with his troops to Tondapur which is only distant five cos from the Phardapur pass. But I have not the least idea of his daring to ascend that ghat. However I shall immediately inform Col Stevenson of this movement on the part of Sinde. The Raja of Berar has marched towards the Badauli pass. . .

Should my quondam friend Sinde be brought to a proper sense of his danger by the capture of Ahmednagar and in consequence make any overtures to me for the purpose of effecting a reconciliation with the British government, in what manner shall I answer him? Such an event is possible though improbable. I most sincerely hope that General Lake may be as successful in his military operations as you have been. Your arrival here will afford me infinite pleasure. It is long since we have met, and you will find me strangely altered in person.

WP 3/3/53 p. 173

236

Arthur Wellesley to Jonathan Duncan

Ahmednagar
17 August 1803

I have had the honour of receiving your letter of the 12th inst and I am happy to find that you approve of the suggestions contained in my letter of the 2nd and of Colonel Murray to command the troops to the northward. I beg leave to recommend that he may be appointed and that he may go to Surat at the earliest possible period and in most expeditious manner.[6]

Parl Pps [5, 22 June 1804] p. 547

237

Arthur Wellesley to Colonel Stevenson

Camp at Ahmednagar
17 August 1803 [received 20 August]

I have received your letters of the 13th and 14th the last of which is more satisfactory than the first.[7]

In my opinion the best thing you can do is move forward yourself with the Company's cavalry and all the Nizam's and a battalion and dash at the first party that comes into your neighbourhood. You will either cut them up or drive them off and in either case you will provide more effectually for the security of your convoys than by detaching your troops to bring them in. Keep the infantry collected in a central location and let your supplies collect upon them.

If you adopt this plan and succeed in cutting up or in driving to a distance one good party the campaign will be our own. A long defensive war would ruin us and will answer no purpose whatever. By any other plan than that above proposed we shall lose our supplies do what we will.

The cavalry will reach the river this day. I shall march with the infantry tomorrow and shall be at Toka before they will have crossed and with you a few days afterwards. I shall order Major Hill's battalion which is coming with supplies from the Kistna to Khurdla to march upon Paithan; this will give security to everything there. They will not be at Paithan for a fortnight at soonest.

Grwd (1837) ii 210 (1844) i 640

238

Colonel Stevenson to Arthur Wellesley

Nygaum
17 August 1803 [received 20 August]

Agreeable to the instructions contained in your letter of 18th July I have proceeded with the whole of the force under my command, with the exception of the troops under the orders of Raja Mohipat Ram which I have left for the protection of Aurungabad, towards the Ajanta ghat. I have reason to suppose that this movement has had the effect that you proposed it should, as the enemy have shown no disposition to enter the Nizam's territory by that ghat but have withdrawn their troops in the direction of Burhanpur for the purpose as it is generally reported of avoiding some rocks and ravines and of gaining the road that leads to the eastern ghats.

By the intelligence that I have received for some days past it is their intention to enter by the Badauli ghat and in consequence of the prevailing reports and the movements they have lately made, I have detached a battalion of native infantry and the Mogul troops commanded by Salabat Khan Behaunder and Nur ul Umrah consisting of about 2000 horse 1500 infantry and six guns, the whole under the command of Lt Col Kenny, with orders to proceed to Jafarabad where they will arrive this forenoon. I find it necessary to detach these troops to convince the enemy that I am prepared to defend all passes leading to the Nizam's country, Jafarabad being well situated to make an expeditious movement to any of the eastern ghats.

I have remained here with the rest of my force in order to bring up my supplies. It appears an opportunity being on the Ajanta road of being informed of the real situation of the enemy in regard to their movement to the eastward, as my intelligence from their armies arrives within twentyfour hours. I expect that my banjaras and other supplies will be forward in the course of this day and I have taken measures to direct all that cannot join this evening to return to Aurungabad, which will leave my rear clear, and tomorrow morning I shall march with all my force to join the advance at Jafarabad, which will employ three days.

From there I propose marching by Jalna towards Basmat and after securing 6000 bullock load of rice which I expect to find with my banjaras in that direction, I shall march towards Paithan if necessary or send a detachment to bring forward the grain and treasure that I expect to arrive there before I shall have made three marches. This is the route which I propose to pursue if my attention is not engaged by any movements of the enemy, in which case I make no doubt I shall find resources to support my detachment till your appearance on this side of the Godavari. I shall engage the attention of the enemy and effect an opportunity for my supplies of rice and treasure to join my detachment.

WP 3/3/84 p. 388

239

Lieutenant-Colonel Close to Arthur Wellesley

Pune
17 August 1803 [received 19 August]

I am this instant favoured with your despatch of the 15th and must say that I am greatly rejoiced to find that you approve the Peshwa's proposition relative to Bundelkhand.

I shall attend to your hint about the propriety of my taking some steps towards facilitating the levy of the 5,000 horse to serve with your army. The Peshwa appears to be in good humour about everything except our wishes to arrange with Amrit Rao, and on this point I am concerned to say he is as unaccommodating as ever. All reasoning appears to be lost upon him. However I shall continue to stem his headstrong temper and absurd but obstinate objections with all the force of argument I am capable of.

I sent off 94,000 rupees to you this morning, and as the escort will proceed by long marches, I trust this supply will be in time to catch you in the neighbourhood of Ahmednagar. I am in hopes that the sum which you propose advancing to Goklah will prove to be sufficient for his purposes for a time. However, should it be necessary, I will pay Balaji Pant [Goklah] the remainder of the 75,000 rupees here; the payment may no doubt be made in the manner you recommend . . . Colonel Coleman has shown me your letter to him containing your directions for the supply of Nuggur with rice and other articles of provision. Coolies in any number are happily procurable here at a moderate hire, and parties will be sent in succession from here to Panvel, in as large numbers as can possibly be loaded at Panvel, without the necessity of detaining them there for a period which might be inconvenient to them . . .

WP 3/3/45 p. 506

240

Lieutenant-Colonel Close to Arthur Wellesley

Pune
17 August 1803

I send you herewith 94,000 rupees on thirty five coolies under an escort of a jemadar's party. The above sum is in rupees 38,201, gold mohurs 1,673 and Venetians 4,810.[8] The escort is desired to hasten and overtake the European party that marched from hence for Nuggur on the day before yesterday, so that I hope the cash will soon reach camp.

WP 3/3/45 p. 510

241

Colonel Stevenson to Arthur Wellesley

Hasnabad
18 August 1803

I arrived at Hasnabad this morning after a march of fourteen miles and intend proceeding to Jafarabad tomorrow. The enemy are at the foot of the Deul ghat and intend entering the Nizam's country by that pass but have been delayed on account of some difficulties about arrears of pay.

I cannot determine how I shall proceed till I arrive at Jafarabad and learn further of the movements of the enemy but shall always attend to the instructions conveyed in your letter of the 18th July to prevent the enemy from entering the Nizam's country by all the means in my power. The Deul ghat is 14 kos or 28 miles from Jafarabad.

WP 3/3/84 p. 392

242

Arthur Wellesley to Colonel Collins

north of the Ninderrah ghat
18 August 1803 [received 20 August]

I have received your letter of the 16th. I am sincerely desirous of peace and will certainly conclude one when I can, but we must proceed with caution, because I am afraid that we shall miss our object if we appear too desirous to attain it.

If any overtures should be made to you let them know that you will communicate them to me, but that you are convinced that mere pacific professions unaccompanied by facts will not persuade me that their intentions are sincere. If any such overtures should be made to you favour me with your opinion regarding them at the time you will communicate them.

You see the advantages which we derive from the commencement of hostilities during the season in which the rivers are full. We have got possession of Sinde's only hold in the Deccan. He cannot receive assistance from Holkar, supposing that chief to be inclined to assist him, and he is confined by the Godavari in the execution of his plan of predatory war, supposing him to be capable of carrying it into execution.

In the meantime I shall fill Ahmednagar with provisions and when that is completed all the Marathas in India would not be able to drive me from my position. I believe also that although Colonel Stevenson has suffered much in his equipments lately, and we have all suffered more or less from the severity of the weather, it has done more harm in Sinde's army and he is more crippled by it than any of us.

SD iv 158

243

Jonathan Duncan to Arthur Wellesley

Bombay Castle
19 August 1803
[summary]

In response to a letter from Arthur Wellesley of 13th August, Duncan reported that Songhur had been reprovisioned, and that although the troops lacked a full range, they were adequately equipped. He confirmed that orders had been sent to move forces towards the Narbada, leaving Surat, Songhur and Parneira garrisoned. Colonel Murray was about to leave for Surat.

Parl Pps [5, 22 June 1804] p. 540

244

Lieutenant-Colonel Close to Arthur Wellesley

Pune
19 August 1803

I have to acknowledge your packets of the 16th and 17th . . . Raghunath Rao was taken ill two days ago. Having many things to say to him, I gave him a call this morning, but found him in a violent fever scarcely able to speak or touch on business.

Your propositions for an arrangement with Amrit Rao appear to me to be as judicious as necessary in effect. I have from the beginning seen that you would find this measure indispensable to the support of your operations, and have omitted no occasion to remind Raghunath Rao that in the event of hostilities, Amrit Rao would probably join your camp. The points which you of late wished me to explain to him, I introduced into my short conversation with him this morning. Ill as he was, he says that he will have the intimation conveyed to the Peshwa this evening. He then begged me I would give him another call tomorrow morning, when Suddasheo Munkaiseer would be present, to which I assented. At this proposed meeting I shall endeavour to confront the ministers on Amrit Rao's subject in the manner you desire.

Your reasons for having taken possession of Ahmednagar and districts in the name of the Company and the Peshwa are certainly conclusive. Under this impression I have left both your Proclamations with Raghunath Rao for the Peshwa's information.

If I succeed in reconciling the durbar to the proposed arrangement with Amrit Rao, we may possibly procure his assent to your proposed settlement with that killedar. The object is extremely pressing.

I trust the supplies from Panvel will proceed briskly to their destinations. Raghunath Rao told me that 5000 banjara bullocks were assembled and were about to be loaded by Captain Young, but on this point I shall soon receive intelligence from the Captain himself. I hope to see Malcolm here tomorrow. He tells me that he is much recovered since he left camp . . .

WP 3/3/45 p. 512

245

Colonel Stevenson to Arthur Wellesley

Camp 8 miles west of Jafarabad
19 August 1803

I marched about fifteen miles this morning and have still eight or nine miles to march tomorrow to arrive at Jafarabad.

The enemy were at the bottom of the Badauli ghat yesterday morning and it was reported in their camp that they were to enter the Nizam's country by that ghat this morning. I have received your letters of the 14th and 15th instant and am very glad to find that you begin your march in this direction at so early a period. Raja Mohipat Ram shall have instructions to lay in stores of grain in any strong place where it can be collected, but I must confess that I do not think his influence extends far from Aurungabad.

I have ordered Lt Col Kenny to advance two or three kos towards the Badauli ghat tomorrow morning. If on my arrival at Jafarabad I find there is any risk in that position I shall recall him, but the movement may create delay in the movements of the enemy and perhaps change their route.

WP 3/3/84 p. 390

246

Colonel Collins to Arthur Wellesley

Camp at Aurungabad
19 August 1803

Although Daulat Rao Sinde has been informed that you have invested the fort of Ahmednagar after taking the pettah, yet he has not dismissed my agent from his camp . . .

Sinde had not marched on the 17th but orders for moving had been issued to his troops, in what direction is not known. The Bhonsle had proceeded eight kos towards the Badauli ghat which is about half way, on the 17th of this month. These are all the particulars I have learned respecting this chieftain since I last wrote to you . . . Your presence in this quarter would be of infinite use in quickening the measures of the Nabob's agents who it seems are very tardy in furnishing supplies of grain.

WP 3/3/53 p. 175

247

Arthur Wellesley to Colonel Stevenson

Camp at Carwoody
20 August 1803

I have received your letter of the 17th. There is only one part of your plan which I should wish to see altered and that is your intention to retire to Paithan.

Depend upon it no pindari or straggling horse will venture to your rear as long as you keep the enemy in check and your detachment well in advance. Dash at the first fellows that make their appearance and the campaign will be our own . . .

Grwd (1837) ii 219 (1844) i 646

248

Colonel Stevenson to Arthur Wellesley

Camp at Jafarabad
20 August 1803

I have arrived at Jafarabad with the whole of my force except Raja Mohipat Ram's party left at Aurungabad to protect that place and its provisions, and Salabat Khan's party left at Phulambri to give protection to provisions moving from Aurungabad to join the camp at Nygaum. He has received orders to move forward and join me but has not yet arrived. I have kept a party in advance consisting of Lt Colonel Kenny's battalion and Salabat Khan and Nur ul Umrah's troops.

I shall march tomorrow to Barroor about six kos and next day to Chikhli about five kos. I shall then have passed the Deul ghat but can still give effectual protection to it and be within three kos of the Badauli ghat, to which I can move forward immediately after my arrival at Chikhli if necessary. But I am of the opinion that the enemy march in an easterly direction towards the Lakhanwada pass, after which the chain of mountains cease and they will have the country open to them.

I have received your letters of the 17th and you may depend on my using the most active movements to prevent the enemy entering any of the ghats and if a fair opportunity should offer I shall not fail to confront their advance. We are always prepared to clash with them in such a manner as I trust will effect all your wishes. I have taken means to bring forward my grain from Aurungabad in the direction that I am moving as there is no impediment at present. I have reason to hope that I should not have occasion to relinquish the duties you require of this force on account of a failure of supplies.

WP 3/3/84 p. 394

249

Colonel Collins to Arthur Wellesley

Camp at Aurungabad
20 August 1803

. . . Be assured that I shall most carefully avoid giving Sinde any reason to believe that you are in the least desirous of peace and should that chieftain write to me with a view of accommodating existing differences, my reply shall be exactly as you have suggested. But at present I have little hope of Sinde's adopting any measures of a pacific tendency, his pride being hurt at the loss of 'the impregnable fortress of Ahmednagar.'

Daulat Rao Sinde has joined the Berar Raja at a place distant about eight kos from the Badauli ghat. My newswriter still attends the camp of the Maharajah and my dak hircarrahs in that quarter have hitherto been permitted to remain unmolested at their usual stations.

I was always well aware of the advantage you would derive by commencing your military operations during the rainy monsoon. At the same [time] however I thought it might be prudent to put the Maratha chieftains altogether in the wrong, previously to any hostilities on the part of the British Government.

WP 3/3/53 p. 177

250

Lieutenant-Colonel Close to Arthur Wellesley

Pune
21 August 1803

. . . The Peshwa and his minister, I am sorry to say, are either really or politically ill, and I am obliged in consequence to communicate with the durbar on paper. I am told that I shall have the services of 100 horse to proceed to the Kistna, but

I cannot depend on this till I see them parade to go off. The banjara maestri who engaged to produce 5,000 bullocks by the 20th of this month holds off on account of the deepness of the roads in the Konkan, and I am afraid that none of the bullocks will appear till some time in September. Major Malcolm arrived yesterday morning. He is as well as I expected to find him, but requires being refreshed by the sea air. He will leave us in a day or two for Bombay. I keep him from writing or giving his thoughts to business as much as I can.

WP 3/3/45 p. 528

251

Arthur Wellesley to Secretary, Bombay Government

22 August 1803

. . . Major Walker has proposed a variety of operations, namely firstly an expedition against Canoji, secondly an expedition against Mulhar Rao and thirdly an expedition into Kathiawar combined with one against Bhuj and the Dwarka pirates.

I cannot enter into these operations, firstly because the Governor General has given orders and it is expedient that Sinde's fort of Broach should be attacked, and that he should be deprived of his possessions in that quarter, secondly because I do not see adequate resources of men or means for any of these operations, and thirdly because it is by no means certain that Holkar will not join the confederates and if the troops should be employed against Canoji or Mulhar Rao or in Kathiawar the whole province will be left defenceless to his ravages . . .

These are my sentiments upon the plan of operations for Gujerat. I can have but little local knowledge of that country and Major Walker must have much, but I object on military principles to the separation of our small forces in that quarter and to undertaking many distinct operations with inadequate means. If the Governor in Council should think it proper to adopt the suggestions of Major Walker they must be carried into execution and I hope that I shall not be considered responsible for the consequences.

Grwd (1837) ii 223 (1844) i 649

252

Colonel Collins to Arthur Wellesley

Camp at Aurungabad
22 August 1803

I received your letter of the 19th inst with its enclosures yesterday evening. I think it will be practicable to convey copies of the Proclamation of the Governor General to Major Brownrigg Major Smith and Captain Grant.

The first commands a corps consisting of four battalions of infantry. The second is attached to Colonel Dudrenec's brigade and in fact commands it, he being a very active good soldier whereas the Colonel has not a military idea. Captain Grant is brigade major to, and in great favour with, Colonel Pohlman, an Hanoverian. The latter commands one of Sinde's best brigades and would I know be glad of an opportunity of leaving his present situation, at least so he assured me for I met him on my morning rides several times when I was encamped at Jalgong.

Colonel Sutherland has already resigned the service of the Maharajah. Colonel Hessing the elder a Dutchman who has seen much service died a short time ago. His son a halfcaste also commands a brigade and as he is a wretched officer I hope he will continue where he is.

In short, with the exception of Frenchmen, I believe Pohlman Brownrigg and Smith are the only experienced officers in the service of Sinde. There are several English gentlemen attached to the corps commanded by the two former, who of course would be glad to accept of the benefits held forth in the Proclamation. As to the natives I am doubtful though it is likely that many of them will follow their European officers.[9]

WP 3/3/53 p. 181

253

Colonel Stevenson to Arthur Wellesley

Camp 2 miles east of Chikhli
22 August 1803

I marched from Jafarabad to Barroor about fourteen miles yesterday and this day about the same distance in an easterly direction and am now encamped two miles east of Chikhli about ten miles south of the Badauli and Deul ghats and 24 miles west of the Lakhanwada ghat. The enemy are about ten miles from the Badauli and Deul ghats. It is reported that they are determined to ascend the ghats but no time is fixed. At present they are engaged in sending off Bhonsle's nephew to Nagpur partly on account of sickness and partly because they know the English troops are moving towards it. I propose tomorrow to get more particular accounts of the enemy.

WP 3/3/84 p. 390

254

Colonel Stevenson to Arthur Wellesley

ten miles south of the Badauli ghat
23 August 1803 10 am [received by 26 August]

The enclosed letter contains confirmation of the enemy's having marched in a westerly direction towards Goomlah Peepree. Their movement to the eastward may have been intended to engage my attention while their guns and infantry marched back to

Burhanpur, and having effected that, they may have some future plans for ascending the Ajanta ghat.

The ghats to the eastward, Sirsooli and Lakhanwada, are much easier of ascent than the Ajanta or Peepree ghats and open immediately on a rich and well cultivated country, and if the enemy were prepared and determined upon entry in the Nizam's country I think they would give the eastern ghats the preference, particularly at this time when you are entering upon the Ajanta road. Their western movement may be for the purpose of meeting Holkar.

I am this instant informed by travellers that there is a party of about 5000 of Bhonsle's horse at the Sirsooli ghat and I think it necessary to remove them before I make a westerly movement. I think your movement to Aurungabad which leads to Ajanta or Nizamabad will prevent them from entering upon that ghat. Lt Colonel Haliburton is a march to the rear at Barroor with the brigade and two twelve pounders. I shall order him back to Jafarabad as much to secure my supplies coming immediately from Aurungabad to that place as to keep watch on the western ghats.

WP 3/3/84 p. 401

254A

Captain Johnston to Colonel Stevenson

22 [August 1803] received at 7 pm

The letter to Salabat Khan mentions that Sinde and Bhonsle have gone back to Goomlah Peepree. The man who brought the letter says he left the camp at 8 o'clock this morning when they had already marched. Peepree is 10 kos from Ajanta and on the road to Burhanpur. The letter is from the Deul ghat man.

WP 3/3/84 p. 397

255

Lieutenant-Colonel Close to Arthur Wellesley

Pune
23 August 1803 [received by 26 August]

. . . Colonel Murray was to leave Bombay for Broach by a sea conveyance this morning. I hope Major Walker's numerous packets of extravagant intelligence will be properly appreciated by the Colonel, who you know has not yet had much experience in respect to correspondence with the natives.

Malcolm left us yesterday evening for Bombay. He showed me a letter from you he received just before he set out.[10] Gopal Bhau's force appears to be less than was generally imagined. It will be high fun if you could sweep up his guns and bazaar.

I am now giving 10,000 rupees to Balaji Pant Goklah and 17,000 to Appah Dessaye's karkun agreeable to your draft upon me which arrived yesterday.

Rice and other articles are coming in fast from Panvel, and a handsome convoy goes off from hence today for Ahmednagar. You will find the requisite supplies collect rapidly at that fortress. The banjaras will not assemble at Panvel till the beginning of next month, but when they do, they will be numerous. I hope to have a few good bullocks for you ere long. I shall send them without saddles to Ahmednagar, but I know not whether they should be supplied with a proportion of drivers or whether you have got drivers for them already in your camp.

Raghunath Rao is still invisible and the Peshwa too, but I think I shall hear from Suddasheo Munkaiseer in the course of today or tomorrow, in reply to my last memorandum.

WP 3/3/45 p. 538

256

Jonathan Duncan to Arthur Wellesley

Bombay Castle
23 August 1803
[summary]

In response to the letter from Arthur Wellesley of 17 August, Duncan explained that he felt precluded 'from authorising the Colonel [Murray] to proceed to his intended command with the powers you wish to assign to him, until you shall be pleased to take the measure wholly upon yourself.'

'I think it my duty to enter in this place into some more precise detail of the reasons as they appear to me for judging the system you have proposed in some respect dangerous and in others unnecessary.

'First then I deemed it dangerous in leaving at the discretion of the local commanding officer how far he shall comply with Major Walker the Resident at Baroda's requisitions, and in leaving the movement of the subsidised force independent of and unconnected with the said Resident's approbation . . .

'Secondly, I deem the proposed alteration at Surat unnecessary because the superiority of the civil over the military authority at that station is a principle established . . . by the express authority of the Governor General in Council which has been for some time past exercised by a commission . . .

'Thirdly I am not satisfied that, as a mere system of defence is in contemplation, the uniting of two present distinct local commands in the Attavesi and Gujerat proper can be attended with advantages commensurate to some of the opposite consequences which I have above stated . . .'[11]

PRC x 128 Parl Pps [5, 22 June 1804] p. 547

257

Colonel Murray to Arthur Wellesley

Bombay
23 August 1803 [received 29 August]

I make no doubt that you will be surprised to learn than Mr Duncan still detains me here, under what plea I am at a loss to know, but I am sure that if it is possible to delay he will continue to do so. I should not have troubled you on this subject had I not been anxious to convince you that the delay does not originate with me. I confess I am the more surprised at this sudden objection on the part of Mr Duncan as he both in conversation and by letter has given me every reason to believe that your arrangements met his approbation. I hope when he receives your next letter that all further objections will cease.

WP 3/3/79 p. 110

258

Colonel Murray to Arthur Wellesley

Bombay
23 [August 1803] [received 29 August]

Since I wrote you this morning I have seen Mr Duncan's letter to you. I was glad to find that there are no personal objections and as you were acquainted with all the circumstances he states, I venture to hope that I shall still be placed in command. Of this I may venture to assure you, that the civil authority whether at Baroda or Surat shall be supported and their requisitions attended to. Indeed I shall feel doubly interested in the present measures and I hope that you will find no reason to regret the present recommendation to Mr Duncan.

WP 3/3/79 p. 112

259

Colonel Stevenson to Arthur Wellesley

ten miles south of the Badauli ghat.
23 August 1803 [pm?] [received by 26 August]

I have the honour to inform you that I have followed your instructions advised in your letter of the 18th July and [moved] the troops under my command to my present ground yesterday about noon. I am encamped about ten miles south of the Badauli ghat and eighteen miles from the place where Sinde was encamped near the foot of that ghat. I have great satisfaction in informing you that this movement has had all the good effect that you expected from it except a successful clash with the enemy, who have taken effectual means to prevent it for the present, as they marched from their camp at Rohankedh at eleven o'clock yesterday morning in a westerly direction to Goolah Peepree, making a march of ten kos. The only troops that are to the eastward consist of about 5000 horse belonging to Raghuji Bhonsle and are at the end of the Sirsooli or Undri ghat about halfway to the Lakhanwada ghat.

Having heard yesterday that a party of the enemy's had appeared at Badauli ghat, I ordered two squadrons of native cavalry and 500 Mogul horse to march there at daylight this morning to make an observation on the Badauli fort at the head of the ghat and the road through the ghat. An officer has this instant returned and reports Badauli to be a common mud gurry and the road very easy and practicable for carriages.

An officer and a party went three or four miles into the country beyond the ghats but saw no remnants of the enemy's camp who he was informed had marched in a north-westerly direction yesterday. The party picked up a few horses and bullocks loaded with grain . . . I intend moving at ten o'clock this night with a party of my horse to Undri ghat to endeavour to surprise the party there. The remainder of my force will follow at daylight. I have detached the light brigade consisting of three battalions of 1000 firelocks in each battalion and attached two twelve pounders with their complement of artillery and ordnance stores to Jafarabad to give protection to the brigade coming from Aurungabad and to be a check on the enemy to the northward.

WP 3/3/84 p. 399

260

Colonel Stevenson to Arthur Wellesley

Camp near Chikhli
24 August 1803

I have not received any reports respecting the movements of Sinde and Bhonsle's troops after their arrival at Goomlah Peepree that I can depend on, but common report as well as a letter that I have received from Raja Sukhruder mentions his [Sinde] being pretty well advanced up the Ajanta ghat and that Holkar is advancing towards him to join him as a friend and ally with the pindari horse to the numbers of from ten to fifteen thousand.

It is not likely that they would prefer entering the country by that difficult ghat when the eastern ghats of Sirsooli, Undri and Lakhanwada which are broad and easy roads are open to them, and on my arrival near the Badauli ghat it would have been as easy for their troops to have entered by either of the above named ghats as to have made a retrograde movement towards Ajanta.[12]

As the troops of the enemy have however forsaken this part of the frontier and marched to the westward I shall in obedience to your instructions of the 18th July march towards them and hope to arrive near Ajanta in good time to prevent their entering the Nizam's country by that ghat. I did not find it necessary to march to the Undri ghat last night agreeable to my intention as communicated to you in my letter of yesterday, having received intelligence on which I could depend that the enemy had left that place.

WP 3/3/84 p. 403

261

George Barlow – Memorandum

[before 3 August received by Arthur Wellesley 24 August]
[summary]

In a memorandum possibly prepared earlier, Barlow set out some of the main requirements of a peace settlement. There were two significant annotations by Richard Wellesley. Barlow noted that an element of a peace settlement concluded by Arthur Wellesley should be acceptance of treaties made by Lake and Mercer with subordinate rulers in Hindustan. Tributaries of either Sinde or Bhonsle who had aided the military operations of the Company should be guaranteed non-molestation. If Baji Rao was to flee from Pune, in the setting of an attempt to render his government more effective, Amrit Rao should be appointed Dewan until the Peshwa returned to Pune. It was expected that Baji Rao would soon tire 'of being carried about by Sinde as a pageant or instrument in his hands.' Barlow raised the issue of the need for an alliance with Jaswant Rao Holkar.

Richard Wellesley noted 'We must establish an efficient government at Pune, and I am inclined to think that it may become necessary to employ Amrit Rao in some mode. It appears also that Holkar must be conciliated. At all events, Amrit Rao and Holkar must be separated from Sinde. The Peshwa must not be suffered to escape, and the government must be conducted in his name.'

Barlow stressed the need for a settlement with the southern jagirdars, and commented that Sinde and Bhonsle might withdraw 'under circumstances which may preclude us from demanding the cession of Cuttack, Broach and the Doab.' He considered that the best security of Company power at Pune was an alliance with Jaswant Rao Holkar and the 'introduction of Amrit Rao, Moraba Phadnavis and their party into authority' there. He noted finally that Bhonsle was rumoured to have accumulated treasure and this might make possible the demand of a war indemnity. Richard

Wellesley commented marginally that 'this suggestion merits General Wellesley's special attention.'

A Mss 13,722 f. 1, WP 3/3/5

262

Arthur Wellesley to Merrick Shawe

Toka
24 August 1803

. . . To consider the memoranda included in your letter of the 3rd, in case I should have an opportunity of negotiating a peace, I will attend to the first two articles.

In respect to the third, I have no idea that the Peshwa will attempt to fly from Pune, or that if he be so inclined, he could carry his plan into execution without the knowledge of his ministers. You will have observed from my letters to Colonel Close, that I have urged him to pay the ministers, in order to have accurate information of what passes. We cannot contrive to settle the government of Pune till the conclusion of the war. Bad as the situation is, it must be allowed to continue. If we were to attempt to alter it now, we should have a contest in our rear, which would be ruinous . . .

With respect to the fourth article, before you have received this the Governor General will have heard that the southern chiefs have kept aloof, and that all we can expect from them is their neutrality during the war. I have written to them since the fall of Ahmednagar, but I have as yet received no answer. If I find them disposed to join, upon condition that their possessions should be confirmed and guaranteed to them, I will enter into engagements accordingly . . .

With respect to the seventh article, I have to tell you that the confederates have moved to the eastward, and Colonel Stevenson has moved in a parallel line with them, and he will fall upon them as soon as he can. He will continue that course even to Nagpur, if it should be necessary, and I shall be able to move in a day or two, which will probably induce Sinde at least to return.

The confederates cannot make any serious impression upon the Nizam's territories till the middle of October, when it may be expected that the river Godavari will fall, and I have strongly recommended to the Resident at Hyderabad, that a corps should be collected at that city to protect it effectually in case the enemy should contrive to pass round us. If they should go to the northward to invade Bengal, some of us must follow them . . .

Grwd (1837) ii 231 (1844) i 657

263

Colonel Collins to Arthur Wellesley

Aurungabad
25 August 1803

I have received no advices from the camp of Sinde since the 18th instant which in itself looks suspicious. But Raja Mohipat Ram assures me that Daulat Rao Sinde moved towards the Badauli ghat in order to deceive Col Stevenson, and has since returned to Phardapur and that part of his horse has actually ascended the ghat at that place. Yesterday I sent off four of my own horsemen towards Phardapur for the purpose of obtaining more certain intelligence. When they return I shall write to you again. In the meantime I forward a letter to you from Raja Mohipat Ram, who appears to be an alarmist, but whether through timidity or disaffection I cannot pretend to determine.

WP 3/3/53

264

Colonel Stevenson to Arthur Wellesley

Dewalgaon
25 August 1803

Sinde and Bhonsle with their whole force came up the Ajanta ghat yesterday and have made a march on the Aurungabad road. My march to Dewalgaon this morning was intended to interrupt them in getting up the ghat but as I am too late to effect that point I must march on their left flank keeping them to the westward and take any opportunity afforded of attacking them whether by day or night or till your advance can move upon them in a westerly direction.

Colonel Haliburton was at Jafarabad yesterday with his brigade but supposing it might be necessary for him to advance with his whole brigade towards Budnapur to meet the escort with grain. But whether he remains at Jafarabad or advances to meet the grain, his force with this will form a chain to keep the enemy to the west and expose them to your advance. They are at present too far in a westerly direction for me to march right upon them, as it will give them the opportunity of marching round me to the southward and getting immediately to Jalna and Budnapur and the whole eastern country will be open to them. I shall therefore march to Jafarabad and if I find it practicable keep on their left and press them further to the southward which will be towards you or to the westward towards Chandore.[13]

WP 3/3/84 p. 405

265

Colonel Stevenson to Arthur Wellesley

25 August 1803 [pm]

I marched fifteen miles this day towards Jafarabad without an interruption from the pindari horse; they were very troublesome yesterday.

Reports are that the enemy's horse have advanced betwixt Ajanta and Aurungabad and that they were yesterday at Phulambri. I am satisfied with the movement [of] which I informed you yesterday and which is most likely to drive them towards your advance. I find this movement absolutely necessary as I have only dry grain with the detachment to last to the end of the present month, and hope to find this supply at Jafarabad, to secure which I left Colonel Haliburton's brigade at Jafarabad when I moved to the ghats.

I shall encamp on the Jalna side of Jafarabad tomorrow as I propose moving in that direction so far as I know you will advance, as it leads to the richest grain countries, from which I expect 6000 bullock loads of rice for which I have made advances to the banjaras. But if I find that by advancing on the enemy I can press them closely betwixt your force and this for us to expect any immediate and important benefit I shall do so. Otherwise the securing of so large a quantity of rice will claim my particular attention.

WP 3/3/84 p. 412

266

Lieutenant-Colonel Close to Arthur Wellesley

Pune
27 August 1803 [received 30 August]

. . . The Peshwa and Raghunath Rao still sick and no prospect of my receiving any reply to my memorandum of the 20th. The detachment for Erroor marched yesterday morning. It is accompanied by a party of horse from Sham Rao Rastiah's corps by order of the durbar, and the young man Soabhaun Rao who commands it [says?] that it is 100 strong. Should it be weaker even I am happy it has been furnished as so much accommodation on the part of the durbar shows that the Peshwa is not much out of humour. I gave Soabhaun a handsome present at his departure, which will probably have a good effect.

In consequence of your hint to me about the expediency of my beginning to raise part of the 5000 horse to serve with your army, stated in the proposition from the Peshwa, I took steps to ascertain whether it would be pleasing to the Peshwa if I should begin to levy 500 horse to be in charge of Maukaji Sindhia one of his Highness' mankaries here who bears a good character. I received an answer that the Peshwa had not much confidence in any of his mankaries here, but he would be pleased if the cavalry under Goklah should be reinforced by a new levy, that as Goklah has agreed to serve with you, and appeared to give you satisfaction, it would be well to trust him in preference to any other sirdars under the government.

You can turn this subject in your mind and determine whether it might be advisable to authorise Goklah to increase the number of his cavalry, the augmentation to be considered as part of the 5000 proposed by the Peshwa and paid accordingly. I have given Balaji Pant Goklah 30,000 rupees, that is 10,000 from money which I had procured for you, and 20,000 for which you will have to send me a bill on Calcutta. I have mentioned this to your paymaster . . . Our coolies from Panvel come in daily, but not in the numbers that could be wished . . .

As you are now far off, the shroffs have made a difficulty about the delay which occurs in receiving your bills of exchange for the cash which they give me on your account. It would be very convenient if you would either authorise me to draw bills on your account, or send me some blank ones to fill up as occasion might require, informing your paymaster of the particulars . . .

WP 3/3/45 p. 542

267

Colonel Collins to Arthur Wellesley

Aurungabad
27 August 1803 [received 28 August]

In my letter of the 26th I apprised you that I had sent four horsemen towards the Ajanta ghat . . . They report that they could not proceed further than Seloor which is about twenty kos from hence and ten from the Ajanta ghat on account of the pindari who infest the intermediate country. My people were pursued several kos by the pindari who according to the report of the villagers were in the service of Sinde.

I have received no advices whatever from my agent in the Maratha camp since the 18th of this month and I conclude that this man has either been confined or dismissed.

Yesterday I had a conversation with Raja Mohipat Ram in which I suggested to him how necessary it was that he should exert his utmost endeavours to supply your armies with grain etc. The Raja assured me that he had already forwarded to the camp of Colonel Stevenson all the grain he had been able to collect in the vicinity of this place and on my urging him further on this head he said that any quantity of grain might now be procured at Bir and Perinda and that he thought it would be a prudent measure to purchase immediately to the amount of one or two lakhs of rupees.

He further observed that the grain thus purchased might be lodged in forts and be convoyed occasionally to your camp or Colonel Stevenson's by the banjaras as circumstances might require. He concluded by remarking that if these purchases were not shortly made, the grain at Bir and Parenda would most probably be plundered by the Maratha troops.

I asked him why he did not instantly secure the grain in question. He replied that he had no money to make the necessary purchases. I have advised him to write to you for instructions on this important subject . . . On my pressing Mohipat Ram to make advances of cash on this occasion he swore that he had no money but that if Azim ul Umara[14] would order the amil of Bir and Parenda who I believe is Sukhruder Pundit to direct the talukdars of the districts to deliver the grain and to charge the cost in their accounts with government there would in this case be no difficulty in the business particularly as Sukhruder resided in the camp of Colonel Stevenson . . .

WP 3/3/53

268

Arthur Wellesley to Colonel Collins

Camp at Julgong
28 August 1803

I have just received your letter of the 27th. I received intelligence yesterday morning that Daulat Rao Sinde had ascended the Ajanta ghat on the 24th. This was confirmed in the evening by two men who returned from Holkar's army which they say was on its march from Myhissur to join Sinde. They left Holkar's army on the 18th one march beyond the Dhaukote [Dhulkot] ghat on the road to Burhanpur.

The intelligence that Sinde is above the ghat is further confirmed by your letter. But the account of Holkar's movement does not agree with accounts which I have received from Amrit Rao's camp which state that Holkar has crossed the Narbada and gone to Indore. But I have little doubt that a part at least of his army is on its march to the northward.

I am obliged to you for the trouble you have taken with Raja Mohipat Ram to induce him to supply grain for the use of my troops. I will give the lakh of rupees required with pleasure provided he will point out the places at which I can get the grain. I have some bullocks coming through the districts of Bir and Parenda which may bring some of it up. I hope however that though I should not bring it up immediately Mohipat Ram's fears have exaggerated the chance of its being seized by the Maratha armies.

I shall be at Aurungabad tomorrow where I hope to shake hands with you. Have there been any accounts of Colonel Stevenson lately[?] The last letter I received from him was of the 23rd . . .

SD iv 163

269

Lieutenant-Colonel Close to Arthur Wellesley

Pune
29 August 1803 [received 1 September]
[summary]

Close reports that to aid both Goklah and Appah Dessaye he had been forced to utilise a bill sent to him by Arthur Wellesley and so is unable to send cash to camp. 'I cannot draw on Bombay myself.' He needed either blank bills or an authorisation to draw on Arthur Wellesley's account. The Peshwa contended that he had no money to pay Goklah, who was due to receive 70,000 rupees a month.

'It is painful for me to say that I cannot expect to see the Peshwa disburse any money for any purpose except to feed brahmins and to forward his pleasures. His menial servants are actually starving. As for Appah Dessaye, the Peshwa conceives that his seranjami is sufficient to support his party and on this presumption has never promised to give him any monthly allowance. That you have the means of deriving much service from Goklah or Appah Dessaye under any circumstance I conceive to be very doubtful. The Peshwa now seems indifferent whether any of his sirdars here procure employment or not, and is only confident of Goklah because he imagines this chieftain gives you entire satisfaction.' Close added that he was really uncertain whether it would be best to let both Goklah and Appah Dessaye 'return to their jagirs' and for the Company to recruit Maratha horse directly. He thought resources might permit the retention and payment of one of the two chiefs.

WP 3/3/47 p. 550

270

Colonel Murray to Arthur Wellesley

Bombay
29 August [1803]

I have at last got my orders, a copy of which I know will be sent by Mr Duncan . . . I have declined all interference with the Gujerat districts till your final decision shall arrive. Everything is done to cramp the operations that may be necessary, and the result will probably be unpleasant unless speedily rectified. From every communication I have had with Mr Duncan I perceive that it is at your authority he is hurt, and he cannot understand the necessity of one officer directing the whole system.

I shall proceed to Surat tomorrow morning. I understand some orders have been given to the cavalry which is raising at Gujerat. I conclude that most necessary corps will come under my command with the rest of the troops. Government have sent me a copy of your letter of the 13th in which you direct the troops to be moved towards the Narbada, the garrisons of Surat, Songhur and Parneira excepted. This shall be my first object and I shall have them in readiness to secure that river in case of invasion by Holkar or, which may occur, the appearance of the chiefs during the absence of the troops from Baroda.

WP 3/3/79 p. 114

271

Lieutenant-Colonel Close to Arthur Wellesley

Pune
30 August 1803
[summary]

Close outlined the topics that he had raised at a meeting with Raghunath Rao on the evening of 29 August. He had tried to learn the Peshwa's reaction to the proposed meeting of Arthur Wellesley and Amrit Rao, and had pressed for the completion of arrangements which would bring the soucars back to Pune.

'Letters arrived here yesterday from a soucar house at Nagpur which mention that British troops were on the Jumna and that they were soon to take possession of Delhi, also that a British army was about to enter Cuttack . . . Raghunath Rao is now properly disposed and you may confidently rely that if anything wrong should be in agitation here, he will not fail to give us full and early information. I expect that the Peshwa will be long sullen about Amrit Rao, but this will not be of material inconvenience to us.'

WP 3/3/47 p. 561

272

Colonel Stevenson to Arthur Wellesley

[Donegaum]
30 August 1803

The . . . report that I sent you yesterday[15] has not been confirmed by the movements of the enemy, as their principal force accompanied by Sinde and Bhonsle has marched from Budnapur in an easterly direction. They have however detached 6000 horse to Moongy Puttan [Paithan] and detachments the number not specified to Bir. The enemy were encamped yesterday morning at Kalegaum about three kos east of Jalna and having heard of our arrival at Jafarabad marched yesterday morning at nine o'clock with an intention as it is reported to march to Patri and from thence to Baswunt and Nandair.

This appears to be the best opportunity I shall have of getting the lakh of pagodas under the charge of Lt Oliver and also three lakhs of rupees that I have now to expect is arrived at Aurungabad from Hyderabad. I have therefore detached the 2nd Regt of the native infantry with three guns and the allies under Sultan Eer Jung, who commands Nur ul Umrah's party during his absences, with orders to proceed to Aurungabad and bring the treasure and the escorts to join my detachment.

To favour the march of the detachment I marched with my force in a southerly direction to Donegaum where I propose remaining until joined by my treasure, if no particular information draws me from hence. If that should happen I shall give timely notice to Colonel Desse who commands the party to provide for the security of the treasure and the detachment.

WP 3/3/84 p. 410

273

Lieutenant-Colonel Close to Arthur Wellesley

Pune
31 August 1803

Raghunath Rao being unable to quit his room has sent me a message to the following effect . . . Goklah was taken into pay by the Peshwa on the . . . 6th June, has received in all three months' pay, that is two here and one from you, and his fourth month's pay will accordingly be due on the 6th September.

The Peshwa has determined to grant cowle immediately to all the soucars belonging to and now absent from Pune and these cowles shall be sent to me. The Peshwa having lost all his cannon [would be gratified?] if you would direct his being furnished with a few pieces either from Nuggur or Bombay. On the subject of Amrit Rao's proposed meeting with you I shall receive a communication from the durbar.

These points of intimation you see are of a pleasing kind, if they originate in sincerity. If the soucars return, as I trust they will, our means of raising cash here will be much augmented. If any old guns at Nuggur can be spared for the Peshwa he will send for them from hence. If a little powder can be spared to him also it would be acceptable.

The durbar intelligence of this morning is that the enemy have come in through the Ajanta ghat. I have assisted Captain Graham with two men who I think will be useful to him. 2000 coolies and 100 asses loaded with rice and I believe a small quantity of arrack are sent off to Nuggur today. I shall in two or three days send to Nuggur the 25,000 rupees you demand and besides a small supply of cash for yourself, perhaps 50,000 rupees.[16]

WP 3/3/45 p. 565

274

Colonel Collins to Arthur Wellesley

Aurungabad
31 August 1803

In consequence of your intimation, I sent for Mohipat Ram this morning and have the pleasure to inform you that he has already written to the different zemindars under his authority directing them in the strongest terms to come to no sort of compromise with the Marathas but to defend themselves to the last extremity relying in the meantime on being shortly relieved by the troops under your command. Mohipat Ram seems quite on the alert since his interview with you and I really believe will exert himself for the good of the service . . . I wish it would rain and the Godavari would overflow its banks; you might then catch the Maratha chieftains napping . . .

WP 3/3/53 p. 187

275

John Malcolm to Arthur Wellesley

Bombay
31 August 1803

I am much recovered . . . I enclose you a long letter from Shawe[17] which will satisfy you respecting his Lordship's sentiments of your conduct in the negotiation. The opportunity which this rupture affords of crushing the only remaining nest of democrats in India is glorious and this circumstance more than any other will tend to make the war palatable at home . . . Your letter of the 26th to Close is most favourable. I have not a doubt of your successful progress to Burhanpur. The Concan is in peace; Angria will not disturb it [unless?] forces in Sinde's camp make an appearance in person to support him. The only alarm the inhabitants have is about Amrit Rao and his junction with you will put an end to all their fears from that quarter.

I am delighted to learn that General Campbell's detachment has been so powerfully reinforced. I am anxious to learn how you will dispose of that corps. It is too large to be kept idle and pursuing the plan of non-interference with the southern countries as you have hitherto done . . .

I have had a long conversation with Mr Duncan on Gujerat and am sorry to find that he is wrong on that subject. He has mistaken your meaning on some points and has confused himself on others. I shall try to put him right.

WP 3/3/70 fldr 1 p. 18

276

Lieutenant-Colonel Close to Arthur Wellesley

Pune
2 September 1803

I have just received your very interesting letter of the 30th [August]. Yesterday all was quiet at Ahmednagar and no reports whatever have reached Pune yet of the enemy having come to the southward even of Aurungabad. I trust therefore that you will [be] in time to give the gentlemen a turn, and thus save our convoys from interruption. I have given a perusal of your letter to Coleman and sent it on to Malcolm. The 1000 banjara bullocks with rice from hence must now be near Ahmednagar, where I hope they will arrive safe. If the communication continues we shall send off another convoy in the course of two or three days.

WP 3/3/47 p. 3

277

Colonel Collins to Arthur Wellesley

Aurungabad
2 September 1803 [received by 4 September]

. . . I learn from Colonel Desse who arrived here yesterday that Colonel Stevenson was to be at Jalna this morning. The same officer informs me that Gopal Bhau has ascended the Ajanta pass which intelligence is confirmed by Mohipat Ram. Colonel Desse has also been informed that Jaswant Rao Holkar is only twenty kos from Aurungabad but I fancy this news cannot be true, since Mohipat Ram has not learnt that he has yet arrived on this side of the Cassabarri ghat. I am rejoiced to learn that the Godavari still continues high. God send it may not fall for the next two months by which time General Lake ought to settle affairs in Hindustan.

Colonel Desse requested I would present his best respects when I wrote to you. On his march to this place he fell in with some hircarrahs who had come from Surat and were going I believe to Pune. These men reported that Broach had been taken by the British troops. As you expected that this event would soon take place I doubt not but the news is true.

Colonel Desse moves from hence with the treasure tomorrow morning. This battalion is 900 strong and he has about 800 of the Nizam's horse with him, but the latter are six months in arrear and by the Colonel's account cannot be depended on for actual service. If you intend to cross the Godavari let me know in time that I may join you and afterwards proceed to Bombay, since this city must fall into the hands of the Marathas when you and Colonel Stevenson march to any considerable distance from it.

Although I have sent out many hircarrahs in various directions yet not one has returned with intelligence. They have now been out about six days.

WP 3/3/53 p. 196

278

Deposition of John Roach and George Blake

[Aurungabad]
[2 September 1803]

Deposition of John Roach Englishman and George Blake Scotsman lately commanding each a gun in the service of the Begum.

Begum's encampment 31st [August] at night. The night before last, name of place unknown, under orders to march twelve kos and to start at nine o'clock. Hearing the detachment was to march to oppose the English, left camp by permission upon remonstrance against being employed to fight. Immediately after robbed of everything. Went to sleep till past four o'clock yesterday morning. Started then and marched twelve kos to a village distant from this place seven kos due west. Left it this morning at daylight. From half past six o'clock heard a brisk and heavy cannonade for an hour and a half.

We imagine it must have been an action betwixt the united forces of Sinde, the Begum, and Dupont opposed to Wellesley's army joined near Jalna by the Nizamites under Salabat Khan and Rajah Ram Rhumlah . . . We have never heard any mention of Colonel Stevenson's detachment.

Colonel Pohlman with seven battalions of regular infantry two battalions of matchlock men with five guns to a battalion of calibres from three to five pounds was in the rear of the Begum, when we left her campoo, two days march. We do not think it possible for them to have joined in this action.

Sinde and Bhonsle have swarms of horse, a lakh and a half of all descriptions of fighting men. Every battalion of infantry [has] four or five guns and park of thirteen heavy cannon which we saw at Ujjein and believe to have been with him.

We, on the first instance of probability of being opposed to the English, protested against our employment. We were hurried on many marches latterly by night, and it was not until the period specified above that we knew against whom we were sent. When we knew it, we determined on throwing ourselves on the clemency of our countrymen encamped, as were told, at Aurungabad.

WP 3/3/53 p. 195

279

Colonel Murray to Arthur Wellesley

Surat
2 September 1803

I have at last the pleasure to acquaint you that I have assumed the command here and from little I have seen it was highly necessary that some officer should do so. I cannot as yet make any correct report either of the troops or stores in this district. I hope however in a day or two to be enabled to lay a state of them before you and likewise to inform you when I shall be enabled to move towards the Narbada. There is as usual a total lack of money. I hope however to procure a sufficiency to enable me to commence. I look with anxiety to your orders to unite the districts. I feel the inconvenience of the separation already.

WP 3/3/79 p. 120

280

Lieutenant-Colonel Close to Arthur Wellesley

Pune
[3] September 1803

I enclose a letter for you from Malcolm who I am happy to find has a fair prospect of a speedy recovery. You see what Shawe says about the Peshwa, and Malcolm about the southern force. Our effective strength here is 600 firelocks of four battalions. Colonel Coleman has sent for two howitzers which have arrived at Panvel. Until Colonel Hill's battalion joins us, we shall be obliged to continue in our present position, which can be strengthened if necessary, and shall I fear have scarcely the means of protecting the city should we be opposed by any numerous force. We hear nothing from Hill, but Griffiths was nine or ten days ago at Tuljapur. The news of the town today is that the enemy is at Paithan. I have just received a letter from Piele[18] mentioning that on the 27th ult he had despatched a lakh of pagodas for you escorted by 75 horse and 600 peons. This convoy will reach Erroor probably about the 8th or 9th inst at the same time as Lt Page, who will be directed to take charge of the whole and come on hither with all expedition.

WP 3/3/47 p. 23

281

Arthur Wellesley to James Kirkpatrick

Rakshasbhuwan [Rackisbaum]
3 September 1803

. . . Upon hearing of my arrival at Aurungabad, the enemy moved a considerable distance to the eastward of Jalnapur to a place called Ambergaum. They halted there the day before yesterday. Colonel Stevenson was yesterday at Jalnapur and I believe took that place.

The enemy have nothing but cavalry and I am informed are considerably distressed. They have been kept out of the fortified villages by the peons and I have circulated letters to the different amildars in which I have promised rewards to those jemadars who oppose them.

I marched to the river yesterday and I propose to remain on its bank. By this position I hope to secure the junction of all the supplies, to check the incursions of the enemy into the southern countries and, as I shall have my boats on the river, it will be in my power either to fall upon the enemy's troops as they are crossing, if they should attempt to cross it in boats, or to cross it myself if they should be able to ford it. At the same time I shall draw near to them and if an opportunity of striking a blow should offer I shall seize it.

Colonel Stevenson is well placed at Jalnapur to impede the junction of some of their troops particularly of their infantry and guns. But I cannot hope to remove this body of horse from the Nizam's territories till either Colonel Stevenson or I am enabled to commence an offensive operation against the territories of the Rajah of Berar by the junction of our supplies.

These have been much delayed, indeed I may add almost destroyed by the badness of the weather, but I still hope that some of them may soon arrive.

Grwd (1837) ii 261 (1844) i 677

282

Colonel Collins to Arthur Wellesley

Aurungabad
4 September 1803

Two of my hircarrahs returned yesterday from Sinde's camp where they had been discovered and confined. These men report that Sinde and the Bhonsle marched from Ambarh on the 1st and were proceeding in the direction of Hyderabad along the northern side of the Godavari. They state the forces of these chieftains to consist of 50,000 horse, but probably this account is exaggerated. My hircarrahs saw very few tents in the Maratha camp. Sinde and Bhonsle had each a small one. Neither have they much baggage of any description and not a single gun . . .

Begum Sumroo's four battalions were at Seloor yesterday morning, of which circumstance I apprised Colonel Stevenson by express. Also that Gopal Bhau was within six kos of that place. If the Colonel could but fall in with either or both of these detachments he might easily give a good account of them. The Begum's battalions were regarded in a very contemptible light by the European officers in the service of Sinde.

Notwithstanding the deposition of the deserters I am inclined to believe that Pohlman's brigade has not ascended the Ajanta ghat.

WP 3/3/53 fldr 4

283

Lieutenant-Colonel Close to Arthur Wellesley

Pune
4 September 1803

I had the pleasure of writing to you yesterday and shortly after, having had a conversation with Colonel Coleman, I learnt that as our detachments that were out had come in, our effective force now consists of at least 1000 firelocks, so that at all events we are strong enough for present purposes.

Your letter of the 1st is this moment come to hand. I infer from it that there was no certainty of the enemy having approached to the Godavari. We shall therefore continue our convoys to Nuggur, escorted perhaps by parties of infantry or cavalry. In my last I told you that a lakh of pagodas are on their way from Harihar and shall be sent to Nuggur and I have now got more than a lakh of rupees for you here . . .

I am delighted to find that you are joined by Appah Dessaye. You must, my dear General, pay both him and Goklah. The

Peshwa will be debited for the expense, and the Gaikwar fund is good security. To be deprived of any of your present cavalry would be dreadful. You ought to have many more.

WP 3/3/47 p. 4

284

Arthur Wellesley to Lieutenant-General Stuart

Rakshasbhuwan [Rackisbaum]
4 September 1803

. . . The enemy are to the eastward at Partur. They still talk of crossing the Godavari and of marching upon Hyderabad and although the river is fordable in many places, which was never known before at this season of the year, they see by my position on it that I shall cross it likewise, and they are apprehensive of the consequences of being cut off from their own territories and exposed alone to my attacks when the river shall rise again, of which there are no doubts.

Begum Sumru's campoo has come up the ghats and I am afraid has passed the Subah's camp and joined Sinde yesterday. Two deserters from it who came into Aurungabad on the 2nd declared that Pohlman's campoo was following it and two days march in its rear, but I doubt this as I believe Pohlman's campoo was sent to Hindustan.

The arrival of these campoos will retard the enemy's movements and give us something more solid than cavalry to operate upon, but I think we shall not be able effectually to relieve the Subah's country till we can invade Berar, and I am endeavouring to arrange an expedition into that country. Whether I shall be able to effect it or not will depend much upon the state of Colonel Stevenson's equipments, and upon the assistance of grain and provisions which he is to receive from Salabat Khan, the jagirdar of Elichpur . . . .

Grwd (1837) ii 264 (1844) i 678

285

Colonel Murray to Arthur Wellesley

Surat
5 September 1803

I had the honour of receiving your letter of the 26th August this morning. Upon the subject you first mention I shall not fail to be on my guard. The intelligence procured here, from the means employed, could not be depended upon. I hope to make such arrangements as shall enable me to act with some degree of certainty.

Since my arrival here I have been principally occupied in examining the castle, works etc all of which, as well as the garrison, are in the worst possible order. On this subject, as well as my proposed alterations, I shall address you at length in some days. At the same time I am making every effort to equip the field detachment. I now want only tents; I might add men, for by Mr Duncan's private arrangement I cannot order the 2nd battalion of the 6th regt to the southward of the Narbada and the extreme sickly state of the corps will much diminish the proposed force on several points. There were 511 sick Europeans in the Surat hospitals when I took the command.

Another advantage of Mr Duncan's system is that Colonel Woodington has been obliged to leave a detachment of the 86th in Broach, whilst the 88th is here, whom you destined for that garrison as well as Baroda. Colonel Watson agreeable to his orders was on his march to Surat when he received a letter from Major Walker . . . He did not think himself authorised to return. I have however sent him an order to that effect. This will delay his return but he will be here before the 65th and sepoys can come to any great distance . . .

There has hitherto been no connection formed between our government and the Bheels. I find however that there is a vakil from the Mandairi Raja and a naik from a Bheel officer here at present, through this man I shall endeavour to open a communication . . . I am perfectly convinced of the necessity of activity on this side, destitute as we are of cavalry. Everything must depend upon it and I hope that you will not have reason to complain. I hope when the final arrangements are made that I shall meet with a more ardent cooperation on the part of the Bombay government. I hope when Mr Duncan sees the necessity of your measures he will be reconciled.

WP 3/3/79 p. 124

286

Lieutenant-Colonel Close to Arthur Wellesley

Pune
6 September 1803

I am this moment favoured with your public letter of the 3rd and shall act on and reply to it soon. I send you a packet from Malcolm, one from the Bombay Government and one from Major Walker. Yesterday I sent off 60,000 rupees to Nuggur for you. 2000 loaded coolies accompanied them, and I trust the whole will arrive safe. The cash is escorted by twenty of our troopers. Coleman is anxious to accomplish your wishes, and you must send him instructions when necessary. Rice and other grain become cheaper in the city, and a considerable quantity of rice is now on its way from Panvel and must arrive ere long . . . The Peshwa has sent me a paper of cowle for the different soucars who are about Pune, so that I shall soon have them assembled here, which will add to our resources . . .

We have no news of Hill yet, but I hope that you have heard of Griffiths. Coleman, I believe, will soon move out and occupy the position which you formerly inspected and approved. I understand you heard some firing on the 3rd to the eastward.

WP 3/3/47 p. 7

287

Arthur Wellesley to John Malcolm

6 September 1803

. . . I made a march yesterday and another this day to the eastward from Rackisbaum and I am now about six miles north of the Godavari and shall have a fair start with the enemy for Hyderabad. The enemy have done but little mischief hitherto to the country. The pindaris have been driven away from many villages, grain is very dear in their army, which is a certain sign that they get but little plunder; they are terribly alarmed and I am told much dissatisfied. They certainly intend to avoid an action with either of us if they can, unless Colonel Stevenson's movement of yesterday towards Aurungabad should encourage them to blows with him . . .

Whether they go to Hyderabad or not, I have determined to commence an offensive operation against Berar, and I have accordingly arranged that Colonel Stevenson shall march with his corps towards Elichpur and thence to attack the Raja's fort of Gawile or Gawilghar, and possibly plunder Nagpur. If they should march upon Hyderabad I intend to reinforce Pune with three battalions and move to Hyderabad with the rest of my corps. If they do not, I shall endeavour to bring them to an action on this side of the river, and if I find that they lead me far to the eastward, I shall still detach to Pune . . .

I have some hopes however that the invasion of Berar will check the expedition to Hyderabad. Collins, whom I saw at Aurungabad, declares that Raghuji is the only one of the three who cares one pin about his country, or has anything to lose by an invasion of it, and I declare that from what Collins told me I am of the opinion that we are involved in this war because Raghuji saw plainly that if the Maratha armies did not subsist this year in the Nizam's country, they must have subsisted in his . . .

Grwd (1837) ii 273 (1844) i 684

288

John Malcolm to Arthur Wellesley

Bombay
7 September 1803

I have received your letters of the 29th and the 1st from Colonel Close and am now in a state of powerful anxiety which I cannot describe to hear of the success which has attended your pursuit. One good blow will suffice, and even partial success would dispirit warriors like Sinde and the Bhonsle while it would fix the wavering faith of the Dessaye and Goklah.

Your letter of the 29th to this Government[19] had all the effect which it was calculated to produce and I failed not in my endeavour to improve the impression which it had made on Mr Duncan's mind. In my note . . . I recommended to him a plan which I thought would satisfy his conscience while it preserved all the essential principles of your plan of operations, and I was on the point of transmitting it when I received a note requiring me to read and give my sentiments on a voluminous minute where he gives a history of the question ab origine and concluded by proposing some directions of a general nature to be sent to Colonel Murray and Major Walker, to both of which he earnestly recommended the propriety of keeping the peace.

As some of the sentiments expressed in this minute showed a change in his mind, I took courage to send the notes of instructions and in a few hours I had a visit from the Chief Secretary who informed me that Mr Duncan would send the instructions which I had proposed with very little deviation in the letter and none in the sense, provided that I would consent to his stating in a minute that he had taken advantage of Major Malcolm, late Private Secretary to the Governor General being at Bombay to ask his advice, [and] that he had concurred in the propriety of the instructions to Colonel Murray . . .

I have now done with this subject. My packets on it have already been of a size that would not discredit the Secretary's office at Bombay . . . I enclose you a letter from Shawe . . . I am greatly recovered. I have been at my desk writing letters to England by a vessel that sails tomorrow for six hours and am not fatigued. I am not yet permitted to ride . . .

WP 3/3/70 fldr 1 p. 41

289

Colonel Murray to Arthur Wellesley

Surat
8 September 1803

I had the pleasure of receiving your letter of the 29th this morning.

Your surprise at Mr Duncan's objection must have been great after the cordial cooperation he promised in his letter of the 12th. With your letter, which has been sent by express, I have not received a line from government and I am now at a loss what to do. The arrangements which I have made and should still continue may neither please the Surat Committee or the Resident at Baroda, when they resume their commands, which I presume will immediately be the case. Under the control of either of these powers I am sure that you will not expect that I should act and if any attempt is made I shall immediately resign my command and return to Bombay.

If Mr Duncan was to see or could judge the state of affairs in this part of the world I think his respect for his Committee would be much diminished. This whole part of the force, and I have every reason to believe that part north of the Narbada, is so disjointed and in such a state as to be unserviceable in case of any serious attack. It cannot indeed be otherwise.

From every appearance and from all the accounts which I have had I think there is no doubt that a very serious attack is planned on the Gujerat district. Colonel Woodington informs me that Canoji has 6000 men and expects to be reinforced by many more.

A body of Sinde's troops have by every account very much reinforced the fort of Powanghur and large bodies are collected at Godra, Dohad etc to the eastward of Powanghar.

On this side of the Narbada the enemy appears at present quiet. But it is well known that there are bodies of Holkar cavalry near the ghats to the southward of this district. Whilst the season advances so rapidly, nothing is in a state of readiness to move. There are no tents, not a bullock purchased, no public followers and no money at least that I can get. The corps under Colonel Woodington are still dispersed; I know not how they are provided. The garrison is extremely sickly and as it has been lately managed cannot fail of continuing so, and of ruining at the same time the discipline of any regiment; that of regiments here is dreadfully relaxed.

I shall delay troubling you with my ideas relative to Surat till I hear from Mr Duncan which will probably be in the course of tomorrow. Whatever his answer may be, I assure you that I shall ever feel myself extremely indebted to you and shall at all times be happy to serve under your command. Mr Duncan will I think feel himself a little puzzled how to act after the orders he has given out, and I am much mistaken in his character if he will not shrink from the responsibility.

WP 3/3/79 p. 134

290

Arthur Wellesley to John Malcolm

9 September 1803

. . . Colonel Stevenson beat up a pindari camp on the night of the 6th, but from private accounts from his camp I suspect that the Subah's cavalry as very bad and very useless. What do you think of the pickets having been obliged to defend themselves with cannon during the whole of the 6th? I believe the same thing happened yesterday, as one of my hircarrahs has reported that he saw an action between our infantry and the enemy's cavalry yesterday morning in which there was much firing of cannon, and the latter were driven off, but Colonel Stevenson from whom I have just received a letter of the 8th, does not mention it.

The enemy are far distant to the northward. The sirdars of the silledar are much discontented and swear they will not serve unless the campoos are brought forward. Not a horseman has come near me yet. Indeed they will not allow me to get within forty miles of them. Every hircarrah who comes in brings accounts of reports of the filtur [treachery?] of the Nizam's sirdars, particularly of Sukhruder.

SD iv 172 Grwd (1844) i 695

291

Lieutenant-Colonel Close to Arthur Wellesley

Pune
10 September 1803

I am this moment favoured with your letter of the 7th . . . Within these few days past I have received a dozen complaints from the durbar against Amrit Rao who, the Peshwa says, has lately taken Nasik . . . and plundered the town, and is now going against Trimbuck. Under these circumstances I really fear that it will not be possible to establish rules of neutrality between the two parties. Indeed on every point I meet with extreme difficulty. The Peshwa is still sick and invisible now on account of the death of Raghunath Rao . . .

WP 3/3/47 p. 16

292

Arthur Wellesley to Colonel Stevenson

Goondy
[10 September 1803]

In my letter of yesterday in which I proposed that you should send to my camp for money and heavy artillery, if you should want them for the expedition into Berar, I omitted to tell you where the detachment coming for these articles would find me. I am still encamped upon the Godavari and am marching to the eastward. I am this day at Goondy at the junction of the Godavari and Galatti, and purpose to move on daily to the eastward, till the enemy shall cross the river, when I shall cross likewise. It is obvious I cannot tell you at what place, but if you direct the march of the detachment from your corps on this place, or upon Ramusgaum on the Godavari, it will certainly find me. Let me know by what route your detachment will march.

Grwd (1837) ii 311 (1844) i 714, undated in WP 3/3/83 fldr 3 p. 80

293

Arthur Wellesley to Colonel Stevenson

12 September 1803

I find that the enemy have moved off from Jalna and are now to the northward of Budnapur. Some of my light troops fell in with some of theirs on the night before last, in consequence of which they found out my intended march and went off. I doubt however whether my movement will have been of any benefit to you as they appear to be equally close to you only to the northward.

The doubt expressed in the latter part of your letter of yesterday has annoyed me a good deal, as I am afraid that it will oblige me to alter my plan, at least till we have brought the enemy to an action. The fact is that if you are not sufficiently strong for them when they have neither their infantry nor their guns, [nor] been joined by Holkar, I cannot expect that you will be able to undertake a siege while they can keep the field against you.

It is true that your movement towards the territories of the Rajah of Berar will create a diversion in favour of those of the Subah of the Deccan, but if you are not strong enough it may be one which will cost us an army.

I wish to have your sentiments upon this subject.

Grwd (1837) ii 289 (1844) i 699

294

Arthur Wellesley to John Malcolm

12 September 1803

. . . I am glad to find that you are so much better, but you must restrain your pen. Stevenson attacked the enemy on the night of the 9th and did great damage, as the hircarrahs come from their camp say, not much in his opinion. They have some pindaris in my neighbourhood now, who have done us but little mischief themselves, but they have set the village people a-going and these have attacked our supplies, but a gallows or two will remedy that evil. The main body keep away from me and remain to the northward about fifty miles from hence and not far from the passes.

I enclose you a curious letter which I got last night.[20] I made the movement therein suggested yesterday morning and accordingly they went off. But this letter, however contradictory, has annoyed me considerably, as it gives room for doubt whether the plan I had in contemplation for the campaign is practicable. If the doubts contained in the last paragraph are [well] founded it certainly is not.

Grwd (1844) i 699 [not in 1837 edition], SD iv 174

295

Arthur Wellesley to Colonel Collins

13 September 1803 [received 16 September]

. . . I regret exceedingly the circumstances which occasion your desire to return to Calcutta. If you wish it I will take upon me to give you leave to return immediately . . . You mentioned in our conversation at Aurungabad that you had a secret communication with one of Sinde's munshis. It would be very desirable to renew this communication and to keep it up if possible during the war . . .

SD iv 174

296

Colonel Murray to Arthur Wellesley

Surat
13 September 1803

I received Mr Duncan's final instructions a few days ago. They are the most unpleasant I ever served under and I am sure the public service must be much injured were they literally to be attended to. I have stated my objections to which I expect no attention will be paid, and I have finished by informing government that I must make the public good the rule of my conduct. They must conclude from this that I will not act in a manner detrimental to it. I assure you however that I am [as] strongly impressed with the necessity of a hearty cooperation as Mr Duncan and I feel confident that he will not venture to complain on this score.

Things begin to wear a regular appearance here, though far from what they ought to be, and much is I fear wanted in the northern district. The 65th and detachments of the 60th and 88th march tomorrow for Baroda. I follow in the evening. Lt Colonel Anderson remains in command to the southward of the Narbada with the 75th and the 1st of the 6th. I have increased the magazine at Broach as more convenient for the present intended operations which are against Canoji and the fort of Powanghar. Colonel Woodington is already marched against this fort, a measure of which I cannot judge, but he has in my opinion a force by no means adequate.

Your instructions of the 2nd August shall be my guide. You will permit me to say that in spite of Mr Duncan's fears there could not be devised another plan for the salvation of this country . . .

WP 3/3/79 p. 136

297

Lieutenant-Colonel Close to Arthur Wellesley

16 September 1803

I yesterday perused and forwarded your letter of the 12th to Malcolm. As Colonel Murray is furnished at length with a proper position of authority, I trust your instructions in regard to Gujerat will be successfully exerted. Walker will have it that Ambaji Inglia is destined for Champaneer and it is certain that a report prevails here that this person has been recalled by Sinde.

We yesterday despatched a convoy of rice etc to Ahmednagar and I took the occasion to forward 54,000 rupees for you to that post, so that if the garrison has not expended any of the cash I have transmitted to you, Mr Carfrae will soon have 2,05,165 rupees at your command. Yesterday 1000 banjara bullocks arrived here on their way to join your camp from Harihar. They are escorted by one naik and four [sepoys?]. Some of these bullocks are unloaded; they will take up rice from Major Spen's depot.

About an hour since Chinavas Rao with the treasure from Purniah came in here. He met with no material interruption on the road. He has come on very quickly and conducted himself admirably. These two convoys will proceed on to Nuggur in a few days accompanied by a convoy of rice etc from hence . . .

The Peshwa is so far recovered as to take the air in his palanquin and I hope to have an interview with him ere long. Since writing the above I have seen your letter of the 13th to Colonel Coleman. Chinavas Rao with the treasure will be sent off to Nuggur with the least possible delay.

WP 3/3/47 p. 32

298

Colonel Collins to Arthur Wellesley

Chickwen
16 September 1803 7 pm

I received your obliging letter of the 13th inst about an hour ago at this place which is forty four miles from Rackisbaum [Rakshasbhuwan] . . . The communication I had with Sinde's munshi was through the channel of my agent Gunput Roy who was obliged to quit me nearly two months ago on account of a severe illness. But were this man now with me, he could not keep up this communication for in the first place Sinde's munshi would never commit himself in writing and in the second he grew very cautious and reserved as soon as he saw that there was a great probability of a rupture between his prince and the English.

Gunput Roy had resided sixteen years at the durbar of Sinde during which period he contracted an intimacy with this munshi whose name is Kavalnyn, but this fellow is too well paid by the Maharajah to hazard the loss of his situation by carrying on a clandestine correspondence with any of our native agents during a war. I write this note in great haste that your cossids might not be detained.

WP 3/3/53 p. 210

299

Richard Wellesley to Arthur Wellesley

Fort William
26 August 1803 [received about 17 September]

[Richard Wellesley assures Arthur Wellesley of 'firm confidence that you will prosecute the war now commenced against Sinde and the Raja of Berar with the same ability promptitude and success which have distinguished your conduct on every occasion.']

It will be satisfactory to you to know that the Commander in Chief probably commenced operations against the territories of Sinde in the Doab of the Jumna and Ganges on the 25th inst and that the operations against Cuttack will probably commence about the 30th inst. Every prospect exists of the immediate success of the Commander in Chief and of Lt Colonel Campbell, who commands the expedition against Cuttack.

I request that you will transmit to me a regular note of your despatches to the Commander in Chief as well as of such as you may receive from him by the route of Hindustan. It is extremely important that your communication with the Commander in Chief by that route should be maintained and accelerated by every possible precaution. I am aware that the passage of the dak through Hindustan[21] will be subject to risk under present circumstances, but it is highly desirable that every exertion should be employed to secure your intercourse with the Commander in Chief by that route.

WP 3/3/1 fldr 3 p. 61 [partly in cipher]

300

Colonel Stevenson to Arthur Wellesley

Budnapur
17 September 1803

. . . Sinde and Bhonsle have continued on the same ground. I was encamped on the same place the day before I arrived at Jafarabad on my way to the Badauli ghat. It is six miles two furlongs by the wheel from Jafarabad. The place is called Naleniah in my orderly book but my hircarrahs in general call it Naulniah. I marched from Hasnabad about 15 miles 2 furlongs to Naulniah on the route to Jafarabad 18 August and the next day 6 miles 2 furlongs to Jafarabad.

If he [Sinde] awaits an attack at that place you will come on his left flank by keeping Jafarabad on your left about a mile and a half where you will find a good road across the river and if I come on his flank at the same time it will have every probability of a successful termination . . .

Sinde was joined yesterday by Gopal Bhau. I expect Captain Maitland's battalion will join at eight this morning. I recommended that he should rather be three days on his march than leave my shot and powder on the river . . . he made three marches from Paithan which is 30–40 miles from Budnapur. I expect to be joined this day by the banjaras that marched with Sukhruder's troops and about 1000 from Jalna – all dry grain.

WP 3/3/84 p. 407–9

301

Lieutenant-Colonel Close to Arthur Wellesley

Pune
18 September 1803

A clashing of officers here and a difference about emolument has obliged me to alter the arrangements I had adopted respecting the bullocks I procured for you. I have taken them back from Colonel Coleman and am training them to carry and shall despatch them to Nuggur ere long loaded with rice . . .

While writing I am favoured with your packet of the 15th. The enclosure for Malcolm shall go on immediately. As Sinde is bringing up his infantry it would be melancholy to be obliged to break up your line. We are strengthening ourselves in front of the 84th barracks and will soon be secure against anything but guns. The right of the line is low and commanded by all the ground on the opposite side of the river. With another battalion I think we might occupy the high ground on the east side of the river which you formerly approved. We should also be able to give some protection to the city which might offer some resistance if the troops within would fight. I continue to bore the durbar to give the creatures some pay and may possibly succeed.

I shall get a few guns for the Peshwa from Bombay. Chinavas Rao with the Mysore treasure marches for Nuggur tomorrow morning. I shall forward the 56,500 rupees by him. The 1000 banjara bullocks that arrived here a few days since from Harihar resumed their march this morning to Nuggur. A convoy of rice etc from Major Spens moved at the same time, so that you perceive the Nuggur depot increases fast. A little while longer and I trust it will be completed. All your arrangements must be backwards I fear, till the junction of Hill whom the Lord pursue and speed . . .

WP 3/3/47 p. 44

302

Colonel Stevenson to Arthur Wellesley

Budnapur
18 September 1803

Captain Maitland's battalion joined yesterday morning and brought hither the 12 lb shot that was left at the river before the stores were delivered to him. He brought forward 380 bullock loads of rice from Paithan for the Commissariat of grain department, which was all that had arrived at that place. I do not hear of the Baswunt rice coming forward nor can I get any report of the 26 casks of arrack that left Hyderabad on the 12th of last month . . . I expect to receive 5000 bullock loads of dry grain this day from the banjaras with Rajah Sukhruder's party which with

1000 received from Jalna which together with what I have received from this place will make more than 7000 loads [and] with what I may pick up from the country will supply the troops by regular issue at a seer a day gratis and subsist the followers for about forty days. My hircarrahs report that Sinde and Bhonsle remain in the same situation that I described in my former letter yesterday morning.

WP 3/3/84 p. 418

303

Colonel Stevenson to Arthur Wellesley

[Budnapur?]
19 September 1803

Sinde and Bhonsle have marched 8 kos from Naulniah in a north-westerly direction which may lead to the Ajanta ghat or to Phulambri.

I expect 5000 loads of dry grain this morning which will enable me to march tomorrow to Lolsangwi about five kos also in a north-westerly direction, where I shall be able . . . to prevent the enemy from marching by Phulambri to Aurungabad or getting to the southward by that route. It will also give me the opportunity of annoying their rear if they go down the ghat. Or should their movements be intended to join their infantry and guns I shall take such advantages as their position will admit.

I have received a letter from my banjaras . . . about eighty kos to the eastward. They are backward but responsive to our needs. [Monack Chanda?] whom I [sent?] with a large party of horse foot and guns to give them protection has not been nearer the banjaras than 25 kos. The subahdar that was with the banjaras offered to bring them further but they would not move unless the subahdar would give them a written assurance that the rice should be the loss of government and they should be paid for any of their bullocks that may be lost.

Having so large a party as [Monack Chanda has ?], 1000 horse 500 foot and 2 guns, they were certainly strong enough if they would do their duty. It might be attended with loss if I was to send two companies to reinforce the subahdar and it might happen that they were not strong enough to effect a junction. I shall therefore endeavour to prevail on [Monack Chanda] to join the banjaras and march by a safer route to join the detachment.

I have little doubt that I shall get the 5000 bullock load of grain this day, which will enable me to move forward in any direction for thirty or forty days, in which time I may adopt some other means of loading my bullocks . . .

WP 3/3/84 p. 414

304

Colonel Stevenson to Arthur Wellesley

Budnapur
20 September 1803

. . . I have received 200 loads of rice from Paithan which with what I had is equal to 16 days issue and I have eight days issue of dry grain. I have received no account of Sukhruder's dry grain but he is seriously alarmed and has taken such measures as will I think bring it forward.

I shall march tomorrow some kos beyond Lolsangwi in a northwesterly direction which is the [best route?] I can find towards the enemy who is at Bhokrdan. It will also lead me upon the advanced guard of horse at Chandli [?] which are reported to have increased to more than 20,000. Bhokrdan is not a place of much importance and other hircarrahs may describe the situation of the enemy by the name of Jarni[?] a small village. Bhokrdan is about four kos west and a little northerly from Lonegaum (not Donegaum) a place better known than either Bhokrdan or Chandli.

If you keep your route directly north from Jalna you will be considerably to the eastward of the enemy at Bhokrdan but by keeping Jalna to your right and inclining to the westward it will bring you nearer to the enemy. Provided that the enemy keep their station, which I dare say is strong, I am in hopes you will fix on a day when both your division and the subsidiary force may be near enough to the enemy to attack on the same morning and as nearly as possible at the same hour. In the meantime I shall not fail to take advantage of every circumstance and situation which may offer.

Rajah Mohipat Ram has advanced an extraordinary story and persists in his [assertion?] that he cannot be deceived. He says that the officer that was taken belonging to Colonel Collins' bodyguard will be sent back and that Sinde will request that Captain Johnston, my Persian interpreter, may be sent to afford him an opportunity of sending some proposals to you, which the impetuous conduct of Colonel Collins prevented him from doing before. The Rajah first said that he had a letter but on being asked to produce it said it was a messenger but from such authority as could not be doubted.

I have this instant got information that Sukhruder's grain has arrived at Jamkier about 14 kos from here and I think will join without loss.

WP 3/3/84 p. 419

305

Lieutenant-Colonel Close to Arthur Wellesley

Pune
21 September 1803

I send you copies of two letters which I yesterday addressed to Mr Duncan. I also enclose copies of two packets which I this morning received from Mr Edmonstone. You will perceive from the latter that his Excellency has accepted the Peshwa's proposals relative to Bundelkhand and will proceed to act immediately on these proposals.

You will perceive also that I am by no means confident that the Gaikwar state will ever discharge regularly the rent of the Peshwa's share of the subah of Ahmedabad, and that I have accordingly proposed that the said territory should be brought under the management of the Company's government in order to afford us a satisfactory security for the payment of the sums you have disbursed, and will be obliged to disburse, for the Peshwa's troops under Goklah and Appah Dessaye . . . I fear it will be impossible to prevail on the Vinchor man to accept an equivalent for Oolpar; could we offer him land from the territory annexed to Ahmednagar ?

I think I could raise Maratha horse here to serve with your army, but I fear it would be necessary to pay the common horsemen about 35 rupees per month per man, especially as you do not permit plundering.

I have now sent in all about 2,50,000 rupees to Nuggur and will send more as occasions offer. Since writing the above I have received your letter of the 18th.

WP 3/3/47 p. 44

306

Arthur Wellesley to Richard Wellesley

Assaye
24 September 1803 [received 30 October 1803]

I was joined by Major Hill with the last of the convoys expected from the river Kistna on the 18th, and on the 20th was enabled to move forward towards the enemy, who had been joined in the course of the last seven or eight days by the infantry under Colonel Pohlman, by that belonging to Begum Sumru and by another brigade of infantry . . . The enemy's army was collected about Bhokrdan and between that place and Jafarabad.

I was near Colonel Stevenson's corps on the 21st and had a conference with that officer in which we concerted a plan to attack the enemy's army with the divisions under our command on the 24th in the morning, and we marched on the 22nd, Colonel Stevenson by the western route and I by the eastern route round the hills between Budnapur and Jalna.

On the 23rd I arrived at Naulniah and there received a report that Sinde and the Raja of Berar had moved off in the morning with their cavalry and that the infantry were about to follow, but were still in camp at the distance of about six miles from the ground on which I had intended to encamp. It was obvious that the attack was no longer to be delayed, and having provided for the security of my baggage and stores at Naulniah, I marched on to attack the enemy.

I found the whole combined army of Sinde and the Raja of Berar encamped on the bank of the Kaitna river nearly on the ground which I had been informed that they occupied. Their right which consisted entirely of cavalry was about Bhokrdan and extended to the corps of infantry which were encamped in the neighbourhood of Assaye. Although I came first in front of their right I determined to attack their left, as the defeat of their corps of infantry was most likely to be effectual. Accordingly I marched round to their left flank, covering the march of the column of infantry by the British cavalry in the rear and by the Maratha and Mysore cavalry on the right flank.

We passed the river Kaitna at a ford beyond the enemy's left flank and I formed the infantry immediately in two lines with the British cavalry as a reserve in a third, in a open space between that river and a nullah running parallel to it. The Maratha and Mysore cavalry occupied the ground beyond the Kaitna on our left flank and kept in check a large body of the enemy's cavalry which had followed our march from the right of their position.

The enemy had altered the position of their infantry previous to our attack; it was no longer as at first along the Kaitna but extended from that river across to the village of Assaye upon the nullah which was on our right. We attacked them immediately and the troops advanced under a very hot fire from cannon, the execution of which was terrible. The pickets of the infantry and the 74th Regiment, which were on the right of the first and second lines, suffered particularly from the fire of the guns on the left of the enemy's position near Assaye. The enemy's cavalry also made an attempt to charge the 74th Regiment at the moment when they were most exposed to this fire, but they were cut up by the British cavalry which moved on at that moment. At length the enemy's line gave way in all directions and the British cavalry cut in among their broken infantry, but some of their corps went off in good order and a fire was kept up on our troops from many of the guns from which the enemy had been first driven, by individuals who had been passed by the line under the supposition that they were dead.

Lt Colonel Maxwell with the British cavalry charged one large body of infantry which had retired and was formed again in which operation he was killed, and some time elapsed before we could put an end to the straggling fire which was kept up by individuals from the guns from which the enemy were driven. The enemy's cavalry also which had been hovering round us throughout the action were still near us. At length when the last formed body of infantry gave way, the whole went off and left in our hands ninety pieces of cannon.

The victory which was certainly complete has however cost us dear . . . The enemy are gone off towards the Ajanta ghat and I propose to follow them as soon as I can place my captured guns and wounded in security. Colonel Stevenson arrived this morning at Bhokrdan and I imagine that he will be here this evening.

Grwd (1837) ii 323 (1844) i 723

306A

Letter from an unknown cavalry officer

Camp near Jafarabad
24 September 1803

We had yesterday a brilliant and decisive engagement with the confederate armies of Daulat Rap Sindhia and Raghuji Bhonsle who both commanded in person. It was understood that Colonel

Stevenson's division and ours were to march to a point on this day, but on reconnoitring yesterday we discovered no less than three camps. The baggage and the 1st and the 2nd [Madras Native Infantry] were left under charge of Lt Colonel Chalmers and the remainder, two regiments of Europeans, 4 battalions of sepoys, 4 regiments of cavalry, with four brass twelve pounders and our light guns, moved to attack the enemy. At one [pm] our line was formed consisting of the whole of the infantry and supported by a second line composed of the cavalry.

After sustaining a most dreadful and destructive cannonade till near three o'clock from a hundred pieces of cannon, we succeeded in bringing the confederate army to a close engagement. The picquets and the 74th regiment were charged by a wonderful fine body of infantry and cavalry. The picquets lost all their officers except Lt Colonel Orrock and another officer and had only 75 men left. The 74th out of 400 men have only about 100 who are likely to survive. Every officer of this corps except Major Swinton and Mr Grant the quarter-master were either killed or desperately wounded.

At this awful moment, when the enemy had succeeded in their attack on our right, which was so hard pressed as possibly to have been little longer able to sustain so unequal a conflict, the cavalry charged those advancing and made dreadful slaughter. They also attacked an immense body that surrounded the elephants of the principal chiefs who were posted in a nullah. Here however owing to the difficulty of getting at them, all were killed and wounded, both Europeans and natives on our side, that attempted it.

Captain Mackay of the 4th regiment fell nobly within two yards of the muzzle of one of their guns. Captain McGregor of the 7th was badly wounded. Lt Bonomi of the 5th regiment was killed. Captain Colebrooke, Lts Mcleod and Dark wounded, the latter his leg shot off, and a number of men and horses killed and wounded.

We then made another charge upon a body of infantry and guns. The enemy's infantry faced and received us with a [severe?] file firing as did their artillery with a terrible discharge of grape which killed numbers. We succeeded however in getting possession of their cannon, 70 field pieces and 4 howitzers and retaining them till our line of infantry came up. In this latter conflict fell the gallant Colonel Maxwell our Brigadier and Captain Boyle of HM 19th Dragoons. Captain Cathcart and Lt Wilson of the same were wounded.

You may suppose what a day we had of it when I tell you that our loss is about 20 officers killed and 30 wounded and about 1000 men. Not an officer of the cavalry but was either killed or wounded or lost a horse shot under him. It was indeed a glorious day but dearly purchased. The whole country is strewn with the killed and wounded both European and natives, ours as well as the enemy's. Their loss is supposed to be about 2000 killed.

Never was artillery more destructively served or better defended. Had their numerous cavalry but supported them as they ought to have done, God knows what would have been the issue. The enemy had 17 fine battalions and about 20,000 horse. Lt Colonel Mcleod and Major Macaulay of the 12th were wounded. The 7th I understand have lost Captain Douglas killed and a great many men killed and wounded. Captains Steele and Fowler and Lts Lindsay and Griffiths of the artillery were killed at their guns . . .

NLW Clive 2107

IV
An Interim Settlement – October to December, 1803

The measure of the extent of the victory of the battle of Assaye literally lay about Arthur Wellesley on 24 September. It took some weeks to assess, from a variety of sources, some of them given here [343, 344], the degree of destruction of the 'formed brigades' of Daulat Rao Sinde that had been achieved, and the effect that the victory would have on the military ventures of the two Maratha rulers. Somewhat later Arthur Wellesley wrote to a colleague who had distributed intelligence which he should have been able to realise was questionable. 'An hircarrah can know nothing except what he sees, and he generally exaggerates that.'[1] October 1803 was to provide adequate evidence of this.

After his belated arrival at the field of battle, the detachment commanded by Stevenson was moved northwards through the Ajanta pass [310, 311]. From the intelligence messages received it began to be possible to assess the surviving military structure of the two Maratha armies, and to speculate on their next moves. Perhaps a new threat was about to emerge, that of a southward movement through the passes to the northwest of Aurungabad (the Cassabarri passes). Uncertainty over this threat led Arthur Wellesley initially to move southward from the Ajanta pass, reaching Phulambri by 12 October [331, 332]. That day he explained to the Madras Government that a further move southwards as far as Aurungabad might discourage the prospective movement of the two Maratha rulers, but that if his position led them again to send their cavalry northward, he too would turn north.[2]

During the night of 15/16 October, Arthur Wellesley received 'a particular account of the disposition of their troops' from which he deduced that a combined Maratha move to interrupt the operations against Burhanpur and Asirgarh being undertaken by the detachment commanded by Stevenson was in prospect. Arthur Wellesley reported to Barry Close his desperate shortage of intelligence hircarrahs, complaining that some recruited near Pune, presumably with local geographic and linguistic skills, had deserted [338, 344].[3]

The detachment therefore retraced its steps northwards, passing through the Ajanta ghat and reaching Phardapur. Here Arthur Wellesley learnt of the capture of Burhanpur and Asirgarh [345, 349]. It was also possible to assess the extent to which the officers in Sinde's infantry had responded to the Governor-General's Proclamation of August 1803. This had guaranteed pensions to these officers, of various nationalities, following surrender to the Company's forces. Probably few of them had received word of the Proclamation while serving Daulat Rao Sinde, but once captured accepted the terms offered [350]. It now became clear that the forces of Raghuji Bhonsle, although not of Daulat Rao Sinde, had indeed moved south. This recreated the threat to Pune that had existed in early September, and perhaps also gave Bhonsle an opportunity, by a meeting with Amrit Rao, to attempt to divert him from his newly found alliance with the Company, which had been agreed through intermediaries in August, but had still to be implemented by junction with Company forces. The detachment commanded by Arthur Wellesley therefore journeyed south again [360]. By the end of October both armies, that of the Raja of Berar and that commanded by Arthur Wellesley were in the Godavari valley near to Aurungabad [366, 367].

Word also began to arrive of events in Hindustan; both the defection of Perron and the victories of General Lake at Aligurh and before Delhi at Patpanganj were known in the Deccan early in October [347]. Operations in the Deccan were essentially defensive of the territories of Hyderabad [362] but the lukewarm support, or worse, of the major feudatories of the Nizam, and his court, led Arthur Wellesley to protest in the strongest terms to the Resident [366, 367]. James Kirkpatrick was not one of the politicals with whom Arthur Wellesley was in a confidential relationship, but he regarded as creditable his attempt to bring the 'young Nizam,' who had succeeded to the throne in August, to a realisation of the obligations of the alliance treaties with the Company. Arthur Wellesley wished later to include in the peace settlement an enhanced role for the Resident at Hyderabad, under which both the readiness of the forces of the Nizam and the scale of stores provision in the frontier forts in his territories would be directly subject to Company inspection; but this objective was not achieved.

In Gujerat, Colonel Murray was faced with severe sickness among his European forces [307, 314]. In the first days of October 1803, he was able to move northeastwards from Baroda and secure Godra [330, 333]. He was aware of the presence of isolated forces loyal to Sinde above the Western Ghats and set out to Arthur Wellesley his plan by control of the passes to safeguard Gujerat from any attack [339, 341]. But at the point which Arthur Wellesley described as 'the most precious time of the campaign' [342] Murray felt bound to give priority to the defence of Gujerat from the guerilla attack on its territory by Canoji, a relative of the Gaikwar [339, 341]. Alarm at the movements of Canoji forced Murray to move from Godra towards the northern frontier of Gujerat [359, 363]. These movements forced a withdrawal by Canoji, but Murray became increasingly concerned at the ineffectiveness in this contest of the forces of the Gaikwar. He clearly totally doubted their willingness and capacity to contribute to the defeat of Daulat Rao Sinde [364, 365]. Despite the lack of support from the forces of the Gaikwar of Baroda, Murray had so moved as to force the withdrawal of the rebel Canoji out of the Gaikwar's territory and into that of Holkar. He now felt able to concentrate on creating a threat against Sinde, stating slightly prematurely on 12 November that Canoji was 'now off my hands' [370, 375].

Even before Assaye there had been hints that Daulat Rao Sinde would welcome a return to negotiation rather than warfare, as Collins had foreseen. In early October an attempt was made to negotiate, in Maratha fashion in a form that could be either exploited or disowned. But these initial ventures at peace making were rebuffed; later correspondence from Fort William showed that their handling by Arthur Wellesley was endorsed by the Governor-General. After the loss of Burhanpur and Asirgarh the attempts were resumed, and by early November Arthur Wellesley could report to Fort William that he knew that an agent who appeared to be accredited would soon arrive in his camp [369].

Drawing on the detailed instructions which Richard Wellesley had sent to him in June [175] Arthur Wellesley now set out the approach which he intended to adopt in peace negotiations [374]. Many of the points he made echoed those of the Governor-General. But there was an area of significant difference. Richard Wellesley had suggested that the Narbada should become the southern boundary of the territory of Daulat Rao Sinde, and that lands between the Narbada and the environs of Pune should be divided between the Nizam and the Peshwa. Arthur Wellesley proposed markedly to vary this approach, taking to the Company the fortresses of Broach and Ahmednagar, both recently taken by siege, and the territories directly depending on them, rather than the entire tract. He saw a frontier on the Narbada as difficult to defend and also urged the importance of preserving 'a part of Sinde's strength, to enable him to support himself against Jaswant Rao Holkar.' This was to anticipate the difference of view with the Governor-General which both Arthur Wellesley and John Malcolm were to demonstrate early in 1804. These territorial concessions were also seen as inducements that could bring Sinde to join the Company promptly in a joint attack on Berar. This did not happen, since the agents when they reached Arthur Wellesley were in no way prepared for a reversal of alliances, and this was in any event an approach which the Governor-General later indicated he did not favour.

In the period before the first tentative peace negotiations took place, the detachment commanded by Stevenson was moving cautiously eastwards in the Purna valley, towards the objective it had been set earlier, the siege of Gawilghar. Stevenson reported frequently to Arthur Wellesley, in letters often brought by runners and so prepared that they could be concealed. Some are written on minute scraps of paper. The letters are repetitive, since Stevenson could have no certainty of his runners and their messages reaching Arthur Wellesley. There were short letters designed to be sent by runner who might elude interception, and fuller accounts when the means of communication was believed to be more secure. In these longer letters Stevenson reported the style of the capture of both Burhanpur and Asirgarh, where the arrears of pay of Sinde's forces made possible the use of a 'golden key' [345, 349, 353].

Shortly after Arthur Wellesley had set out, in a letter to Fort William which would take almost a month to reach its destination, his objectives in any peace negotiations [374] further guidance arrived, amplifying that given in August [385, 386]. Arthur Wellesley was now reassured that his own proposals would not now 'seem tame' [387]. It was on this interim guidance that Arthur Wellesley had to rely in the peace negotiations, for which he had been given extensive delegated authority [174]. Arthur Wellesley received also, and to some degree discounted, advice from Malcolm [384]. The later extensive and detailed instructions of 11 December 1803, often quoted as if they were available to Arthur Wellesley during the negotiations, were received only in mid-January 1804, after treaty settlements with both Daulat Rao Sinde and Raghuji Bhonsle had been concluded.[4]

The notes of the discussions on the peace settlements, which Arthur Wellesley appears to have written out himself after each meeting (perhaps Elphinstone took notes, but if so they do not appear to have survived) are not here printed in full. The initial discussions yielded little, but led on to an armistice with Daulat Rao Sinde applicable to hostilities in the

Deccan and Gujerat [393, 394, 398]. This arrangement was eventually ratified by Sinde, but had not been honoured at the time of the second major battle of the campaign, that fought before the town of Argaum on 29 November [404]. This battle was far less costly to the Company forces, European and Indian, than Assaye, and in it the forces of the allies of the Company, Maratha and those of Mysore and the Nizam of Hyderabad, took some part at least in the pursuit of the enemy.

After the battle of Argaum, the siege of Gawilghar, long planned, was prepared and initiated. The Raja of Berar now opened peace talks [410, 414]. After very appreciable difficulties in bringing artillery to bear on the northern side of the fortress had been overcome, Gawilghar was assaulted and captured [416, 417]. After this success, the negotiations with Raghuji Bhonsle of Berar were rapidly concluded [422]. Arthur Wellesley now despatched Elphinstone, who had been with him throughout the campaign while Malcolm had been recuperating at Bombay, as Resident at Nagpur [425].

The peace negotiations with the agents of Daulat Rao Sinde moved more deliberately, due in Arthur Wellesley's view to 'haughtiness.' A significant matter at issue was the scale of territorial cession to be sought in northern India, clear in principle from the instructions of Richard Wellesley, but made complex in negotiation by lack of information in the Deccan on the treaties concluded by Lake with subordinate rulers in Hindustan [415]. A later dispute at the court of Daulat Rao Sinde in 1804 followed from the rather broadly drafted sections of the treaty used to handle this matter, to which Arthur Wellesley directed the attention of the Governor-General [430].

Peace had thus been secured, and it is a proper question why Arthur Wellesley hastened it on. Almost certainly he saw the moral effect of the defeat at Assaye as a formidable but waning asset, and was anxious to secure peace with Daulat Rao Sinde promptly, knowing that he had limited capacity to move into southern Hindustan on what would have been lengthened supply lines. He saw Raghuji Bhonsle of Berar as the initiator of the confederacy, and had been anxious to pursue him into his own territory, and inflict defeats that brought him to the negotiating tent.

To a marked degree the extensive territorial objectives which Richard Wellesley had outlined before the campaign had begun [175] had been secured. As events were to move later, these settlements, and especially that with Sinde, were seen by the Marathas as interim and even contingent in character. In creating the settlement, Arthur Wellesley and John Malcolm, as is very clear from their later correspondence, had assumed that Daulat Rao Sinde could be conciliated to the Company, was anxious to secure an effective alliance with the Company, and indeed would, if circumstances so required, elect to ally with the British against Jaswant Rao Holkar. These assumptions were not soundly based, and the military achievements of both Arthur Wellesley and Gerald Lake were to lose their full political effect, in significant measure as a result of misreading by Richard Wellesley in 1804 of the prospects of further advance against the Marathas. The fruits of an interim settlement were imperilled by mistaken adherence to a long-term objective.

307

Colonel Murray to Arthur Wellesley

Baroda
26 September 1803

I had the pleasure of receiving your letter of the 14th two days ago and I hope that you will believe that it gave me great pleasure to feel that you had assumed the command of the troops in this province.

Since I received my last instructions I have been occupied in carrying your plan into execution. The troops were however so spread and the whole so disjointed that I have not yet a corps equipped for the movements I propose. I expect in four or five days to join the principal force encamped at Jerod about 12 miles from hence. My advanced troops consisting of the 2nd of the 1st, two six pounders and some of the Gaikwar's cavalry is at Halol, nearly eight miles further, where the roads from Malwa, Godra etc meet. Major Holmes is directed to reconnoitre these roads and keep a strict eye on the movements which the enemy may make in that quarter.

I am extremely sorry to say that the troops are very unhealthy. There are now above 1000 sick in the different hospitals. This is severe in so small a corps as mine, and I feel it the more that I do not expect above 1,200 or 1,400 of the Gaikwar's troops. On the frontier to the southward of the Narbada everything appears quiet. Songhur and Paneira are provisioned and garrisoned by this time. Colonel Anderson is encamped with a small corps consisting of 150 Europeans and 850 sepoys and with 2 six pounders and 2 howitzers, to move where any small body may appear, with instructions to reinforce Surat if he is unable to keep the field.

On the frontier there are two corps. Canoji is in the neighbourhood of Lunavada with something between 8000 and 10,000 men of all descriptions. He has lately been joined by [blank in text] who has brought with him a few pieces of cannon; this is in our favour. At Dohad there is a party of Sinde's troops under the command of Ambaji Inglia amounting probably to 7000 or 8000.

I propose that my first object shall be to drive back the corps under Canoji. He threatens an invasion. If successful in this attempt and if the southern frontier continues unmolested, I propose advancing to the neighbourhood of Bariya from whence extending to our left a strong frontier may be established. This I conceive to be an important point and from Colonel Reynolds' communications I expect that it may there be found. In the peninsula of Gujerat, Mulhar Rao is in arms but there is a corps of the Gaikwar's troops sufficient it is thought to keep him in check.

In addition to the garrisons you pointed out I have been obliged to leave troops in Sunkeera which is a frontier and of importance and in Powanghar . . . I shall have with me only 25 of the Company's cavalry. This regiment, which I find is solely under the Resident, goes on very slowly indeed. These 25 are nearly all they have fit for service.

In consequence of the operations being to the northward of the Narbada I have requested our supplies to be sent to Broach which becomes the principal depot of the district, but a magazine of considerable importance will be established at Surat. I hope that these arrangements will meet with your approbation. I think it unnecessary to trouble you with the details, but as soon as the garrisons are formed I shall have the honour of forwarding to you a complete return of the troops.

It gives me much pleasure to acquaint you that my equipment in point of cattle is very good and increasing. I have not a single brass 12 pounder in the district. My train will consist of 8 pounders and four 5½ inch howitzers.

On my last instructions I shall not say anything more . . . I confess that I did not like the 10th, 11th, or 12th paragraphs,[1] but I find Major Walker so little inclined to increase or occasion difficulties and so ready to give me any assistance, that I hope the inconveniences generally arriving where authority is so divided will not be experienced. I wish you all manner of success.

WP 3/3/79 p. 185

308

Arthur Wellesley to James Kirkpatrick

Assaye
27 September 1803

I am concerned to be under the necessity of making a formal complaint of any of the officers in the service of the Subahdar of the Deccan, but justice to the troops under my command and to the service the conduct of which is entrusted to me obliges me to do so.

Some time ago having observed that the city of Aurungabad was by no means in a state fit for defence and as it was probable that the course of the operations of the war would draw the troops to a distance from it, I desired Colonel Stevenson to remove the hospital to Daulatabad and to place the sick in the lower fort. Application was accordingly made to the killedar in my name by Raja Mohipat Ram to admit the hospital into the place proposed for them and he positively refused to receive them.

Raja Mohipat Ram has made a report upon the subject to the durbar and possibly orders may be sent in consequence of this report. But I think it proper to mention the subject to you now, as the consequences of this refusal to admit the sick and wounded troops into Daulatabad at present is that I must either send them to Ahmednagar or I must leave these brave men exposed in an open place to the violence and ferocity of a barbarous enemy. I have also with me about seventy pieces of brass ordnance captured. These must likewise be sent to Ahmednagar or I must leave them exposed to be retaken in Aurungabad . . .

Grwd (1837) ii 346 (1844) i 734

309

Arthur Wellesley to Lieutenant-Colonel Close

Assaye
28 September 1803

. . . Lord Wellesley has taken up the question of paying the Peshwa's ministers upon a great scale. The Peshwa is certainly sincere in his intentions to adhere to the alliance, but there is a crookedness in his policy, and the feelings of his mind are so far different from those which guide our conduct, that with the best intentions it must be expected we shall frequently clash. Besides under the instructions from the Governor General we have adopted measures in respect to Amrit Rao and Holkar which must be highly disagreeable to him, and might occasion a desire to alter the alliance.

The Peshwa has no ministers. He is everything himself and everything is little. In my opinion therefore we ought to pay those who are supposed to be and are called his ministers, not to keep the machine of government in motion in consistence with the objects of the alliance, as we do at Hyderabad, but to have intelligence of what passes in the Peshwa's secret councils, in order that we may check him in time when it may be necessary . . .

Grwd (1837) ii 351 (1844) i 737

310

Colonel Stevenson to Arthur Wellesley

2 miles north of the Ajanta ghat
29 September 1803

I reported to you that the enemy was encamped within ten miles of the Ajanta ghat at three o'clock yesterday. At four their tents disappeared and they marched off on the Burhanpur road. At nine o'clock last night they were twenty miles from me and I cannot move forward till twelve o'clock at noon this day by which time

I may reasonably suppose they will be thirty miles in advance and although I shall move with a light party I cannot overtake them till they will have arrived at Burhanpur which is eighty miles from here. I judge it better therefore to halt today and shall march with the whole force tomorrow on the Burhanpur road and hope to be favoured with your orders on arrival at my new ground early tomorrow morning.

I informed you that Ajanta affords excellent and safe accommodation for the sick and wounded with an octagonal brick fort with about sixty [bays?] such as may contain two cotts and the enclosure would contain tents. Many other places are equally safe and convenient for the natives and the octagon might be given to the Europeans. Two strong gates serve the fort.[2]

If the intelligence I receive shall promise any advantage by advancing I shall move forward but if the enemy are reinforced or strongly positioned at Burhanpur it seems advisable that I should be reinforced by your division and the whole of your force advance together to the north. I enclose the intelligence I have received. We marched 13½ miles yesterday including the ghat which makes about 29 miles from your encampment at Assaye. The pioneers are employed in clearing and improving the ghat. I have just received confirmation that the enemy were 24 miles at daybreak, which satisfies my mind in my resolution of not advancing.

WP 3/3/84 p. 421

311

Intelligence by Colonel Stevenson's hircarrahs

[29 September 1803]

The enemy was encamped yesterday about ten miles from the Ajanta ghat. They marched off about 3 pm towards Burhanpur and marched until nine [pm] distant about 5 kos where the hircarrahs left them. They are said to have gone off in great confusion. Gopal Rao with a party of horse remained within four or five miles of our camp until the whole of the enemy's force marched off.

A campoo from Burhanpur is said to have joined them yesterday. They are also said to have the Maharajah's campoo, the Begum's campoo and one other campoo with upwards of twenty guns. Jadu Rao Bhaskar is said to have died yesterday of the wounds he received in the late action. The loss of this sirdar is said to have affected Sinde very greatly.

The above information is confirmed by two of Salabat Khan's hircarrahs who came in from the enemy's camp this morning. A sepoy of the enemy's taken yesterday reports that Jadu Rao Bhaskar was killed in the late action with General Wellesley's army and that two of the battalions [that] belonged to the Begum's campoo were completely cut up and the remaining corps [is] in a state of mutiny being seven months in arrears. The sepoy says there are only ten or twelve guns with the different campoos.

WP 3/3/84 p. 423

312

Colonel Stevenson to Arthur Wellesley

[Pahur]
30 September 1803

Two of Mohipat Ram's hircarrahs are this instant come in from Sinde's camp which they report to be 16 kos from here. Hircarrahs arrived at Sinde's camp from Holkar yesterday. They were well received and had presents of money and trumbrils. These hircarrahs say that Gopal Bhau is dead and his nephew wounded. But on our arrival at this ground it was reported that he was with his party and very active in covering the rear of all Sinde's troops with a party of horse. Sinde marched immediately towards Burhanpur on receiving Holkar's letter.

Captain Palmer has offered his services and the services of his garrison to forward grain from Toka or any other place to Ajanta and says there are some banjaras at Aurungabad who are very likely to come forward to supply grain if they have encouragement. I shall enquire from them the nature of the arrangement they require.

It is possible the hircarrahs may have heard of the death of Jadu Rao Bhasker and confused it with Gopal Bhau.

WP 3/3/84 p. 424

313

Colonel Stevenson to Arthur Wellesley

[Pahur]
30 September 1803

Enclosed is Rajah Mohipat Ram's note to the killedar of Ajanta to admit the sick and if he rejects [this] you are requested to remove him and appoint another. He was very civil when I passed and his gates were open. I arrived at Pahur this morning. It is ten miles from my last ground and 13½ from Ajanta. Sinde and Bhonsle with their armies were to arrive at the Tapti this day and at Burhanpur tomorrow.

I have accounts of twenty six casks of arrack arrived at Ajanta ghat this day for my force and have sent my pioneers to bring it safe down tomorrow. Rajah Sukhruder's party has arrived with 1200 bullock load of grain. I have found abundance of cattle in this village and shall purchase such as are required and have also account of sheep which I shall send for. I shall have a [survey?] of the country on this side the Tapti and shall endeavour to secure as much grain as possible . . .

WP 3/3/84 pp. 431–2

314

Colonel Murray to Arthur Wellesley

Baroda
30 September 1803

I had the pleasure of receiving your letter of the 16th September yesterday morning . . .

Canoji has begun his movements. I shall march on the 4th towards Godra in which neighbourhood he is at present.

Major Walker has just been with me with a letter he received from Mr Duncan. It is upon the subject of conciliating Canoji, and he mentions it as your opinion that this should be attempted. I find that it has already been tried and that he has treated our overtures with the greatest contempt. A confidential person sent lately by Major Walker is a prisoner in his camp and his servants in irons. Under the circumstances, Major Walker is of opinion that an attempt would be fruitless and would serve only to raise the spirit of his party and encourage the petty Rajas of Lunavada, Bariya, Eder etc to join him.

Whilst our army is at a distance, an offer of reconciliation might be so interpreted, but when I get near him and it is seen that we are in a state to punish [him] and protect our allies, I think an overture might be made, and I shall accordingly do so. If he is prevailed upon to desist from attacking the Gujerat, it will probably be an easy step to engage him in our operations against Sinde. This would be the safest way of disposing of his troops.

The accounts I have to give you of the troops is melancholy indeed. The 65th marched into camp at Jerod yesterday evening 264 strong. The 86th will not take the field above 500. The grenadier battalion when joined by its outparties probably 400. The 2nd of the 1st about 500, and I shall not be able to take more than 200 of the 2nd of the 6th. I have at present only 23 of the Company's cavalry, fit for nothing but orderlies, and the Gaikwar troops assemble very slowly indeed. However I shall do all in my power to turn this small force to account. It is well situated to annoy the enemy, and if of sufficient strength might prove of the greatest advantage . . .

The affair of the Patans will I hope be settled this day. When I directed Colonel Watson to assure these people that the ransom should be paid, I was determined it should be so, had I in the first instance been obliged to take it from the Military Chest. I am well aware of the consequence of a breach of faith, but it was never intended by Major Walker, although it probably was so [intended] by the Gaikwar government that the ransom should not be paid. Major Walker proposes to take some of the Patans into his service as sebundi. I shall know the answer before I despatch this letter.

Since I had the honour of writing to you last I have received letters in very friendly terms from the Rajas of [Maderire?] and Banswara, and the Raja of Bariya has offered to send a vakil, which of course is accepted. Mr Duncan is very particular in directing me not to counteract any prior arrangement that might have been made with the Bheels. He is very safe in this respect for I do not believe that there was the smallest attempt made to the southward of the Narbada at least. Colonel Anderson is authorised to treat with these people and he is so well acquainted with their interests and number I hope he will succeed . . . The vakil from the Bariya Raja is arrived at Halol. I expect him the day after tomorrow. I have heard nothing more of the Patans. They are encamped close to the town . . .

WP 3/3/79 p. 141

315

Lieutenant-Colonel Close to Arthur Wellesley

Pune
1 October 1803

[Word had arrived of the battle of Assaye]

. . . I have been particular in making it known here that the whole was effected by your own division and that, as you left the rear guard and a battalion with your baggage, [you] had not more than five infantry corps in action . . . I conclude that you have got possession of the equipment of the whole of Sinde's force on this side of the Narbada. It is likely that either Brownrigg or Dudrenec's brigade pursued its march to Ujjein although the akbars gave no specific word of such an event. It is true that Colonel Collins' statements [3] include a great park of 25 guns and 100 field pieces and if these guns really exist they may no doubt be at Burhanpur . . .

WP 3/3/47 fldr 3

316

S. Johnston Persian Interpreter to the Subsidiary Force

Intelligence from the enemy's camp by Colonel Stevenson's hircarrahs.

1 October 1803

The hircarrahs arrived in the enemy's camp at Jamner on the morning of the 29th at daylight. The campoos were all in readiness to march and they moved off about one hour after. Sinde and Bhonsle remained on the ground and after breakfast followed the campoos to Gurhayrack [Garkheda?] where the campoos encamped. They then proceeded with the cavalry to Burrangaon 6 kos where they arrived about sunset. They halted there near an hour and their elephants were brought close together. After a long consultation Sinde moved off to the left and Bhonsle went to the right. They both quitted the Burhanpur road and Sinde proceeded to Jalgaon Soneygaon 6 kos where one of the hircarrahs accompanied him. He arrived there about nine o'clock at night. The other hircarrah followed Bhonsle and has not yet returned.

Sinde halted yesterday at Jalgaon and was joined by Gopal Bhau, Myral Pant and Nabalkar. His force is supposed to consist of 15,000 horse. It is reported in Sinde's camp and the hircarrah heard it on the road that the campoos were ordered to Burhanpur. There were 15 guns and two howitzer with the campoos. Jalgaon Soneygaon 15 kos from Pahur on the Cassabarri ghat road. The hircarrah left Sinde's camp before daylight this morning and it was reported they were to march today.

The hircarrah who followed Bhonsle returned about 12 at night. He reports that the consultation took place at Gurhayrack eight kos from Jamner and it was there [that] Sinde and Bhonsle separated, the former went to the left and the other went on to Burrangaon where he halted on the 30th. The campoos are gone to the Tapti. On the 1st Bhonsle made a march of three or four miles on the Yedabad road. After his jundar was pitched he returned to Burrangaon where his dewan had remained with about 5000 troops. The hircarrah left them at noon when he came away. Bapu Fharkyah with 4 or 5000 troops went off to Sinde early in the morning. A Pathan chief with 2000 horse also quitted Bhonsle's party and went towards Mulkapur. The hircarrah saw a party of Arabs and Rohillas who had escorted some of Sinde's family down the Badauli ghat. They amounted to near 1500 and were to join Sinde.

WP 3/3/84 p. 427

317

Colonel Stevenson to Arthur Wellesley

Pahur
2 October 1803

I have been much deceived in regard to the intentions of the enemy as will appear by the accompanying report of two of my hircarrahs. The enemy having arrived at Burrangaon on the 29th which is only one march or seven kos on this side the Tapti and on the Burhanpur road gave me reason to suppose that they intended to proceed to that place and from the hasty consultation and sudden movement from that direction it is reasonable to suppose that their original intention was to have proceeded to that place. As I could not at any rate have moved from the foot of the Ajanta ghat till 12 o'clock at noon on the 29th, the same day that the enemy changed their route, it is not likely that such movement would have been known to them early enough to have made any alteration in their plans.

The manner in which Sinde and Bhonsle are said to have participated in Bhonsle's short march to the eastward and returning again to his dewan who remained at Burrangaon with a greater force than accompanying his master suggests that there is great dissatisfaction and discussion among the parties. But Sinde seems to have been accompanied by the most inconsiderable number of troops. They are composed however only of horse and by their movements may be going towards the Cassabarri ghat or perhaps towards Pune although from the precautions that you have taken that plan must be in doubt.

As I am better situated where I am now encamped to proceed either to the eastward towards Bhonsle's country or to the westward towards the Cassabarri ghat and am nearer to you to receive your orders and forward any measures you may determine on, I think it more advisable to remain here than advance towards Burhanpur. I am however partly inclined to suppose that the recent movement of Sinde may be intended to divert your attention from Burhanpur till he bring forward troops and ordnance from the northward. But should I advance to Burhanpur under this supposition I may remove myself from the means of a more immediate compliance with your orders which I may receive by noon tomorrow if you find it expedient to send them with fresh horsemen.

WP 3/3/84 p. 425

318

Colonel Murray to Arthur Wellesley

Baroda
2 October 1803 [received by 15 October]

Amongst the Pathan cavalry who accompanied Futteh Sing there are about 200 who are good, for these sort of people at least. I have authorised Major Walker, provided their terms are not exorbitant, to engage them. I have not only their immediate service in view, which however in our situation is most desirable, but I conceive it may form some connection between us and the chiefs you mention above the ghats. Another reason no less important is that it would have been very dangerous to allow these people to return to Songarh without sending with them a considerable detachment to prevent their plundering the country. I hope these reasons will be considered by you as a sufficient justification of the expense. In the event of clearing the frontier of the troops under Canoji, my object will be to advance and attempt a diversion. For this purpose, at least to do it effectively, large bodies of cavalry may be necessary. But were I to mention this circumstance to Mr Duncan I should probably be recalled. The public money shall on this occasion be most sparingly used, but if it can be employed to advantage I hope you will have no objection to my engaging these people by small presents or even pay . . . I join the corps at Jarod this day, and shall march on the 4th to Halol unless I am detained by a want of pack saddles. My cattle are good and I think I may depend upon plenty of them.

WP 3/3/79 p. 146

319

Colonel Stevenson to Arthur Wellesley

Pahur
3 October 1803

Some difficulties have arisen in respect to the value and exchange of the Star Pagoda, in which coin the troops received their last issue of pay. I ordered a committee of field officers to determine the value and exchange of Star Pagodas, and they report the loss to the troops to be 10%. I cannot see there is such a difference . . . without further enquiries., but find it necessary to fix the value of a Star Pagoda at 3¼ rupees.

. . . Two of my hircarrahs have come in from Burhanpur and give the following account of the position of the enemy's troops which differs very much from what I have conjectured from previous reports. The whole of the troops are on this side of the Tapti. The burrah campoo or Sinde's is at Jasnubad on the south side of the Tapti immediately opposite to Burhanpur which is on the north bank. The force consists of 6000 infantry and 14 guns. Begum Sumru's campoo is 4 kos on this side the Tapti [with] the same number of infantry and 16 guns. 22 guns are described as in a park called the Gingee [Jinsee] with men to work the guns but not attached to the infantry. Their state is not described.

Sinde and Bhonsle have again united their horse and are on this bank of the Tapti 4 kos to the westward of Jasnubad. There are no troops at Asir but the hill fort is garrisoned. Burhanpur is described to have a brick wall and bastions . . . but has no troops in it except for a few fresh parties of horse.

The hircarrahs say it was reported at Burhanpur that Holkar is levying contributions at Ujjein and is removing Sinde's tannahs in the towns north of the Tapti . . . I think I may advance to Jamner five kos from hence on the Burhanpur road and receive your orders at that place, and if I do not receive any instructions from you before daylight tomorrow shall advance to Jamner where I may possibly meet encouragement to move forward.

WP 3/3/84 p. 429

320

Arthur Wellesley to Colonel Collins

3 October 1803 [received by 11 October]

I have not written to you since the action of the 23rd September because I have had much to do and I thought it probable that some time would elapse before you would arrive at Hyderabad and that my letter would not reach you upon the road.

I attacked the united armies of Daulat Rao Sinde and the Raja of Berar on that day and gained a complete victory, having taken ninety-eight pieces of cannon, all their ammunition etc. My division alone was engaged. The battle was the most severe that I believe was fought in India and my loss was very great. Sinde's infantry behaved well, they were driven from their guns only by the bayonet and some of the corps retreated in great order and formed again. The campoos engaged were Pohlman's, Begum Sumroo and another which has been called by the hircarrahs Monkely's, Macquire's, and the Maharajah's. I rather believe that as Mr Grant was the brigade-major of one of the campoos engaged, the one of which I have not ascertained the name is Dodernaigue's [sic].

I enclose a list of officers belonging to the campoo of which Mr Grant was brigade-major,[4] which has been made up by taking, from a few leaves from an old orderly book, the names of officers ordered for duty. From a perusal of this list you will probably be able to form an opinion what this brigade was, and as everything relating to this action is a matter of curiosity I shall be glad to hear from you on the subject.

I have some reason to complain of Sinde's English officers, and I shall bring the matter forward publicly as soon as I can ascertain the matter more completely. My soldiers say that after they were knocked down by cannon or grape shot, they were cut and piked by the horse belonging to the campoos, which indeed is perfectly true, and that horse was cut to pieces by the British cavalry. But they say besides that they heard one English officer with a battalion say to another 'You understand the language better than I do. Desire the jemadar of that body of horse to go and cut up those wounded European soldiers.' The other did as he was desired, and the horse obeyed the orders they received.

It is bad enough that these gentlemen should serve the enemies of their country, particularly after the British government had offered them a provision, but it is too bad that they should make themselves the instruments, or rather that they should excite the savage ferocity of the natives against their brave and wounded countrymen . . .

SD iv 184

321

Colonel Murray to Arthur Wellesley

Jarod
4 October 1803 [received by 23 October]

I have been obliged to send the 65th Regiment into Baroda on account of the sickly state of the corps. 100 men is all that I have thought fit for service. To replace this corps in some measure I have ordered the small details of the 61st and 88th to join me. The sickly state of this corps I in great measure attribute to the barracks at Surat in which they lately have been quartered, which are in every respect, except as to the buildings themselves, very ill calculated for their present purpose. The . . . state of the 65th when they took the field is one of the strongest proofs that can be adduced. Although there is no [other] corps in so bad a state, the whole are more or less sickly and my disposable force is considerably reduced almost to a shadow. It will not exceed 1600 men and probably about 500 of the Gaikwar cavalry. More indeed are promised but it is extremely doubtful if they will join and still more so whether they will act. Common report says that the principal people are much disaffected and they have shown much reluctance to take the field.

Under these circumstances I fear much that I shall fall far short of your expectations and my weakness is the more to be regretted [in] that the friendship of the Bariya Raja would so much facilitate my march to Ujjein. In the course of a month I hope this corps will recover and the moment I have the smallest hopes of success you may depend upon my making every attempt. The vakil of the Bariya Raja is with me in camp. He has been sent with offers of friendship and is directed to remain for the purpose of procuring guides and safeguards to our cattle and followers. The road to Ujjein passes though his country which is a strong jungle. He is one of the most powerful of the Bheel Rajas . . . Colonel Anderson has taken the field with . . . his corps. He will encamp about 25 miles to the eastward of Surat and act against any marauders that may appear and reinforce the garrison of Surat if attacked by a large force.

I march tomorrow morning to Halol and if the account is true that Canoji has made a movement to the southward and westward it may not be long before we meet. Major Walker has given me the cypher so that any orders you may wish to convey to me may be sent through the country which will be more expeditious than sending them by Bombay.

WP 3/3/79 p. 150

322

Colonel Stevenson to Arthur Wellesley

Pahur
4 October 1803

I lose no time in forwarding the accompanying letters from Sinde's camp.[5] I have also received letters of which I shall acknowledge the receipt but add that I am under your authority and have received no orders from you to enter into any correspondence and that agreeable to my duty I shall continue to advance until I receive instructions from you. I send the letters directed to me and the Persian letter from Muhammed Mir Khan and the Marathi letter from Balaji Kunjar the Peshwa's vakil. The assembly is beating and I march to Jamner.

WP 3/3/84 p. 439

323

Arthur Wellesley to Colonel Stevenson

4 October 1803 [received 5 October]

I have just received your letter of the 3rd . . . The doolies returned this morning and I shall move myself with the second division of sick on the day after tomorrow. I must halt however on the 7th in order to get up another supply by Captain Baynes and I shall then descend the ghat. Colonel Lang shall take on the doolies belonging to the 94th regiment. The dooley boys did not get their provisions but they appear well satisfied with the treatment they have received. I could not give to them without also giving provision to my own dooley boys and that I could not do as I have literally no dry grain excepting what comes in from the bazaar.

I shall send to Ajanta 300 18-pounder shot and I shall take on from hence 2000 12-pounder shot. I wish that you would send bullocks and gunny bags to Ajanta to take on the 18-pounder shot.

I shall also send a large quantity of 6-pounder shot to Ajanta but this may remain there as neither of us I believe want it.

We ought to have three companies of infantry at Ajanta and I shall be obliged to you if you will give them from your corps. There is one company at Ajanta belonging to Lang's battalion but you may possibly find it more convenient to make up this garrison by detachments from different corps. I have sent five companies of Colonel Lang's corps to the Godavari with forty of the captured guns. They will be back I imagine about the 7th . . .

I wish you not to go too far forward. Your news about Holkar is very good and I hope it is true.

Grwd (1837) ii 373 (1844) i 755

324

Colonel Stevenson to Arthur Wellesley

Jamner
4 October 1803

The letters I despatched to you this morning from Sinde's camp arrived after the assembly had beaten and the troops had begun to march off. The Persian letter was written by Mir Muhammed Khan, a man I understand employed by Colonel Collins in all his communications with Sinde, and the Marathi letter by Balaji Kunjar the Peshwa's vakil. The letters written to me which I forwarded at the same time were from the same persons. Rajah Mohipat Ram has also letters from the same people. They were explained to me and were merely to make him the channel of communication. I am sorry I neglected to send his letter for your perusal.

In the note which I wrote you this morning and which accompanied the above mentioned letters I signified that I should acknowledge the receipt of letters addressed to me but on deliberate consideration it appeared to me that I possessed no authority to enter into any sort of communication or correspondence and that the intention of addressing letters to me was meant as the most direct method of forwarding, and at all events without your particular order or permission I cannot receive or send letters to the enemy although depending on your indulgence I should on subsequent occasions do so. I have just read the letter to Mohipat Ram which I send for your perusal.

I enclose a copy of the intelligence of this day. The movements of the enemy seem more intended to puzzle and perplex than to answer any good purpose for their own interests. I am still of opinion that their divided movements are to divert attention from Burhanpur and that moving towards that point will distress the enemy more than a pursuit of any of their more active parties. I am this instant favoured with your letter of the 3rd and am in a good position to observe the movements of the enemy . . .

WP 3/3/84 p. 433

324A

S. Johnston Persian Interpreter to the Subsidiary Force

[Intelligence]
4 October 1803

A hircarrah of Salabat Khan's who left the enemy's camp yesterday evening about 4 o'clock reports that Sinde and Bhonsle with 30,000 horse two battalions of infantry and 12 guns were at Ahonah [?Asoda] on the Girna river in the Nasirabad pergannah, 7 kos from Nasirabad. Ahonah 9 kos from Jamner 8 from Pahur and 5 from the Tapti.

Sinde's campoos guns heavy baggage etc were all gone to Burhanpur and Bhonsle's baggage, treasure, and the principal soucars who accompanied him from Nagpur, are gone to Mulkapur towards Nagpur. It was generally talked of in the enemy camp that they were going to the Cassabarri ghat which they were to make in two marches and that they were to march today. The Cassabarri ghat [is] 20 kos from Ahonah.

Two of Colonel Stevenson's hircarrahs who have just come in from the enemy's camp confirm that part of the intelligence relating to the situation of Sinde and Bhonsle. They say there were no guns or infantry with them, that the whole had gone to Burhanpur. They arrived in the enemy camp yesterday evening about five o'clock and left them at daylight this morning, when the enemy moved off to Andoore Durrungaon on the road to the Cassabarri ghat. It is also in a direction towards Chandore and Nasik. Dry grain sold in the enemy's bazaar yesterday at one seer per rupee.

WP 3/3/84 p. 434

325

Colonel Stevenson to Arthur Wellesley

Jamner
5 October 1803 9 pm

Thirty bullocks with proper assistance will be sent tomorrow morning for the 300 eighteen pounder shot under a jemadar guard who will have a letter addressed to Captain Noble from the Commissary of Stores of this force. Three companies of native infantry formed by detail under the command of a Captain and two subaltern officers will march in the course of tomorrow to garrison Ajanta.

WP 3/3/84

326

S. Johnston Intelligence

6 October 1803

The enemy were encamped at Yerrundole on the 4th when the hircarrahs arrived there. It is the same place often called Andole

Durrangaon. They marched from there on the 5th to Nargaysar 9 kos. The whole of the force under Sinde and Bhonsle is not supposed to exceed 30,000 men. They have no infantry or guns with them excepting five or six small guns with Gopal Rao. The pindaries are also gone to Burhanpur.

It is the general report in the enemy's camp that they intend to go to Pune to be guided by the advice of the Peshwa whom they acknowledge as their master. Another report mentions that they intend to proceed to the Cassabarri ghat with a view to draw off the attention of the British troops from Burhanpur and Nagpur but that if they persist in going on to those places they will return and endeavour to enter into negotiations.

WP 3/3/84 p. 443

327

Colonel Stevenson to Arthur Wellesley

6 October 1803 7 pm

All the information that I have received lately has stated that the enemy's horse without infantry or guns has marched towards the Cassabarri ghat and I have uniformly considered their movement as intended to draw your attention from the infantry and guns at Burhanpur.

If you approve of my marching to the Tapti in advance it may be the means of discovering their intentions. I shall act with caution and take such advantage as may offer. I have not expressed a desire to advance whilst their cavalry and infantry were together or whilst their cavalry could advance to the support of their infantry, and it did not seem prudent to put it in the power of fortune for this force to meet with a check or sustain a loss when victory will be certain if reinforced by your division.

At present their cavalry are so far removed that I may move forward with caution and not be obliged to engage in any enterprise unless I see a fair opportunity of gaining some advantage and a forward movement may press them to show their real intentions by moving the horse in the direction which they have gone.

I have received your letters of yesterday's date and shall forward your Persian and Marathi letters to Sinde's camp within an hour of the present time.[6]

WP 3/3/84 p. 437–8

328

Colonel Stevenson to Arthur Wellesley

7 October 1803

I was disappointed of getting grain by the party that went out yesterday. The country as far as the eye could reach abounded with grain . . . and the grain ripe in the fields but none to be found in the villages. My stock of grain is getting so low, not having ten days issue for the fighting men, that I find myself under the necessity of marching five or six kos toward Boder [Bodvad?] which is on the road to Mulkapur as that place was likely to afford grain. But as there is a party of 2000 horse and some infantry belonging to the Bhonsle at Mulkapur (who were kept out by the inhabitants) it will be necessary for me to move forward to afford protection to the banjaras. Boder is a little to the eastward of the road to Burhanpur and should I go by Mulkapur it will not occasion more than an additional march. It is difficult to account for the movements of Sinde and Bhonsle with their horse. I have always considered [them?] a diversion in the Nizam's country to draw your attention from Burhanpur. It may proceed from a mistaken pride, wishing to negotiate for peace in the Nizam's country or on the borders. Should they fail in their negotiation they may be prepared to plunder and destroy the Nizam's country as an inducement either to you to apply to them to withdraw or to listen to their proposals.

If it is possible that the enemy have such expectations they may be counteracted by the cavalry from this detachment joining your cavalry at the head of the ghat, and being joined by one or two battalions lightly equipped they might proceed directly to Cassabarri in pursuit of the enemy. You would still have a sufficient train of infantry to undertake the siege of Asir. Should the enemy's horse return with an intention to annoy the besieging army, our cavalry would be close on their rear. My march tomorrow towards Boder is rather in opposition to the possible junction of my cavalry with that of your division. But a forced march may make amends particularly if successful in procuring a few days grain for the horses. The cavalry have a long time depended entirely on the banjaras as they cannot send out their grain bullocks for grain without a strong detachment which cannot well be spared . . .

WP 3/3/84 p. 444

329

Colonel Stevenson to Arthur Wellesley

Jamner 23 miles north of Ajanta
7 October 1803 10 pm

. . . Having received information that the enemy's cavalry and some infantry and guns as detailed in the enclosed intelligence were still advancing toward Cassabarri and by the agents report were within four kos of the ghat when the intelligence left their camp I determined not to march tomorrow but to remain where I was till I know what you determine.

I think the party to watch the movements of the enemy should be strong in cavalry and that no more cavalry should be kept with the line of infantry intended for the assault of any place than to cover the cattle and the followers and make excursions of a few miles for the benefit of forage. I am still of opinion two battalions with their guns and the gallopers attached to two regiments of cavalry, including the brigaded six pound gallopers attached to the Subah's force, would be sufficient to keep Sinde and Bhonsle in check and prevent their designs on the Nizam's country. But if you intend to attack Asir the cavalry should be made as strong as possible to enable them to follow up Sinde and attack him.

If there is any probability of the enemy going to Surat your division is already on the road and I think I should endeavour to destroy some of the infantry that still remains on this side the Tapti near Burhanpur before I proceed to Berar. The infantry have remained so far on this side the Tapti that it is possible that they may be moving off by detachments to join Sinde, who may have some intention to the westward but I have received no information that favours this opinion. At all events the army with Sinde and Bhonsle have advanced so far towards Cassabarri that a force should be sent immediately for the protection of the Nizam's countries and to follow them up if their views are against Pune or Surat, and under these considerations it will be most convenient for your force to march in that direction.

In the meantime I may keep moving towards Burhanpur and eventually to Asir. If Sinde has made his recent movements to draw your attention from his guns and infantry at Burhanpur my march that way will engage him to return in which case you will follow up his rear. By following up these movements with your division towards Sinde and mine towards Burhanpur you will not forsake your original plan and intentions against Asir unless he moved towards Surat which may make it expedient for you to follow him. If you [determine upon?] moving towards Sinde I will be obliged to you to send me such rice as you can spare to be lodged for me at Ajanta. I have accounts from Major Kirkpatrick of great stores of rice advancing but I am very low in grain at present.

There is great reason to think Rajah Mohipat Ram must have proposed himself as mediator and it is likely that he joined Captain Johnston's services to his own but I believe without consulting him. I will send a detachment to meet my doolies.

WP 3/3/84 p. 446

329A

Intelligence by Colonel Stevenson's hircarrahs

7 October 1803

They arrived in the enemy's camp on the 5th at Yerrundole and found them all in readiness to march. The hircarrah went with them to Nargaysar 7 kos where they halted yesterday. They were to march this morning but the hircarrah came away before daylight and did not see them move off. It was the general opinion in camp that they were going to Pune by the Cassabarri ghat. The hircarrahs report that they saw two battalions of infantry and 16 guns with their camp and that Sinde had always 4 guns in front of his tent. Gopal Bhau, Mehyral Pundit and Ledohao Rao were encamped about 4 kos to the rear of Sinde at Kassadah Phurkunder. Nargaysar 23 kos from Jamner.

WP 3/3/84 p. 448

330

Colonel Murray to Arthur Wellesley

Halol 10 kos from Godra
7 October 1803

Your plan of conciliating the Bheels has succeeded much to our advantage. We have marched through their country these two days past without the least molestation, not even a stray bullock has been lost, although the country is a complete jungle in many places.

I mentioned to you in a former letter than the Raja of Bariya had sent me a vakil. We have since concluded a treaty with a man of no less consequence, the Raja of Bomrea. I have proposed to send to each 200 men which I shall pay. This will effectually secure our convoys. Sinde raised a considerable revenue from this district. I propose following your example and establishing a collection when Godra is taken but I shall exempt from taxation all the Bheel Rajas. I have been requested to do this, and as both money and grain may be required, I think I shall not be blamed for turning the conquest of a fine district to some advantage.

There are still some of Sinde's troops in Godra but I do not believe they will make any resistance. If they do your instructions for Carnalla shall be adopted as my rule of conduct. Canoji has not made any movement lately. He is with 10,000 men, it is said, near Lunavada. A report prevails here that a large force under Hurnaut is in the neighbourhood of Ujjein. Holkar was himself said to be with this army, which the Baroda gazette[7] makes 40,000 men and destined for Gujerat. I shall ascertain this fact before I leave Godra as my future measures must in great measure depend upon it.

WP 3/3/79 p. 132

331

Arthur Wellesley to Merrick Shawe

Ajanta
8 October 1803 [received 2 November 1803]

. . . Sinde and the Rajah of Berar after making two marches to the westward along the Tapti have turned to the southward and it is said intend to pass the Cassabarri ghat. They have with them the greatest part of their horse, some infantry, and some guns, which they got out of Burhanpur. They have sent into that place the remains of the campoos.

It is possible that this movement may be intended to draw my attention away from Burhanpur and Asirgarh and they may return to the northward upon finding that I do not follow them. On the other hand these things called allied governments are in such a state of deplorable weakness, they depend so entirely upon us for the defence of their territories, and their power is so feeble over their own servants, who have much connection with and even dependence on the enemy, that I have not means to move forward at once upon Asirgarh with my whole force, although I know that if I could take that step with safety it would put an end to the war.

But not one of the Subah's forts is sufficiently garrisoned. He has not a soldier in the country excepting those belonging to the Company and his killedars and amildars would readily pay the money they have just to be allowed to sit quietly in their forts and towns. As for the Peshwa he has possession of his palace at Pune and nothing more, and he spends the little money he receives either upon Brahmins or upon women rather than give any to his troops or even to his menial servants. The consequence then of my proceeding to the northward with my whole force might be that the enemy would get possession or levy contributions upon some important place belonging to the Nizam, or they might move down upon Pune itself. They would certainly stop our supplies and the consequence of such a movement might thus be fatal to us. In this manner does the radical weakness of these governments operate against us. I have therefore determined to return to the southward . . .

Grwd (1837) ii 387 (1844) i 765

332

Arthur Wellesley to Colonel Stevenson

Ajanta
8 October 1803

. . . I recommend the following objects to your attention; firstly, either to beat or drive back any infantry that may be at or near Burhanpur; secondly, levy a contribution on Burhanpur; thirdly, reconnoitre Asirgarh and if it holds any prospect of success lay siege to it, and if it does not, move to your right upon Gawilghar and lay siege to that place; fourthly levy a contribution upon Nagpur . . .

Grwd (1837) ii 391 (1844) i 768

333

Colonel Murray to Arthur Wellesley

Godra
9 October [1803]

I have the pleasure to acquaint you that we got possession of the fort and town of Godra this morning without opposition. The last of Sinde's troops evacuated the place yesterday. The fort is totally out of repair but will secure our stores from plunder, if I should find it necessary to move light from hence. I shall place a small detachment here when I march; it is the capital of the district which consists of five valuable parganahs.

The behaviour of the inhabitants has everywhere been most friendly. We have not lost a single bullock by plunder nor [has] any follower been robbed. I am attempting to collect information relative to the revenue which I shall forward to you and the Bombay government as soon as possible. The country is everywhere in the highest state of cultivation.

I have not yet decided on my future movements. Canoji has certainly decamped and is gone to the northward but I have no certain information where. I expect intelligence every hour. There is certainly a force at Ujjein or in its neighbourhood which is said to be destined for the Gujerat, but other accounts state it is to be collected only for defence against an invasion on this side. I hope in a few days to have it in my power to give you more satisfactory accounts from this quarter.

Sinde has no possession nearer than Dohad.

WP 3/3/79 p. 157

334

Colonel Stevenson to Arthur Wellesley

Jamner
9 October 1803 7 pm

I have received both your letters of the 8th and waited for my hircarrahs to come in from Sinde's camp before I wrote to you. Enclosed are reports from his camp as well as from Burhanpur . . . I shall be attentive to the advice you have given me respecting the charging of guns and unless a fair probability of success offers itself I shall desist. I shall also be attentive to the four articles of advice contained in your letter respecting my operations . . .

I have this evening despatched an English copy of the Proclamations. They are directed to the European officers in Sinde and the Rajah of Berar's service or serving with any of the Maratha states. It will be handled in the enemy's camp in the most probable manner of coming before the British and European officers. I shall send the copies and translations of the Proclamation addressed to the native troops.

I propose marching towards Burhanpur tomorrow and have left instructions to Colonel Lang to join me at Barragaon on the 11th. I sent off 1000 bullocks this evening to Ajanta for the rice you left them for this force. When in possession of 3000 bags I shall not be alarmed about the means of marching in any direction. I have written to the officer commanding the five companies of Colonel Lang's battalion - that escorting the forty guns to the Godavari - to bring forward the 1000 bags of rice from Ajanta. But should you have detained those five companies for any other service I shall take some other method for giving security to that rice.

I shall hear of the movements of the infantry and guns as I advance to Burhanpur and on my arrival there I shall act according to circumstances. The Rajahs[8] have commenced a plundering war without authority. I shall endeavour to keep it within bounds as far as possible.

WP 3/3/84 p. 451

335

S. Johnston Intelligence from Sinde's camp

9 October 1803

Two hircarrahs who left the camp on the 7th report that great discontent prevails among the troops: they are all calling out for money. Gopal Bhau and a dewan of Bhonsle's remained behind at Yerrundole with 5000 horse. Sinde and the Berar Rajah were at Nargaysar 32 kos from Jamner. It was their intention to have gone to the Cassabarri ghat but hearing that our troops had moved that way they have altered their intention and propose moving to the Tapti. Their force is supposed to consist of 40,000 horse of all descriptions.

A hircarrah from Burhanpur reports that he left it on the 7th in the morning. The Maharajah's campoo was encamped on the Tapti to the southwest of Burhanpur about one mile. They have about 6000 men and 16 guns. The Begum's campoo was to the southwards of the town about three miles. They are supposed to have 6000 men and 14 guns. The park and stores were about two miles further to the northwards and have 20 guns. It was the general report in the campoos that they were going to Ujjein but an idea of joining Sinde is also entertained among them.

WP 3/3/84 p. 454

336

Josiah Webbe to Arthur Wellesley

Fort St George Madras
10 October 1803
[summary]

Webbe congratulated Arthur Wellesley on the battle of Assaye.

'I now feel, and I presume to indulge the feeling with some degree of personal pride, that the wisdom of Lord Wellesley will have accomplished in the course of his government all the great purposes of his counsels by the final attainment of peace in the permanent foundations of security, and the degree in which your own achievement have contributed to this great work has fixed the military fame of his family in the rank of those who by their illustrious exploits have founded maintained and established this empire.'

WP 3/3/93

337

Colonel Stevenson to Arthur Wellesley

11 October 1803

I send you a letter from Kawder Beg . . . I opened it supposing it might contain intelligence of importance. I trust that Kawder Beg may find an opportunity of joining me soon. I attempted to get the letter that is rolled and accompanied the Persian letter translated but was not able to find any person that understood the writing.[9]

I march this morning to Burrangaon and tomorrow to Changdee on the Tapti river. I find that Sinde and Bhonsle are not returning with their horse but the river makes a bend and although I cross the river at Changdee and continue on a northerly route I must make two marches of six or seven kos each to come to Burhanpur on the north bank of the Tapti. I shall halt a day to refresh the troops at Changdee . . . At all events I shall endeavour to strike a blow at the infantry before they are joined by the horse. My latest hircarrah describes the infantry and guns to be near Burhanpur but inclining to the northwards.

I sent two hircarrahs of my own yesterday to Sinde's camp with orders to carry intelligence to you at Aurungabad. This evening I shall send two more of my own and tomorrow two of Mohipat Ram's. This day I will send directly to you from Barragaon two hircarrahs from Salabat Khan and two from Rajah Sukhruder. These four sets will have orders to remain with you.

Colonel Lang with the five companies and convoy arrived yesterday at the ground I left 7 miles in my rear and I expect he will join me today at Barragaon. My marches are determined by the needs of securing water. I sent a thousand bullocks in Company's hire the night before last towards Ajanta for the rice you left there. 700 of them were driven off by the pindari horse and the rest are returning with Colonel Lang. The rice continues at Ajanta.

WP 3/3/84 p. 455

338

Arthur Wellesley to Lieutenant-Colonel Barry Close

Phulambri
11 October 1803

. . . I am within one march of Aurungabad. The enemy has not yet passed the Cassabarri ghat. The majority of my intelligence hircarrahs have either deserted or have been taken and four days have elapsed since I heard from their camp, but they were then on the road to that ghat and as far as I can learn forty miles from it. . . .

Gwrd (1837) ii 399 (1844) i 773

339

Colonel Murray to Arthur Wellesley

Godra
12 October 1803

I congratulate you most sincerely on the splendid victory of the 23rd which we heard of yesterday and have made as public as possible. I make no doubt that its consequence will be as important to our interest as it is honourable to our arms. Your loss, the particulars of which I received this morning, is severe but it is [to] be hoped that the lesson you have given them will prevent their making such an opportunity in future.

This certainly would be a most favourable opportunity for my advancing upon Ujjein, but the weakness of my corps renders such an attempt dangerous, as there is no doubt a very large force at Jhabua and Dohad under one of Sinde's officers and a still larger body under Hurnauth, who is in Holkar's service not far from those places. Upon our approach, as I mentioned in a former letter, Canoji removed from Lunavada and is now encamped . . . in the Eder parganah; he will not risk an action. I had yesterday very pressing letters from two of the Gaikwar's sirdars to join them near Ambersomba[10] where they had halted in consequence of the movement made by Canoji, but I do not think it prudent to leave this centrical position till the news of the force at Dohad are more clearly discovered. I shall endeavour to prevail upon Amir Saheb and Kakoji to oppose Canoji which will allow me to move forward and occupy the defiles of Bariya . . .

I am extremely sorry to acquaint you that the sickness continues amongst the troops. By the returns of this morning the 65th Regiment have near 600 in hospital, and in camp although I marched without a sick man I have now near one hundred and fifty . . .

WP 3/3/79 p. 159

340

Colonel Collins to Arthur Wellesley

near Hyderabad
12 October 1803 [received 23 October]

Many thanks for your obliging letter of the 3rd which I received yesterday . . . After a careful examination of the returns you sent me I am inclined to believe that the officers whose names are therein specified belong to Colonel Pohlman's corps of which Grant is major of brigade. I have reason to think that Dudrenec's battalions were not in the action. The other brigade which you allude to must therefore have been the late Colonel Filose's. This corps was denominated the Maharajah's from not being subject to the authority of General Perron. The brigade commanded by Dudrenec was at Ujjein on the 5th August and Major Brownrigg was expected to arrive at that place on the 18th . . .

I am shocked and surprised at what you state respecting the savage cruelty of the English officers in Sinde's service. I thought our countrymen incapable of action with so much inhumanity . . . With the exception of Grant and Beckett I know none of the English officers whose names are inserted in the return . . . With sincere good wishes for your continued success . . .

WP 3/3/53 p. 216

341

Colonel Murray to Arthur Wellesley

Godra
14 October 1803

. . . I have undoubted intelligence of a considerable body of Sinde's troops being at Jhabua and in that neighbourhood. One of my cossids returned from thence this morning. Holkar's troops are near Ratlam. It is said that he is there but I have that from no authority. This body of troops arrived at Ujjein on the 22nd and marched towards Ratlam . . . on the 24th. The latter part of this intelligence is from Major Walker. The report in the country is that this force is destined for Gujerat.

To enable you to judge of the propriety of my remaining here I think it necessary to give you some account of the country. There are three roads that lead from Sinde's territories into Gujerat, one to the southward of Godra leading to Sunkeera or Champaneer, one by Bariya and Godra, and one by Lunavada and Balasinore.

The first of these is extremely difficult for an army and if the Bheels make opposition may be considered impracticable. A great part of the road leads through the Bheel Raja of Bomrea's country, and his vakil with a body of his troops are now in my camp. The Raja has promised to make every opposition; I consider that road therefore as nearly secure.

The second road is extremely good if the Raja of Bariya is friendly, but if hostile it will be necessary to force the defiles of his country which are very strong. We have likewise his vakil and a body of his troops with me. But the troops are not exactly what I required and he is alarmed at the idea of defending his country fearing our success. I conceive therefore that it would be dangerous to leave this place till he has consented to admit a body of our troops into his country, which I have proposed. If he consents I shall immediately detach 400 or 500 men to take possession of the passes, which will open the enemy's country to us and shut up that passage to Sinde.

The third road by Lunavada is not so favourable for an army but is practicable. The Lunavada Raja has however promised that four or five thousand Bheels shall join my corps if it is found necessary to march in that direction. But this position at Godra besides being so centrical has a good communication with these roads and I can intercept an enemy on either before he clears the enclosed country where with my small numbers it is in my interest to engage.

With regard to Canoji I am likewise well posted. He left Lunavada when he heard of the march of the troops from Jarod and is now in the jungle in the skirts of Gujerat. He may pillage a village or a district but if he advances at all in the country he will expose himself to be cut off as there is a direct and good communication with Balasinore, Kapadvahj and so on through the country. At these places, it is said, there are about 3,000 Gaikwar cavalry and infantry. But even allowing that he should advance and plunder a district, it is undoubtedly better than to open the country to any deluge which might be poured in from Ratlam and Dohad.

These considerations have induced me to remain here; I had other reasons likewise but of less importance. It was necessary to give some government to the country, to secure our rear and convoys. The Bheels might not have joined me had I removed to a greater distance and, what had great weight, the Gaikwar's cavalry refused to march; in the unsettled situation of affairs I was unwilling that this should appear.

I have mentioned my intention of occupying the passes of Bariya. As soon as these important points are secure, I propose marching to Balasinore and perhaps further. But I have no other view in this movement than to force him [Canoji] to retire which I am sure he will as soon as he hears of our approach. I propose then to return with all expedition to the frontier of Bariya and if I can prevail on the Gaikwar cavalry to accompany me, and if I shall have been enabled to bring up some more troops, I shall advance upon Dohad.

Such is my plan of operations from which I shall not deviate but for important reasons. I have raised and am raising sebundi for the interior protection of the country, and have determined to take into pay a body of silledar horse. I can procure them easily if I was authorised to any extent. I am afraid that you may think me not sufficiently active and that I should penetrate at once to Dohad, but I am really too weak at present for such an undertaking. For Canoji I am fully strong enough, but to follow him would take me too far from my principal object.

I sent a hircarrah to you through the country with a letter in cypher. My principal reason for this was to ascertain if it were practicable and to get an account of what was going on when he returns. This country is extremely useful in a military point of view . . .

WP 3/3/79 p. 165

342

Arthur Wellesley to Colonel Murray

15 October 1803

I have received your letters of the 30th September and 2nd inst. It is very probable that you will do nothing with Canoji by negotiating. I suggested this means only because I observed that he was extremely weak in troops, and was absolutely destitute of money, and that he could procure none. At the same time the few troops he has were likely to keep in employment all our troops in Gujerat during the most precious time of the campaign and thus divert them, from the prosecution of the general war, to domestic purposes. If you should negotiate I anxiously hope that you will not stop your operations on that account. That mode will never answer any good purpose . . .

I suspect that you will not find the Patans of much use; however a few of them can do you no harm, and they may be the means of opening the communication with their friends on the frontier.

Gwrd (1837) ii 420 (1844) i 786

343

Lieutenant-Colonel Close: report from Lieutenant Stuart

Pune
15 October 1803

Mr Stuart arrived in Sinde's camp at Edilabad on the 1st June 1803. About 25 days after, he was appointed to do duty with the Burhanpur battalion of the 1st brigade commanded by Colonel Pohlman. The Bhonsle's army was then, Mr Stuart believes, at Mulkapur.

The force at Edilabad was then as follows

8 battalions of the 1st brigade
4 battalions of Begum Sumru
4 battalions of the brigade of the late Filose commanded by M Dupont a person of Dutch extraction born in Ceylon
4 or 5 battalions of the fifth brigade commanded by Major Brownrigg
6 or 7 battalions of the 4th brigade commanded by the Chevalier Dudrenec

> Sinde with his cavalry was at this time not in sight probably at Mulkapur.
>
> The ordnance was as follows
>
> With the 1st brigade there were five guns to each battalion besides a park to the brigade consisting of eight or ten pieces, 18 and 12 pounders. The ordnance of the other brigades was not quite so numerous, probably about three to each battalion, besides which was Daulat Rao Sinde's own park called the Jinsee under Man Singh Chaudhari about forty or fifty pieces.

This was the whole force in infantry and ordnance when Mr Stuart joined. The cavalry was very numerous . . .

In the month of July the whole force moved on towards Ajanta, the 1st brigade having halted within 6 kos of that pass. After a halt of some days the 4th and 5th brigades under Brownrigg and Dudrenec were ordered to Hindustan. They accordingly marched towards Ujjein. The 1st brigade received orders to march back to Burhanpur the same night that Colonel Collins left Sinde's camp; they accordingly marched to Burhanpur. Two of the battalions crossed the Tapti, when the whole brigade was remanded to Sinde's camp, Sinde himself having by this time penetrated through the Ajanta pass with his cavalry, the Begum's battalions, and the four [battalions] under M Dupont. The 1st brigade marched to Ajanta where it encamped, Sumru's and Dupont's being encamped in the neighbourhood.

When Colonel Collins left camp, Mr Stuart asked Colonel Pohlman to give him his discharge. Colonel Pohlman said he could have his discharge from General Perron only. Mr Stuart continued to press Colonel Pohlman for his discharge telling him that hostilities might commence before he could hear from General Perron and that if Colonel Pohlman persisted in refusing him his discharge, he was determined to go and in the best manner he could. At length on the 12th of September Colonel Pohlman was induced to give him his discharge and Mr Stuart immediately quitted camp and went to Burhanpur. Mr Grant and Mr MacCullough obtained their discharge at the same time and went back with Mr Stuart to Burhanpur.

In the ghat Mr Stuart met Sinde's Jinsee park . . .

PRC x 154, SNRR i 374, WP 3/3/47 fldr 5

344

Lieutenant-Colonel Close to Arthur Wellesley

Pune
15 October 1803

. . . You engaged all the infantry and guns that Sinde could collect, so that he must feel seriously indeed the loss of his equipment. The brigades under Dudrenec and Brownrigg it would appear are off to Hindustan. At Ujjein there can be nothing but the brigade under Baptiste and the other brigade forming at that capital, and at Burhanpur there can be nothing but the defeated infantry, by this time I suppose not very numerous. . . I shall send you the hircarrahs you have called for but I am sorry to find that those I previously sent to camp have failed to give satisfaction. I shall endeavour to ascertain whether any of them that are missing have returned to their former homes. . .

WP 3/3/47 fldr 5

345

Colonel Stevenson to Arthur Wellesley

Burhanpur
16 October 1803

I arrived at Burhanpur yesterday with cavalry a battalion of native infantry and 1500 of Rajah Sukhruder's horse. The detachment followed and arrived this morning. I expected to have met some of the principal inhabitants but was disappointed. On coming near the fort I first saw some of the principal people but they did not come on and on advancing to the gates forced their closure. After explaining to the inhabitants that I was disposed to treat them with indulgence if they behaved with proper respect, but if they showed any opposition to my orders I should expose them to plunder, they apologised for not opening the gates as the man who had charge of the keys was absent. I offered them a gun which was in readiness but they objected to that means and broke off the locks and bolts and threw the gates open. They then appeared to receive me with great joy and said the day was arrived that they had long wished for when they [should] be under the protection of the English government.

A great number of inhabitants proceeded towards the gates and at the request of the principal inhabitants I went with them to the Chauki, the streets lined with many people. They all appeared to express great satisfaction and begged for a guard which I granted by placing the battalion at the gate and in other parts of the town.

As I propose marching towards Asirgarh tomorrow in search of the campoos, I have not signified my intention of demanding a contribution but shall send the Ajanta man to enquire into the state of the town and revenues of the country, but to give particular attention to securing as much grain as I have the means of carrying, against my return. Any attempt on the fort of Asirgarh will depend on the appearance and the probability of speedy success. . .

Rajah Sukhruder informed me this evening that he had received intelligence that Bhonsle has been joined by horse from Jaswant Rao and other Marathas which with his own amounts to 25,000 and that he ascended the Cassabarri ghat three days ago with the intention of cutting off your supplies and that Sinde is to march this way to harass my detachment and cut off my supplies. They neither of them have any guns or infantry as I learn from every information that has been lately received.

The person who managed business for Colonel Collins and has since corresponded with, or rather written to, Captain Johnston arrived here yesterday [and] said he was sent by Sinde to know what terms would be listened to. He added that he was desired to get an answer to the letter formerly written to me and as you have explained on former occasions your pacific intentions I shall write to say that I am not authorised to answer any sort of negotiation but I am assured that you are willing to pay due respect and attention to any proposals that Sinde may send directly to you. The man seems to come as a supplicant to entreat for terms although without any letter or apparent authority. He hints that Sinde would be glad of a separate peace and has brought five hircarrahs with him for the purpose of corresponding but I shall not be induced by any means to write more than I have above described. The man also declares that he has authority from Sinde to say that whatever progress I may make in his country he shall remain quiet till he receives some reply. . .

WP 3/3/84 pp. 457–8

346

Colonel Murray to Arthur Wellesley

Godra
17 October 1803

. . . Everything in this country will I hope be quiet. I have taken Bheels into pay and they have agreed to escort all convoys through the country. We experience a great advantage from this friendship. I have sent on 300 sepoys with two six pounders to occupy the defiles of Bariya, which with the Raja's troops will be fully sufficient to check anybody till I can march to their assistance. I have assessed the country at four-fifths of last year's revenue. The deduction was made on account of the failure of the crops, the desertion of the inhabitants, and the loss by the march of our troops and those of Sinde, but above all to secure the goodwill of the inhabitants. Four of the five parganahs are perfectly arranged.

WP 3/3/79 p. 181

347

Josiah Webbe to Arthur Wellesley

Fort St George Madras
17 October 1803

. . . Close will have sent you the report he received by the way of Surat regarding General Lake's success at Delhi and I have this morning had the satisfaction of receiving a confirmation of it from Shawe . . . This is following your success most gloriously and it cannot fail of bringing things to the conclusion desired by Lord Wellesley. It is therefore possible that before you receive this you may be cutting up the ox by a partition treaty, and enable his Excellency to finish his government in a manner consistent with itself. Everything will have succeeded before our friends in Leadenhall Street can have invented objections to the Maratha war . . .

WP 3/3/93

348

Lieutenant-Colonel Close to Arthur Wellesley

Pune
18 October 1803
[summary]

Close has reported to the Governor-General the determination of the Peshwa not to be reconciled to Amrit Rao. 'We get no money for bills on Bombay, the long sight having disgusted the schroffs'. Duncan was reported to be in negotiation with 'some soucars at Bombay' to send Rs 2 lakhs to Pune each month. Close has 1½ lakhs ready to be sent to Ahmednagar by the next convoy. Malcolm was due to leave Bombay on 21st October.

WP 3/3/47 fldr 5

349
Colonel Stevenson to Arthur Wellesley

near Asirgarh
19 October 1803

I informed you in my letter of the 16th that I arrived at Burhanpur with the cavalry the second battalion 2nd Regiment of native infantry and 1000 Mogul horse on the 15th and was well received by the inhabitants although they hesitated at opening the gates till I have offered them a gun . . . They requested me to hoist the English colours to give confidence to the inhabitants.

The detachment marched about four miles from Burhanpur on the 15th and on the 16th passed it and crossed the Tapti. On the 17th the whole marched to Asirgarh with the exception of a detail of 300 effective native infantry . . . On the 18th I marched out with the pickets to reconnoitre the fort . . . and take such advantage as might offer, and as the enemy came out from the fort and pettah to seize some heights, I ordered two companies of native infantry to drive them down, after effecting which and seeing the pettah directly under them with very few troops for its defence, the guns of Captain [Lindsay?] who commanded the two companies and of Captain Dalrymple who had my permission to volunteer, urged them down the hill and they got easy possession of an open pettah immediately under the walls of the fort.

I then ordered them to be supported by the European pickets and another company of the native infantry and followed up with the other two companies having previously ordered a battalion without their guns to support and ultimately relieve the pickets. I have this morning ordered another battalion with the 18 and 12 pounders down to the pettah and the whole of the Mogul horse with two squadrons to reconnoitre the other side of the hill.

The fort has a very formidable appearance and if the garrison determine to keep it I must acknowledge that I despair of taking it by assault and have not ordnance enough to take it by a regular attack. The enemy fired very briskly all day yesterday from heavy guns as well as from musketry but with little mischief. As they have not commenced any fire this morning I have reason to think they will accept terms that I have offered, which is that every man shall carry off his private property and that the arrears of the troops shall be paid if it does not exceed 20,000 rupees. I thought it better to get the fort on these terms than either to have it in possession of the enemy or waste much time in the attack. If they give it up I shall put in a proper garrison, return directly to Burhanpur, endeavour to raise a contribution and proceed directly towards the Berar country.

I am sorry to observe that all the campoos with the guns have advanced too far towards the Narbada to give me any hope of overtaking them. I should have considered the destruction of that party of more consequence than the fort. Captain Dupont, Lieutenant Mercier, two European Portuguese officers, Ensign Marrs and some other officers and sergeants have surrendered themselves. Colonel Pohlman and other officers are in irons. Gopal Bhau is marching this way with 5000 men. Sinde and Bhonsle remain near the Cassabarri ghat. The brinjaras are receiving grain at Burhanpur.

WP 3/3/84 p. 461

350

J. Colebrooke – Roll of Europeans late in the service of Daulat Rao Sinde who have surrendered themselves as prisoners of state.

(The two who surrendered in September, see [278] above, were John Roach and George Black both English and both gunners.)

The list of those surrendered at Burhanpur on 16th October, all after the first three from Portugal, reads

'Captain John James Dupon [sic] from Holland, Lieutenant Mercier from France, Ensign Alexander Marrs from England, Ensigns John Berdard, Jookeen Caumbra, John Padroos, Francis

Carvoile, Manuelle Souza De Ball, Joaza Cartoos, Sergeants Joseph Roman and Joseph Vareirement, and Gunners Antony Dalmaid, Joseph Antony, and John Ammaral.'

WP 3/3/84

351

Colonel Murray to Arthur Wellesley

Godra
20 October 1803

. . . Major Holmes had an interview with the Raja of Bariya and now occupies the defiles, which shuts up the best road into Gujerat. As my Gaikwar allies refuse to march towards Ujjein, I am collecting silledar horse. I shall conclude tomorrow with 200 Scindians who have never been in any other service.

WP 3/3/79 p. 183

352

Arthur Wellesley to Lieutenant-Colonel Close

Phardapur
21 October 1803

. . . I am obliged to you for Mr Stuart's report. I have sent orders to Pune that he may enjoy the benefits held forth in the Governor General's Proclamation of 29th August. The only brigade that escaped on the 23rd was part of the Begum Sumru's. They were with the baggage and got off in safety. I knew this on the day of action and saw them go off. There may also have been one battalion of Pohlman's with the baggage but I am not certain of that. Dorsan was certainly killed and the bodies of other Europeans who did not belong to us were seen . . .[11]

Stevenson took possession of Burhanpur without opposition on the 16th and he was going the next day to look at Asirgarh. By the last accounts the enemy were still about Parola. They have made another offer of peace, in the same style with the last, which has been answered in the same manner. Colonel Lang met Colonel Collins' newswriter in the road between this and Edilabad with letters for me which he said contained propositions for peace. This man is arrived in Colonel Stevenson's camp but he has not produced these letters although he certainly has them.

Grwd (1837) ii 432 (1844) i 797

353

Colonel Stevenson to Arthur Wellesley

Asirgarh
21 October 1803 11pm

I have the satisfaction to inform you that the British colours were deployed on the upper works of the fort of Asirgarh this morning. Previous to marching from Burhanpur on the 17th one of the principal inhabitants informed me that the garrison of Asirgarh was in long arrears and if I were to engage to pay these arrears he was of opinion they would give up the place. As the immediate possession of the place seemed to me of the highest importance to the interests of government, I wrote to the killedar, jemadars and garrison to say that to prevent the effusion of blood on both sides that must be occasioned by a siege and to release them from their present distress, I would comply with these proposals and pay off the arrears of the troops if it did not exceed the sum of twenty thousand rupees . . .

On the 17th I encamped near the fort and some shot was fired into the army. I sent to know if they had received my letter which they did not acknowledge but said that although they were servants of Daulat Rao [Sinde] they would be happy to receive any communication from me. On the 18th I took possession of the pettah, on the 19th sent down all my 18 and 12 pounders and commenced erecting a battery to bear on the upper and lower works of the fort. At 3 pm on the 20th I commenced firing and pressed on the garrison hard with the fire of the battery, whereupon they finished in sending a reply to my summons at the promised time. I had determined to [open?] the gates and allow the garrison and [the] inhabitants who had taken refuge in the fort, to march out without their effects and, although they had fired on my horse and bullocks, [to] perform my engagements in respect of the honours of the garrison.

On the evening of the 20th they offered to open the lower gates and [invited?] me to send five soldiers into the lower fort. I detained the bearer of such an extraordinary message and determined on taking possession of the lower fort at an early hour the next morning, but after making preparations for commencing the fire, a messenger arrived to inform me that all the gates were open and that I might send any troops to take possession of the fort when I thought proper. A flank company of the 94th and two companies of native infantry were ordered to march up immediately and take possession of the gates. Two other companies were ready to give protection to the garrison and [to] the inhabitants in carrying off their [property?], and I have great satisfaction in informing you that this was conducted with the greatest order. One of the inhabitants marching with a camp follower was detected in plunder and I ordered him to be hanged immediately. Except for this circumstance, not an inhabitant has reason to complain. They were [taken into?] the pettah where they were met by two squadrons of native cavalry who escorted them in safety six or seven miles in the rear towards Burhanpur. There is some property belonging to Sinde in the fort. It is [reported] to me by one of the officers of the committee ordered to [safeguard?] the property that it will amount to four or five lakhs of pagodas, but this I fear is too sanguine.

I have received your letters of the 14th and 16th by the latter of which I understand that you have made a march to the northward. My late intelligence says that Sinde has marched towards Burhanpur which we confirmed by a messenger from Kawda

Newas Khan who says he was in Sinde's camp about 35 kos from Burhanpur on the 19th and he was to march the next day. Kawder Beg's letter says Sinde was to halt on that ground four days. As his intention was most likely to interrupt my operations against Burhanpur and Asirgarh, he will most likely halt when he hears that they are both in British possession.

My only consideration will be to preserve the troops in a state for the further opportunities of the war and I shall put in a garrison and provisions for their support with all convenient expedition, after which I shall return to Burhanpur to press the business of the contribution in the manner you have recommended, and it will bring my detachment together to oppose the enemy if they should advance towards it. I have reason to hope that the detachment is strong enough to oppose Sinde's and Bhonsle's present force, but it is very desirable that you should march this way and in order that you may take such decisions as you think best for the future security of these important places, and determine on the future operations of the troops. If any circumstance shall [lead?] you to march in a different direction I shall finish my negotiations at Burhanpur as speedily as possible and march with my detachment by Mulkapur, leaving the range of mountains on my left towards Gawilghar which will carry me through rich grain country belonging to Sinde.

In two or three days at furthest I can settle everything necessary for the security of this place and finish all business at Burhanpur. The guard is so strong at this place and at Burhanpur and on the road between them that no horse can hurt me. But if Sinde should advance towards me I can provide for this place in a few hours and act as circumstances may require either offence or defence.

WP 3/3/84 p. 463

354

Arthur Wellesley to Colonel Murray

Phardapur
23 October 1803

I have received great satisfaction from the perusal of your letters of the 4th and 7th [October] and I assure you that you are getting on much better than I could have expected with your defective means.

I think that Canoji will not engage in an action with you, but he will retire. You must then guide yourself according to the circumstances of the country, the state of your supplies and resources and of your force compared with that of the enemy, whether you will move upon Ujjein. It is not possible for me at this distance from the scene to do more than give you a general outline and communicate to you the information I have of the enemy's actual force. To beat or drive away Canoji must be your first object, the security of Gujerat your next.

If there were not in that quarter a number of little low objects which are always in view with native governments and which the British influence in that quarter rather encourages and promotes than discourages, I should think it very possible to connect the security of Gujerat with an invasion of Ujjein. However I have not sufficient information upon the subject and I must leave the decision to yourself . . .

Grwd (1837) ii 438 (1844) i 802

355

Arthur Wellesley to Colonel Collins

Phardapur
23 October 1803

I received in due course your letter of the 6th [October] and this day your letter of the [12th], for which I am obliged to you.

Mr Grant and Mr Stuart were not in the action of the 23rd September. The latter is arrived at Pune and says he and Mr Grant and Mr McCulloch quitted Sinde's camp on the [12 September] and went to Burhanpur. From thence Mr Stuart went to Pune, but he does not say in his report what became of the other gentlemen. He says that they had not heard of the Governor General's Proclamation of the 29th August, and regrets that they had not, as he is convinced that many natives would have come away with him. The motives with these gentlemen for coming away were their reluctance to serve against their country, and the fact that the English officers in Hindustan had gone to the British settlements, of which Colonel Pohlman received intelligence from General Perron on the 12 September. The brigades engaged were Pohlman's, Dupont's, and Begum Sumru's, in the whole sixteen battalions.

Wahed Beg, if that be the man to whom the Proclamations were sent has deceived you, and I suspect him of playing tricks in another instance very lately . . . He had been sent from Sinde's camp with letters for me in answer to those I wrote on the subject of the first propositions for peace. He showed the directions on the letters to Colonel Lang who met him on his march to this place to receive a convoy. He afterwards went on to Colonel Stevenson, swore that he had no letter for anybody, and pretended that he was come only to supplicate for peace. His object with Colonel Stevenson, I see clearly, was to try if he could not prevail upon him to write a letter to Sinde upon the subject of peace different from that which I had written him. But it happened that I had sent the Colonel a translation of my letter and if the Colonel has written at all, it is in corresponding terms. However whatever his object was, he has deceived Colonel Stevenson, as letters directed to me were positively seen in his hand . . .

Who is the Nabob Muhammed Mir Khan Mueen ud Daulah, who interests himself so much in the affair of the peace? He says that he is a great friend of yours and has forwarded all your objects.

SD iv 206

356

Colonel Stevenson to Arthur Wellesley

Asirgarh
23 October 1803

An hircarrah belonging to Salabat Khan arrived in camp yesterday and reported that he left your camp at Phardapur four days ago. It will afford me the highest satisfaction if you advance far enough this way to give me an opportunity of waiting on you to receive your instructions about our further opportunities. As I have no reason to expect any interruption from the enemy and as your march will be very difficult after leaving Barragaon, I recommend you not proceeding further with your division in this direction unless you have some views to the northward, and then I believe Mulkapur will be the best route. If I am to proceed from here towards Gawilghar I must return by the route I came beyond Yedlabad and I believe to Burrangaon and there I would choose the route by Mulkapur and keep the chain of hills on my left by which means I shall benefit from villages of Sinde's stored with grain and get well provided till I get near Elichpur and the Berar country.

From Barragaon to Yedlabad is twelve miles six furlongs and from Yedlabad to Burhanpur 22 miles, the latter part of the last march very much interrupted with deep ravines. From Burhanpur to this place about 14 miles, ravines almost the whole way. I have made these remarks that you may avoid any unnecessary fatigues. But if your views are to clear the country as far as the Narbada all these impediments will vanish. I have not had any of my own hircarrahs arrive lately from the enemy's camp or from the infantry camp that went towards the Narbada. But the following report was made to me last night by two hircarrahs belonging to Salabat Khan.

'Bhonsle and Sinde quarrelled and parted seven days ago at the camp at Nargaysar. Bhonsle made a march to Barragaon to which place the hircarrahs accompanied him and stayed one day in his camp at that place. It was reported that he intended to go to [?Nasik] to meet Amrit Rao. The hircarrahs then returned to Sinde's camp at Jelode on the north bank of the Tapti. It was said in Sinde's camp that he intended going by the Scindrid ghat which is near Coprail and to cross the Narbada towards Chooli Myhissur and ultimately to Ujjein.'

Captain Johnston writes me from Burhanpur as follows

'Hircarrahs have just come in from the enemy's camp. They report that Sinde was the day before yesterday the 20th at Rawail on the Ramaysir[?] river 10 kos from Parolah. He was to march yesterday 5 kos in this direction but they had not marched when the hircarrahs left camp. Gopal Bhau was with Sinde. Bhonsle had left Sinde at Parolah and it was said had made four marches towards the Cassabarri ghat. Parolah is northwest 16 kos from the Cassabarri ghat. Bapu Sinde with 10 or 12,000 horse was 12 kos from him near Rawail. It is said that he is going to Hindustan.'

In another part of Captain Johnston's letter he writes 'it is said that Sinde's infantry were staying on this side of the Narbada and have been joined by some battalions and guns from Hindustan under Colonel James in the favour of Ambaji Inglia.' The latter name is without any particular authority and I suppose it a fabricated story of the inhabitants of Burhanpur. As Sinde and Bhonsle wished me to advance to this position when their forces were together and these places not in my possession, it is not likely that Sinde, now divided from Burhanpur and the British colours flying on Asirgarh, will offer to attack or oppose . . .

If it is your intention to drive all the enemy beyond the Narbada I shall be ready to march to the northward when I receive your instructions. But as this fort will be left in perfect security and as the capture of Gawilghar will totally destroy all the power and influence of Bhonsle and deprive him of the means of supporting an army, I am rather inclined to think you will turn your views that way and under that opinion I shall march from this place to Burhanpur tomorrow leaving plenty of provisions of all descriptions for a garrison of a Captain, two subalterns, three native officers, twelve havildars, and 300 rank and file native infantry for the defence of this place. There are provisions enough in the fort to last them six months certain and I believe twelve months.

I shall summon the inhabitants of Burhanpur for a contribution. Our force cannot afford a garrison for it and it may not perhaps be advisable to make it over to the Nizam and if the town is kept on account of either a contribution cannot be raised. It may at all times be taken possession of and it will be as safely kept at the expense of the enemy as at the expense of the British or their allies. Salabat Khan . . . says he will raise horse and foot for its defence. Mohipat Ram is prepared to defend it for the Nizam and I have authorised Captain Johnston and the Raja to press the business of a contribution. It may be too late for fresh accommodation.

It will afford me infinite satisfaction if your distance from Burhanpur admits of my waiting on you to receive your instructions for our future opportunities. Or if your leisure admits of your coming forward with an escort which may be met by another from this camp at Yedlabad in order that you may form your own opinions in respect to the disposal of Burhanpur and Asirgarh it will be still more satisfactory. If neither of these expedients are convenient it may be assumed that I shall have no other guide for my conduct than the most zealous desire to promote the British interests and the success of the troops under your command.

WP 3/3/84 p. 467

357

Colonel Stevenson to Arthur Wellesley

Asirgarh
24 October 1803

I was very sorry to learn by a letter from Barclay dated Phardapur the 20th that you were indisposed and hope to hear of your speedy recovery.

Sinde and Gopal Bhau have moved to the northwest from their former situation. Bhonsle and Baba Furkia have gone to the westward . . . The campoos are reinforced with some horse but every intelligence I receive tends to confirm Sinde's intention of crossing the Narbada. But until that event has really taken place it may not be prudent to march to the eastward.

As I am not acquainted with your opinions and intentions in respect of marching to the Berar country, I think that I shall preserve this station. If I should follow up the infantry they have it in their power to return across the Narbada when they think proper beyond a point I think you would wish me to advance, and there is no necessity for my falling back to Burhanpur and I have reason to think the business of contribution is going as well as if I was present. If you were to advance as far as Barragaon you could then determine whether it was advisable for you to advance and drive everything beyond the Narbada before you proceed to Berar or whether the already advanced situation of the enemy to the northward leaves you at liberty to proceed with your plan to the eastward.

If you advance to Barragaon I shall be glad to pay my respects to you at that place which I can do in a short time if you will have the goodness to send a palanquin to Yedlabad for me with a fresh escort. I am favoured with sufficient grain to advance upon the campoos if I shall think I shall have time before you propose going to Berar. Mulkapur seems a good situation for Colonel Lang's battalion as he can intercept the convoys from the Berar country.

WP 3/3/84 p. 471–2

358

Arthur Wellesley to Colonel Stevenson

Phardapur
24 October 1803

I received last night your letter of the 21st and I sincerely congratulate you on your success against Asirgarh. My letter of yesterday will have apprised you that I had received a report of it to which I gave credit.

The first object of your attention must now be to establish a garrison in Asirgarh. Possibly 300 men of the Company's troops and a small detail of artillery with a careful non-commissioned officer and 400 or 500 of Raja Mohipat Ram's infantry would be a very sufficient garrison. Throw into the post a sufficient quantity of provisions for these troops and desire one of your officers of artillery to see that the most useful guns on the works are properly arranged and provided with the necessary quantity of ammunition. I conclude that the granaries at Asirgarh are already well stored. If they should be so, I recommend that you should not take the bags for your supply on your expedition into Berar if you can get grain in the country or in Burhanpur, as in case it should be necessary hereafter to push our operations into Hindustan the depot at Asirgarh will be very useful to us.

In respect to Burhanpur, after you shall have levied a contribution on it I mean that it should be given over to Raja Mohipat Ram. The British troops may be withdrawn from it and a garrison of the Subah's infantry established there. I mean the country depending upon Burhanpur and Asirgarh should be delivered to the charge of Raja Mohipat Ram for the Subah of the Deccan. I will request you to speak to him on the subject and desire him to make his arrangements for placing his tannahs in the different villages belonging to Daulat Rao Sinde for establishing in the country the government of his Highness the Subah of the Deccan and for collecting the revenues . . .

It is said here that you found at Assaye an account book of Lieutenant Stuart which proves that he was in camp on the 22nd September; I wish you would let me know if that be true.

Grwd (1837) ii 443 (1844) i 805

359

Colonel Murray to Arthur Wellesley

Godra
24 October 1803

I have remained in this encampment since I had last the honour of writing you. I detached Major Holmes some days ago to the Bariya country which he has now traversed and which he has not found so strong as he expected. He proposed going to Dohad yesterday from whence Sinde's troops had retired when they heard of the advance of Major Holmes' corps.

A report prevails that Holkar is in person gone to Hindustan, and my hircarrahs report that he is to the northward of Ujjein collecting his revenues which I believe to be the most likely story of the two. However there are two of his corps at Jhabua and Ratlam. Canoji has lately made a movement towards the Gaikwar corps which is to be with me and they are so alarmed that I shall march to join them tomorrow. Canoji I have every reason to believe will immediately retire . . .

The small body of Gaikwar cavalry refused to advance with me towards Ujjein and it has been difficult to get them to go towards that body which I propose joining. They declare they will not return should they be required. I have in consequence engaged two hundred Scindian cavalry which I can increase to one thousand if the Bombay government will consent.

I am happy to acquaint you that the sickness which rendered us so low begins to diminish. I hope in the course of a fortnight or three weeks to add above four hundred Europeans to my corps in the field.

WP 3/3/79 p. 198

360

Arthur Wellesley to Colonel Stevenson

[Ajanta]
25 October 1803 [received 27 October]

The march of the Raja of Berar to the southward and the fear that I may be detained in the southward for some time, during which all this country would be exposed to Sinde, make it necessary that we should revise our plan to some degree. Accordingly I wish you for the present to watch Sinde and to prevent him from undertaking anything of consequence, or doing any material mischief till I can give the other a turn to the northward when all will be safe. You may in the meantime make all your arrangements for the Berar expedition, all your enquiries respecting roads distances etc upon which you shall certainly go as soon as I have brought up the Raja; this I may possibly do in a few days.

I leave with Captain Scott for you 75,000 pagodas in various gold coins and 25,000 in silver, the whole 30 bullock loads, and I leave all the medicines for your corps 54 bullock loads. You will do well to send an escort and carriage for that money and medicines.

Grwd (1837) ii 453 (1844) i 813

361

J. Colebrooke

28 October 1803 7 pm

General Wellesley's letter of the 25th was received last night and the duplicate by the bearers just now. Colonel Stevenson is somewhat better but still confined to his bed and unable to attend to business. A detachment will be sent for the money and medicines and General Wellesley's letters answered tomorrow.

WP 3/3/84

362

Arthur Wellesley to Colonel Stevenson

Phulambri
28 October 1803

. . . It is unpleasant that we cannot take all the advantage I could wish of our success. But the fact is that offensive operations are not expected of us in this quarter and although I am willing and have undertaken them already I must take care not to risk, by attempting too much, that for which I am sent here and the failure of the service expected of me, namely the defence of the Nizam's and Peshwa's territories . . .

It is therefore peculiarly incumbent on me to act with caution. I think that in a day or two I shall drive off Raghuji Bhonsle. I shall give you notice of everything that passes and as soon as ever I make it certain that he is out of the country you may begin your march upon Gawilghar. We may eventually invade Hindustan but I think that before we do that we ought to secure our right flank by taking Gawilghar and if possible forcing Raghuji to a peace. I wrote to Mohipat Ram to desire him to take possession of the taluks depending on Burhanpur and Asirgarh in the name of the Subah of the Deccan.

I shall be near Aurungabad tomorrow. Your Baswant rice was to be at the Godavari on the 25th, I shall forward it to Ajanta to which place you might send for it.

Grwd (1837) ii 459 (1844) ii 817

363

Colonel Murray to Arthur Wellesley

Camp on the Myhie
29 October 1803

I marched from Godra on the 25th. Tomorrow I go to Balasinor where I expect to meet some of the Gaikwar cavalry and the officer who commands their forces in this part of the country. I know he will press me much to march to the northward, which will serve no other purpose than enabling them to raise contributions on the neighbouring Rajas.

Major Holmes has established himself in the Bariya country which with his small corps he thinks he can defend till supplemented by me. All our reports at present agree that Holkar is at Kotah but I do not think it clear that he is going to oppose General Lake. He has left this corps to cover Ujjein and Indore.

Our friendship with the Bheels increases. Major Walker informs me that overtures of peace have been made to you by Sinde. I hope that you will hear that we have possession of this country before anything is concluded. It is of the utmost importance to Gujerat.

WP 3/3/79 p. 193

364

Colonel Murray to Arthur Wellesley

Balasinor
29 October 1803

I have had the pleasure of receiving your letter of the 13th [October] this morning. As soon as I received my instructions from Bombay I began to act upon them and after having stated what appeared to me objectionable I determined to say nothing more, in which I was the more confirmed when I found that they met with your approbation. It is extremely fortunate that Major Walker is of the disposition that he is, for if he chose to be troublesome he might depend upon every support from Mr Duncan . . .

When I wrote to you on the 26th September that I should immediately attack Canoji, it was my firm intention to do so, but he put it out of my power by moving off to a distance of sixty kos. I was prevented from following him by Holkar's appearance in Malwa and it was not till I had secured the road through

Bariya that I thought it safe to move in this direction. My instructions pointed out Ujjein as my principal object, but that was supposing my corps much stronger than it is. I had proposed employing the time necessary for the recovery of the troops in drawing Canoji from the frontier, keeping always in train my prescribed invasion.

Your letter of the 13th now points him out as a principal object and I should immediately follow him, had I not what appears to be good intelligence that he has retired on my march and that his present intention is to join Holkar who it is said has [incited?] him to this measure. Upon this important point I shall have more intelligence in the course of the day and tomorrow.

I am obliged to halt to arrange my movements with the Gaikwar's corps. I had appointed their chief to meet here, which however he has failed to do. If this information proves correct it will be perfectly useless to go further to the northward. I shall with the utmost expedition march to Dohad, and if possible proceed to Ujjein . . .

I have given Major Holmes who is on the frontier of Bariya the most positive orders relative to Holkar and I shall careful[ly] avoid giving him any cause of offence. It is however generally supposed and reported by the natives that he has joined the confederacy; I shall not however be guided by such authority.

Besides the depots at Broach and Surat I have formed another at Baroda and have directed grain to be collected at Powanghar and Godra. Cambay is not at present sufficiently secure to form large magazines nor is it at present requisite. I hope that Godra and Bariya will be the line of communication . . . There is as yet very little alteration in the health of the troops. I had flattered myself that it was improving. We continue however to lose men very fast, and those which recover [from] an attack of a few days are so weak after it as to be incapable of fatigue. This is the case with almost all the Europeans in camp.

I am much obliged to you for the account you have favoured me with of your movement since the action of the 23rd. I see all the advantages of moving towards Ujjein and it is distressing not to be in a state to afford the cooperation. I will not however fail to push forward the moment I am at liberty by the removal or destruction of Canoji . . .

WP 3/3/79 p. 206

365

Colonel Murray to Arthur Wellesley

Balasinore
31 October 1803

The accounts I had received of Canoji's retreat are confirmed. He is now in the immediate neighbourhood of Gallicotte which is far beyond the Gujerat frontier and when my last hircarrahs came away he was still retiring and it was confidently said towards Malwa.

I had yesterday an interview with Kakoji the Gaikwar commander and I decided on advancing to Beerpur two marches in the direction Canoji is gone. Kakoji marches this day, I march tomorrow. The only advantage of this step will be to force Canoji a little further back. He will go probably to Purtaabghar, a strong fort belonging to Holkar. It is confidently reported that Canoji has resisted every effort of the Arabs to induce him to engage us, and as it appears he is supported in his opinion by the other chiefs, I fear there is no hope of bringing him to action. His army has been very much harassed by the Bheels, who daily kill his men and cattle. It is rather extraordinary that I have received no answer to my letters. The first I sent was I know interrupted by the Bheels. Of the fate of the second I have heard nothing.

Your letter of the 15th October is this instant arrived. I assure you I shall lose no time in negotiating. Indeed Canoji does not appear willing to give me an opportunity either of negotiating or fighting . . . The engaging of the Pathans failed from their enormous demands. I have engaged two hundred [Scindians?] whom I find extremely useful, for upon the Gaikwar cavalry I cannot depend. Indeed they are in such a state for want of pay that I do not think we shall be able to induce them to enter Malwa . . .

WP 3/3/79 p. 224

366

Arthur Wellesley to James Kirkpatrick

[Cheesekair]
2 November 1803

. . . I cannot express to you how much I am distressed and how much the public cause suffers by the total want of means of defence in this country. In order to save it this last time I have been obliged to march 120 miles and to pass through the Ajanta and Chavak ghats in eight days, and when I arrived all the amildars were in treaty with the enemy to pay contributions . . .

I am fully aware that it is very desirable to carry the war into Berar and I have no doubt that unless we carry it there we shall have no peace. But the question is can the war be carried into Berar unless the Subah of the Deccan defends his country, and [unless] he or his ministers [are] willing to submit to the loss which must be incurred by exposing it to invasions, undefended by a British army, in its present state.

If the war should be carried into Berar I conceive that the Subah will not be exonerated from the necessity of storing his forts with grain, and I certainly think the expedition into that country a matter of some risk, if the only dependence of the subsistence of the troops was the grain which they should find in the Rajah's territories. Although the smaller forts are in the hands of amildars and others it is to be supposed that there is some mode of obliging them to keep them in repair, to have garrisons in them, and to defend them. If something is not done on this subject I must confine the operation of the troops to a strict defensive . . .

Grwd (1837) ii 463 (1844) ii 823

367

Arthur Wellesley to Richard Wellesley

Cheesekair
2 November 1803 [received 26 November 1803]

. . . The Raja of Berar has moved to the eastward and I think he is going to his own territories. I have no doubt that he would have been obliged to do so even without my presence in these districts, if any one step had been taken by the [Nizam's] government for their protection, or I might add if there existed any government in the country. It is now obvious that horse alone cannot make any impression on a country, and if there had been only a few peons in the villages, as has been frequently recommended to the government of Hyderabad by the Resident, the Raja must have lost the whole of his baggage in the confused and precipitate flight which he has made since I have been in the neighbourhood.

The government of Hyderabad appears determined to do nothing in their own defence . . . even the city of Aurungabad in which so many of his Highness's relations and the families of so many of his sirdars reside, is held by 500 men of the old French infantry[12] who I have every reason to believe are a part of the corps which ought to be in the field.

This conduct in the government of Hyderabad will I much fear put it out of my power to carry the war into Berar as I wish unless the Raja should retire towards Nagpur. I am convinced however that until I am enabled to carry the war into that country no progress will have been made towards procuring a peace.

Daulat Rao Sinde moved to the eastward as soon as I ascended the Ajanta ghat and he was at Edilabad on the 29th October.

Grwd (1837) ii 466 (1844) ii 825

368

Colonel Murray to Arthur Wellesley

Camp at Beepur
3 November 1803

The Bombay government have so altered your plan of conciliating Canoji that I do not intend to take any further steps. I wrote to know how far they would authorise me to go. My answer is that they will inform Major Walker who will consult the Gaikwar government and get their concurrence to the terms [that] Mr Duncan will grant and that I am to refer Canoji's letter to Major Walker. This latter part I understand, but of the rest I can make nothing except that I am to treat with a man without knowing the terms and if from necessity I make a promise I risk its being broke and Canoji deceived.

The messenger I sent is now in his camp and I this day received accounts that he proposed returning with a munshi of Canoji's who may possibly be authorised to treat. I have lately had some communication with a brahmin who frequently visits him and he says that in his opinion Canoji would be glad to treat with us on liberal terms and provided the negotiation was kept secret from the Arabs. The consultation with the Gaikwar government precludes the one as much as the necessity of its occurrence precludes the other.

I have been obliged to halt here one day for the Gaikwar troops. Their delay is intentional and impertinent. They have not arrived and I shall march tomorrow towards Canoji without them. I find that contrary to his normal action he has not moved; perhaps he may give me an opportunity of attacking him.

If you have not already done so, allow me to beg of you to press Mr Duncan on the subject of cavalry. I am convinced that Gaikwar's principal officers are decidedly hostile to us and would regret our success. I have daily proofs of the little dependence that can be placed upon them. I have raised about 200 men who at a very moderate price are of the greatest utility.

Some of my cossids lately come in mentioned General Lake's

army as rumoured [to be] in the country. I shall write to him in cypher to ascertain that my cossids traverse the country . . .

WP 3/3/79 p. 230

369

Arthur Wellesley to Merrick Shawe

6 November 1803

. . . A vakil from Daulat Rao Sinde is now on his road to camp and I expect will be here in a day or two. You may believe that I am anxious to receive from Bengal accounts of the state of your negotiations with the Rajput, Jats etc and of your military operations of which I know nothing since the 18th September, particularly how matters are going in Bundelkhand.

The Raja of Berar is flying to the eastward as fast as he can along the Godavari. I have not heard that he has yet turned to the northward but I expect he will as Sinde marched to the eastward in the valley of the Tapti and Purna rivers. I know that he passed Mulkapur on the 30th October as it is said on his way to Berar. This movement relieves us from all apprehension of his attacking the territories of the Nizam or the Peshwa and immediately sets at liberty Colonel Stevenson's corps who will follow Sinde into Berar. I think it very possible that four armies may be in that country in a few days which will be delightful to the Raja of Berar. . .

Grwd (1837) ii 481 (1844) ii 838

370

Colonel Murray to Arthur Wellesley

Camp Baerour
9 November 1803

I proceeded as I mentioned to this place. I was joined on the 7th by the Marathas who had halted two days on account of rain they said but I believe it was for plundering. Even those expressly attached to me would not march from Beepur. On the 8th I proposed marching to Peit and had actually struck the tents when I received undoubted information that Canoji had retreated as soon as he heard that this corps had advanced to Baerour and passed the ghat which is now in the rear. This retreat shows evidently that he has no intention of engaging us and as Holkar's country is within a few kos in his rear I propose returning to Beepur from whence by Lunawara I shall march towards Bariya.

The confidence which the Bheels place in us and the friendship they have everywhere shown would I am convinced enable an English army to march unmolested through the whole country. I have heard from all quarters and numbers of the Bheels had assembled to join me. But the conduct of the Marathas has been such that I shall probably be obliged to fight my way tomorrow through the very jungle that I passed two days ago led by the Bheels themselves. They burned two villages as they came up and in spite of every remonstrance on my part they have continued systematically to plunder since their arrival. Were these desultory parties it might be prevented but it is countenanced and done by order of Kakoji their commanding officer. I have therefore no means left to me but to attack them by force which would not be advisable at present. I have represented their conduct to Major Walker that some notice of it may be taken at Baroda but I have little hope of amendment . . .

Daily experience convinces me of the little dependence that can be placed on the Maratha cavalry . . . the money proposed to be expended in paying these vagabonds will be much more usefully employed in raising a corps of our own. Mr Duncan has given me no answer on this subject; I hope he is consulting you. As everything appears favourable to the southwards of the Narbada, I have ordered the 84th from Paneira, 250 of the 75th from Surat, and all the 88th fit for duty from Broach. Our sickness in camp diminishes but the men die fast in the hospitals.

WP 3/3/79 p. 232

371

Colonel Stevenson to Arthur Wellesley

Yedlabad
9 November [1803]

I have this instant received your letter [from] Naundair Barri 4 kos northeast of Paithan. You are likely to have some trouble in your hunt after Raghuji Bhonsle.

I was rejoicing at the prospect of finding my Busmunt rice at Ajanta but a note just received from Captain Scott at Ajanta inclosing a letter from Captain Barclay dated near Goondy 3 November in which he says that Captain Seton is before a court martial for disobedience of orders, which gives me reason to apprehend the rice has miscarried. I have however secured some grain at Balapur which place is safe in the possession of Salabat Khan's troops. I shall not therefore be in want, nor shall I be prevented from watching Sinde's motions or pursuing your plan of operation upon Gawilghar, but my ultimate dependence is upon the Busmunt rice. I shall take the earliest opportunity of sending a detachment to Ajanta to meet the rice, the instant I hear of its arrival there. In the meantime I shall take up my grain at Balapur.

My force is now collected at Yedlabad. I arrived here this morning with the 2nd of the 7th and shot and ammunition for the siege of Gawilghar. Captain Dalrymple arrived at Burhanpur from Asirgarh on the 7th with about 700 rounds [for] each gun for your 12 pounders as well as my iron guns. The powder is made up in cartridges and packed in boxes well secured.

I marched on the 8th from Burhanpur to Antomarri and this morning to this place. I shall detach two battalions (the 2nd of the 2nd and the 2nd of the 9th) tomorrow to Ajanta for treasure and medicines, and the grain if the brinjaras have arrived there, with instructions to the officer to join me at Balapur on the 19th or 20th. On the 11th I shall march with the rest of the force from this place to Mulkapur and from thence to Balapur.

At Balapur I expect some assistance of guns and ammunition as well as grain and can either proceed to the siege of Gawilghar or follow up Sinde's marches, or I can go directly against Nagpur or if it is found necessary march up the Serail ghat into the Nizam's country. My principal objects . . . will depend on the orders I may receive from you.

The inhabitants of Burhanpur had entered into written agreements to pay ten lakhs of rupees but I found the early collections attendant with so much distress to the inhabitants and that it would also interfere with objects of more material consequence to the general interest that I annulled the engagements provided the inhabitants would pay Rajah Mohipat Ram two lakhs and a half of rupees immediately. More is on hand besides jewels to a considerable amount.

Sinde on the 7th marched from Jellgaon . . . 7 kos and 30 kos from Yedlabad on the Amrauti to Elichpur road. The Berar Rajah had arrived at Nagpur and Mana Bapu it was said has ascended the Serallah ghat with an intention to join Bhonsle. Govind Rao Bhakshi with 4000 horse was at Takael Keyorah 5 kos from Mulkapur.

WP 3/3/84

372

Arthur Wellesley – Conference with Jaswant Rao Goorparah and Naru Pant Nana

10 November 1803
[summary]

In the initial conference with representatives of Daulat Rao Sinde, there was discussion of the circumstances in which relations had been broken off in the last days of July 1803, the contention of the agents of Sinde being that breakdown had been due to 'the violence and precipitation of Colonel Collins'. Arthur Wellesley contested this, pointedly noting that far from having hurried away, Collins had 'stayed much longer than he was authorised.' He then sought confirmation that Jaswant Rao Goorparah had authority to negotiate, and learnt that he had not. Arthur Wellesley finally agreed as a gesture of conciliation to inform Daulat Rao Sinde that his agents had arrived in his camp.

SD iv 221

373

Arthur Wellesley – Conference with Appah Dessaye

11 November 1803
[summary]

In a conference on which Appah Dessaye[13] insisted, Arthur Wellesley was given an indication of the supposed propositions for peace that the vakils of Daulat Rao Sinde had brought, and was told that Sinde was accustomed to negotiate for Raghuji Bhonsle and Jaswant Rao Holkar. He clearly doubted the validity of both points.

SD iv 224

374

Arthur Wellesley to Richard Wellesley

Jaum
11 November 1803

. . . I proceed to state to your Excellency the demands which I propose to make to Daulat Rao Sinde . . . I shall demand from him the cession of all his territories north of those of the Rajas of Jodhpur and Jynaghur: the cession of the fort of Broach and a territory depending thereon . . . and the fort of Ahmednagar and a territory depending thereon: the cession of all his territories situated southward and eastward of the hills called the Ajanta hills including the fort and district of Jalnapur and all districts in which he may have a joint right with the Subah of the Deccan and collects the revenues: a renunciation of all claims of chaute and all other claims of whatever denomination upon the Subah of the Deccan and all the allies of the British government.

[I shall also demand] an acknowledgement of the independence of the Rajas of Jodhpur and Jynaghur, a renunciation of all claims upon the Rana of Gohad who is in future to be dependent upon the British government, an engagement never to entertain in his service any Europeans belonging to a country which may be at war with Great Britain: that his Majesty [the Mugul Emperor] is to be under the protection of the British government, that he [Sinde] shall not molest the chiefs who may have assisted the British government in the war of whom I shall include the names of as many as I can procure. I propose also to settle some plan for ascertaining what districts in Khandesh and Malwa belong to the Peshwa and what to Sinde . . .

This plan appears to provide for all the material objects in your . . . instructions of the 27th June . . .

Grwd (1837) ii 408 (1844) ii 853, WP 3/3/2

375

Colonel Murray to Arthur Wellesley

Lunavada
12 November 1803

I have the pleasure to acquaint you that Canoji is now off my hands. He conceived probably that I should not follow him across the hills but finding that I was within fifteen kos he went off in a great hurry. The greater part of his troops have left him. He is gone so far my spies retired thinking it unnecessary to follow him further. A body of Holkar's horse have however appeared on the frontier and I shall remain till some troops which I have ordered forward shall come up. I propose then advancing by this route and joining Major Holmes beyond the Bariya country. When united I shall if possible push on to Ujjein or act in the rear of Sinde's army as you may direct or circumstances point out.

It gives me much satisfaction to acquaint you that the Bheels everywhere have received us with the greatest cordiality. I have everywhere prevented plunder and this treatment is so different from what they are accustomed to that their takurs have promised me every assistance should we return amongst them, and on the morning I proposed marching towards Canoji large bodies were ready to join us.

I find that the Raja of Lunavada has a most extensive influence in this country and his friendship is essential to our interests. His tribute to Godra is 7000 rupees annually. In consequence of the Marathas having plundered some of his villages and Canoji having forced him to pay 25,000 rupees he has requested that his tribute should for this year be remitted. It would be sufficient to ruin the Rajah if I recommended such a measure unless through you and I therefore take the liberty of requesting that you will order me not to call for it. Half is now due, but I have told the Rajah that I will take nothing till your orders arrive . . .

I should be extremely obliged if you would inform Mr Duncan that I am under your orders. There is hardly a post that I do not receive some unpleasant letter, and his making every attempt to reduce me to that situation which must tie me up completely. He has by last post directed me that no agreement I may make with the Bheels or any other person is to be sanctioned unless approved by the Resident, who he adds will consult the Gaikwar government. Now it is well known that the very name of the Gaikwar is detested by the Bheel Rajahs and that they will not agree to any thing where they are concerned. This is a well founded dislike for they [put forward?] unjust claims wherever they appear and pillage whatever they can lay their hands on.

Besides I do not see why that government should be consulted on our transactions with chieftains dependent only on ourselves . . .

As Mulhar Rao is taken, Gujerat is now perfectly quiet but I assure you that the chiefs who have been with me are determinedly hostile to me, and I have no doubt will soon shew it. A very considerable body of them were ordered with me; sixty only came. The remainder positively refused and that detachment which came with me from Baroda refused to march. If I can get 1000 good cavalry dependent on ourselves I shall prefer it to the Gaikwar's whole army. Government has sanctioned this levy.

WP 3/3/79 p. 226

376

Colonel Collins to Arthur Wellesley

near Hyderabad
12 November 1803

Ever since the 29th . . . I have been confined to my bed by the gout . . . Nabob Muhammed Mir Khan is the son of Shah Nizam ud Dein, an old and confidential servant of the late Mahadji, Sinde's predecessor. Shah Nizam ud Dein was subah of Delhi for a considerable time and during the period that he held this situation, of which he was deprived by the influence of M Perron, I kept up a regular and friendly correspondence with him. Muhammed Mir Khan brought me a letter from his father when I was at Ujjein in 1801 and on my arrival at Burhanpur . . . he waited on me with offers both from Shah Nizam ud Dein and himself of every assistance they could afford in forwarding my views at Sinde's durbar. Nor have I the least doubt of the sincerity of these offers since both wished to re-establish their interest by forming a connection with the English Resident at Sinde's court. Unfortunately however neither Shah Nizam ud Dein nor his son possessed the smallest influence with the Maharajah or his ministers . . .

Of Wahed Beg I know very little, having never met him but a few days previously to my leaving the camp of Sinde. He thought proper of his own accord to follow me to Aurungabad where I left him having no occasion for his service. In fact I regarded him as a spy on the part of Balaji Kunjar with whom he is intimately connected. Wahed Beg is also well acquainted with Muhammed Mir Khan.

WP 3/3/53 p. 222

377

Arthur Wellesley to Richard Wellesley

13 November 1803

I have the pleasure to inform your Excellency that Amrit Rao joined me yesterday and that I had a meeting with him in the neighbourhood of his camp. I am to visit him this day . . .

Raghuji Bhonsle is gone towards the Wausim ghat on the road to Nagpur and Sinde is by last accounts with a body of cavalry to the east of Mulkapur, likewise on his road to the Berar country. Colonel Stevenson has by this time completed his equipments for the siege of Gawilghar from the stores at Asirgarh, and I hope that we shall now be able to carry on that operation and to make the Berar country the seat of war in the Deccan . . .

Gwrd (1837) ii 506 (1844) ii 859

378

J. Colebrooke [signing for Stevenson] to Arthur Wellesley

Two miles North East of Mulkapur
13 November 1803

I had the honour to advise you on the 26th [October] detailing the operations of the subsidiary force in taking possession of Burhanpur and in the subsequent capture of Asirgarh . . .

My first object in getting possession of the place was to make arrangement for detailing the garrison and for the necessary equipments, and to direct the artillery officers to make a selection of shot and powder which we should require for the siege of Gawilghar. A good deal of my attention was also required to watch the movements of the enemy, and as I had reason to apprehend they were meditating an attack on the details and Mohipat Ram's troops which I had left at Burhanpur, I determined on marching there on the 27th [October].

On the 30th I learnt that Sinde had marched to Jellabad and the same day I received a letter from Lt Colonel Lang at Mulkapur informing me that the enemy had moved towards that place, and were at Chickhli only four kos from him. In this letter he gave me to understand that he considered his situation perfectly secure unless the enemy had infantry and guns, and I had every reason to believe that they had not. But as I did not deem it prudent to trust to report, I determined upon sending the force to his relief, with the exception of one battalion and the Rajah's troops, which I kept for the security of Burhanpur. It marched accordingly on the 31st under the command of Lt Colonel Maclean (Colonel Haliburton and myself both being too unwell to proceed with it) and Lt Colonel Lang with the 1st battalion 11th Regt joined on the 3rd [November].

My letter of the 9th [November] . . . will have apprised you of my having joined the force at Yedlabad on the 9th, of my having detached two battalions to Ajanta on the 10th and of my intention to march to Balapur where they were to join me. On the 11th I wrote to you from camp eleven miles west of Mulkapur and yesterday I made a short march and encamped two miles to the northeast. I have halted today but intend marching towards Balapur and expect to arrive there about the 20th. I have had the honour of receiving your letters of the 4th and 6th . . .

WP 3/3/84 p. 474

379

Colonel Stevenson to Arthur Wellesley

North East of Mulkapur
14 November 1803

The enclosed letter could not be got ready in time to be despatched yesterday. I have found it necessary to halt today as the whole of the grain I expect from Mulkapur had not come into camp. Fifteen hundred bullock load has been filled by the banjaras and I trust that I shall get a good deal more.

My hircarrahs brought me a report that last night there was a disaffection in Sinde's camp. They say that Annaji, Appoji Nebalkar and Sadashi Rajoji had left his camp and told him if he did not choose to fight they would and were determined to march to Burhanpur. They are said to have encamped yesterday at Jellgaum 13 kos to the eastward of Mulkapur. I have sent hircarrahs to watch their motions and this morning I ordered the cavalry brigade, Salabat Khan's horse, and 300 of his infantry to move out 8 miles on the Jellgaum road.

I have this morning received both your letters of the 9th and immediately wrote to Lt Colonel Maclean to take charge of the rice if it arrived at Ajanta before he came away. He was at Pahur on the 12th and would be at the foot of the Ajanta pass the next day. I have desired him in the event of his having left Ajanta to halt wherever he may receive my letter and send back six companies and a gun for the rice and to proceed, after it joins him, to Balapur. Salabat Khan has [undertaken?] to furnish me with 2 brass twelve pounders at Balapur and an 18 or 24 pounder at Elichpur with bullocks and ammunition complete, besides a supply of grain for the force. As I have ever found him to possess a steady and zealous attachment to the cause we are engaged in, I have no reason to think he will deceive me.

I shall march tomorrow and shall not be later than the 19th or 20th in reaching Balapur. Manu Bapu with the force under his command is said to be between that place and Elichpur.

Mohipat Ram is still at Burhanpur. He writes me that Mr Clementi had made an attack on a party of the enemy's horse, killed and wounded a good number and took some horses. Captain Johnston has been desired to write to him to refrain from any interference with the pergannahs you mention. I am much obliged for your kind enquiries after my health. I had a slight return of my complaint yesterday but find myself much better today and hope with a little care to be perfectly restored to health in a short time.

WP 3/3/84 p. 475

380

Arthur Wellesley to Colonel Stevenson

14 November 1803

Raghuji has decidedly gone towards his own country through the Wausim ghat and I am on my march that way likewise but I think that I shall pass by the Lakhanwada ghat. I shall be at Tulni on the 16th and most probably at the Lakhanwada ghat on the 18th or 19th unless I find on my arrival at Tulni that the enemy hang about the Wausim ghat in which case I shall go that way. I conclude that you will have begun your march along the Purna river into Berar as soon as possible after the rice shall have arrived at Ajanta, and in that case we shall probably be at no great distance from each other again when I shall pass the Lakhanwada ghat. Your best mode of communicating with me however till you are certain that I am in Berar will be by the Deul ghat and Jafarabad.

Grwd (1837) ii 511 (1844) ii 863

381

Colonel Murray to Arthur Wellesley

Lunavada
15 November 1803

I was in hopes that I should have been enabled to inform you that I should commence my march into Malwa in a few days. I have however just received intelligence that the Bhau has again joined Canoji and that he has been reinforced by a corps of Holkar's under Balchund. The whole are said to be encamped near Banswara. It is possible that Balchund may not march with Canoji should he advance but it would be imprudent in me to leave this force in my rear. I shall endeavour to get the Gaekwar's troops to encamp within one march of me and if I find it necessary when joined by some detachments which are coming up I shall march against this united body . . .

Government have consented to allow me to engage cavalry. I shall accordingly raise about 1000; I should hope that I shall soon get that number. I had some while ago many offers but the people have now left me . . . I have received no answer from Canoji nor am I at all certain that he received my letter.

I ought perhaps to have acquainted you that my reason for declining all further interference was from a conviction that Canoji would never treat if the Gaekwar's government was concerned, and from some circumstances which have taken place I rather doubt whether without your guarantee or that of some other officer he would accept of any terms offered by Major Walker or the Government of Bombay. This I mention to you in confidence and as explanatory of my own conduct. The circumstances I am sure have not been made known to you.

The Bheels everywhere are friendly but it will be necessary that substantial favours be conferred upon those who can essentially serve and who have weight with the others. The tribute of the Lunavada Raja ought to be lowered or given up altogether on condition of his keeping a larger body of troops . . . The Raja of

Bariya might receive the parganah of Jellode on the same terms in lieu of his claim on the other parganahs . . .

With these Rajas in our favour and attached to us by interest, and a camp at Godra to support them, a barrier will be formed which it would not be an easy task to force.

WP 3/3/79 p. 196

382

Colonel Murray to Arthur Wellesley

Camp at Lunavada
17 November 1803

I had the pleasure of receiving your letters of the 23rd and 28th [October] last night. Everything is going on well in this quarter except that there is a report that Canoji has been joined by Balchund one of Holkar's sirdars with four or five thousand men.

From the rapidity of your success I think it probable that you may find it more convenient to draw your supplies from hence than from Panvel. At all events there is no harm in preparing for it, as we can consume what you do not require. I have ordered the Surat magazine to be transferred to Broach and shall bring on the supplies for Europeans to Godra that they may be ready to forward. I have mentioned this to General Nicolls and if he is of my opinion I have requested him to send large supplies of spirits.

WP 3/3/79 p. 234

383

Colonel Stevenson to Arthur Wellesley

Camp at [Agndae?]
17 November 1803

I was seized yesterday with another cold fit and my faculties impaired in the same manner as I described to you before. On that account I desired Colebrooke to write to you. I enclose letters that were brought in the night from Sinde and of which the accompanying are copies. They were accompanied by a respectable old man who came to me at Burhanpur to know if a vakil would be received from Sinde. I assured him that if he had anything to propose to you and sent a respectable vakil that he would be received with due respect.

The man declared that a vakil had been sent from Sinde to you but that he has many people about him who will engage in going to you as a vakil to endeavour to prevent any negotiation from taking place. I hope Sinde's letter will reach you before the vakil leaves you as Captain Johnston's correspondent Mirza Wahed Beg writes that it is Sinde's intention to write to you not to receive any person from him unless he carries proper authority for being received as such.

I am at present in a good situation for affording protection to the two battalions on their march from Ajanta to Balapur and as it is a large village belonging to Bhonsle and can furnish a considerable quantity of grain I may therefore halt here tomorrow . . .

WP 3/3/84 p. 480

384

Major Malcolm – Notes on General Wellesley's letter of the 11th [November 1803]

[mid-November 1803]
[summary]

To conclude peace with Sinde at this stage would be highly advantageous, and to return to him lands in Kandesh Gujerat and the Deccan could be an important inducement.

'But however circumstances may authorise some deviation from Lord Wellesley's instructions respecting the terms of peace, it would appear of great consequence to maintain the leading principles of these instructions, which is to keep in the general arrangements, as distinct as circumstances will admit, the territory of the different chiefs in order that there may be an end to that clashing of authority and that mixture of power which constantly generates disputes, and an attention to this principle would perhaps make it advisable neither to restore the districts of Ahmednagar or of Broach to Daulat Rao Sinde as both would be situated in the midst of the territory of the allies of the British government.'

If Sinde were to be allocated territory of the value of Godhra and Champaneer, this land revenue income could be taken from his northern territories in Malwa, or taken in credit against the cost of a subsidiary force, should he subsequently sign an alliance treaty. If a separate peace were to be signed with Sinde, his cooperation with the Company against the Raja of Berar would be helpful.

Compensation to the Nizam, who had not fulfilled the terms of his alliance, would have to come from the lands between the Godavari and the Ajanta range, and if more were involved, from the territory of the Raja of Berar. The scheme of mustering the forces of the Nizam under the supervision of the Resident, proposed by Arthur Wellesley, could cause 'irritation' and it might be preferable, while giving territorial gains to the Nizam 'from our acquisitions to the northward' to agree to maintain a body of horse, at Company expense, as had been done in the recent agreement with the Peshwa.[14]

It would be important, in any agreement, to make an arrangement which freed the Nizam from the obligation to pay chaute to the Peshwa. 'But under any event I trust that we shall never be obliged to transfer to the Peshwa's wretched government any of our late acquisitions in Gujerat or the Attavesi as these acquisitions appear to be of great value to the British government whether they are considered in a revenue, commercial or political point of view. The possession of them, connected as they are with other territory in Gujerat over which our influence is now established, will . . . lead to the formation of a power in that quarter which will have the great political advantage of enabling us to check better than from any other position in India, the future ambition of either Daulat Rao Sinde or Jaswant Rao Holkar.'

WP 3/3/70, A Mss 13,748 f. 3

385

Richard Wellesley 'Some hints respecting peace'

Fort William
27 October 1803 [received 18 November 1803]

We must <u>now</u> positively retain
From Sinde
- the doab of the Jumna and Ganges
- Delhi
- Agra and the whole line of the right bank of the Jumna to the junction at Allahabad
- The King [the Mughal Emperor]
- The Marathas must be expelled from the northern parts of Hindustan altogether, the boundary to be formed by the petty states, Rajputs Jats etc.

From the Berar man
  Cuttack with a good frontier
  A crore or two of rupees if he possess so much
  The frontier of Bundelkhand

On the western side of India
  Sinde's maritime possessions and his possessions in Gujerat
  Ahmednagar for the Peshwa
  All intermixed territories and forts for the Nizam (from Sinde and Berar)
  Exemption of chaute for the Nizam

SD iv 188

386

George Barlow – Memorandum on the Peace

16 October 1803 [received by Arthur Wellesley 18 November]
[summary, with annotations by Richard Wellesley]

Barlow set out a listing of further requirements of a peace settlement. These included provision that Sinde and Raghuji were to be obliged to exclude French and other Europeans from their service, that there should be a strong and connected frontier of Cuttack towards Berar and that the northern frontiers of Nizam and of Peshwa should also be compact and connected. By the settlement Sinde was to be deprived of territory south of the Tapti and also of Champaneer and his possessions in Gujerat. The peace settlement should include acceptance of the admission of a Resident.

Barlow noted that Arthur Wellesley had already been informed of the requirement to secure the Ganges-Jumna Doab and territory from Jat and Rajput chiefs, and Gwalior, Jansi and Kalpi.

On this point Richard Wellesley noted 'the occupation of the right bank of the Jumna will secure the tranquillity as well as the safety of the whole Doab. Our garrisons must be Delhi, Muttra, Kalpi and some position in Bundelkhand.'

On the issue of the confirmation of treaties signed with lesser rulers, who had sought British protection, by British detachment commanders, Richard Wellesley noted 'an article in the treaty must provide for this; peace ought not to be delayed for the specification of every name.'

Barlow also commented on the requirement for there to be separate treaties with Sinde, Raghuji, and Jaswant Rao Holkar.

'By the conclusion of separate treaties with Sinde Berar and Holkar further jealousies might be excited between them [and] any future union of their interests might perhaps be prevented. Would it under present circumstances be advisable to admit either Raghuji Bhonsle or Sinde to the benefits of the Treaties of Hyderabad or Bassein? Would it not be advisable to leave Sinde at least exposed to the attacks of Holkar in his present formidable situation with respect to Sinde. It cannot be doubted that a contest would immediately take place between these two chiefs if the war with the British Government and its allies be terminated.

'The expediency of admitting Sinde to the benefit of the treaties above-mentioned appears to depend on the determination of this question, whether we are likely to be secured against any future attempts on the part of Sinde by maintaining him in the state of power in which he may be left at the conclusion of peace, or by leaving him to settle his own differences with Holkar, who would probably prove too powerful for him. Perhaps there is no objection to the addition of the Raja of Berar to the benefits of the Treaties of Hyderabad and Bassein. This observation is founded on considerations of policy, and not on the claim or merits of the Raja of Berar, who deserves to be annihilated for the part he had taken against the British government.'

On this Richard Wellesley commented

'I think it would be advisable to admit Sinde to the benefits of the Treaties of Hyderabad and Bassein and also to admit Berar and Holkar to the same. Holkar might destroy Sinde, or Sinde Holkar, and in either case a power would be formed of a magnitude exceeding the due scale; the same reasoning applies to Berar . . . .'

A Mss 13,722 f. 27, WP 3/3/5

387

Arthur Wellesley to Merrick Shawe

18 November 1803 [received 11 December]

I have received . . . the memorandum and the notes thereon by the Governor General on the subject of the peace. Until I received the Governor General's letter of the 27th I was afraid that my dispatch of the 11th would have appeared tame, and that the demands which I proposed to make were below what we were entitled to expect. But I find by the notes contained in his letter that there is but little difference between his plan and mine, and in fact I intended to amend my plan before I received your memorandum according to that contained in the Governor General's notes.

The principal difference in the plan contained in my dispatch and that in the memorandum consists first in the article regarding Europeans. I took the restriction contained in my plan from the Treaty of Bassein but on reflecting further on the subject, and upon recollecting that the Peshwa would have been restricted from taking into his service any Frenchmen, if we had not been at peace with France, I determined to alter my plan so far as to demand that Sinde should never have any Frenchmen in his service, nor Dutchmen, nor Italians, nor Spaniards, and in fact that he should not have in his service the subjects of any nation, the government of which shall be at war with Great Britain. It appears however that the Governor General is desirous that they should not have any Europeans at all.[15] This prohibition will go to their having no infantry or artillery, and this is a point which I think deserves consideration.

Sinde's armies had actually been brought to a very favourable state of discipline and his power had become formidable by the exertions of the European officers in his service. But I think it is much to be doubted whether his power, or rather that of the Maratha nation, would not have been more formidable at least to the British government, if they had never had an European, as an infantry soldier, in their service, and had carried on their operations in the manner of the original Marathas only by means of cavalry. I have no doubt whatever but that the military spirit of the nation has been destroyed by their establishment of infantry and artillery, possibly indeed by other causes. At all events, it is certain that those establishments, however formidable, afford us a good object of attack in a war with the Marathas, and that the destruction of them contributes to the success of the contest, and to the re-establishment of peace. [This is] because having made them the principal object of their attention, which they must do in order to have them at all, and that part of their strength on which they place most reliance, they become also the principal reliance of the army, and therefore when they are lost the cavalry, as is the case in this war, will not act.

Two questions occur here

one, whether the Maratha cavalry were ever better than they now are

[the other] if they were, would they regain their spirit if the infantry establishment were to be destroyed.

I believe they were formerly better than they now are. In regard to the second point, I have to observe that if there were no infantry in a Maratha army, their cavalry would commence those predatory operations for which they were formerly so famous. Although I am aware of the greater difficulties which they would now have to encounter than their ancestors formerly had, from the practice which is universal in the Deccan and I believe in Hindustan of fortifying every village . . . I should still consider these operations to be more formidable to the British government than any they can carry on by means of the best body of infantry that they can form. On this ground therefore I think that they should be encouraged to have infantry rather than otherwise. As however the Governor General has given a positive opinion upon this subject, I shall make a demand in conformity to his wishes, but this shall be the last of my demands, in hopes that I may hear further from you on the subject, before the peace shall be concluded . . .

Grwd (1837) ii 517 (1844) ii 868

388

Colonel Murray to Arthur Wellesley

Camp at Lunawara
19 November 1803

Mr Duncan has sent me your letter . . . you must conclude I dare say that I have, in spite of all orders, insisted on the management of the country. It is so much the reverse that previous to my march I informed Major Walker that I proposed arranging and settling affairs as I went along except Champaneer which being in Gujerat I had nothing to do with. He requested me to settle that with the others and when at Godra he sent me people to employ . . .

You can easily conceive that I am personally speaking extremely glad to be relieved from trouble and responsibility on this occasion. I never should have thought of interfering had I assumed that any plan had been in agitation, and I have only pressed a continuance of things as arranged from feeling that I had much more weight and consideration among the natives than I possibly can have when they conceive that there is an appeal to Major Walker from whatever I may order. The insignificance to which all commanding officers in this quarter have of late been reduced renders it necessary that some consequence should be attended to my present situation.

The nature of the country which is not yet conquered, the intractable spirit of the inhabitants, their fear of Sinde's vengeance, all make it necessary that it should be guarded with a strong and vigorous law for some time to come. I cannot omit mentioning that Major Walker himself sent me the zemindars of Callal who had gone to Baroda in order that I should make the arrangements for that parganah. I beg you will excuse my giving you any trouble on this subject but I am extremely anxious that you neither think me officious or disobedient to orders.

I believe that some of the troops from the south of the Tapti and Burhanpur have reached Ujjein. At least, bodies of Sinde's army had arrived when my last accounts came away. By intelligence received this morning a large body of pindaris are arrived at Ratlam but of this I am not at all certain. Canoji is encamped near Balchund in the Banswara country but whether Balchund means to act with him or not I have not learnt. A very large body of Holkar's army and it is said Holkar himself is in the Udiapur country. It is currently reported that he has had some actions with the Bundi Raja on account of tribute and current report says that [once] that business [is] ended he means to proceed towards Gujerat. I confess however that I place no further faith in it from its being currently reported. Canoji having taken refuge in Holkar's country will prevent my disturbing him till that chieftain's views are more declared . . .

Major Walker and I differ much respecting the Gaikwar forces. I have had a good specimen of their obedience lately. I wrote to Kakoji acquainting him of the necessity of his remaining near me and requested him to come to Baerour enclosing at the same time an order from Baroda to that effect. He acknowledged the letter and went off in the opposite direction next morning. From the Dewanji who will now command I am to expect a different line of conduct, but of this I am certain, that our cause is not popular amongst the chiefs and that they are extremely unwilling to enter Malwa.

WP 3/3/79 p. 236

389

Colonel Stevenson to Arthur Wellesley

near Balapur
20 November [1803]

. . . I determined on halting a day or two at Balapur to watch the enemy and form the best plan of executing your instructions regarding driving Sinde further to the northward or into the Berar country which I supposed could be done by carrying all my grain and stores to Elichpur and after lodging them there with a battalion to have advanced on the enemy with a light detachment.

I have however received intelligence this morning that . . . about 8000 pindari horse are about ten kos from me on the road leading from Balapur to Elichpur. This will make it necessary for me to lodge my heavy baggage at Balapur till I could clear the road to Elichpur. Besides the pindaris I have mentioned, Manu Bapu is also betwixt those places. I do not however from any report find that there is any communication betwixt the troops of Sinde and Raghuji Bhonsle. Your letter of the 17th informs me I shall be near enough to receive your further advices.

WP 3/3/84

390

Colonel Stevenson to Arthur Wellesley

½ mile east of Balapur
21 November 1803

I arrived here this morning and delayed writing till this hour in hopes of hearing by which ghat you had descended, but have not yet obtained that knowledge. I received a letter from Lt Colonel Maclean who will arrive here with the treasure and medicine and the Ajanta rice on the 23rd. He was delayed one day by having left Ajanta before he heard of the arrival of the rice and halting to send a detachment back for it.

I shall on the 23rd have everything together and be ready to advance. I am still of opinion that your twelve pounders and some howitzers and artillery men to work them [would be of value in the forthcoming siege.]

Colonel Maclean did not see a pindari horse after the first day that he left Yedlabad, and only six have shown themselves since I left Mulkapur, but I hear no more of the vakil. Your letter of the 17th declaring your intention of moving down the Lakhanwada or Sirsooli ghat is the last I have received.

WP 3/3/84 p. 483

391

S. Johnston to Colonel Stevenson

21 November [1803]

I have the pleasure to send you a letter from Muhammed Mir Khan addressed to you with a translation also a letter from Mirza Wahed Beg to me . . . I think they should be forwarded to General Wellesley as soon as possible but I did not wish to do so without first consulting you.

I have had some hircarrahs from Sinde's camp who say that he has fallen back to Waugkayrah near Patolah, the place he remained at so long after leaving the neighbourhood of Mulkapur. The hircarrahs who brought the letters say that they left him at Muttee Undoorah last night. Annaji's party is at the Purna, Govind Rao Bhakshi at Dugal Kayrah about three miles from Sinde. Manu Bapu has gone to Gawilghar.

WP 3/3/84

392

Colonel Stevenson to Arthur Wellesley

Balapur
21 November 1803 9 pm

I send two letters received this day.[16] The conduct of Jaswant Rao Goorparah and Mirza Wahed Beg is very unaccountable; there is strong argument on the part of Mirza Wayed Beg but I cannot account for his professed desire to promote British interests. My correspondent seems far in the background of this scene. I wrote you this evening that Colonel Maclean will arrive here on the 24th. I shall then have all I want and be ready to advance. I am desirous to hear of your descending the ghat.

WP 3/3/84 p. 491

393

Conference between Arthur Wellesley and Jaswant Rao Goorporah

21 November 1803
[summary]

In this conference with vakils of Daulat Rao Sinde, Arthur Wellesley insisted that the war was one of aggression by Sinde and that any peace settlement should give the Company and its allies compensation and security. Once it had been established that the vakils had no powers to negotiate such terms, Arthur Wellesley refused to indicate to them 'the extent of the compensation' until they were so empowered. The vakils sought and secured an armistice.

SD iv 228, PRC x 165 [the part of the discussion dealing with the cessation of hostilities is not printed in PRC x]

394

Captain Barclay to Colonel Stevenson

22 November 1803

Major General Wellesley . . . is particularly engaged just now and has desired me to write to you. The representations of Wahed Beg are in consequence of an intrigue in Sinde's durbar. Jaswant Rao Goorporah has received ample powers as vakil from Sinde. The General had a long conference with him yesterday and has sat down again with him now. He has consented in general terms to a suspension of hostilities between the British troops and Sinde . . .

The General's principal reason for agreeing to the suspension of hostilities with Sinde was that the siege of Gawilghar might be uninterrupted by him, and the General begs that you will order every preparation to be made for commencing it immediately on your arrival and carrying it on with the utmost celerity and activity. But as he observes with much concern . . . that you are much weakened and reduced by your late indisposition, he begs that you will not risk your life in the arduous undertaking of the siege of Gawilghar, if you do not find your strength equal to conducting the operations of it. And if you find yourself too weak for that, he will change situations with you for the period of the siege, by his joining the subsidiary force while you take the command of this division.

He reckons it of the utmost importance that the suspension of hostilities should be kept a secret from the servants of the Subah. You will probably receive an order of this date to suspend hostilities against Daulat Rao Sinde, but this is not to prevent you from attacking him if you find that he will not take up the proposed position and wants to pass to the westward.

Grwd (1837) ii 528 (1844) ii 875

395

Colonel Stevenson to Arthur Wellesley

Balapur
22 November 1803

I am anxious to hear that you have descended the Lakhanwada ghat as I may then hope to have a personal communication with you as it is only 24 miles from Balapur . . .

My disorders may perhaps have had some effect on my opinions lately and my correspondence may not have appeared as steady and connected as it ought, particularly respecting ordnance. I have considered that nothing should be left to chance when you possess the means of moving it forward, and although my present ordnance might be sufficient to batter Gawilghar, yet an unlucky shot may disable a gun or their works prove stronger than we have given them credit for . . . If you should find it convenient to send the iron twelves and one or two howitzers, my artillery officers think they would further our efforts and are already advancing on the powder and shot for them.

I wrote in my last sheet I shall be ready to advance on the 24th, but Colonel Maclean's detachment will require a day to halt and some of further arrangements might be necessary in regard to the stores that he brings with him, and I think that I shall be able to commence my march with better effect on the 25th with the ordnance I can command if you do not find it convenient to send the iron twelves and howitzers.

My disorders are totally removed and by the use of bark I hope to gain strength daily.

WP 3/3/84 p. 482

396

Colonel Murray to Arthur Wellesley

Camp at Lunawara
22 November 1803

I have received yours of the [?28th October]. Sinde by my accounts has not yet crossed the Narbada. Holkar is in the country to the north of Udiapur but he has a corps near [Darwarrah?] and the sirdar is treating with Canoji. I believe they have not yet agreed.

I received a letter this morning from Ujjein pressing me to take possession of it but I cannot with safety advance till I have removed Canoji to a distance. Unfortunately he has taken refuge in Holkar's country. I occupy Dohad which is a good fort and I have ordered it to be put in a state of defence. As soon as I am joined by the 65th and other troops I shall advance about ten or twelve kos which may force Canoji to a further retreat unless he is supported by Holkar. I shall still be in our own country.

As Surat is now safe I have ordered three hundred of the 75th to join me. If it were possible to reinforce me with one or two battalions of sepoys I think I might stop Holkar if he attempts an invasion, as it is the current report that he will . . .

WP 3/3/79 p. 238

397

Arthur Wellesley – Discussion with the vakils of Daulat Rao Sinde

22 November 1803
[summary]

The vakils of Sinde sought a variation in the proposed terms of the agreement for the suspension of hostilities, so that 'Sinde might be allowed to choose a station twenty kos from Elichpur to the westward of that city as he should think proper.' This Arthur Wellesley refused. He commented that territories to the eastward of Burhanpur belonged to the Nizam. The terms of the suspension of hostilities were accepted.

SD iv 232 [not printed in PRC x]

398

Armistice proposed between the Company and its allies and agents of Daulat Rao Sinde

23 November 1803

1.There shall be a cessation of hostilities between the troops commanded by Major General Wellesley in the Deccan and Gujerat and those in the service of Daulat Rao Sinde.

2.To prevent accidents, and in order to ensure the execution of the 1st article, it is agreed that there shall be an interval of twenty kos between the different British and allied armies and that the Maharajah will march with his army and take up a position twenty kos to the eastward of Elichpur and he will forage still further to the eastward.

3.In case the operation of the British and allied armies against other enemies of the British government should draw either of them nearer than twenty kos to the position which the Maharajah will have occupied according to the previous article, previous notice of such operation will be given in order that the Maharajah may take timely measures always to preserve an interval of twenty kos between his army and the British and allied armies

4.In Gujerat the British troops shall not advance beyond Dohad; those of the Maharajah on the side of Gujerat shall not approach nearer to Dohad than twenty kos.

Notice must be given, in case either of the parties should be desirous to put an end to this agreement. This agreement is to be ratified by the Maharajah Daulat Rao Sinde and his ratification is to be given to Major General Wellesley in the space of ten days from this date.

SD iv 234, Grwd (1837) ii 534

399

Colonel Murray to Arthur Wellesley

Lunawara
23 November 1803

A letter was received last night by my pundit from Canoji. A brahmin who had undertaken to deliver my letter and had remained in my camp in full confidence that Canoji would enter into terms went on my arrival at this ground to enquire the reason for the delay. He found that his messenger had delivered it in the presence of some Arabs who without permitting it to be read had destroyed it. The brahmin told him what he understood to be the contents, that he believed no deceit was intended and proposed that he should answer me. Canoji replied that as the contents of my letter was unknown he could not answer me but wrote to the pundit wishing to know what my proposals were. He further commissioned the brahmin to say that if I would send a passport he would despatch a confidential person who might meet anybody I thought proper to appoint. The brahmin added that Canoji complained of the thralldom in which he was held by the Arabs and feared that he would be sold by them.

In answer to this I have permitted the pundit to send a copy of my letter and have given a passport as required. I have likewise written to Major Walker to know the terms on which Government will treat: they did not think it proper to entrust me with so important a secret though I might have been obliged to conclude or break off a negotiation without the possibility of consulting Major Walker. If the terms are such as may be accepted I shall communicate them, but if they are not and the Gaikwar government are concerned, I will inform Canoji decidedly that my powers are not equal to my wishes and that I will not expose him to be[ing] deceived.

Two things prove his sincerity; the first is the return of my messenger who was confined at the instance of the Arabs, the other is the secrecy with which he has requested that the negotiation may be carried on. The brahmin informs me that Canoji has had an interview with Balchund but does not know the result. He has had likewise pressing letters from Amrit Rao, Holkar and Sinde to continue his opposition. That may however be pretended in the hopes of better terms.

The brahmin returns to his camp this evening and I have charged him explicitly to acquaint Canoji that I shall not desist from hostilities till he has actually surrendered himself. Were I now authorised to carry your liberal plan into execution, I have no doubt that I should succeed, but I believe that a treaty made under your sanction, or by those under your orders, will alone be listened to. He will not hear of the security of the Gaikwar's government at present.

I am extremely happy to acquaint you that I continue on the most friendly terms with the different Rajas and Bheels. I do not find that the threatened invasion by Holkar has as yet produced alteration in their conduct . . . Canoji informed the brahmin that it was his intention to move towards Udiapur. If he makes this movement I shall be at liberty to advance without fear into Malwa. I may not perhaps reach Ujjein with my force but it will probably alarm Sinde to find a corps in his rear.

WP 3/3/79 p. 240

400

Arthur Wellesley to Merrick Shawe

Rajura
23 November 1803

Daulat Rao Sinde's vakils have received their powers but they are not so full as they ought to be. I have had a conversation with them on the subject of peace in which I told them that the British government would not make peace unless it received compensation for the unjust aggression of which Daulat Rao Sinde had been guilty. I asked them whether they had powers to make compensation and future security to the Company and their allies the basis of the negotiation for peace. They said they had not and I referred them to Daulat Rao Sinde for further instructions. They then desired that I should agree to a suspension of hostilities including the Raja of Berar. To this proposition I declared that I would never assent.

They then proposed that I should agree to a cessation of hostilities with Daulat Rao Sinde only, to which I agreed upon condition of his going with his army into Berar 20 kos to the eastward of Elichpur and of his keeping at all times at that distance from the British troops carrying on their operations against the other enemies of the British government. They wished the cessation to extend to Hindustan to which proposal I would not consent, but I consented to its extending to Gujerat in which quarter our troops are not to advance beyond Dohad and theirs are not to approach nearer to Dohad than 20 kos . . .

I have already apprised the Governor General that it is not in my power to do anything more against Daulat Rao Sinde. Nothing can be done on the side of Gujerat in particular where we shall remain in possession of the most advanced station we have got and which we hold with only one battalion, while Colonel Murray with the remainder of his corps is obliged to move upon Canoji Rao Gaikwar. Sinde has with him in the field an army of horse only. It is impossible to expect to make any impression upon this army unless by following it for a great length of time and distance. To do this would remove our troops still further than they are already from all sources of supply and would prevent the operations against the Raja of Berar, from which alone in my opinion we are to expect peace . . .

I have received from Malcolm his memorandum upon my proposed plan for a peace . . . I only request that the Governor General, if he should have seen this memorandum, will not make up his mind finally upon on that subject till I shall have had a conversation with Malcolm.

Grwd (1837) ii 535 (1844) ii 879

401

Colonel Stevenson to Arthur Wellesley

Balapur
24 November 1803 7 pm

It was my intention to march tomorrow towards Elichpur, but I shall find it necessary to halt another day in order to load as many of the Company bullocks as I have bags for in the Paymaster's and Commissary of Grains Department with rice from my Baswunt banjaras. I have ordered the Commissary of Grains to increase his bullocks to 2000 agreeable to former orders received from you . . .

I shall observe your instructions if Sinde moves to the westward. My disorders have left me and I am gaining strength and I am persuaded I shall be able to undertake the necessary duties of the siege of Gawilghar for which I have everything in readiness and am well stocked with grain. If you should come near enough I shall particularly be glad to take two of your twelve pounders and some eight inch howitzers.

WP 3/3/84 p. 487

402

Arthur Wellesley to Colonel Stevenson

at the bottom of the Rajura ghat
25 November 1803

I have just received your letter of the 24th and in the night one of the 21st and another of the 22nd. I have already informed you that the whole of Sinde's durbar are intriguing for the office of vakil in this camp, and who shall make the peace. This information will give you the clue to all Mirza Wahed Beg's letters, and will account for his urging us one day to do everything that can be agreeable to Sinde and on the next to attack him with all our forces.

In a military as well as a political view I was never more convinced of the propriety of any measure than that of agreeing at the present moment to the cessation of hostilities with Sinde. I am glad to find by your letter to me of the 24th that you are of the same opinion. Indeed the cessation is so favourable to us and so little so to Sinde that I almost doubt his ratifying it. If I find it is used as a mode to delay the conclusion of the peace, I shall put an end to it directly.

Notwithstanding the arrangement in the cessation of arms, I think it probable that Sinde will endeavour to place himself to the westward instead of to the eastward of Elichpur. If you should find that you can stop him without delaying materially your arrival at Gawilghar it would be desirable to do so, but if to attempt it would be likely materially to delay your arrival at Gawilghar it is better to take no notice of him.

My intention is to move up to Elichpur to cover your operations. I shall be tomorrow at Barsi Takli or at Scindkeira (they are only two kos distant from each other). Next day I shall be at Akola. I conclude that you will leave Balapur tomorrow the 26th and will be at Hatti Andoorah on the Purna river on the 27th. This place is only four or five kos from Akola, and I shall send you two of my twelve pounders and my two 5½ inch howitzers on the 27th. I have no 8 inch howitzers. I shall send with this ordnance some pioneers, but I cannot send you any artillerymen as I have but few of them . . .

I am happy to hear that your health is mended . . .

Grwd (1837) ii 549 (1844) ii 888

403

Colonel Murray to Arthur Wellesley

Lunawara
29 November 1803

Government has sent me your letter of the 11th. I assure you that the difference of opinion between me and the Paymaster has in no way impeded the public service . . . In former service on which I have been employed I was always on the most confidential footing with Mr Duncan. He has now entirely changed in that respect, which I can only attribute to my appointment which he has not yet forgiven. In every little thing he takes an opportunity of showing his illwill, and I could not on many occasions help feeling hurt at this sort of conduct which I did not think deserved. But on this you may depend, that it never shall prevent my doing everything in power to forward the public service. I make no doubt that I shall be removed from my command the moment the war is at an end, which to me will be no disappointment as I could never think of holding it on the footing it formerly was, and probably will be as soon as it is no longer under your immediate command . . .

WP 3/3/79 p. 246

404

Arthur Wellesley to Richard Wellesley

Camp at Paterli
30 November 1803

Having found that the Rajah of Berar was moving towards his own territories, that the body of troops he had with him was but small, decreasing in numbers daily, and not likely to do much mischief to the territories of the Subah of the Deccan, I descended the ghats by Rajura on the 25th, in order to support and cover Colonel Stevenson's operations against Gawilghar in Berar. Colonel Stevenson had equipped his corps at Asirgarh for the siege of that fort, and had marched to Balapur where he was joined on the 24th by the banjaras and other supplies which had been saved from the enemy by Captain Baynes' affair at Umber, and he marched forward on the 26th.

. . . On the 23rd I had consented to a suspension of hostilities with the troops of Daulat Rao Sinde in this quarter and Gujerat. The condition on which this agreement depended, namely 'that Sinde should occupy a position twenty kos to the east of Elichpur' had not been carried into execution, and Sinde was encamped at Sirsooli, about four miles from the camp of Manu Bapu brother to the Rajah of Berar, which was at this place. The army of the former consisted only of cavalry, that of the latter of cavalry and a great part if not the whole of Raghuji Bhonsle's regular infantry, and a large proportion of artillery.

In the course of the 28th the vakils from Daulat Rao Sinde urgently pressed me not to attack these troops, but I informed them repeatedly that there was no suspension of arms with Raghuji Bhonsle, and none with Sinde till he should comply with the terms of his agreement, and that I should certainly attack the enemies of the Company wherever I should find them.

Colonel Stevenson's division and mine both marched to this place yesterday, the Colonel having with great prudence and propriety halted on the 28th at Hatti Andoorah to enable me to cooperate in the attack of the enemy. We found on our arrival that the armies of both chiefs had decamped, and from a tower in Paterli I could perceive a confused mass about two miles beyond Sirsooli and Sinde's old camp which I concluded to be their armies on the march. The troops had marched a great distance on a very hot day and I therefore did not think it proper to pursue them, but shortly after our arrival here bodies of horse appeared in our front with which the Mysore cavalry skirmished during a part of the day. When I went out to push forward the piquets of the infantry to support the Mysore cavalry, and to take up the ground of our encampment, I could perceive distinctly a long line of infantry, cavalry and artillery regularly drawn up on the plains of Argaum, immediately in front of that village, and about six miles from this place, at which I intended to encamp.

Although late in the day I immediately determined to attack this army. Accordingly I marched on in one column, the British cavalry leading in a direction nearly parallel to that of the enemy's line, covering the rear and left by the Mughal and Mysore cavalry. The enemy's infantry and guns were in the left of their centre, with a body of cavalry on their left. Sinde's army, consisting of one very heavy body of cavalry, was on the right, having on its right a body of pindaris and other light troops. Their line extended above five miles, having in their rear the village and extensive gardens and enclosures of Argaum, and in their front a plain which however was much cut by watercourses etc.

I formed the army in two lines, the infantry in the first, the cavalry in the second and supporting the right, and the Mughal and Mysore cavalry the left, nearly parallel to that of the enemy, with the right rather advanced in order to press upon the enemy's left. Some little time elapsed before the lines could be formed, owing to a part of the infantry of my division which led the column having got into some confusion. When formed, the whole advanced in the greatest order; the 74th and 78th regiments were attacked by a large body, supposed to be Persians, and all these were destroyed. Sinde's cavalry charged the 1st battalion the 6th regiment, which was on the left of our line, and were repulsed, and their whole line retired in disorder before our troops, leaving in our hands 38 pieces of cannon and all their ammunition.

The British cavalry then pursued them for several miles, destroyed great numbers and took many elephants and camels and much baggage. The Mughal and Mysore cavalry also pursued the fugitives and did them great mischief. Some of the latter are still following them, and I have sent out this morning all of the Mysore Mughal and Maratha cavalry in order to secure as many advantages from this victory as can be gained, and complete the enemy's confusion. For the reasons stated in the commencement of this letter, the action did not commence till late in the day, and unfortunately sufficient daylight did not remain to do all that I could have wished, but the cavalry continued their pursuit by moonlight and all the troops were under arms till a late hour in the night.

I have the honour to enclose a return of our loss in this action . . . I propose to march tomorrow towards Gawilghar and I shall lose no time in attacking that place.

Grwd (1837) 556 (1844) ii 892, WP 3/3/2

405

Arthur Wellesley to Colonel Murray

1 December 1803

. . . By letters received this day from the Government of Bombay I am happy to observe that you will soon be relieved from the fruitless pursuit of Canoji and that the Resident at Baroda is exerting himself to bring into the field a respectable body of Maratha cavalry. Whatever may be the success of those exertions, you will be enabled by the flight of Canoji to join Major Holmes at Dohud, and I conclude that you will have commenced your march to that quarter as soon as possible. You will be so kind as to make all your preparations for moving forward upon Ujjein from Dohud, when I shall send you orders to do so . . .

Grwd (1837) ii 559 (1844) ii 896

406

Conference with the vakils of Daulat Rao Sinde

1 December 1803
[summary]

In this conference the principal vakil of Sinde, Jaswant Rao Goorparah, sought information on the compensation that Arthur Wellesley would demand. Arthur Wellesley asked whether the principle of compensation had been accepted, and as the document produced by the vakils was ambiguous, threatened to request their removal from his camp if a paper admitting this principle was not produced in two days.

SD iv 239 [not printed in PRC x]

407

Colonel Stevenson to Arthur Wellesley

2 December [1803]

I have read your memoranda which prove the duplicity and folly of Sinde and if it furthers the interest of the British government I should wish to see him reduced to the state of an ordinary partisan.

I do not think I have entered into a sufficient explanation in respect to my conduct at Burhanpur. My general conduct you are acquainted with, but not the particular circumstances associated with it.

The inhabitants in the first instance received the fullest protection to their persons and property and the British flag was hoisted by the request of the principal inhabitants . . . On receiving your order to raise a contribution (I was then at Asirgarh and had left a fresh garrison for the protection of Burhanpur) I did not think it safe to communicate such an order to the inhabitants. But after the surrender of Asirgarh I wrote to Captain Johnston, whom I had left at Burhanpur, to call on the inhabitants for a contribution of ten lakhs of rupees, and they subscribed for that sum according to the abilities of the several tribes. I found that the raising of that sum would detain the detachment from more important duties and would cripple the inhabitants so much that it would reduce an opulent city to a state of beggary that might otherwise have been serviceable to the state as a dependence on Asirgarh. It would in short have reduced it to the same unhappy state as Sinde did to Aurungabad.

I soon after received your orders to deliver it over to Raja Mohipat Ram in account of His Highness the Nizam and it did not appear to me to be creditable to present a town to the Nizam after reducing the inhabitants to such poverty that they could not maintain themselves. Under the ideas of justice and in support of the honour and humanity of the British government I relieved the inhabitants from this seemingly heavy contribution, provided that they paid 2½ lakhs of rupees to Raja Mohipat Ram on account of the British government, a sum which they had previously engaged to pay him in ransom of the town. To which proposal they most thankfully consented, and in the warmth of their gratitude offered to Raja Mohipat Ram a lakh of rupees more, which I consider as an offering to the government which had been so indulgent and to whom their gratitude was meant.

Captain Johnston had by this time received silver and gold, cups and plates and ornament to nearly that amount, which in conformity to my strict ideas of justice I ordered to be returned, but as they had already beat them up for the convenience of carriage, I ordered that they should be made over to Raja Mohipat Ram and he completed the receipts of the 2½ lakhs of rupees which sum he has paid into the Paymaster's chest. Our stay did not admit of his realising the other lakh, the voluntary offer of the inhabitants, but I have informed him that I deem him answerable for that collection or as great a proportion of it as can be made.

These are the plain facts.

WP 3/3/84 p. 494

408

Arthur Wellesley to James Kirkpatrick

Camp at Akote
2 December 1803

I have received and perused your letter to the Governor General of 15th November.[17]

I agree entirely in opinion with you respecting the propriety of resuming parts of the great jagir lands as the best mode of restoring the government of the Subah of the Deccan. But I beg leave to recommend that the first step taken should be to provide some public force for the service of the Subah's government by means of which this measure could be carried into execution. Unless this is done, the execution of the measure will fall upon the British government, whereby a great expense will be incurred, and the unpopularity of the British government which certainly exists already in a great degree will be much increased.

This object is certainly not one referable to me, but I think it possible that at the conclusion of the war some means may be devised to place the public force of the Nizam's government upon a better footing, and it is very desirable that you should turn your thoughts to that subject. In its present state it is no use whatever.

The Subah can do nothing without the assistance of the British government. This inconvenience will increase daily unless some remedy is applied, and in a greater proportion as the extent of the Subah's territories may be greater, or the consequence will be that the British troops must always be in the field. Indeed, if the Subah's military establishments are not improved the subsidiary force as at present will not be equal to the duties which will be required of it.

I hope that you will excuse the liberty I have taken in drawing your attention to this subject, but it is one which I consider of great importance and the evil certainly requires a speedy remedy.

Grwd (1837) ii 562 (1844) ii 897

409

Arthur Wellesley to Lieutenant-General Stuart

Camp at Paundry 15 miles south of Gawilghar
3 December 1803

. . . Sinde has ratified the treaty for suspending hostilities and his vakils say that he is going to the east of Elichpur according to the agreement. I have told them that I shall consider it as void on my part if he does not perform all the conditions. We have advanced no further in the peace than that the vakils have brought forward a kind of consent to treat upon the basis of giving compensation to the Company.

Raghuji Bhonsle has likewise sent a vakil here. I have made the same demand from him. I have sent him to wait at Elichpur till he received an answer to it. They are most terribly alarmed for the loss of Gawilghar etc. On this ground I expect to conclude with Raghuji immediately. His vakil pressed hard for a suspension of hostilities which I positively refused.

Grwd (1837) ii 564 (1844) ii 899

410

Conference with the vakil of Raghuji Bhonsle

9 December 1803
[summary]

Jaswant Rao Ramchandar produced a letter from the Rajah of Berar accepting the principle of compensation to the Company. He asked for details of the cessions sought. These Arthur Wellesley set out; the extension of the boundary of the Nizam of Hyderabad to the northward to the hills on which Gawilghar and Nernulla stood, and to the Wardha river to the east; and for the Company the province of Cuttack. He would also require that treaties concluded with dependents of the Rajah of Berar should be confirmed. The vakil sought a cessation of hostilities, but this Arthur Wellesley refused. He insisted that the Rajah would be required to declare that he no longer adhered to the confederacy he had formed against the British government, and to send a hostage as a security until peace had been concluded.[18]

SD iv 277, PRC x 183

411

Arthur Wellesley to Josiah Webbe

before Gawilghar
9 December 1803

. . . In respect to General Campbell's advance, I have frequently considered that subject, and notwithstanding all my difficulties on account of the want of a reserve on the Godavari to keep the enemy in my front, I have always decided that General Campbell's corps could never be so well posted as in the spot originally pointed out to him.[19]

The foundation of all our success here, the destruction of the enemy's views, and our hopes of peace, depend on the continuation of tranquillity in the Company's territories and in Mysore. That tranquillity might continue if those troops were ordered forward but I am not certain that it would. I am certain it will as long as they remain in their position, because they are superior to all that can be brought against them, and they threaten the safety of all the strongholds of the southern chiefs, if these should presume to declare themselves the enemies of the Company. This was the case before our last success and my present operations which go to [the essence of] Raghuji Bhonsle's existence had brought that chief out of the Nizam's territories. But now that friends and enemies and neutrals are all in Berar, I do not want a reserve on the Godavari, the removal of General Campbell's corps would be useless and all the chances of its being prejudicial to us still exist . . .

This fort has a great name, and has a formidable appearance; it stands on a range and in the midst of hills. The difficulty of attacking it consists in that of encamping near it, on account of the want of water. However I have seized a post within 700 yards of one gate to the southward which is tolerably covered and supported, and I have sent Stevenson over the hills to the northward. We have got him nearly over with great difficulty and labour, but he tells me that he will overlook the fort on that side, so that there is every probability that we shall have the fort in a few days. In the meantime the negotiations, or rather the conversations about peace, are going on.

SD iv 294

412

Captain Barclay to John Malcolm

Camp at Deogaon
10 December 1803

The General received your letters up to the 7th inclusive last night but was so long detained in a conversation with Raghuji's vakil that he had no time to write you, and he went off at sunrise this morning to visit the post on the other side of the fort, a ride of eighteen miles. He therefore desired me to write to you and say that there is every prospect of our taking Gawilghar very soon.

On Colonel Stevenson's side it is ascertained that we can erect batteries from the distance of 800 yards to 300 yards from the wall on a level with some parts and overlooking others, and neither scarped rock or ditch between the batteries and wall; the latter is not very strong. There is also ground and water for a brigade with proper covering distance and abundance of both some miles further off for the whole of the Subsidiary Force. A great part of the terre plein of the fort is also overlooked and all the guns in the detachment can be brought to bear on it.

On this side we are encamped with the infantry within 4 miles of the place, there being no water near for a large force, and have a battalion up under their guns since the 6th. The face of the mountain has been reconnoitred and a place for a battery discovered within 700 yards of a part of the wall, before which there is no scarped rock; the ascent is steep and will be difficult but is deemed practicable. It put me in mind of Colonel Reed's attack on Nundydroog. We began to work [the battery?] this morning and hope to divide the attention of the garrison with Colonel Stevenson. I am directed to write so much in duplicate and to write Baynes about coming on.

NUL Pw Jb 51 p. 311

413

Conference with the vakils of Daulat Rao Sinde

11 December 1803
[summary]

In this conference, the vakils asked for details of the territorial concessions which would be sought in Hindustan. Arthur Wellesley explained that all territory to the northward of Jaipur Jodhpur and Gohad would be required. He refused to accept the suggestion that the support of the Mughal Emperor should continue to be the responsibility of Sinde, or that Sinde should retain the seaport of Broach. He explained the need for a general article in any treaty of peace which would require Sinde to accept cession of territory to individual lesser rulers who had chosen to transfer their allegiance to the British Company.

The vakils indicated that they expected Jaswant Rao Holkar to resume hostilities with Daulat Rao Sinde and sought assistance from the Company. To this Arthur Wellesley responded in general terms that the Company would not wish to see Sinde's government destroyed and that some arrangement might be possible.

SD iv 246 [not printed in PRC x]

414

Conference with the vakil of Raghuji Bhonsle

12 December 1803
[summary]

The vakil of Berar sought either a moderation of the territorial demand on Berar that would benefit the Nizam of Hyderabad, or alternatively that the Rajah of Berar should negotiate separately with the Nizam. These approaches Arthur Wellesley refused, and contended that Hyderabad was entitled to compensation for the devastation to its territories.

SD iv 280, PRC x 185

415

Arthur Wellesley to Merrick Shawe

before Gawilghar
12 December 1803

. . . I think I am getting on towards peace. Raghuji's vakil does not object to the compensation I have asked for the Company, but he does to that required for the Nizam. I have demanded that his boundary should be the Wardha river, from its source in the Gawile hills to its junction with the Godavari . . .

I shall find a difficulty in settling with Sinde on account of the total want of information respecting the countries which I have demanded from him. His vakils declare that he has no countries north of the Rajputs of which the Peshwa and Holkar have not each a third, excepting Perron's jagir which he is willing to make over to the Company. Therefore unless we make war upon Holkar, and deprive the Peshwa of his territories, we shall not succeed in driving the Marathas entirely from these countries, although Sinde should cede his rights. And I acknowledge that if this is really the case, I should prefer to see Sinde remain in the partnership, than to introduce the Company.[20]

However I shall adhere as strictly as I can to the instructions which I have received. But the want of information regarding the proceeding of General Lake, even to the extent to which he has pushed his conquests, and of the country from which he has expelled the Marathas, and taken possession, is a great bar to the progress of the negotiations.

The battle made by Sinde's ministers this day was principally to preserve his influence over the King [the Moghal Emperor] and his territories about Ahmednagar, the last of which they declared being the place of his nativity and the old possession of his ancestors he never could be brought to consent to give up. I think it appears from what they said about the King, that the countries in Hindustan were managed in the name of His Majesty by Sinde [as] his vizier.

The vakils disclosed this day a great apprehension of Holkar's power, and they almost expressed an expectation that Holkar would attack them as soon as the peace with the Company should be settled. They said that in that case they must depend upon the Company for assistance in money and troops. When going away they said they had a proposition to make to draw closer the connection between the two governments after the war, to which they hoped we should consent.

In short everything appears to go on well and I think I shall succeed in settling a peace to the satisfaction of the Governor General.

I shall open upon this place tomorrow.

Grwd (1837) ii 574 (1844) ii 905

416

Arthur Wellesley to Richard Wellesley

Camp at Deogaun
15 December 1803

. . . The fort of Gawilghar is situated in a range of mountains between the sources of the rivers Purna and Tapti. It stands on a lofty mountain in this range and consists of one complete inner fort, which fronts to the south, where the rock is most steep, and an outer fort which covers the inner to the north-west and north. This outer fort has a third wall, which covers the approach to it from the north by the village of Labada. All these walls are strongly built and fortified by ramparts and towers.

The communications with the fort are through three gates; one to the south with the inner fort, one to the north-west with the outer fort, and one to the north with the third wall. The ascent to the first is very long and steep and is practicable only for men, that to the second is by a road used for the common communications of the garrison with the countries to the southward, but the road passes round the west side of the fort and is exposed for a great distance to its fire, it is so narrow as to make it impracticable to approach regularly by it, and the rock is scarped on each side. This road also leads no further than to the gate.

The communication with the northern gate is direct from the village of Labada, and here the ground is level with the fort. But the road to Labada leads through the mountains for about thirty miles from Elichpur and it was obvious that the difficulty and labour of moving ordnance and stores to Labada would be very great. However after making enquiry at Elichpur it appeared both to Colonel Stevenson and to me that this point of attack was upon the whole the most advantageous and we accordingly adopted it.

Colonel Stevenson had equipped his corps at Asirgarh for the siege of Gawilghar for which service it had long been destined, and I therefore determined that he should make the principal attack by Labada while I should cover his operations with my own division and all the cavalry and if possible assist them by other attacks to the southward and westward . . .

On the 12th [December] at night Colonel Stevenson erected two batteries in front of the north face of the fort, one consisting of two iron eighteen pounders and three iron twelve pounders to breach the outer fort and third wall, and one consisting of two brass twelve pounders and two five inch howitzers to clear and destroy the defences on the point of attack. On the same night the troops of my division constructed a battery for 2 iron and 2 brass twelve pounders on the mountain near the southern gate with a view if possible to breach the wall near that gate or at all events to draw the enemy's attention to that quarter. Unfortunately the iron guns could not be moved into the battery notwithstanding the utmost exertions of the troops and the fire of the brass guns produced little effect.

The fire of all these batteries opening on the 13th in the morning and on the 14th at night the breaches in the walls of the outer fort were practicable. All the arrangements were then made for storming on this day. Lt Colonel Kenny of the 11th Regiment commanded the party for the storm consisting of the flank companies of the 94th Regiment and of the native corps in Colonel Stevenson's division supported by the 94th Regiment and Lt Colonel Haliburton's brigade with Lt Colonel Maclean's brigade in reserve.

At the same hour I made two attacks from the southward to draw the enemy's attention to that quarter. One under Lt Colonel Wallace consisting of the 74th Regiment five companies of the 78th and 1st battalion 8th Regiment on the southern gate, and one under Lt Colonel Chalmers consisting of five companies of the 78th and the 1st battalion 8th Regiment on the north-west gate. These last attacks could be of no service except to draw the enemy's attention from that from the north, unless they should succeed in blowing open the gates, and till they should communicate with detachments from Colonel Stevenson's corps as they had no other means of entering the fort.

All the troops advanced at about ten in the morning. The detachment under Lt Colonel Chalmers arrived at the north-west gate at the moment when the enemy was endeavouring to escape through it from the detachment of Colonel Stevenson's corps which had been sent to communicate with Colonel Chalmers, and he entered without difficulty. The wall of the inner fort in which no breach had been made was then to be carried. After some attempts upon the gate for communication between the inner and outer fort a place was found at which it was possible to escalade the wall. Captain Campbell with the light infantry of the 94th Regiment fixed the ladders against this place escaladed the wall opened the gate for the storming party and the fort was shortly in our possession.

The enemy's garrison was numerous. It consisted of Rajputs and of a great part of Beny Singh's regular infantry which had escaped from the battle of Argaum, commanded by Beny Singh himself. They were all well armed with the Company's new muskets and bayonets. Vast numbers of them were killed particularly at the different gates. This service has been performed I hope with small loss on our side . . .

Grwd (1837) ii 583 (1844) ii 913

417

Letter from an unknown officer

Gawilghar
16 December 1803

I am extremely happy to have it in my power to inform you that this extensive fortress is in our possession. It was taken by storm yesterday morning at 10 o'clock. I will as nearly as I can give you the particulars.

I believe that in my last letter I informed you that Colonel Stevenson's batteries had been erected in a very commanding place. It was I believe on the 12th a working party of 4000 Europeans from the 74th and 78th Regiments and 500 sepoys were ordered down under Captain Beauman to construct the batteries on one side and to put in the guns. The battery was ready by the next morning but on account of the steepness of the road the guns were not up until about 10 o'clock. I mean the four brass twelve pounders (it was utterly impossible to get up the iron ones) when we began to cut a trench to get them into the battery. The General came up soon after and was extremely anxious to get one in, as he wished to see what effect it would have upon them. We soon got them all in, the General's presence animating the men, who were I assure you extremely fagged having worked the whole night.

After we had completed our work the General ordered us back to camp and I expected to have had a rest the next day, but was awoke that night to look at orders which were that the 74th and 78th Regiment with the 2nd battalion the 10th Regiment [native infantry] were to move away the next morning and encamp close to the fort, which we did, and were horribly annoyed by their guns which played upon us very smartly but without effect, in expectation to have been ordered up to the fort about two o'clock. But Colonel Stevenson not having reported the breach practicable we did not.

But about twelve o'clock that night orders came saying that Colonel Stevenson's detachment was to storm the north face of the fort at 10 o'clock the next morning, that five companies of the 78th with the 74th were to move under Colonel Wallace, the remainder with the 2nd and 10th Regiments under Colonel Chalmers, at 3 o'clock the next morning the party under Colonel Wallace to move beyond the battery and get under cover near one of their gates, the party under Colonel Chalmers with a six-pounder was ordered to move up a road round the hill towards the Delhi gate and likewise to get under cover before daybreak. Both parties were to show themselves at the time Colonel Stevenson should move to the breach in order that we might as much as possible draw off the attention of the enemy from that quarter.

The right wing went with Wallace, the left with Chalmers; as the light company had no officer with them, Captain Fraser having been ordered up the night before as a covering party to the battery and the Grenadiers had four, I was ordered to take charge of them and consequently went with Colonel Chalmers. We were got under cover when Colonel Chalmers informed me that he was ordered to take the gun at 10 o'clock and blow open the gate.

While we were sitting talking one of the enemy came down, not knowing anybody was there, and we immediately seized him, when he informed us that the killedar and all his troops intended making their escape at that gate, not supposing we would take the trouble to go so far round to guard the road.

A short time after some more came, but saw us in time enough to get back to the fort and alarm them. They immediately recommenced firing from the garrison, but we were so well secured that the whole of their shot went over our heads. At about a quarter before ten we began moving. We soon found it impossible to get in the gun, so left it. After running about a couple of miles, during which the enemy was firing at us with their matchlocks, we arrived at the gateway and had at the same time the pleasure of seeing the 94th upon the hills inside the fort.

We could only get the wicket open when a dreadful sight presented [itself]. Actually I stepped over dead bodies to get in at the wicket and when I was in had to walk many paces over them. I am certain that there could not be less than one hundred dead and dying of enemy close to the gate. It appeared that at the commencement of the storm they had flocked there to get away. The people of Colonel Stevenson's detachment knew we were there and rushed on that way, when they massacred the whole of them. When we got in we found that the remainder of the garrison had retired to the inner fort which was excessively strong . . .

NLS 13,631 f. 238

418

Conference of Arthur Wellesley with the vakil of Raghuji Bhonsle

16 December 1803
[summary]

The vakil sought to reduce the scale of territorial cession in Cuttack, and to vary the cession to the Nizam of Hyderabad to be in money and not territory. On both these points Arthur Wellesley was insistent and prevailed. On the article in the treaty dealing with treaties concluded with 'subjects and feudatories of the confederated Maratha chiefs' Arthur Wellesley explained that the requirement was indispensable but that its implementation should be 'as little injurious . . . as possible.'

SD iv 281, PRC x 186

419

Colonel Stevenson to Arthur Wellesley

Camp at Gawilghar
16 December 1803

I have the honour to enclose you a copy of the orders issued and the disposition I made for the assault of the fort of Gawilghar on the side attacked by the Subsidiary Force . . .

The breach in the outer wall was reported practicable on the evening of the 14th and I apprised you of my determination of storming the following day. The troops were accordingly ordered into the trenches before daylight and moved out to the attack at half past nine o'clock in the morning. The whole advanced in the most regular order and gained the breach under cover of the fire of the batteries and were instantaneously joined by Lt Colonel Kenny. The right attack commanded by Lt Colonel Lang and HM 94th Regiment under Major Campbell pursued the enemy to the Road gate and were met by the attack from your division under Lt Colonel Chalmers, while the left were led by Lt Colonel Kenny towards the third wall and the Delhi gate and near which he determined on escalading.

In performing this the troops had a deep chasm to pass over and were opposed to a heavy fire from the walls and gate, but their advance was greatly assisted by the judicious manner in which Lt Colonel Haliburton had formed his brigade to fire on the parapet and defence of the gate. One brass twelve pounder and two six pounders were run down to the front of the batteries and were also of great service in keeping down the enemy's fire. Every part of Lt Colonel Kenny's instructions were executed with the utmost promptitude and zeal and I have to regret that the attack was early deprived of the animating example of that gallant officer from his receiving two wounds while leading on the troops to the assault of the inner wall. In the performance of this duty the attack was lead by the light company of HM 94th Regiment under Captain Campbell, and they are justly entitled to a considerable degree of praise for the gallant manner with which they surmounted the difficulties in escalading this wall.

Lt Colonel Kenny had his thigh broke and lost a thumb by musket shots and I am happy to have it in my power to add that his wounds are not pronounced dangerous. I have to lament the loss of Lt Young of the 2nd battalion the 7th regiment, a young officer of promising abilities who fell mortally wounded nearly at the same time; these were the only casualties that have yet been reported among the officers . . .

WP 3/3/84 p. 502

420

Colonel Stevenson – Order of the day

16 December 1803

Colonel Stevenson congratulates his brother officers and soldiers of the Subsidiary Force on the success which attended their gallant conduct in the assault of the fort of Gawilghar yesterday, and which he considers an honourable reward for the incessant labour the troops have experienced from the commencement of the operations against that place. The difficulties they had to overcome have been such as must give them that applause they so justly deserve, and he will not fail to report their very meritorious conduct to the Commander in Chief and to the Honorable Major General Wellesley.

Colonel Stevenson is highly sensible of the spirited and intrepid manner in which Lt Colonel Lang led on the storming party and regrets the event that so early deprived the service of his animating zeal and example, not however until he had arranged his plan for surmounting the difficulties of escalading the interior wall of the fort and driving the enemy from the defences of the Matchly Gate. In performing this service Captain Campbell with the light company of HM 94th Regiment is justly entitled to a considerable degree of praise. The meritorious services of Lt Colonels Lang and Desse and Major Campbell in performing the duties assigned to their several attacks and in forcing open the Perpeety and [Delhi?] Road gates claim his most gratifying acknowledgement, and he cannot be unmindful of the regular and orderly manner in which HM 94th Regiment and the whole of the troops advanced to the attack.

The able manner in which Lt Colonel Haliburton formed his brigade and the support he gave to the attack justly entitles that officer to his warmest thanks and he hopes to return them also to Lt Colonel Maclean for the regular and judicious manner in which he posted the reserve under his command. To Captains Burke and Dalrymple and the officers and men of the artillery the greatest praise is due for the incessant labour in the batteries, their numbers not permitting regular relief.

The services performed by Capt Heitland and the officers and men of the corps of pioneers and Captain Johnston of the Engineers have been equally arduous and Colonel Stevenson will feel the greatest satisfaction in making his report of the obligations he is under to these officers and not only for their zealous exertions during the siege but also in the assault . . .

WP 3/3/84 p. 504

421

Colonel Stevenson to Arthur Wellesley

[Gawilghar]
16 December 1803 ½ past 6 pm

You desired that Colonel Lang should be left in charge of the fort yesterday and no officer could be more fit both for the defence of the place and the collection and protection of the captured property. I know not if it is your intention or wish that he should be left in command when the troops march from hence. The place is extensive and may require a battalion for the defence, nor is it likely [that] five native battalions may be sufficient for the services I am hereafter to be employed on.

The property may be removed from that part of the fort that was breached and a small guard left in it, and the defence confined to the upper fort, or that next to the Peerputy gate, and as it is in general defended by the precipices and strength of the [gardines?] a company garrison may be sufficient. The battalion can however be spared and I cannot name an officer fitter for any military duties or duties of trust than Colonel Lang. I will be obliged to you if you could favour me with your instructions in this hour.

WP 3/3/84 p. 498

422

Arthur Wellesley to Richard Wellesley

Elichpur
17 December 1803

I have the honour to enclose . . . a treaty of peace which I have this day concluded with Jaswant Rao Ramchandar, the vakil of the Rajah of Berar.

I have made the treaty in the name of the British government and its allies generally . . . the reasons for omitting to name the allies in the treaty and to engage that they should ratify it, will become sufficiently obvious when the character and conduct of the government of these allies are recollected . . .

I wished to be able to define more accurately the bounds of the cession of the province of Cuttack but I had no information upon the subject . . .

By the third article the Company and its allies gain on this side the whole province of Berar and the frontier of the Subah of the Deccan will be carried forward to the Wurda river. The countries thus ceded are old possessions of the Subah of the Deccan, the revenues of which have been collected by them and the Rajah of Berar in different proportions at different times . . . It appeared to me to be an object of greater importance to get rid of the Rajah of Berar entirely from this fine country than to secure an additional barrier for Cuttack.

The revenues of Berar on this side of the Wurda are computed to amount to about one crore of rupees. The Rajah has appropriated entirely to himself countries, the revenues of which are computed to have been ten lakhs of rupees, and the remainder under different treaties was to be divided equally between him and the Subah of the Deccan. However I have reason to believe from the conferences during the negotiations that the Rajah of Berar never received more than thirty lakhs as his share of the countries on this side of the Wurda . . .

By the fourth article I have agreed that the Rajah shall have possession of the forts of Nernulla and Gawilghar. In fact these forts are of greater importance to the power which remains in possession of the mountains than to that which possesses the plains . . . I consented to the fifth article because the districts in the plains immediately under the hills will always be liable to the depredations of the inhabitants of the hills. The loss to the Subah's government will be but trifling in comparison with what it would incur if the Raja were not interested, as he will now be, to restrain the incursions of the hill people into the plains.

The seventh article provides that the Hon Company are to arbitrate between the Rajah and the Subah of the Deccan and the Peshwa. The Rajah's minister was desirous that I should consent to confirm all grants and treaties made heretofore by these powers, but I refused this on the ground that I could not consent to anything of which I had no knowledge . . .

The tenth article is of considerable importance.[21] The Rajah's ministers appeared to feel the full extent of the engagements to which it bound the Rajah and expressed the greatest uneasiness on the subject. He said that after ceding Berar and Cuttack the Rajah had no territories excepting what he had conquered from the zemindars rajahs etc, and that by this article he might be bound to give up the whole of his territories. I told him that whatever might be the consequence the article was indispensable and must be agreed to, that peace would not have been agreed to if the British government had wished for the destruction of the Raja's state, and that it certainly was not intended that the article should apply to more cases than were absolutely necessary to preserve the good faith of the British government, and I promised him that the British government would apply it to as few cases as possible consistently with an adherence to good faith. The vakil was satisfied with this assurance which I requested him to convey to the Rajah, as I think it probable that this article will be that to which his durbar will have the strongest objections . . .

I hope that your Excellency will approve of and ratify this treaty . . .

Grwd (1837) ii 591 (1844) ii 916

423

Arthur Wellesley to Lieutenant-Colonel Close

Camp 14 miles east from Elichpur
20 December 1803

When the peace shall be ratified by Raghuji Bhonsle I propose to send Mr Elphinstone to his camp to act as Resident till the arrival of Webbe. I may also have occasion to request Malcolm to go to one of these chiefs, and in that case, I shall be much in want of assistance. Malcolm tells me that you would have no objection to allow Mr Strachey to come here, and if this be the case, I shall be much obliged to you if you will ask him . . . I have no doubt but that Raghuji will ratify the treaty.

Grwd (1837) ii 599 (1844) ii 923

424

Arthur Wellesley to Richard Wellesley

23 December 1803

I have the honour to inform Your Excellency that I this day received the ratification of the Rajah of Berar of the treaty of peace, signed on the 17th inst by myself on the part of the Honorable Company and their allies, and by Jaswant Rao Ramchandar on the part of Rajah Raghuji Bhonsle.

Daulat Rao Sinde's ministers, Vithal Pant and Kavalnyn arrived in my camp this afternoon for the purpose, as they say, of making peace for their master. I yesterday gave notice to Sinde's vakils, Jaswant Rao Goorporah and Naru Pant Nana, that I was desirous to put an end to the agreement made on the 23rd November for suspending hostilties, and that I should consider it as null and void from the 27th inst.

Grwd (1837) ii 609 (1844) ii 930

425

Arthur Wellesley to Mountstuart Elphinstone

Deogaun
24 December 1803

Peace having been concluded with the Raja of Berar I have appointed you to go to the camp of that chief and act as Resident till the arrival of Mr Webbe. You will accordingly commence your march as soon as will be convenient to you attended by the troops appointed in this day's orders as your escort.

A principal object of your attention on your arrival in the camp of the Raja of Berar should be to endeavour to convince him of the sincere desire of the British government to consolidate the peace. You will omit no opportunity of assuring him that the British government is desirous that he should continue a respectable power in India and that if he should fulfil the articles of the peace and perform the common duties of friendship the British government will never break with him.

If he should make any propositions, such as you have heard his vakils make in the conferences during the negotiations, to draw more closely the alliance between the two governments you will encourage him to speak plainly upon that subject. Inform him that it is probable his Excellency the Governor General will be inclined to attend to his wishes provided that you are enabled to state them to him distinctly. At the same time apprise him that all governments must consider their own interests in such a case and unless bound by previous engagements it might be . . . that to give him assistance in the moment of danger might be inconsistent with those of the British government. On this ground you will urge to the Raja the necessity of providing by previous engagements for the support and assistance of the British government and of his stating his wishes on this point in the most distinct manner . . .

I think there is every reason to believe that the Raja is sincere in his desire for peace with the British government and that he will adhere to his treaty even if the war should continue with Sinde. But his treachery is notorious and the sacrifices which he has made are very great and he might be induced to renew the war in hopes to regain part of what he has lost. For this reason it is necessary that you should do everything in your power to be accurately informed of all that passes in his durbar particularly with the emissaries of Sinde and Holkar and the southern chiefs . . .

In regard to the modes of acquiring this intelligence I have but little to say. You must employ those which your own experience and discretion will suggest, and as I know that no intelligence can be gained without expense I beg you to incur such as you may think absolutely necessary to obtain that which is required. I beg leave also to recommend to you as much as possible a constant personal intercourse with the ministers of Raghuji Bhonsle's durbar instead of communicating by means of any native servants. The establishment of this mode of communicating at an early period if it does not immediately lay open to you sources of information which would otherwise be wanted will at least give the government the advantage of them hereafter. It is vain to hope that any native in the situation of a minister at a durbar will ever trust another in the situation of servant to the British Resident, and it is equally so to hope that the British Resident will ever be able to gain any useful intelligence from the ministers at any durbar if his intercourse with them is to be a matter of state or parade or anything but a daily occurrence for the transaction of the daily business . . .

Gwrd (1844) i 930, SNRR i 3, SD iv 302

426

Conference with the ministers of Daulat Rao Sinde

24 December 1803
[summary]

In this initial conference with ministers of Daulat Rao Sinde, Vithal Pant first sought a general guarantee by both states of each others territories. Arthur Wellesley explained that such an alliance could not be offensive in character, and that Sinde would be bound to inform the Company of all his relations with foreign powers and attend to Company advice.

Arthur Wellesley reassured the ministers that he had no intention to enquire into the title of Daulat Rao Sinde to all his territories, but that the treaty of peace must provide that he should have no claims upon the Nizam of Hyderabad or upon the Peshwa, and that he must give up claims upon rulers with whom the Company during the war had concluded treaties. He also enquired about the reported agreement between Sinde and Jaswant Rao Holkar, by which it was understood that Sinde had agreed to restore territory which he had seized.

The vakils asked whether once peace had been concluded Sinde would be free to visit the Peshwa at Pune. Arthur Wellesley explained that this journey could not be undertaken with an army, and suggested that Sinde would be better employed settling the affairs of his own government.

SD iv 251, PRC x 168

427

Conference with the ministers and vakils of Daulat Rao Sinde

26 December 1803
[summary]

After a discussion about the retention by Sinde of some territories near Ahmednagar, which were regarded as the family estate of the Maharaja, Arthur Wellesley again asked the vakils about the treaty with Jaswant Rao Holkar. Jaswant Rao Goorporah explained that the central condition of the treaty, that Holkar should join in the attack on the British government, had not been fulfilled.

Arthur Wellesley then put to the ministers the proposition that provided all territory north of the the line Jaipur Jodhpur and Gohad were ceded, Sinde would not be involved in any further expense in consequence of a treaty of defensive alliance, if he elected to enter one, and that a range of pensions in total value of not more than fifteen lakhs of rupees would be granted to his principal servants. He repeated his insistence that treaties concluded by other Company officials with lesser rulers would have to be accepted by Sinde.

SD iv 254, PRC x 171

428

Discussion with the ministers and vakils of Daulat Rao Sinde

28 December 1803
[summary]

A draft treaty had been prepared and this was read 'article by article.' There was a long discussion about the second article, which determined the alignment of the northern boundary of the territorial cessions being demanded. A revised wording was accepted. A compromise wording also dealt with the issue of the claims of Sinde against the Peshwa and the Gaikwar.

Arthur Wellesley responded to a request to increase the scale of the pensioning of some of Sinde's principal sirdars by enlarging the total available to seventeen lakhs of rupees. He insisted upon the renunciation by Sinde of titles he had held from the Mughal Emperor. He agreed to ask General Lake to permit the retention by Sinde of guns in forts in Hindustan provided they had not been captured by the time of the arrival of word of the treaty.

SD iv 258, PRC x 175

429

Discussion with the ministers and vakils of Daulat Rao Sinde

29 December 1803

. . . The copies of the treaty and of the schedules were read and compared, and they were signed at about one in the morning of the 30th December . . .

SD iv 263, PRC x 180

430

Arthur Wellesley to Richard Wellesley

30 December 1803

. . I have this day concluded, with the vakils of Daulat Rao Sinde, and signed, a treaty of peace . . . This treaty like that with the Raja of Berar is concluded in the name of the British government and its allies generally and the cessions are made to all the allied powers . . .

By this treaty . . . all the important objects detailed in your Excellency's instructions of the 27th June are secured, and the ground is laid for a more complete alliance with Sinde's government, or supposing that he should omit to take advantage of the terms offered to him, to ally himself more closely with the Company's government, such an influence will be established in his as will render it very improbable that its means will ever be again directed against that of the Company.

By the second article of the treaty, Sinde consented to cede to the Honourable Company all his territories north of the countries of the Rajas of Jaipur Jodhpur and the Rana of Gohud. A schedule is annexed to the treaty which contains the best account that can be procured of the revenue of those territories . . .

It would have been impossible to arrange this great cession in the disturbed state of Sinde's government under all the circumstances of his misfortunes in the war and of the great diminution of his military power and reputation, in comparison with that of his rival Holkar, without determining [either] to provide in some degree for those who reaped benefits from the revenue of the ceded territories, or making up my mind to throw into Holkar's hands and to add to his armies all the sirdars and troops who had been subsisted by the resources of those countries, and who must have been forthwith discharged from Sinde's service and would have looked to Holkar for protection and future employment.

I chose the former which I think is most consistent with your Excellency's policy, and it appears that besides avoiding the evil of increasing the numbers of the followers of the only freebooter that remains in India, it tends to establish an influence in the Sinde's durbar . . . In the course of this war Sinde's power reputation and military resources have been greatly diminished, while his rival Holkar after having recovered the possessions of his family by his treaty of peace with Sinde remains with undiminished power and increased reputation. Comparatively with those of Sinde his power and military resources are much greater than they were previous to the war and I have little doubt but that the contest between those chiefs will be revived . . .

There was considerable difficulty . . . in settling the ninth article respecting the treaties made with the Rajas. The ministers appeared to be aware of the loss which Sinde's government might incur under this article, and they contended strongly against it, till at last I was obliged to tell them that unless they agreed to it I could not make peace. The advantage which it appeared to me that your Excellency expected to derive from the independence of the Rajas of Jaipur and Jodhpur and the Rana of Gohud was that these chiefs should connect themselves by treaty with the British government.

From the different accounts however which I have received I observe that treaties have not been concluded with any of these chiefs notwithstanding the rapid and astonishing success of his Excellency the Commander in Chief. The consequence of their independence, unless they should have connected themselves with the British government, would be that the annual contest which they have had with the Marathas for the peshcush[22] would cease and the British government would derive no additional security. I therefore deemed it best to stipulate generally for the independence of every Raja with whom a treaty should have been concluded, by which your Excellency's object is secured in respect to all of this description; and in regard to the others they are left to their fate . . .

Grwd (1837) ii 616 (1844) ii 933

Notes

Introduction

1 Cornwallis to Shore 10 June 1796. Ross, *Correspondence of Charles, first Marquis Cornwallis* (1859) ii 305.

2 Dundas to Cornwallis 19 January 1797. Cornwallis to Dundas 19 January 1797. Ross op. cit. pp. 317–19. Scott to Dundas 22 January 1797. C.H. Philips (ed), *The Correspondence of David Scott* (Camden Society 1951), vol. 1, p. 94.

3 Ross op. cit. ii 317–27. R. Callahan, *The East India Company and Army Reform 1783–1798* (Harvard 1972) pp. 200–5. C.H. Philips, *The East India Company 1783–1834* (Manchester 1940) p. 93.

4 The text of the Treaty of Bassein can be found in PRC x 258, Martin iii 627.

Prelude – Introduction

1 O.H.K. Spate *India and Pakistan a General and Regional Geography* (1954) p. 35.

2 Memorandum on Operations in the Maratha territory dated September 1801 Grwd (1837) i 357 (1844) i 295.

3 Close to Clive 25 October 1802 Home Misc 466 p. 43, Close to Duncan 25 October 1802 Parl Pps [5, 22 June 1804] p. 341, Close to Kirkpatrick 25 October 1802 Mss Eur f. 228/76.

4 Arthur Wellesley to Stuart 4 December 1802 Grwd (1837) i 384 (1844) i 311, Arthur Wellesley to Clive 19 December 1802 Grwd (1837) i 387 (1844) i 318.

5 Arthur Wellesley to Malcolm 11 December 1802 Grwd (1844) i 316. On the character of Lord Clive, see Richard Wellesley to Dundas 16 May 1799 in *Two Views of British India* ed E Ingram (1970) p. 151.

6 Arthur Wellesley to Stuart 3 March 1803 and accompanying memorandum Grwd (1837) i 413 (1844) i 338.

7 Arthur Wellesley to Stevenson 14 March 1803 Grwd (1837) i 435 (1844) i 354, Close to Governor-General 31 March 1803 Home Misc 616 p. 279.

8 Arthur Wellesley to Close 7 April 1803 Grwd (1837) i 474 (1844) i 383.

Prelude

1 Josiah Webbe, although dismissed by the Court of Directors from his position as Secretary to the Governor, was probably still acting in that capacity. He had seen Edmonstone to Close 30 December 1802 Parl Pps [5, 22 June 1804] p. 76.

2 Colonel Sir William Clarke had been sent as senior officer to the occupied Portuguese territory of Goa.

3 Stuart is here responding to a memorandum of Arthur Wellesley of 15 February 1803 SD iv 1.

4 Presumably Stuart had received the letter from Richard Wellesley of 8 February at Martin iii 48. The date of the despatch from Colonel Close cannot be determined; its content must have been comparable to that to Arthur Wellesley of 14 February at [10].

5 The 'detailed arrangements' are in Arthur Wellesley's memorandum of 3 March 1803 Grwd (1837) i 414 (1844) i 338. Clive's instructions to Stuart of 27 February 1803 are at Parl Pps [5, 22 June 1804] p. 432. Richard Wellesley's instructions to Clive of 2 February 1803 are at Martin iii 41.

6 It is clear from a further letter from Stuart of 9 March 1803 at WP 3/3/87 p. 51 that Arthur Wellesley had seen these instructions in draft.

7 Stevenson had reported to Close that he commanded a force of 'two regiments of native cavalry consisting of 800 or upwards, sixteen field pieces twelve and six [pounders] besides two six-pounder gallopers and four three pounders attached to the cavalry, and six battalions of native infantry consisting of 6000 firelocks.' Stevenson to Close 7 March 1803 Parl Pps [5, 22 June 1804] p. 431.

8 A revolt in Malabar, following a revenue assessment and imposed rates of exchange between different currencies, led to the senior judge in the territory revoking both in an attempt to forestall further disturbances. OIOC Abstract of Madras Letters Received vii 338.

9 Stuart did not leave Madras until the autumn of 1804.

10 Malcolm set out the 'animosities' of the southern jagirdars in a letter to Lord Clive of 3 April 1803, and its attachments, Parl Pps [5, 22 June 1804] p. 110, Grwd (1837) i 462 (1844) i 376, PRC x 89. The Ninderrah ghat was on the road between Ahmednagar and Toka.

11 Stuart sent Arthur Wellesley a copy of letter from Stevenson of 22 March written from '8 miles east of Kurdlar' which reported that 'some of my hircarrahs who arrived yesterday in four days from Holkar's camp describe it to be about 40 kos in a northeasterly direction from Pune, that his force consists of 60,000 of his best horse and that he has ordered his infantry and guns to follow him from Pune and has summoned Mir Khan and his commanders in the Akul Cottah country to join him with an intention of pursuing the Burhanpur route to meet and engage Sinde.' Stevenson to Stuart 22 March 1803 WP 3/3/87 p. 115.

12 The 'letter from the brahmin' is at PRC ix 175.

13 Close's letter to the Governor-General of 8 April is printed at PRC ix 174. The letter of Arthur Wellesley to Close of 16 April probably wrongly dates this letter of Close. Grwd (1837) i 498 (1844) i 399.

14 The statement of Sinde of 24 March is reported by Collins in a despatch of 25 March in PRC ix 162. Made after considerable pressure from Collins, it was to the effect that 'he had no intention whatever to obstruct the completion of the arrangements lately concluded between the Peshwa and the British Government.' The despatch of Close to Richard Wellesley of 10 April is at PRC x 95.

15 Collins to Richard Wellesley of 9 April is at PRC ix 176.

Confrontation – Introduction

1 Close to Arthur Wellesley 3 August 1803 (in part of letter not at [207] below).

2 Arthur Wellesley's recommendation of 3 May 1803 [62] was accepted by Stuart (Stuart to Clive 14 May 1803 PRC ix 209) and endorsed by Clive (Clive to Stuart 19 May 1803 PRC ix 214). In two contingent situations, an invasion by the Maratha rulers of the lands of the Nizam, or a confrontation sufficient to endanger the two advanced detachments, Stuart was to advance to their support.

3 Arthur Wellesley to Stuart 19 June 1803 Grwd (1837) ii 18 (1844) i 510.

4 Arthur Wellesley to Richard Wellesley 8 July 1803 Grwd (1837) ii 74 (1844) i 544, in that part of the letter not here printed at [156].

5 Arthur Wellesley to Richard Wellesley 24 July 1803 Grwd (1837) ii 130 (1844) i 572 here summarised at [190].

Confrontation

1 The 'return' of Murray's force at the beginning of April 1803 has not been found.

2 The terms in which the Resident at Hyderabad had written, to which Arthur Wellesley objected, were 'I see no reason whatever to alter the opinion I have long entertained of a general confederacy among the Maratha chieftains against us. There is but too much reason to suppose that an accommodation has already taken place between Holkar and Sinde through the machinations of Bhonsle . . . It is not impossible that Holkar may return to Pune with his army before General Wellesley reaches it, in which case hostilities will be inevitable. But if you can provide forage for your cattle there will be no difficulty in retaining Pune, though there will still be a great deal to achieve ere the Peshwa can be considered restored in the true sense of the word.' WP 1/147.

3 This listing of Sinde's force should be compared with that on 25 July at

[193]. At that latter date both Brownrigg and Dudrenec had left the Deccan on a march to Hindustan.

4 The despatch from Collins was that to the Governor-General of 25 April 1803 PRC ix 184.

5 The account of Sinde's forces was that sent to Arthur Wellesley by Collins with his letter of 25 April, and is given at [47].

6 In his letter, Sinde informed Collins that he planned to have an interview with Raghuji Bhonsle of Berar at Badauli and that they both planned then to move to Pune.

7 The correct dating of this letter is 8 May, as is evident from James Kirkpatrick's acknowledgement of it.

8 This listing can be compared with a more extensive one prepared by John Malcolm for Lord Clive at Miraj on 3 April 1803, printed at Parl Pps [5, 22 June 1804] p. 112, the supporting memorandum of which is printed also in PRC x 89.

9 John Malcolm also reported, commenting that the Peshwa had 'confounded us all, but none so much as Colonel Close' and had 'spoken on all subjects with great good sense and propriety.' (Malcolm to Shawe 16 May 1803 A Mss 13,746 f. 156).

10 This letter is undated by Collins, and noted as such by Arthur Wellesley. The 'Doab' is the territory between the Jumna and the Ganges.

11 Two letters from the subahdar of Aurungabad to his brother at Hyderabad of 16 and 23 May, and available to the Company later, are at Parl Pps [5, 22 June 1804] p. 467.

12 This despatch was copied to Collins and to Arthur Wellesley.

13 The reference is to Arthur Wellesley to Richard Wellesley from Akluj of 15 April [34], which had evidently not been copied to his Commander-in-Chief.

14 The Court of Directors had instructed the Governor of Madras that he must act in concert with his Council, some of whom were believed by both Richard and Arthur Wellesley to be more than willing to thwart policy. Richard Wellesley had begged Clive to stay at Madras to avert 'weak or wicked counsels at Fort St George [which] might affect the whole system of our political relations with the native powers.' (Richard Wellesley to Clive 4 April 1803 A Mss 13,622 f. 10, NLW Clive 664).

15 In the event nothing came of the proposal of Mir Khan that he should enter the service of the Nizam. The Nizam, who had been partially paralysed for some years, died in August 1803.

16 Collins' letter to Close of 30 May 1803, at PRC ix 238, reported Sinde's appreciation at the immediate notice that Arthur Wellesley had taken of some alleged plundering.

17 Malcolm had evidently sent to Arthur Wellesley the letter sent to him by Merrick Shawe on 5 May 1803, in which was recorded the very favourable reaction of Richard Wellesley to the letter written from Akluj on 15 April. His

letter was seen as giving 'a masterly review of the state of our interest and of the present posture of affairs with the Maratha empire, together with a most able opinion with regard to the political conduct and to the military operations which it may be proper to adopt.' Shawe added that the instructions of 5 May 1803, already in draft, were despatched after Richard Wellesley had read the letter. (Shawe-Malcolm 5 May 1803 A Mss 13,602 f. 4).

18 The 'minutes' of the meeting with the Peshwa have not been found, but Close's despatch to the Secretary to the Governor-General of 10 June reports that he expressed concern that none of the southern jagirdars had yet joined Arthur Wellesley, and reported to the Peshwa on Collins' discussion with Daulat Rao Sinde of 28 May. Directly challenged, Baji Rao denied having written to Sinde and Bhonsle seeking their presence at his capital since his return to Pune, and stated that he approved of the policy towards Sinde initiated by Richard Wellesley. He agreed to write to Sinde and Bhonsle asking them not to come to Pune. For Malcolm, who was present, the meeting 'added to the evidence we already possess of [the Peshwa] being firm to his engagements.' (Close to Governor-General 10 June 1803 A Mss 13,598 f. 151, Malcolm to Shawe 10 June 1803 A Mss 13,746 f. 172).

19 An enclosure to this letter gives the 'state' of the treasure at 10 June. 10,000 'dollars' at 233½ per hundred were valued at 23,350 rupees, and there were in addition 9,214 rupees 2 annas, 'exclusive of the 18,000 due to the Paymaster of General Wellesley's detachment.'

20 In a letter to Lake of the same date Collins noted that 'this durbar wishes to amuse me until the Maharajah be joined by Jaswant Rao Holkar who is I understand on his march hither' and added that 'General Wellesley marched from Pune unattended by a single sirdar in the service of his Highness the Peshwa, who seems altogether indifferent to the interests of the general defensive alliance.' A Mss 13,742 f. 37.

21 By 'flattering' Close means 'reassuring'.

22 The letter from Shawe was of 29 May, as appears from Malcolm to Shawe 4 July 1803 A Mss 13,746 f. 194.

23 The despatch from Collins was that of 13 June PRC ix 266.

24 Collins' letter of 16 June to Lieutenant-Colonel Close is at PRC ix 271. It reports a dispute at the durbar as to whether Baji Rao had invited Sinde to visit Pune.

25 A 'very strong remonstrance' given to the durbar, dated 28 June 1803 is at Parl Pps [5, 22 June 1804] p. 490.

26 The letter from Close to Malcolm has not been found.

27 The letters to the Governor-General are in Martin iii 250 PRC ix 311,312.

28 The reference is probably to Collins' report to the Governor-General of 15 June 1803, presumably copied to Close, where he forwarded a minute by his munshi of a discussion with Raghuji Bhonsle of the previous day. PRC ix 269, Parl Pps [5, 22 June 1804] p. 485.

29 Mohipat Ram was the principal officer of the Nizam in the area north of the Godavari.
30 The direction of Richard Wellesley to which Collins refers is that of 21 June 1803 PRC ix 280.
31 On the text of this letter in WP 3/3/1, which is totally in cypher, there is a PS in clear 'you will furnish a copy of this dispatch to Lieutenant-Colonel Close. No other person has received a copy of it.'
32 Arthur Wellesley had written to General Stuart on 7 July Grwd (1837) ii 101 (1844) i 563.
33 The report to the Governor-General from Collins of 17 July is at PRC ix 337.
34 Major Walker was Resident with the Gaikwar of Baroda.

The Road to Assaye – Introduction

1 Arthur Wellesley to Duncan 25 July 1803 SD iv 145, 31 July 1803 NLS 13,643 f. 35
2 Duncan to Arthur Wellesley 12 August 1803 [222] President's Minute 12 August 1803 Parl Pps [5, 22 June 1804] 527.
3 Walker to Duncan 7 August 1803 NLS 13,665 f. 1, Duncan to Walker 16 August 1803 ibid, Close-Duncan 19 August 1803 NLS 13,643 f. 57.
4 Arthur Wellesley to Duncan 29 August 1803 Gwrd (1837) ii 248 (1844) i 666, PRC x 131.
5 Duncan to Malcolm 31 August 1803 NLS 13,643 f. 55, Malcolm-Duncan 2, 3 September 1803 ibid f. 73, 61, Duncan-Malcolm 2 September 1803 ibid f. 55, Malcolm-Arthur Wellesley 3 September 1803 WP 3/3/70 enclosing these letters.
6 Collins to Richard Wellesley 31 August 1803 PRC x 132.
7 This quotation is from the 'Notes Relative to the late Transactions . . .' dated 15 December 1803, Parl Pps [5, 22 June 1804] pp. 220–55. It is at p. 242.

The Road to Assaye

1 The message from the newswriter, sent as an enclosure to the letter of 7 August, is given at [213A].
2 The 'very judicious paper' is the memorandum of 6 August 1803 Grwd (1844) i 618. It sets out Arthur Wellesley's case against the two Maratha rulers and their style of negotiation. 'Malcolm's convoy' included money (Arthur Wellesley to Malcolm 16 August 1803 SD iv 152, Grwd (1844) i 638).
3 The 'Cassabarri ghat' is the pass to the west of the Ajanta range in which can be found the modern town of Kasari.
4 Collins' letter of 13 August has not been found, but its content is clear from Arthur Wellesley to Stevenson 15 August 1803 Grwd (1837) ii 205 (1844)

i 636. The 'Badauli ghat' is in the Ajanta range near the modern Buldana.

5 Malcolm explained the terms of the treaty with Amrit Rao to Shawe in Fort William in a letter of 15 August which reached Shawe on 5 September (A Mss 13,746 f. 245). The meeting of Amrit Rao and Arthur Wellesley was delayed until November 1803 (Arthur Wellesley to Richard Wellesley 13 November 1803 Grwd (1837) ii 506 (1844) i 859).

6 Arthur Wellesley had taken Duncan's letter of 12 August [222] as an acceptance of the proposals he had set out in his extended note of 2 August [205]. It was not an acceptance, as Duncan explained on 23 August.[256].

7 Stevenson's letters were both of 14 August [227,228] the first enclosing letters from Kelly of the 13th [227A,B]

8 A valuable table of the comparative values of coins used in India in the decade 1783-93 can be found in H. Furber *John Company at Work* (Harvard 1948) p. 349. A Bengal gold mohur was then worth one pound twelve shillings, a 'Venetian' was a sequin or gold ducat worth about 9 shillings, the Bombay rupee worth about 2 shillings three pence.

9 Arthur Wellesley's letter to Collins of 19 August has not been found. The Proclamation of the Governor-General is printed in PRC ix 332 and in Parl Pps [5, 22 June 1804] p. 534. The attempt to send it to the European officers serving in Sinde's army in the Deccan probably failed [355]. The listing of British officers in the service of Daulat Rao Sinde should be compared with that in Smith *Sketch of the Rise Progress and Termination of the Regular Corps . . . in the service of the Native Princes of India . . .* (Calcutta 1804) p. 49. See also [350].

10 Arthur Wellesley had written to Malcolm on 20 August (Grwd (1844) i 646, SD iv 160). He had opened Shawe's letter to Malcolm of 26 July. This had reported that the principles of the Malcolm memorandum of 30 June/4 July [150] were seen as appropriate at Fort William, and had added on Baji Rao 'you must act . . . if he will not act for himself.' (Shawe to Malcolm 26 July 1803 A Mss 13,602 f. 25).

11 Duncan wrote in similar terms to Richard Wellesley protesting that the arrangements suggested by Arthur Wellesley in his letter of 2 August [205] removed 'from the Resident [at Baroda] all the local influence and control which he has hitherto had.' (Duncan to Richard Wellesley 22 August 1803 A Mss 13,701 f. 147).

12 Collins had explained to Stevenson on 10 August that he considered the Ajanta ghat was 'not practicable for guns and will prove difficult to loaded cattle' [217]. Later movements suggest that this was not an accurate assessment. The location of the Sirsooli ghat has not been determined.

13 This letter presents difficulties of interpretation. Stevenson is presumably describing his movement southwestwards from Chikhli where he had been on 24 August [260] and as headed towards Jafarabad. The letter may have been written at Pattanka Dewalgaon.

14 Azim ul Umara was the principal minister of the Nizam of Hyderabad.

15 Stevenson's letter of 29 August has not been found.

16 There was panic in Pune late in August following reports of a southward movement of Gopal Bhau with a large body of pindaris. The 'cowle' sought by the soucars is a safeconduct.

17 The letter from Shawe was that of 16 August; it acknowledged the arrival of Arthur Wellesley's letter of 24 July [190]. It reported that his 'proceedings and intentions are highly approved of.' (Shawe to Malcolm 16 August 1803 A Mss 13,602 f. 41). General Campbell's detachment was that placed near Mudghal in the Kistna-Toombuddra doab after the rest of the army under the command of Lieutenant-General Stuart had returned to the Carnatic (Stuart to Richard Wellesley 8 August 1803 Grwd (1837) ii 189 (1844) i 629). In a letter to Close of 1 September, which was forwarded to Arthur Wellesley, Campbell reported that on 27 August he had encamped three miles from Mudghal with the 1st battalion of native cavalry, a detachment of HM 33rd, and two battalions of native infantry and six field pieces (Campbell to Close 1 September 1803 WP 3/3/47 p. 14).

18 Piele was acting Resident at Seringapatam. Later movements of this convoy are reported [297,301].

19 Arthur Wellesley in his letter of 29 August had dissociated himself from responsibility for military actions in Gujerat and the Attavesi (Arthur Wellesley to Duncan 29 August 1803 Grwd (1837) ii 247 (1844) i 665, PRC x 131). Malcolm now forwarded to Arthur Wellesley the instructions for Colonel Murray dated 6 September printed at PRC x 141 which followed from the minute of Duncan's of 5 September printed at PRC x 137. The letter from Shawe would have been that dated 26 August (Shawe to Malcolm 26 August 1803 A Mss 13,602 f. 46).

20 Stevenson's letter to Arthur Wellesley of 11 September 1803 does not seem to have survived. Presumably it both sought immediate help, which Arthur Wellesley provided, and also argued that his force was of inadequate strength to attempt a journey northeastwards, from his position near Budnapur, into Berar.

21 The dak line across Hindustan from the Deccan was not retained.

An Interim Settlement – Introduction

1 Arthur Wellesley to Sir William Clarke 2 December 1803, SD iv 292.

2 Arthur Wellesley to Adjutant-General Madras 12 October 1803, SD iv 198. The 'Cassabarri ghat' led through the Ajanta range near to the modern town of Kasari.

3 Arthur Wellesley to Richard Wellesley 24 October 1803, Grwd (1837) ii 446 (1844) i 808.

4 Richard Wellesley to Arthur Wellesley 11 December 1803 Martin iii 497 with its attachments, was presumably the content of the 'numerous and

voluminous packets from Bengal' which Arthur Wellesley noted as arriving on 12 January 1804, at the summit of the Badauli ghat, Arthur Wellesley to Malcolm 13 January 1804, Grwd (1837) ii 659 (1844) ii 964. He subsequently prepared a detailed statement of the extent to which the settlement he had concluded met the requirements of the instructions of 11 December. Arthur Wellesley to Shawe and attachments 16 January 1804, SD iv 317.

An Interim Settlement

1 The instructions to which Murray objected were those issued by the Secretary to the Bombay Government on 6 September 1803 printed at PRC x 141. By them, Lieutenant-Colonel Woodington was responsible for the internal details of the subsidiary force with the Gaikwar of Baroda; although subject to the operational command of Colonel Murray, troops at Baroda were to comply with requisitions made by the Resident, and guard detachments there were also subject to the authority of the Resident.

2 Stevenson's description of Ajanta can be set beside that in the *Maharashtra State Gazetteer Aurungabad District* (Revised Edition 1977) p. 835: 'A spacious and well built serai is near the northern gate and bears an inscription recording that it was the work of Asaf Jah. It has sixty four recesses for travellers . . . The barradarri overlooks the Ajanta ravine and was occupied by Arthur Wellesley immediately after the battle of Assaye to lodge and treat the sick and wounded. Immediately outside the northern gate are the tombs of two or three officers who died as a result of their wounds.'

3 Barry Close is referring to the listing of Sinde's forces given by Collins on 25 July and here inserted at [193].

4 The listing prepared by Arthur Wellesley is here omitted.

5 Stevenson had received the first tentative attempt by Daulat Rao Sinde to initiate peace discussions.

6 Stevenson sent forward to Sinde's camp the letters Arthur Wellesley wrote on 5 October to Balaji Kunjar and another correspondent, Grwd (1837) ii 382 (1844) i 761.

7 The 'gazette' was probably an akbar message. The 'instructions for Carnalla' are in Arthur Wellesley to Murray May 1803 at [67].

8 The reference to 'the Rajas' is presumably to the troops of the Nizam of Hyderabad.

9 Kawder Beg had been sent by Arthur Wellesley in July on a mission to Jaswant Rao Holkar but had been unable to secure a safe journey. As Arthur Wellesley subsequently explained to Stevenson, Kawder Beg had written to him in a south Indian language as a coded safeguard.

10 Given by Murray as Ambersomba is probably the modern Antasumba, WNW of Kapadvahj.

11 As John Pemple points out ('Resources and Techniques in the Second Maratha War' *Historical Journal* vol. 19 pp 375-404 at p. 393), Dorsan was not killed at Assaye.

12 The 'old French infantry' were the formed battalions originally under French officers, who were disarmed at Hyderabad in October 1798 and subsequently remustered.

13 Two days later Arthur Wellesley noted in a letter to John Malcolm 'You may well suppose that I shall soon put a stop to this go-between style of going on through Appah Dessaye.' Grwd (1837) ii 509 (1844) ii 861.

14 Arthur Wellesley's proposals for mustering the forces of the Nizam under the supervision of the Resident, were set out in his letter of 11 November to the Governor-General, in that part not here printed, Grwd (1837) ii 498 (1844) ii 853. The terms of Malcolm's comments suggest that he had *not* been shown the Governor-General's instructions of 27 June, printed in part at [175].

15 In the event, the Treaty of Sarji Arjangoan provided in its Article 13 that 'The Maharajah Daulat Rao Sinde engages never to take or retain in his service any Frenchman, or the subject of any other European or American power, the government of which may be at war with the British government, or any British subject, whether European or native of India, without the consent of the British government.'

16 The two letters to which Stevenson refers have not been found. They evidently related to the proposed embassy of Muhammed Mir Khan.

17 In this despatch to Richard Wellesley, James Kirkpatrick reported that the total holding in the treasury of the Nizam was reported to be nearly 39 lakhs of rupees, adding that 'this state still possesses considerable resources if honestly and ably managed and applied to proper purposes.' The remedy which the Resident recommended was the 'gradual assumption of the great jagir lands to the collective amount of near two crores of rupees of revenue.' (Kirkpatrick to Governor-General 15 November 1803 Mss Eur F 228/62.).

18 Arthur Wellesley did not in the event seek a hostage from Raghuji Bhonsle of Berar.

19 The recommendation to Campbell of the position he should occupy was given in the letter of 5 October 1803, Grwd (1837) ii 375 (1844) i 757.

20 The difficulty to which Arthur Wellesley here refers was resolved in discussion.

21 The tenth article of the treaty, which gave rise to controversy later, was that which required Raghuji Bhonsle to accept treaties which had been made by the Company with his feudatories in Cuttack. The text of the treaty of Deogaun is at Martin iii 633, Grwd (1837) ii 588.

22 Peshcush, the ruler's demand of land revenue. This is one of the few misprints the present editor has detected in Gurwood (both editions). The Treaty of Sarji Arjangaon is printed at Martin iii 634, Grwd (1837) ii 612, PRC x 268.

Biographical Notes

British military and civil officers

(Where no further details available, appointment that held in 1803)

Baird, Sir David (1757–1829). Ensign 1772, served at Gibraltar 1773–6, Lieutenant 1778, Captain of the 73rd (afterwards 71st) Highland Light Infantry in India under Munro 1780. Joined Colonel Baillie's force, and after its defeat by Hyder Ali was captured, released 1784. Major 1787; in England 1789–91, commanded brigade against Tipu Sultan 1792, took Pondicherry 1793. Colonel 1795, at the Cape 1795–8, Major-General 1798. Took part in the seige of Seringapatam, commanded force in Egypt against the French 1801–2, command of northern division of Madras army 1802. Resigned and returned to England 1803, knighted, Lieutenant-General in expedition to recapture Cape of Good Hope 1805, commanded first division in expedition invading Denmark 1807, second in command under Moore in Spain 1808, wounded at Coruna, KB 1809, created baronet 1810, General 1814, Governor of Kinsale 1819, and of Fort St George 1829, Commander of Irish forces and Privy Councillor 1820.

Barlow, George (1762–1846). Bengal Civil Service 1778, Sub-Secretary Revenue Department 1788, Chief Secretary to government 1796, Member of the Supreme Council 1801, baronet 1803, Governor-General 1805–7, Governor of Madras 1807, recalled 1812.

Bentinck, Lord William Cavendish (1774–1839). Second son of William Henry third Duke of Portland, Ensign 1791, Captain 1792, Lieutenant-Colonel 1794, campaign in Flanders 1794, garrison duty in Ireland 1795–8, attached to Suvorov's army in Italy and Switzerland 1799, and to the Austrian commander Bellegarde, 1801, posted to Egypt 1801. Governor of Madras 1803, recalled after mutiny at Vellore 1807, commanded brigade at Coruna. Lieutenant-General, Commander-in-Chief of forces in Sicily 1811, served in Spain 1813, commanded expedition against Genoa 1814. Governor-General of Bengal 1827, returned to England 1835, MP for Glasgow 1837.

Campbell, Major-General Dugald, commander of an advanced force of the Madras army, 1803.

Clive, Lord Edward (1754–1839). Eldest son of Robert Clive; succeeded to the Irish barony 1774, MP for Ludlow 1774–94, created Baron Clive of Walcot in the English peerage 1794, Governor of Madras 1798–1803, created Earl of Powis 1804.

Close, Sir Barry (died 1813). Cadet 1771, took part in the seige of Seringapatam 1792, Adjutant-General Madras 1796–9, campaign in Mysore 1799, Resident with Raja of Mysore 1799–1801, Resident at Pune 1801–11, returned to England 1811, created baronet.

Collins, Colonel John (died 1807). Cadet Bengal army 1769, Captain 1780, Major 1794, Lieutenant-Colonel 1796; Resident at the court of Daulat Rao Sinde 1798–1803, Colonel 1800, Resident with the Nawab of Oudh 1804–7.

Dallas, Major Peter, 10th Regiment Native Infantry Madras.

Desse, Lieutenant-Colonel Peter, 10th Regiment Native Infantry Madras.

Duncan, Jonathan (1756–1811). Resident and Superintendent Benares 1788–95, Governor of Bombay 1795–1811.

Edmonstone, Neil Benjamin (1765–1841). Writer 1783, Persian translator to government 1794, Secretary to the Foreign Political and Secret Department 1801, Chief Secretary to Government 1809, Member of the Supreme Council 1812–17.

Elphinstone, Mountstuart (1779–1859). Appointed to the Bengal service 1796, Assistant Residency with the Peshwa 1801, Political Assistant to Arthur Wellesley 1803, Resident with Raghuji Bhonsle of Nagpur December 1803, Resident with the Peshwa 1810–16, ordered to annex Maratha territories 1817, Governor of Bombay 1819–27; author of a history of India.

Haliburton, Lieutenant-Colonel, 7th Regiment Native Infantry Madras.

Harness, Lieutenant-Colonel William, HM 18th Regiment.

Kenny, Lieutenant-Colonel William, 11th Regiment Native Infantry Madras.

Kirkpatrick, Major James (died 1805). Resident with the Nizam of Hyderabad 1798–1805.

Lake, Gerald, first Viscount (1744–1808). Ensign 1758, service in Germany 1760–62, Lieutenant 1762, Captain 1776, service in America 1781, Major 1784, MP Aylesbury 1790–1802, Lieutentant-Colonel 1792, service in Flanders 1793, invalided home 1793, Colonel HM 53rd Regiment; Lieutenant-Governor Berwick-on-Tweed, Governor of Limerick 1795, Commander in Ulster 1796, Lieutenant-General 1797, Commander-in-Chief Ireland 1798, accepted capitulation of Humbert, September 1798, brought into the Irish parliament to vote for union. Appointed Commander-in-Chief and second Member of the Supreme Council in India 1800, ordered to commence operations against Daulat Rao Sinde June 1803, captured Alighur, Delhi and Agra 1803, victory at Laswari November 1803, pursued Holkar after seige of Delhi October 1804, routed Holkar at Farruckabad November 1804, besieged Bharatpur January 1805, pursued Holkar into the Punjab, concluded peace settlement January 1806, embarked for England 1807.

Malcolm, John (1769–1833). Entered military service of East India Company 1782, Lieutenant 1788, Persian interpreter to auxiliary battalions of the Nizam of Hyderabad 1792, returned to England 1794; secretary to Sir Alured Clarke 1796–8, town major Madras 1798, Assistant Resident

Hyderabad 1798–9, envoy to Persia 1799–1801; private secretary to the Governor-General 1801–2, political adviser to Arthur Wellesley 1803, Resident with Daulat Rao Sinde 1804, political advisor to General Lake 1805; attempted embassy to Persia rebuffed 1807, further mission to Tehran 1810. Published *A Sketch of Political History of India from 1784* 1811, worked on a study of Persia later published as *A History of Persia* in 1818. Sailed for England 1812, KCB 1815, sailed for India 1815, Agent to the Governor-General in the Deccan and Brigadier in command of the third division of the army of the Deccan 1817, fought at Mehidpoor, negotiated with Baji Rao 1818; wrote *Report on the Province of Malwa and Adjoining Districts* 1819; returned to England 1821, published *Memoir of Central India* 1823, Governor of Bombay 1827–30, MP Launceston 1831–2, published *Administration of India*, 1833.

Maxwell, Lieutenant-Colonel Patrick, 19th Light Dragoons.

Murray, John (1768–1827). Ensign 1788, Captain 1793, served in Flanders 1793–4, Lieutenant-Colonel HM 84th Regiment 1794, commanded the 84th at capture of Cape of Good Hope 1796, took 84th to India, sent with small force to Aden 1798, British Commissioner in the Red Sea 1799, appointed Quarter-Master general of the army sent to Egypt under Baird 1801; joined Arthur Wellesley at Pune May 1803, command in Gujerat September 1803, advanced into Malwa June 1804, reached Ujjein July 1804, captured Indore August 1804, advanced to Kotah January 1805, Major-General 1805. Returned to Britain, commanded a brigade in the eastern counties 1806–7, commanded expedition to Sweden 1808, joined army in Portugal 1809, returned to England 1811, MP 1811–18; Lieutenant-General 1812, appointed to the army in Sicily 1812, sailed from Alicante to before Tarragona, but reembarked June 1813, courtmartialled and ordered to be admonished 1815, General 1825.

Nicolls, Major-General Oliver, Commander-in-Chief, Bombay.

Piele, an official acting at the Residency to the Raja of Mysore.

Stevenson, Colonel, commander of the subsidiary force of the Nizam of Hyderabad.

Shawe, Merrick (1771?–1843). Ensign 1782, HM 76th Regiment 1789, present at the seige of Bangalore 1791, and at Seringapatam 1792, Lieutenant 1792, joined the staff of the Governor-General 1799, Captain 1800, Major 1803; returned to England 1805, Assistant Adjutant-General Ireland 1806, Lieutenant-Colonel, took part in the Walcheren campaign 1809, employed as a staff officer at the Horse Guards, Commissioner of Stamps 1819, private secretary to Lord Lieutenant of Ireland 1822–8 and later.

Stuart, Lieutenant-General James (1741–1815). Served in America, Major HM 78th Regiment 1782, Lieutenant-Colonel 1782, served against Hyder Ali and at seige of Cuddalore 1782, reduced fortresses of Dindigul and Palghat 1790, commanded central division in assault on Seringapatam, Colonel 1792, Major-General 1795, commanded expedition against the Dutch possessions in Ceylon 1795, appointed Commander-in-Chief Madras 1796, commanded Bombay army in campaign against Tipu Sultan 1799, Commander-in-Chief Madras 1802, Lieutenant-General 1802, returned to England 1805.

Walker, Alexander (1764–1831). Appointed to Bombay army 1780, Lieutenant 1788, Captain 1797, political agent in Baroda 1800–08, returned to England 1810, Brigadier-General and Governor of St Helena 1822–30.

Webbe, Josiah (died 1804), Madras civilian official, secretary to Government of Madras 1797–1800, Chief Secretary 1800–01, Resident at Mysore 1801–3, Resident with Daulat Rao Sinde 1804.

Wellesley, Arthur, First Duke of Wellington (1769–1852). Fourth son of Garrett, first Earl of Mornington. Educated at Eton, Brussels and the Angers Military Academy. Lieutenant, 1787. Captain, 1792. ADC to Lord Lieutenant of Ireland, 1787–93. MP for Trim, 1790–5. Lieutenant-Colonel, 33rd Foot, 1793–1806. Service in Netherlands and India. Governor of Seringapatam and Mysore, 1797–1802. Major-General, 1802. Chief of the Military and Civil Administration in the Deccan, 1803–5. KB, 1804. MP for Rye, 1806. MP for Mitchell, 1807. MP for Newport, 1807–9. Chief Secretary for Ireland, 1807–9. Commander of British forces in Portugal and Spain, 1808, 1809–14. Lieutenant-General, 1808. Created Viscount Wellington, 1809. Earl, 1812. Marquess, 1812. KG, 1813. Duke, 1814. Ambassador in Paris and to Congress of Vienna, 1815. Allied Commander-in-Chief, Belgium, 1815. Master-General of the Ordnance, 1818–27. Governor of Plymouth, 1819–26. Lord Lieutenant of Hampshire, 1820–52. Commander-in-Chief of the British Army, 1827–8, 1842–52. Prime Minister, 1828–30, 1834. Lord Warden of the Cinque Ports, 1829–52. Leader of the Opposition in the House of Lords, 1835–41. Cabinet minister without departmental office, 1841–46.

Wellesley, Richard Colley, Marquess Wellesley (1760–1842). Eldest son of Garrett, First Earl of Mornington. Educated at Eton and Christ Church, Oxford. Succeeds as Earl Mornington in Irish peerage, 1781. MP for Beeralston, 1787. MP for Windsor, 1790. MP for Old Sarum, 1796. Member of the India Board, 1793. Governor-General of India, 1797–1805. Created Baron Wellesley in English peerage, 1797. Created Marquis Wellesley in Irish peerage, 1799. Ambassador to Spain, 1809. Foreign Secretary, 1809–12. Lord Lieutenant of Ireland, 1821–8, 1833–4. Lord Chamberlain, 1835.

Woodington, Lieutenant-Colonel H., commander of the northern division of forces in Gujerat.

Indian

Ambaji Inglia, a major feudatory of Daulat Rao Sinde.
Amrit Rao, half brother of Peshwa Baji Rao.
Appah Dessaye, a feudatory of Peshwa Baji Rao.
Azim ul Umara, principal minister of the Nizam.
Baji Rao. *See* Peshwa.
Bal Kishen Gungar Dhur, former commander of the fort of Dharwar.
Balaji Kunjar, a minister of Peshwa Baji Rao, sent on mission to Daulat Rao Sinde.
Bapoji Sinde, a feudatory of Peshwa Baji Rao.
Begum Sumru, the Indian widow of a German soldier of fortune, a feudatory of Daulat Rao Sinde, whose disciplined infantry formed part of the forces of Daulat Rao Sinde.
Berar, Raja of. *See* Raghuji Bhonsle.
Canoji Rao, a pretender in revolt against Anand Rao, the recognised Gaekwar.
Daulat Rao Sinde (full title Maharaja Alijah) was the ruler of part of Malwa, north of the Narbada, and his capital was Ujjein. Formerly jagirdars, the Sindes were in effect independent.
Fateh Sing Mane, a military commander in the forces of Jaswant Rao Holkar.
Goklah, a feudatory of Peshwa Baji Rao.
Hurnauth Singh, a military commander in the forces of Jaswant Rao Holkar.
Jadu Rao Bhaskar, a principal minister of Daulat Rao Sinde.
Jaswant Rao Holkar was the illegitimate son of Tukhoji Holkar and claimed the heritage in Malwa of the Holkars, also formerly jagirdars, but independent. Their capital was Indore.
Jaswant Rao Ramchand, an agent of Raguji Bhonsle.
Kashi Rao Holkar, eldest legitimate son of Tukaji Holkar.
Khande Rao Holkar, a nephew of Jaswant Rao Holkar.
Khande Rao Rastiah, a feudatory of Peshwa Baji Rao.
Kistnaji Bowanni, a vakil of Peshwa Baji Rao sent to Daulat Rao Sinde.
Marin Singh, a military commander in the forces of Jaswant Rao Holkar.
Mir Khan, a military commander in the forces of Jaswant Rao Holkar.
Mirza Wahed Beg, a vakil of Balaji Kunjar at the court of Daulat Rao Sinde.
Mohipat Ram, a minister of the Nizam of Hyderabad in the area north of the Godavari.
Mulhar Rao, leader of an armed insurrection in Gujerat.
Nagu Jevaji, a military commander in the forces of Jaswant Rao Holkar.
Nanamji, an employee of Barry Close at the Residency at Pune.
Peshwa Baji Rao (full titles Sreemut Baji Rao Raghunath Rao Pundit Pradhan) was the chief ruler of the Maratha Confederacy, nominally under the Raja of Sattara.
Pritti Niddi, a feudatory of Peshwa Baji Rao.
Raghuji Bhonsle (title was Senah Sahib Soubah) was the Raja of Berar, the eastern Maratha territory. His residence was at Nagpur.

Raghunath Rao, a minister of Peshwa Baji Rao.
Ram Dyale, an employee of Barry Close at the Residency at Pune.
Rana of Gohud, the displaced ruler of Gohud, in treaty relationship with the Company.
Salabat Khan, a military commander in the forces of the Nizam of Hyderabad.
Shalamut Khan, a military commander in the forces of Jaswant Rao Holkar.
Suddasheo Munkaisseer, a minister of Peshwa Baji Rao.
Sukhruder, a military commander in the service of the Nizam of Hyderabad.

Bibliography

(all books published in London unless otherwise noted)

1 Manuscript sources

Hartley Library, University of Southampton
Woolgar, C.M. *A Summary Catalogue of the Wellington Papers* (1984).
British Library
Additional Manuscripts.
British Library, Oriental and India Office Collections
Home Miscellaneous Series – Hill, S.C., *Catalogue of the Home Miscellaneous Series of the India Office Records* (1927).
Kirkpatrick Papers.
Abstract of Madras Letters Received.
National Library of Scotland
Walker of Bowland Collection.
National Library of Wales
Clive Collection.
Nottingham University Library
Bentinck Papers.

2 Official publications and printed editions of the letters of Arthur Wellesley

Parliamentary Papers
Sessional Papers 1803/4 xii 'Bengal also Fort St George and Bombay Papers/Presented to the House of Commons/Pursuant to their order of 7 May last/From the East India Company/Relative to the Mahratta War in 1803/Printed by Order of the House of Commons 5 and 22 June 1804.'
Gurwood, Lieutenant-Colonel, *The Despatches of . . . the Duke of Wellington . . . from 1799 to 1818* 13 vols. (1834–9. New edition 13 vols. 1837–9. The pagination between the two editions is not standardised. Second edition 8 vols. 1844–7).
Supplementary Despatches . . . of FM Arthur Duke of Wellington 15 vols. (1858–72).
Owen, S.J. (ed), *A Selection from the Despatches . . . relating to India of FM the Duke of Wellington* (Oxford, 1880).
Brett-James, Antony (ed), *Wellington at War 1794–1815* (1961).

3 Important early source material

(References are to first editions only. The place of publication is London unless otherwise stated.)

Aitchison, C.U., *A Collection of treaties, engagements and sanads . . . relating to India* (Calcutta 7 vols. 1862–65).

Auber, P., *Rise and Progress of the British Power in India* (2 vols. 1836–7).

Broughton, T.D., *Letters written in a Mahratta camp . . .* (1813).

Duff, J.C.G., *A History of the Mahrattas* (3 vols. 1826).

Fraser, H., *Our Faithful Ally, the Nizam* (1865).

Kaye, J.W., *Life and Correspondence of Major General Sir John Malcolm* (2 vols, 1856).

Malcolm, J., *Sketch of the Political History of India 1784 to the present date* (1811).

Memoir of Central India 1784–1823 (2 vols, 1823).

Political History of India 1784–1823 (2 vols, 1826).

Martin, M., (ed), *Despatches Minutes and Correspondence of the Marquess Wellesley during his administration in India* (5 vols. 1836–7).

Mill, J., *The History of British India* (3 vols, 1817).

Thorn, W., *Memoir of the war in India conducted by . . . Lord Lake . . . and Sir Arthur Wellesley . . . from 1803 to 1806* (1818).

4 More recent authorities

Bidwell, S., *Swords for Hire: European Mercenaries in Eighteenth Century India* (1971).

Butler, Iris, *The Eldest Brother: The Marquess Wellesley* (1973).

Callahan, R.A., *The East India Company and Army Reform 1783–1798* (Cambridge Mass 1972).

Chakravorty, U.N., *Anglo-Maratha Relations and Malcolm 1798–1830* (New Delhi 1979).

Choksey, R.D., *A History of British Diplomacy at the Court of the Peshwas* (Poona 1951).

Fortescue, J.W., *A History of the British Army* (13 vols. 1899–1930).

Furber, H., *John Company at Work* (Cambridge Mass 1948).

Gupta P.C., *Baji Rao II and the East India Company* (Bombay 1939).

Ingram, E., *Two Views of British India* (1970).

Kanungo, S., *Jaswant Rao Holkar, the Golden Rogue* (Lucknow 1965).

Longford E., *Wellington: The Years of the Sword* (1969).

Maharashtra State Gazetteer Aurangabad District (revised edition 1977).

Nightingale, P., *Trade and Empire in Western India 1784–1806* (1970).

Philips, C.H., *The East India Company 1784–1834* (Manchester 1940).

– ed. *The Correspondence of David Scott* 2 vols (Camden Society 1951).

Poona Residency Correspondence; English Records of Maratha History.

— vol. 7 'Poona Affairs 1801–1810' (Bombay 1940).
— vol. 9 'Daulat Rao Sindhia and North Indian Affairs 1800–1803' (Bombay 1943).
— vol. 10 'The Treaty of Bassein and the Anglo-Maratha War in the Deccan 1802–1804' (Bombay 1951).
Roberts, P.E., *India under Wellesley* (1929).
Sardesai, G.S., *A New History of the Marathas* (3 vols. Bombay 1948).
Sarkar, J., *Fall of the Mughal Empire* (4 vols, Calcutta 1950).
Sen, Surenranath, *Administrative System of the Marathas* (Calcutta 1923).
— *Military System of the Marathas* (Calcutta 1928).
Sinha, H.N. (ed). *Selections from the Nagpur Residency Records* (3 vols. Nagpur 1950–53).
Spate, O.H.K., *India and Pakistan a General and Regional Geography* (1954).
Thompson, E.J., *The Making of the Indian Princes* (1943).
Weller, J., *Wellington in India* (1972).

5 Other works by A.S. Bennell

Southern India under Wellesley 1798-1805 B.Litt. thesis (Oxford 1951).
'Wellesley's Settlement of Mysore', *Journal of the Royal Asiatic Society* (1952) pp. 124–32.
'Governors General of India 1: Wellesley', *History Today* (February 1959) vol. 9 no. 2 pp. 94–102.
'The Anglo-Maratha Confrontation of June, July 1803' *Journal of the Royal Asiatic Society* (1962) parts 3 and 4 pp. 107–31.
'Factors in the Marquis Wellesley's Failure against Holkar', *Bulletin of the School of Oriental and African Studies* vol. 38 Part 3 pp. 553–81.
'The Anglo-Maratha War of 1803–5', *Journal of the Society for Army Historical Research* (1985) vol. 65 pp. 144–61.
'The Road to Poonah' in *East India Company Studies* edited Ballhatchet, K. and Harrison, J. *Asian Studies Monograph Series* (1986) pp. 183–206.
'Arthur Wellesley as Political Agent 1803', *Journal of the Royal Asiatic Society* (1987) no. 2 pp. 273–88.
'Arthur Wellesley the Sepoy General as politician and diplomat 1797–1805' in *The Road to Waterloo* edited Guy, A.J., National Army Museum (1991).
The Making of Arthur Wellesley (Orient Longman Hyderabad 1997).

Index

ARMY RECORDS SOCIETY
(FOUNDED 1984)

Members of the Society are entitled to purchase back volumes at reduced prices.
Orders should be sent to the Hon. Treasurer, Army Records Society,
c/o National Army Museum,
Royal Hospital Road,
London SW3 4HT

The Society has already issued:

Vol. I:
The Military Correspondence of Field Marshal Sir Henry Wilson 1918–1922
Edited by Dr Keith Jeffrey

Vol. II:
The Army and the Curragh Incident, 1914
Edited by Dr Ian F.W. Beckett

Vol. III:
The Napoleonic War Journal of Captain Thomas Henry Browne, 1807–1816
Edited by Roger Norman Buckley

Vol. IV:
An Eighteenth-Century Secretary at War The Papers of William, Viscount Barrington
Edited by Dr Tony Hayter

Vol. V:
The Military Correspondence of Field Marshal Sir William Robertson 1915–1918
Edited by David R. Woodward

Vol. VI:
Colonel Samuel Bagshawe and the Army of George II, 1731–1762
Edited by Dr Alan J. Guy

Vol. VII:
Montgomery and the Eighth Army
Edited by Stephen Brooks

Vol. VIII:
The British Army and Signals Intelligence during the First World War
Edited by John Ferris

Vol. IX:
Roberts in India
The Military Papers of Field Marshal Lord Roberts 1876–1893
Edited by Brian Robson

Vol. X:
Lord Chelmsford's Zululand Campaign 1878–1879
Edited by John P.C. Laband

Vol. XI:
Letters of a Victorian Army Officer: Edward Wellesley 1840–1854
Edited by Michael Carver

Vol. XII:
Military Miscellany I
Papers from the Seven Years War, the Second Sikh War and the First World War
Editors: Alan J. Guy, R.N.W. Thomas and Gerard J. DeGroot

Vol. XIII:
John Peebles' American War 1776–1782
Edited by Ira D. Gruber

RATTA COUNTRY, The COUNTRY of the NYZAM, also, of the NABOB of OUDE &c. Together with the BRITI
Explanation.
are marked thus
CALCUTTA
Nattore
Koonda
Plassey
200 British miles
DELHI
AGRA
Gwalior
LUCKNOW
Bareilly
Furruckabad
Cawnpour
Etaya
Calpi
Chitpour
Cheitore
Oudipour
Ryseen
INDOOR
OUGEIN
Bopaultol
Burhampour
BURHAMPOUR
NAGPOUR
Ellichpour
Omrautty
Chanda
AURUNGABAD
Dowlatabad
AMEDNAGUR
POONAH
Sattara
BEJAPOUR or VISIAPOUR
Callian
Beder
HYDRABAD
Golconda
Sollapour
Condavir
Rajamundry
Musilipatam
Gheriah
GOA
Vingorla Rocks
SURAT
Brodera
Dubhoy
Nerbudda R.
Taptee R.
Godavery R.
Krishna R.
Tungebadra R.
Beemah R.
Rewah
Callinger
Chatterpour
Chanderee
Jansi
Narwah
Bancapour
Condanore
Adoni
M A H R A T T A
B E R A R
COUNTRY of the NIZ
of the DECCA
Parts of Europe
OUDE